Praise for THE OUTSOURCING CONUNDRUM

"This book is a must-read for all those trying to secure business in strategic fashion! Enlightening and honest in the description of the outsourcing world, which we strive to understand and align with."

— Clint S. Griffin, CEO, Team Group of Companies

"*The Outsourcing Conundrum* strikes the perfect balance between personal experience, theoretical groundwork, and practical how-to. An excellent guide for any service provider, based on Damian's vast experience in the IOS industry."

— Gerwin Gädigk, Managing Director, Voith Industrial Services (Shanghai) Co. Ltd.

"Damian Scallon has written the authoritative piece on outsourcing. This book combines innovative insights and real-world experiences to give executive leaders and service providers a powerful looking glass into the arena. Damian's ideas are pragmatic and transformative. This book should be on every business leader's bookshelf."

— David Devine, CEO, Devine Group

"Mastering the 3 P's of Purpose, Process, and People should help any manager navigate the labyrinth of outsourcing work. Damian articulates the challenges and provides solutions for each of them with very usable ideas, stories, and tools. Anyone embarking on, or in the middle of, outsourcing would be well served to read and use these excellent ideas."

— Dave Ulrich, Rensis Likert Professor of Business, University of Michigan; Partner, The RBL Group

"Outsourcing is more important today than ever, and Damian has created a guide that will help everyone involved understand the importance of working together. The demand for cost savings is increasing and when we are all working together, we can benefit with increased profitability as well."

— Mary Miller, CEO, JANCOA Janitorial Services, Inc.

"Damian Scallon has written a much needed and valuable book on culture and outsourcing. It is a must-read for every organization in the throes of change and global competiveness. Don't miss it."

— W. Gary Gore, President/CEO, Team Trek, Inc.

"Service is critical to the success of many businesses, but is the key ingredient for non-profits. *The Outsourcing Conundrum* provides a clear path for non-profit leaders ready to take their business to a new level, by following the 3 P's; this book reiterates the importance of leading with purpose, and provides guidance on mastering processes and people. This is a must-read playbook for any non-profit leader!"

— Amy Thompson, Executive Director, Camp Joy (Leader of Hopes & Dreams)

"Finally, a way to navigate the inside-outsourcing 'labyrinth' in today's complex global economy! Damian provides a simple, easy-to-follow plan to achieve your business' needs in sourcing and purchasing. The presentation, 'Purpose, Process, People' approach, and steps included bring clarity for organizations of any size and are transferable across industries. Mandatory reading for anyone currently striving to grow their company efficiently while spinning off non-value-added steps and activities."

— David Velie & Craig Todd, Managing Partners, AMEND Consulting

The Outsourcing Conundrum

THE OUTSOURCING CONUNDRUM

THE OUTSOURCING CONUNDRUM

A PATH TO NAVIGATE THE "INSIDE-OUTSOURCING" LABYRINTH

DAMIAN SCALLON

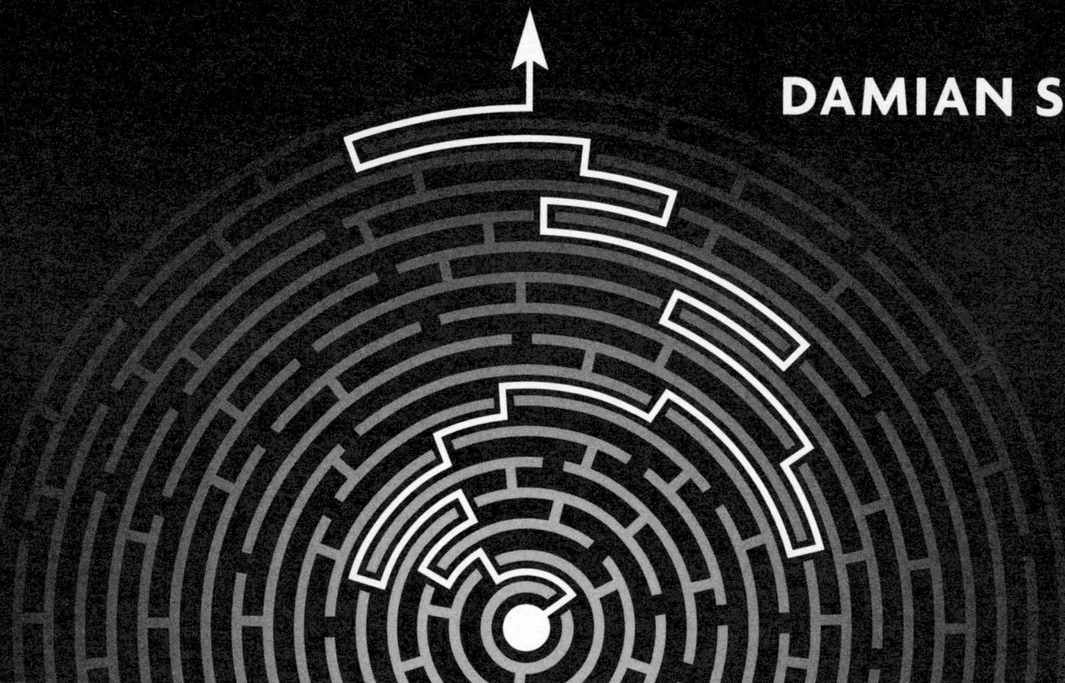

MILNER & ASSOCIATES INC
· EDITING · PUBLISHING · COMMUNICATIONS · CONSULTING

Library and Archives Canada Cataloguing in Publication Data

Scallon, Damian, 1957-, author
The outsourcing conundrum : a path to navigate the "inside-outsourcing" labyrinth / Damian Scallon.

Includes bibliographical references.
ISBN 978-0-9938557-6-4 (pbk.)

1. Contracting out. I. Title.
HD2365.S33 2015 658.4'058 C2014-908438-2

Production Credits
Editor: Karen Milner
Interior design and typesetting: Adrian So
Cover design: Adrian So
Printer: CJK Print Possibilities

Published by Milner & Associates Inc.
www.milnerassociates.ca

Printed in the United States of America
10 9 8 7 6 5 4 3 2 1

To those who deliver inside-outsourcing services, working weekends, holidays and off shifts to add value and meet the need of the customer. Hopefully this book provides a helpful path for you to follow.

THE OUTSOURCING CONUNDRUM MODEL

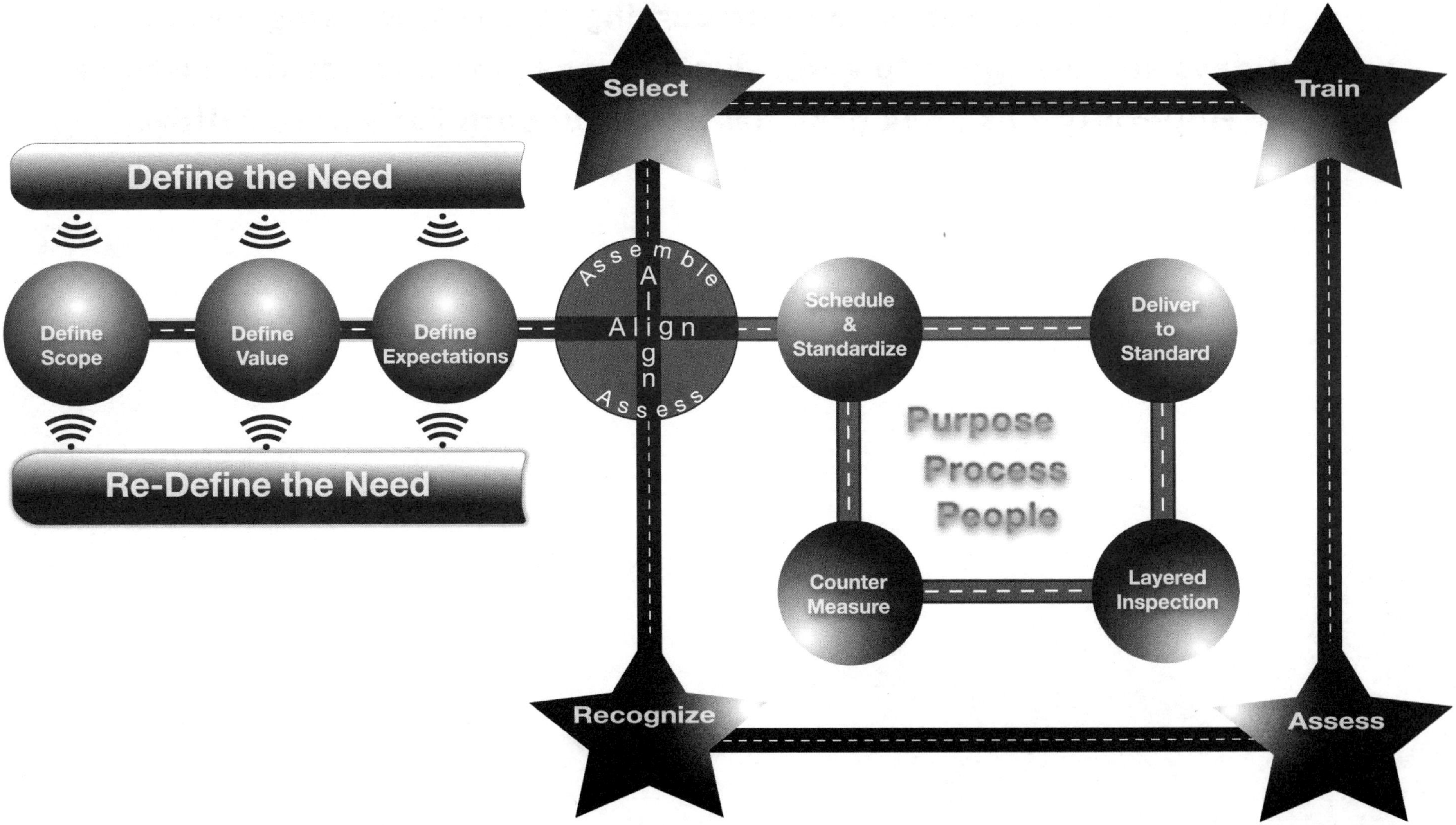

CONTENTS

FOREWORDS

The Outsourcing Conundrum offers great insight around the seismic shift that has been occurring since the '90s in the way that outsourced services are bought, delivered, managed and measured.

The lift-and-shift, labor arbitrage outsourcing model of the '90s has not kept pace with the rapid changes in technology, increased mobility of human capital and sophisticated distribution networks that enable goods and services to flow freely across international borders.

Today, two-thirds of business' revenues are spent with external suppliers, a trend known as Corporate Virtualization. What was once a pay slip is now a supplier invoice. The modern business consists of a small central core conducting a large virtual orchestra of outsourced providers—whether you call them suppliers or partners. This means that the majority of operational activity now takes place outside of the company. So where Henry Ford designed and built every part of his cars, nowadays car manufacturers source nearly everything from third parties—and then assemble.

These external relationships help define the modern company. And smarter management of these relationships can significantly improve business performance.

The Outsourcing Conundrum re-envisions outsourcing as a key lever for business success, breaking the archaic stigma that outsourcing is a transactional processing support function, presenting alternative commercial and operating models for modern business leaders to consider in today's fast-moving, global business environment.

A must-read for anyone who wants to think about outsourcing in a more modern context.

Guy Strafford, FCA, Chief Client Officer, Proxima
London, United Kingdom
www.proximagroup.com

Years ago, Damian Scallon created the "operationally excellent" platform our company uses still today, based upon his Three P's: Purpose, Process, and People. The enemy of great is *good*—Damian's knowledge and approach has driven our company over the "good" wall to achieve greatness, and his book, *The Outsourcing Conundrum*, can help you and your company do the same. It is a must-read for all service providers and buyers.

The evidence of a job well done is to receive the next purchase order; the evidence of a great provider is a recommendation from buyer to buyer to "use these guys—they will never let you down." As companies continue to seek ways to grow and be competitive in the marketplace, they will need to find increasingly creative inside-outsourcing partnerships to deliver excellent service and be recommended over and over.

The map through the inside-outsourcing labyrinth to becoming a great—a *revered*—supplier/partner is here in *The Outsourcing Conundrum*. Damian has captured the essence of the outsourcing mystery and put it into a practical, understandable, and useable guide.

J. Scott Robertson, Chairman and Owner, RCF Group
West Chester, Ohio
www.TheRCFGroup.com

For over 20 years I have been working in the industrial services business. I started off as a nightshift supervisor for a crew of 10 blue-collar guys, with some leadership experience and no technical cleaning know-how at all. Today, I run the very same company as I started up in, but now as CEO and majority owner of an organization that grew from those 10 guys to 350 + people today.

With some amusement, I recognized myself when I read Damian Scallon's stories in *The Outsourcing Conundrum*. I must commend Damian's spot-on analysis of the puzzles and problems an inside-outsourcing company faces in trying to satisfy its customers every day during the course of their relationship. If I had this book in my hands 20 years ago, I could have avoided many mistakes and struggles while striving to be the best possible supplier to my customers. Even so, it will help me tremendously going forward, with coaching and leading my team through the labyrinth of interconnections among Purpose, Process and People—all three of which are so key to earning trust and success with the customer, and so inextricably linked together.

I would recommend that everyone who is planning to start up, or is currently active, in the inside-outsourcing business read this book. Many of the true stories in *The Outsourcing Conundrum* from the author's own experience capture that drama when things are about to turn ugly with your customer, and how they can be changed by using the systematic methods mentioned in the book, if you have the right attitude.

Kjell-Gunnar Granaas, CEO, Premier Service Sverige AB
Gothenburg, Sweden
www.premier.se

PREFACE

A Path to Navigate the "Inside-Outsourcing" Labyrinth

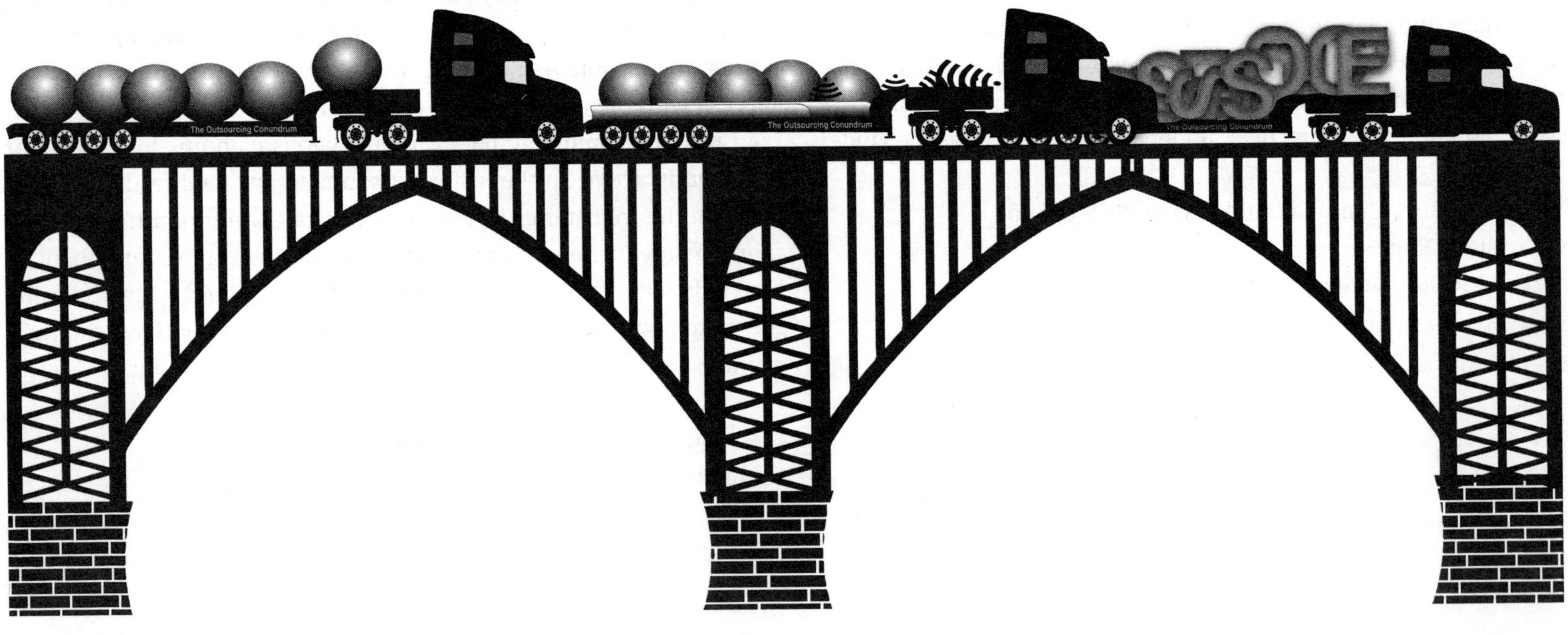

"In our rush to grow, we all need to be careful NOT to lose that essence which makes us special—that essence that somebody is willing to attach value to. If your growth rate exceeds the ability of your experienced people to support, you won't be as successful."

Eric Stevens, Director, Lean Manufacturing Systems—GM Europe
Excerpted from University of Michigan World Class Management Seminar

---

Every company has a strategic goal to grow its business at some measurable rate. This demand for growth has led companies to strategically embrace outsourcing to establish a competitive advantage. Outsourcing certain carefully selected non-core activities to suppliers that are more capable and cost effective than their own internal resources at performing these activities can give companies a competitive edge. Decades ago, one of the largest expenses for any company was the cost of its labor; today the number-one cost for most companies is the cost of its supplier's invoices. Instead of the labor required to manufacture a new product being owned by the manufacturer, hundreds of suppliers who collectively provide the parts and services for a new product now own it.

Yesterday, a company's focus on selection of the right talent was critical to their long-term success. Today, that effort and energy needs to be applied to the right selection of the most talented suppliers—suppliers who will be able to increase the company's ability by providing experienced people aligned with the client to provide value. Only by having a supplier base aligned with them to provide value, can the company focus its time and energy on growing its core business.

A more recent and growing trend is "inside-outsourcing," where companies outsource to service providers business functions that are provided much closer to home, in some cases right in the customer's location. In these cases, the outsourcing provider's employees work right alongside the client's own workforce.

For example, there are very few auto manufacturers who have not now outsourced the cleaning of their automotive facility to a service provider. Most auto manufacturers have not only outsourced the cleaning, but also the complete facilities maintenance of their plants. As this trend continues, auto manufacturers are also using inside-outsourcing service providers (IOSPs) to perform logistics services, including both delivery of all assembly parts to the production line and delivery of the finished product to the shipping line, leaving the plant's employees focused on the quality of assembling a world-class product.

The inside-outsourcing service provider's employees work right in the client's plant, working alongside the car manufacturer's own employees, and are integrated into the client's location and manufacturing processes. In these cases, there is much more at stake than just the price of the service provided; it is critical that buyers and IOSPs be aligned, be partners in the process, and pursue mutual goals.

As the trend towards outsourcing continues—and particularly for companies purchasing inside-outsourcing services—both those who supply and buy desperately need to become aligned on the larger, strategic business reasons and purpose for why the service is being outsourced. A company's ability to choose the right partners to outsource to, partners who have a tried and true model to help navigate the service delivery process, has never been more important.

The Outsourcing Conundrum provides a model that service providers can use as a path to navigate the labyrinth of inside-outsourcing. *The Outsourcing Conundrum* will give the service provider a proven path to deliver service excellence to their customer, and will also provide insight to procurement groups on how to choose an inside-outsourcing service provider.

A competent, professional inside-outsourcing service provider has the ability to reduce the total cost of operating a facility by far more than the cost of the IOSP's invoice. In my 40 years as an IOSP, I have had the luxury of working with a handful of customers who were actually able to tap into the full capability of an IOSP and receive this benefit. *The Outsourcing Conundrum* outlines steps to be taken by both the IOSP and the purchasers of inside-outsourcing services to realize this benefit.

BUT WHAT IS INSIDE-OUTSOURCING?

Inside-outsourcing is a service very often provided within the walls of a customer's facility. That is, a service is being outsourced by an organization to a service provider, but the service is actually performed on the customer's premises, alongside the customer's employees, rather than at some offsite location. Frequently the service provider is working with, and sometimes even training and managing, the client organization's employees.

In many manufacturing scenarios, inside-outsourcing services (IOS) are performed on production processes next to production workers. You might see IOSP employees cleaning aisles, delivering production parts, repairing production equipment, or actually managing the workforce. In institutions, these services are often the first point of contact that a customer has with your organization, or the IOSP may have full responsibility for the facility in which the customer and your employees interact.

One very simple example of inside-outsourcing that any parent can relate to is the choice of a babysitter. You might consider shopping for the lowest price for services such as the oil change for your car or choice of Internet supplier, but you would introduce completely different criteria when selecting the person who will be the nanny or babysitter for your children. This person will be working inside the walls of your home and with your most valuable asset. You would not wish to pull into your driveway to see your children on the front lawn of your burning home, only to hear the sitter explain that calling the fire department was not included in the scope of work you left for them. You would look for and hire a responsible person who not only completed the scope of service you documented, but also understood your needs and was responsible for meeting those overall needs. The total cost of making the right decision far outweighs the amount charged by a responsible sitter at the end of the night.

Similarly, a professional and competent IOSP takes responsibility for understanding the needs of a company, and possesses the skills and capabilities to deliver on the scope of services while continually becoming more efficient and effective, providing customers with an overall competitive advantage.

IS IT VERY VISIBLE?

Inside-outsourcing service providers are very visible, and very often can impact the quality, cost, and delivery of the product. Inside-outsourcing service providers can be seen:

- In airports, performing maintenance, housekeeping, food and beverage, logistics, and greeting services.
- In hospitals, performing maintenance, food and beverage, janitorial, housekeeping, grounds maintenance, administration duties, and gift shop services.
- In universities and colleges, performing clerical duties, housekeeping, facilities, janitorial, and cafeteria services.
- In manufacturing, performing production support, technical cleaning, heavy and light maintenance, dock functions, general-store functions, line-side delivery, housekeeping, and grounds services.
- In office buildings, performing security, facilities, housekeeping, maintenance, property-management, and IT services.

The proximity of service providers to a company's customers and employees makes the need for the correct selection and evaluation process ever more critical. The IOSP becomes an extension of the organization's brand for whom they are providing services. The IOSP's employees are as responsible as the client organization's for the impression the customer gets of the organization's quality of service and friendliness of interaction with the organization's employees. In other words, whether the people the customer is dealing with are employees of the client organization or the IOSP can be totally transparent to the end customer. Both buyers of IOS and providers of IOS cannot afford to make a mistake where they end up in a misaligned relationship.

WHAT'S CHANGED?

The reasons for inside-outsourcing vary as widely as the range of services. Some companies choose to make an inside-outsourcing initiative part of a new product launch, part of a new process addition, part of a new corporate structure or re-organization, or simply because everyone else seems to be doing it.

It is, however, important to recognize that most companies will invest in areas that generate revenue, while starving those considered overhead or expense. It is, therefore, likely that the best IOS provider is one who invests in those areas that the company has chosen to starve. Continuous improvement is key to being cost effective and companies do not usually invest in continuous improvement initiatives in non-core activities. Inside-outsourcing works best if the company making the purchase views it as a management tool that aligns with their overall strategy of being competitive. It has to be a good fit.

KEYS TO A GOOD FIT

Michael F. Corbett of The Outsourcing Research Council states, "If you choose to do something yourself, you should be better at it than the best company that your competitor could hire to do it for them." The choice of the right service provider for the right opportunity is critical.

Michael's advice rings true in my experience with many of the offshore automotive manufacturers who moved operations to North America, and, as part of their strategy, partnered with suppliers who were far more competent in non-production-related functions.

If you are an organization looking to outsource to a service provider, a good strategic fit means that the service they perform:

- Is important to your facility or process.
- Is an ongoing operation.
- Improves your resource utilization by being outsourced.

The best service provider for any outsourcing opportunity will have the required competency, capability, and commitment. It will be:

- Better at the service than the organization themselves, with a proven performance record.
- Committed to the business of providing service.
- Proactively investing in their own special competency.
- Able to deploy and replicate their systems geographically.
- Prepared to scale up to meet customer requirements.

The relationship between the customer and service provider works best when;

- Company cultures are compatible.
- Commercial terms provide synergy.
- Roles and responsibilities are well defined.
- Goals and reward systems are aligned.
- Communication is multi-level and two-way.

WHO SHOULD READ THE BOOK?

This book is primarily for all of the people who work for inside-outsourcing service providers. This includes those who directly deliver the services in an operations group, as well as all those who find themselves in a support role to the operations group:

- Human Resources
- IT Departments
- Business Development / Marketing
- Finance Departments

Buyers of inside-outsourcing services will also find the book valuable in helping to understand how IOS providers work, as well as in selecting the right provider and in developing a productive and effective working relationship with their IOS provider.

If you agree with the philosophy of *The Outsourcing Conundrum*, you will want to show the companion video clip to all of your hourly associates. This is a quick and easy way to educate your broader teams on the process. The clip is available at

www.TheOutsourcingConundrum.com

If you are a member of any procurement department that has, or will have, responsibility for purchasing inside-outsourcing services for your company, you will most definitely benefit from taking time to read *The Outsourcing Conundrum*. It will provide you with tremendous insight on what questions to ask when choosing a supplier, and what is important for inclusion in a request for services by a supplier.

MY INTENTION BEHIND WRITING THE BOOK?

The service industry, although not my original choice for how I was going to spend my career, has rewarded me and allowed me to provide for my family. The 40 years it has taken me to get to this point have been a typical mixture of both good and bad experiences. The inside-outsourcing service industry continues to grow, and, as companies purchasing outsourcing services continue their focus on their own core business, the opportunities for suppliers are unfathomable. Dozens and dozens of excellent business books have been written, and in this book I mention many that have had an impact on my success. This book, though, is not designed to compete with those books. It is designed as a one-stop shop for those in the inside-outsourcing service industry who want a "go to" or "how to" playbook on how to succeed in the service industry.

For 40 years I have seen hourly associates start a career at eight bucks an hour, and achieve senior positions with compensation in the high six digits.

I have also seen managers collapse from stress, hourly associates hurt beyond belief, suppliers go bankrupt, divorces, shootings, etc. One day it occurred to me to write this book, to give back to the industry, and to help the next generation prosper, safely and sanely.

Over the years it has become very clear that all of the pieces that contribute to a well valued inside-outsourcing service provider (IOSP), must be intact. It very much resembles a spider web where each strand, regardless of its length or density, plays a role.

Or, to me, a more appropriate analogy for inside-outsourcing is the image of a labyrinth, and the one I have used in the title and on the cover of the book. Unlike a maze, which has several possible paths and is built to be confusing, a labyrinth has only a single path leading into and out of the center. While the route is still complex and confusing, the one true path is there, a single, clear route to those who know how to navigate it.

The Outsourcing Conundrum provides a step-by-step model to navigate the complex labyrinth of inside-outsourcing; it offers a clear path for you to follow to improve your chances for success by being able to align the needs of customers with the processes required to deliver services, as well as with the people who will deliver the services. Following the process outlined here, step-by-step and in the correct order, will guide you through the potentially puzzling labyrinth of inside-outsourcing, showing you the clear, proven route to becoming a valued service provider and partner to your customers.

The result is an inside-outsourcing service provider where all resources are applied to continually improving the level of service experienced by the customer, creating a longer-term viable partnership between the IOSP and the customer.

The Outsourcing Conundrum also provides a path for those who procure inside-outsourcing services, to better build and assess against the criteria for choosing a provider that can meet the current and future expectations of the organization.

INTRODUCTION

When building a business model, you have to start with what is core to its success or failure.

"Whenever a business is established, it either explicitly or implicitly employs a particular business model that describes the architecture of the value creation, delivery, and capture mechanisms employed by the business enterprise. The essence of a business model is that it defines the manner by which the business enterprise delivers value to customers, entices customers to pay for value, and converts those payments to profit: it thus reflects management's hypothesis about what customers want, how they want it, and how an enterprise can organize to best meet those needs, get paid for doing so, and make a profit."

David J. Teece (2010), "Business Models, Business Strategy and Innovation"

In 1974 while I was in high school, I was given the opportunity for some part-time employment to assist with tuition. The first night on the job I arrived at an automotive assembly plant in Scarborough, Ontario, Canada. All of the other new recruits and I were taken to the roof, handed wet suits, and introduced to two things: a paint stack and high-pressure water blasting guns. We were on the job for about an hour when one of the recruits screamed and dropped onto a pallet. We all rushed over, and I saw a sight I would never forget. The recruit had put the nozzle end of the gun under his arm to pull it free and the trigger engaged, ripping most of his arm from his shoulder.

The injured recruit never regained the use of his arm; quite sadly his is only one of many such stories surrounding the high-pressure water blasting service business at that time.

I began to understand very quickly after that day that the reason I had the part-time job was that it had been deemed too dangerous for the automotive company's full-time employees to perform. To offset the risk, the assembly plant outsourced the work to a service company.

My educational goal at that time was studying to become a teacher, but, as irony would have it, the part-time job became a career that has spanned 40 years.

That night in Scarborough started me on a journey that eventually led to the writing of this book. The incident on the roof of that automotive plant made it very clear to me that if the company I was relying upon for my school tuition was going to prevail, we needed to establish some level of law and order, and an operating system that allowed the employees to work sanely and safely.

As time progressed, I found myself in leadership roles in companies that were providing outsourcing services to others, with responsibility over such things as operations, human resources, business development, technical support and new company start-ups. As my experience in the service industry grew, so did my understanding of what a leader in the outsourcing service industry must do if that company was to be successful. As my career grew and I had responsibility for hundreds of managers and thousands of hourly team members in many countries, the need for a service delivery model grew as well. As you will read, every failure I experienced was due to a lack of compliance to the model. The original kernel for the model grew from the book *Kaizen*, by Masaaki Imai. As time went on and experience challenged the model, it began to grow and evolve. *The Service Profit Chain* that was written in the '90s, outlining the link between employee and customer satisfaction, was a stimulus for even more change to the model, until it has come to rest today with what I call *The Outsourcing Conundrum*.

A LABYRINTH

Many of the inside-outsourcing service providers I worked with over the years view the business as an endless puzzle or riddle. Some even call it a maze, where you spend days making turn after turn but cannot actually find your way out. I prefer to look at it as a labyrinth. A labyrinth is often spoken of as a maze, but that is not totally accurate. A labyrinth has a path in and a path out. A person enters into a labyrinth confused and leaves with clarity, as long as they follow the phases of the labyrinth. The Outsourcing Conundrum Model is a labyrinth with a path in and a path out, as long as the phases are followed. We'll get into exactly how to follow those phases and that path later in the book.

The outsourcing service industry has many channels and forms, and I will explore several that I have been associated with in this book. Regardless of the channel or form, though, every leader in the service industry has to operate with a model that ensures the safe and proficient delivery of service to their customer.

Think of a model as the "how to" for how you will play your game, beat out your competition, and be viewed as a value provider by your customer. Without a model, the service industry can become a real puzzle and conundrum. For example, too often there is a disconnect between those who lead the purchasing process for a customer and the actual

Labyrinth—A Path In and a Path Out

group that is the end user of the inside-outsourcing service, such as production or the facilities group. In these cases, the inside-outsourcing service provider (IOSP) gets caught in the middle. This creates a substantial amount of pain for those charged to deliver the service and for those relying on the delivery of the service. No one wins because no one can agree on what was bought vs. what was sold.

The Outsourcing Conundrum was written as a roadmap for service providers and buyers of inside-outsourcing services. It is a roadmap to close the gap between "why" the service is being outsourced by the buyer of the service, and "how" the service will be delivered by the service provider. One serious lesson I learned is that the confusion of "why" something needs to be done with "how" it will be done usually ends up with the people caught in the middle as victims. The Outsourcing Conundrum Model has worked for decades in many business environments because it naturally adapts to change. It is driven by "why" the outsourcing is taking place in the first place. It is customer-centric and aligns perfectly with customer-intimate businesses, of which service happens to be one.

Over the years I have seen many procurement initiatives come and go from purchasing departments in different companies. Some get it right, but sadly many do not, and their incompetence hurts the service provider businesses. Many purchasing agents come to play with tools designed to get the best price for the service, such as target pricing. Ironically many of these purchasing agents do not understand "why" the service is being outsourced other than for cost-reduction purposes. A better reason to outsource is to align with a supplier who is more competent and expert at the service than the customer, the purchasing company, is currently experiencing. If customers for IOS understood the "why," they would probably be better able to asses the "true cost" for the service, vs. shopping for the lowest invoice cost.

One infamous purchasing leader for a major automotive plant set the service provider/buyer relationship back decades, in my opinion. His reign at a particular company in Detroit lasted only a few years, but the damage that was done lasted for a decade. Every member of his team wore their watch on their right wrist, as opposed to their left, symbolic of the realization they had not yet drained every possible penny out of the service-provider base. The initiative was totally steered to drive down cost at "any cost," with no regard to much else. Hello, target pricing, goodbye, service-provider partnerships.

The Outsourcing Conundrum is based around three intertwined components:

- Purpose
- Process
- People

These three components work together in a similar fashion to a spider's web. Each component is a critical strand and, like a spider's web, if one strand is broken the entire structure becomes broken. It is impossible to weight the value of one of these components over the others, because it is impossible to be a best-in-class service provider and not give equal importance to all three components. As service providers diverge from the model and focus on one component over the others, they become branded as such.

For several of my years in the service industry, I had the privilege of working for a company that built the relationship between Purpose, Process and People into their DNA.

This led them to become the dominant market leader in their space for over two decades, through multiple company acquisitions and changes of ownership. This company outgrew the competition by ten-fold, and became the employer of choice within its niche.

I have also had the opportunity of working with members of the purchasing community who "get it" and work hard with their service

providers in an effort to make the IOSP, and themselves, better companies. These service buyers understand that as the outsourcing of services grows, the need for higher value from the service providers also grows. In any positive relationship, which is what a buyer/ service provider should have, there has to be growth, and growth is based upon understanding. These purchasing groups were able to entice their service providers to remain loyal for decades through many, many, downturns in the industry because they approached the relationship as a true partnership, ensuring that their goals and expectations were aligned at every level, and creating true value together.

PURPOSE

Every decision to outsource a service or an activity has a purpose, a business reason for "why" these particular activities are being outsourced. In the example I gave at the start of this chapter, the service company where I began my career was given the job opportunity because it was deemed too dangerous to have the automotive plant's own employees do the work. Understanding such a motive for outsourcing should set off an alarm for a smart service provider.

The service being outsourced either requires a level of skill that the service provider is capable of, or the situation is inherently unsafe. The latter should be avoided.

During my career, I had the opportunity to be associated with Team Trek, a service provider of adult education that serviced many Fortune 500 companies. Team Trek is a small Arkansas-based company that excels at understanding the purpose for an outsourcing decision. This company's value was based upon the experience of thousands of managers who graced their campus from many different organizations. It was critical to the success of this company to understand fully "why" they were being asked to conduct the education versus their customer doing it in-house with their own resources. I was one of hundreds of managers from my organization who attended leadership training at Team Trek. We used Team Trek because they brought value through their expertise and focus, on an area that we were not expert in and that was not core to our business. So the real reason we outsourced to Team Trek was because of their expertise vs. our own. We will talk more about Team Trek in the chapters to follow.

All smart companies focus on their core. This leads many of them to find alternate ways of getting done what is deemed as non-core by outsourcing to service providers. Outsourcing allows the client company to focus its energy on where it derives profit—the core business—and not to be distracted by the noise surrounding non-core functions and activities. To any service provider who has taken the time to understand this purpose, it should be crystal clear that the buying company expects that their non-core businesses/services should be treated by the service provider as being core to them. It also demands that the buying company's procurement group choose a partner/service provider who can meet that goal, and not just the goal of being low-priced.

During an outsourcing discussion at a recent meeting with the corporate executives of a large tire manufacturer, the head of global production stated that the reason to change service providers was they were above all else looking for a culture change. They wanted an inside-outsourcing company who was strong enough to stand up to their plant management while meeting day-to-day production, as well as to change the role of the service provider in the plant. The production manager saw these things happening as the outsourcing engagement grew, and they became more reliant on the service provider for all non-core activities. Logically, that service provider must be viewed as a valued partner by the plant. The purpose for the change was not cost-driven, but rather motivated by the need for long-term change on the plant floor. The tire producer chose a more expensive service provider, but netted higher production levels. Net-net, the total cost of production was lower.

Every hourly team member or associate who is currently working in the service industry, or has ever worked in the service industry, performs to a much higher standard when the purpose of the work they are performing is explained to them. Engagement of those who perform the work is directly related to how well they understand "why" the work is important, as well as "how" to complete the work to everyone's satisfaction, including their own.

PROCESS

The service provider has to be able to execute on the services being outsourced, and the buyer must choose a service provider who can execute on the services the client is proposing to outsource. The service provider must have a structured approach to the delivery of the service to be provided.

A basic process to deliver on the outsourced services must accomplish certain very measurable goals. The work needs to be completed on time, so it will require a schedule. The work must be done to a set level of quality, so it will require a standard. Those who perform the work must do so in a safe and motivated manner, so they will need to be engaged. The finished services need to be inspected, and any variations require corrective action to bring them back into compliance. This is extremely basic block-and-tackling for anyone who is in the service industry.

In the inside-outsourcing industry, an even more sophisticated process must accomplish all of that, but must also promote the right behaviors from management and hourly associate teams alike. Every system and tool must be designed to underscore the service provider's brand to both the employee of the IOSP and the customer. If you view yourself as a company who empowers its people but you build in inspection systems that disempower your people, then your process is simply working against itself.

A well-oiled process will unify the customer's team with the IOSP team and will be a continual source of suggestions to improve the service delivery. If you are looking for engagement from your team and suggestions for improvement, yet the system surrounding the submission of suggestions takes months before a participant hears feedback on a suggestion, then again your system is competing with your brand.

All tools and operating systems must align with and support the behaviors your company wishes to exhibit as part of their brand promise. In the service industry, and especially when teams are working alongside those of the company for whom they are performing service, the brand is displayed by those who perform the work. It's that simple.

PEOPLE

The service provider's people are critical to the successful delivery of the outsourced services. The people provide the judgment on what gets done, how it gets done, when it gets done, and what can be done to improve it. Without people, there is no service. This is not complicated; it's very simple. Ironic as it may be, it is probably one of the largest unattended ingredients within the service-provider base.

In the service industry there are two categories of people: the service providers' teams who deliver on the services, and the customers who receive the services. The interaction, motivation, and harmony between these two groups will lead down one of two paths: poor service experience with minimal value, or excellent service experience with exceptional value.

Also, ironically, most purchasing groups pay little or no attention to the issues around the people when they are acquiring services. However, and it should come as no surprise, those purchasing groups who get outsourcing right put a tremendous amount of focus on a service provider's people.

One of the biggest mistakes I have seen, and still see, within the service provider community is that within their own companies, IOSP operations teams do not embrace the responsibility of selecting, training, assessing, and recognizing their teams. They allow the HR department to lead these activities, and then spend 80 percent of their time complaining about the HR department and trying to get rid of people who do not fit.

One thing you will notice as you read this book is my distaste for the traditional HR department. During a class on Executive HR Strategy at the University of Michigan, the professor made a profound point: If HR wants to be considered as a player, it needs to figure out how the department impacts the bottom line. For those of us who are service providers, the impact of bad hires, poor performance, high turnover, lack of engagement, misaligned incentive plans, etc., all lead directly to negative impact on the bottom line. Why can HR not see that? This frustration led me to accept a leadership role in HR, which was one of the smartest career moves I made. It allowed me to explore fully and first-hand how to hire, promote, and incentivize behaviors that drive direct improvements to the bottom line.

THE CORE

The core of The Outsourcing Conundrum Model is the three Ps:

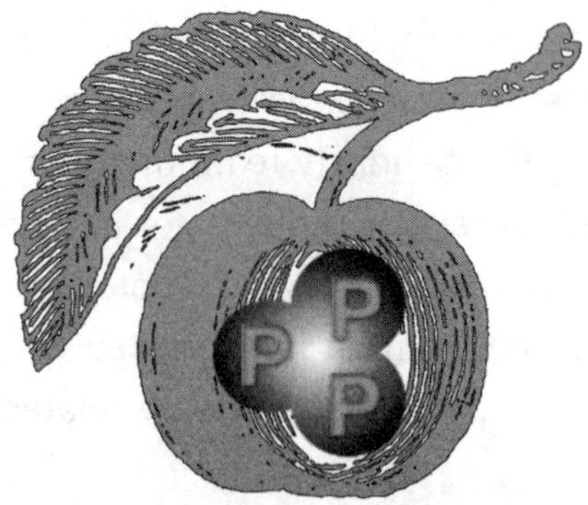

- The **Purpose** is "why" the work needs to be done,

- The **Process** is "how" the work will be done, and
- The **People** are the ones who perform the work.

Adherence to The Outsourcing Conundrum Model forces competing systems from all departments into alignment.

The Outsourcing Conundrum Model directly ties the People system with the delivery Process system and the Purpose for the service.

Imagine the power when why, how, and who is doing the work are all working harmoniously with each other. *The Outsourcing Conundrum* aligns these three components into a straightforward system, allowing both buyers and service providers to achieve their mutual goals.

HOW *THE OUTSOURCING CONUNDRUM* IS ORGANIZED

The book is broken down into three parts. Each part is named after one of the three key components:

Part One	Purpose
Part Two	Process
Part Three	People

The chapters within each part are steps in The Outsourcing Conundrum Model that belong closest to that component. As you move from part to part and chapter to chapter, the model will build one piece at a time.

The book is heavily illustrated to appeal to people who fire on both sides of the brain, as well as those who fire predominantly on one.

It has been my experience that the service industry lends itself more to experiential learners than traditional academic learners, so the book was designed to meet that need. If you are wired in such a way that you never actually read a business book from beginning to end, I suggest you focus on the three chapters associated with each of the main ideas (that is the overview at the beginning of each part), and also read the chapters Assemble, Align & Assess – People, and Re-Define the Need. From that point, you can decide if you wish to delve into any other chapters for further clarification.

This book is drawn from my base of experience being directly involved as a service provider or as a customer of a service provider. To broaden the concept of the model outside of the Original Equipment Manufacturing (OEM) market, I will also reference examples from a company dedicated to experiential learning where I was both a customer and a facilitator.

At the end of each chapter there are what I view to be the key takeaway points for that section. If you are skimming through the book, you might want to check those out.

TAKEAWAYS:

- People are trained on the Process to deliver on the Purpose.
- So, the Purpose must be clear, the Process must align with the Purpose and the People need to understand both fully.

A disciplined focus on the core components of Purpose, Process and People, ensures the model does not stray from its initial intent.

PART 1
PURPOSE

PURPOSE OVERVIEW

"How do you explain how others are able to achieve things that defy all of the assumptions?"

"Do business with people who believe in what you believe."

Simon O. Sinek is an author best known for popularizing the concept of "the golden circle" and Start With Why, described by TED as "a simple but powerful model for inspirational leadership" – Wikipedia

---

After a 17-year career, I left a Toronto-based service company and had the opportunity to join a start-up Cincinnati-based service company. This career change provided me with my first exposure to a leader who led by clearly defining the purpose of the company.

Over the next 20 years, I learned and internalized just how powerful a company can be if it's led with purpose, if employees are educated as to why the company exists, versus what the company provides. The former sounds like "we are here because…" while the latter sounds more like "here is what we do." One inspires, while the other just informs.

I have personally never met anyone who does not know what they do, but very few know why they are doing it. It is the why that pulls on the heart strings.

In his book *Start With Why*, Simon Sinek explains how there is a key part of the human brain, the limbic, that governs our gut feelings. It also helps determine if something feels right. It appears that the old saying, "Go with your gut," actually has a biological basis. This is why we need to know the reason or purpose for why we are doing something before we fully engage. When I failed to clearly define the purpose for a key action or strategic direction to my team, for example, they inevitably filled in the blank for themselves with what they perceived to be the why we were doing it. When a company requires change, it has to retire the "old why" and replace it with the "new why," by clearly communicating the new purpose for a change in direction.

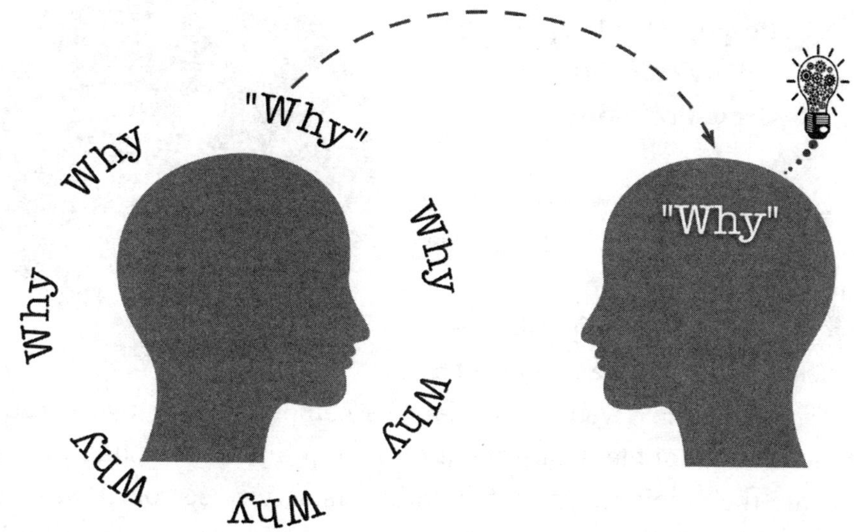

Gone are the days when people did things just because they were told to, or, worse, because they were expected to. We want to know why. Without understanding why, we are not able to be empowered or engaged.

As I stated above, when I made my move to Cincinnati in 1992, I experienced my first purpose-based leader. Although I could not explain it, I loved it—the feeling that what I did mattered and was important. Today it is easier to label. I was engaged and empowered. This style of management was 180 degrees from what I left in Toronto, a company whose primary focus was profit. The Cincinnati company never chased profit, and yet they became the largest and most profitable service company in their niche.

We did not have a meeting where we did not discuss how we could make our customers better, as well as how to align our people with these goals. We operated on four key values:

Be the Best.
Respect Our People.
Satisfy Our Customers.
Grow Profitably.

The last value was always deemed a result of performing the first three, but it was also a requirement to be able to invest in the first three—a perfect circle of cause and effect.

This company went on to defy its competition for two decades by achieving double-digit growth on its top and bottom lines, and it became the employer of choice within its service sector. It was also purchased on three separate occasions, and was still a market leader through the economic downturn in 2009.

Best-in-class service companies know the power of being purpose-driven. By being purpose-driven, they build a great amount of trust that translates into a real asset for the company as goodwill. The reason is simple. Understanding why builds trust. If I trust you, I will give you 100 percent plus, and 100 percent plus means that you will get my hands, my head and my heart; in other words, complete engagement. I do not know too many people who, given a choice, would go to work for a company they do not trust, or stay long-term with a company where they have lost their trust. Not overly complicated is it?

To be a best-in-class company, you have to lead through purpose—engaging and empowering your employees.

Today, most organizations outsource some aspect of what they do to suppliers. In a recent article in *Outsource*, an online magazine, Proxima, a global procurement company, made the point that much of a company's labor is moving from its payroll to being invoiced by suppliers. The new number is roughly 70 percent. That is a big number by any interpretation, and also raises an interesting question: How do we now manage companies where employees, who used to be seen as key to their success, are replaced by the combination of employees and supplier partners who will be key to their success?

The trend is creating a new problem for both suppliers and buyers of outsourced services. *The Outsourcing Conundrum* provides a model for both buyers and suppliers to help make the critical choice of who will be the best partner, by leading with the purpose behind all buy and sell decisions for outsourced services. This choice of the right partnerships for all outsourced services is becoming as important as the choice of the right people for your team. Both provide you with a key competitive advantage.

A company cannot afford to have a bad supplier, and a supplier cannot afford to have a bad customer. In both scenarios, the individual company brands are put at risk.

A good sense of purpose can bridge many gaps between a supplier and buyer of services.

In 2013, I was involved with a project at a high-volume production facility. The company decided to outsource a vital process that sat between where the product was molded and where it was cured. Failure in this area would directly impact production. In a conversation with the head buyer at the plant, she made it clear that she saw no logic in why such a key operation was being outsourced, yet she continued the pursuit for the cheapest supplier. This contract was substantial by any metric. Its value was in the high teens of millions per year. It represented around 20 percent of the plant's workforce. The plant would recruit a large portion of their labor force directly from the supplier's workforce, and, as previously mentioned, the outsourced process could directly impact plant production.

In 2005, I was involved in a different opportunity at an engine manufacturer in southern Michigan. The leader of that operation made one thing very clear to everyone, its purpose. He said, "We are going to work together as a community of employees and supplier partners to build the best engines anywhere. We will outsource to experts where we lack expertise to achieve this goal." The procurement group was tasked with finding a supplier that could meet that purpose. This contract value was also in the high teens of millions per year. It represented around 20 percent of the plant's workforce. The plant would recruit a portion of their labor force from the supplier's workforce, and the outsourced process could directly impact plant production.

In the first example, the company was focused only on what they were outsourcing, not why, and in the second they were focused on why they were outsourcing and not what.

Contemplate the danger of corporations that are heading into a relationship where neither has put in place the basic foundation for trust and mutual understanding. What supplier of services in their right mind would go into business with anyone they do not trust? In the service industry, when buyers and suppliers develop a strained relationship resulting in the termination of the contract, the victims of this judgment become the employees and their families.

Today the topic of customer fit is aired and discussed before we dispatch any resources to a new service opportunity. In many cases we even take it a step further, and the actual physical locations of

potential customers are discussed for "right fit." Will they be a good long-term customer, do they align with our goals—our purpose?

Recently I have seen a lot of books and articles about the war for talent, finding good employees, and retaining good employees. What I think is equally important today is that companies focus on and understand the need for talented and aligned supplier partners. This will become a key to their future success.

QUICK STORY

In January of 2014, I was invited to visit a plastics supplier in the mid-west that supplies front and rear fascia to a prominent auto manufacturer. The plant was experiencing quality and production issues, and was looking for a solution. Within the first 15 minutes of dialogue with the plant manager, he stated he was just looking for "better trained monkeys." I did not have to re-read our company's Purpose statement to understand we were not in the business of supplying monkeys. The meeting lasted 20 minutes in total.

ALIGNMENT: THE IMPACT OF ENGAGEMENT

Don't you hate buzz words? Alignment is one of those buzz words that managers run around spouting to their teams, and purchasing agents spout to their suppliers. It is inevitable that when a supplier contract fails to meet the requirements of the company, the concept of alignment is tossed on the table.

- "You are not aligned."
- "You need to become more aligned."
- "Your team is not aligned with our team."

Okay, alignment is a buzz word, but it's not a bad word, and it would definitely be in the best interest of everyone if we were all aligned.

In his book, *The Power of Alignment: How the Right Tools Enhance Organizational Focus*, George Labovitz's research shows that aligned and integrated companies outperform their nearest competitors by every major financial measure. The organizational effectiveness that derives from alignment is a significant competitive advantage. Labovitz defines alignment as a state of being where strategy, team members, customers, and key processes all work together in a seamless fashion. The results are growth and profit.

Brady Wilson in his book, *Love at Work*, focuses on the idea that, when it comes to benefiting from discretionary effort in the workplace, emotional engagement—engagement that tugs at the heart strings, that involves engaging people's hearts—trumps rational engagement, which involves meeting the intellectual needs of their minds. He describes discretionary effort as the difference in the level of effort one is capable of bringing to an activity or a task, versus the effort required to simply get by or make do.

So for this buzz word, alignment, to truly build up the steam required to meet the types of results as defined by Labovitz and Wilson, a company's leadership needs to start to explain why key strategic decisions are made. Alignment is most effectively created when everyone understands the purpose behind what they are being asked to do.

The decisions involved in outsourcing services are critical to members of both teams, buyers and suppliers, because they impact:

- Those whose jobs are being outsourced.
- Those who are coming into the company via a supplier to perform those jobs.

Many times buyers do not take the time to understand why the suppliers are in business in the first place, and how their cultures do or do not align.

The engagement of the service-delivery team is a key to good service. This is nothing new. We all know that in order for us to get our teams engaged, we need to communicate and get our teams to buy in and follow the purpose of our company, the why behind why we are in business.

As a service provider, we need to align the purpose of our company with the purpose behind the outsourcing opportunity, so the teams involved in the delivery of those services are aligned with our customer. In the chapter on Assemble, Align & Assess – People, we will talk more about just how this can be achieved once we understand the purpose.

The Outsourcing Conundrum is broken into three parts: Purpose, Process and People. The true impact of alignment can be achieved only by starting with purpose. It reminds me of my attempts over the years at trying to master bowling. Only when the ball hit the pocket was I able to impact all ten pins and get a strike.

As an operations leader, I visited my sites on a rotational basis, and, as in most situations, those who were not performing were visited more regularly than those who were performing. During all site visits, I would drill down with the management team and hourly team to find out if the overall team understood the true purpose for our being allowed to service this customer. You can probably guess the outcome. Those sites who were performing well on all metrics knew the purpose of our service offering to the customer, and likewise those who performed poorly did not. Today, I feel very confident in saying this is a pattern.

Jim Womack in his book, *Gemba Walks*, does a terrific job of outlining the importance for an operations leader to go to the floor and see for himself how the operation is running and observe the level of engagement of the overall team.

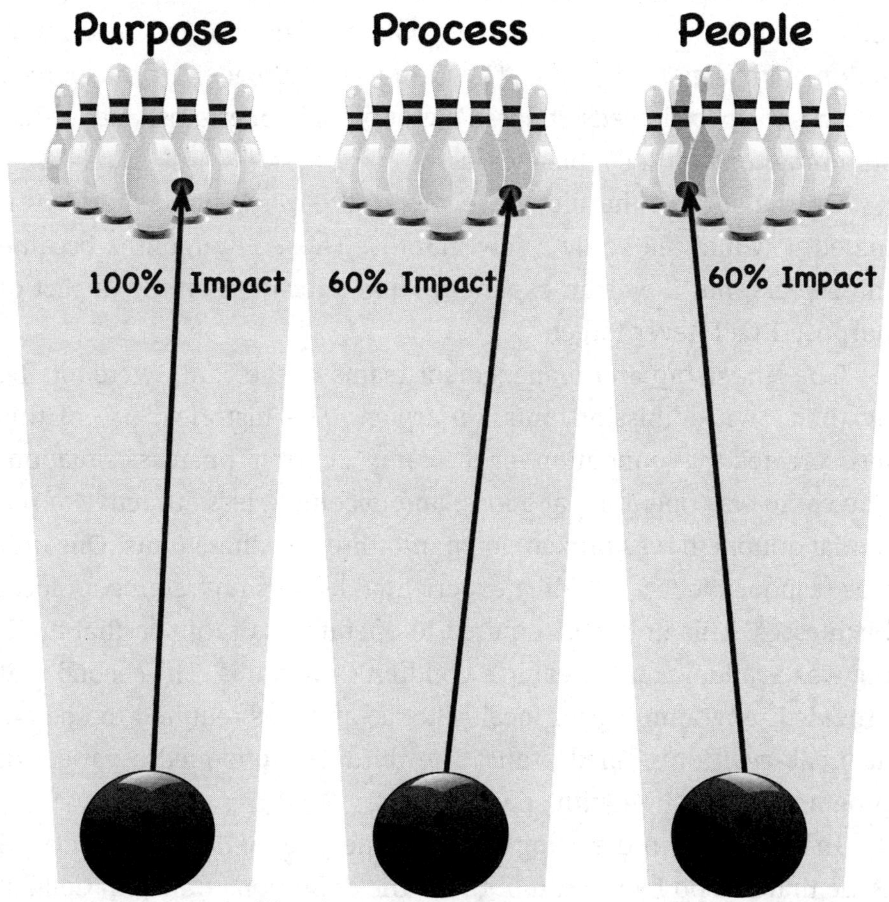

To inspire 100% of your team you must begin with Purpose.

Only when a company starts with purpose will it achieve the impact required to strike the entire organization. In today's environment, that also means that companies who are considering outsourcing their non-core activities to service suppliers must also be able to "hit the pocket" by clearly communicating their purpose with those suppliers to achieve a strike.

In 2001 I was given the opportunity of working for a not-for-profit kids' camp in southern Ohio. This was my first real business interaction with a not-for-profit. The camp is a provider of outsourced services to special needs children's groups, school groups, and leadership programs for local businesses.

On the surface the project seemed to be very simple, and I estimated it would take only a few months. Those few months became three years, but it was an experience and education on the impact of purpose I will never forget.

The leadership and management teams of the camp were totally, by their own admission, mission-driven. The historical use of this term created the foundation for the camp's current business situation. The camp was operating at a loss, and becoming less attractive to potential donors. It was broken down into three business units. One unit was responsible for providing experiential leadership training for local businesses. This unit was required to operate at a profit so that funding was available for the camp's children's programs. The second unit provided programming for local schools, and was required to operate at break-even or a small profit. The third unit provided a variety of programs to children with special needs.

In order to turn the camp around, a new set of definitions needed to be understood by the camp. Using the definitions from Jim Collins' book *Beyond Entrepreneurship*, the camp was oriented to a Vision that contained its Core Values, Purpose and Mission. Core Values were defined as guiding principles, Purpose was defined as the fundamental reason for why the camp existed and Mission was defined as a meaningful goal.

Although the purpose to help kids was crystal clear, the overall business need of running a best-in-class camp was not clear. As a result, the processes, customers, and camp teams were misaligned. To correct this problem, the camp's Board of Directors re-established the vision of the camp with a solid three-year mission/goal. As part of this mission, an operations model was required and someone to oversee its implementation, which became my role.

The Outsourcing Conundrum Model was put in place and targets were set for each of the programs and for those who ran the programs. As a result, the camp experienced turnover in the management ranks, and some of the customers who had previously outsourced work to the camp no longer fit the camp's new model.

Due to the implementation of The Outsourcing Conundrum Model, however, the camp has experienced more than a decade of positive operating contribution. The level of quality realized by the customers is extraordinary, and the camp's ability to attract donor dollars and feed its mission to assist kids is greatly enhanced. This experience taught me to not confuse purpose and mission, and that the benefits from adhering to the model can be realized regardless of the size or type of business.

HOW CAN PURPOSE CHANGE?

For five years, I had responsibility for a contract in our portfolio that provided production maintenance service at a Michigan-based OEM. The corporation had deemed maintenance as non-core to them, and had started an initiative to outsource all maintenance using this one plant as their pilot. It was an extremely successful pilot, and was going to be the springboard for launching us into the maintenance service business. During the economic downturn, however, the corporation was purchased, and the new owner deemed maintenance as core to the company. Within a matter of months the service contract was in-sourced, and our opportunity was lost.

This plant had won several production and quality awards, and was deemed a best-in-class model. But when the purpose for outsourcing no longer aligned with corporate strategy, none of this mattered. Any time there is a change in ownership or leadership, be aware that the purpose driving outsourcing initiatives could change.

TAKEAWAYS:

- Alignment = Engagement
- Engagement = Understanding the Purpose
- If the purpose changes, the alignment will change.

PURPOSE

Define the Need

Define
Expectations
Define
Define
Scope
Re-Define the Need
The Outsourcing Conundrum

> "You can have the latest *Star Trek* production system and most gut-busting sales force in the world. Neither one will mean anything strategically unless everybody on your account team clearly sees the end result he or she is working for."
>
> *Successful Large Account Management*
> Robert B. Miller and Stephen Heiman

Define the Need

The Outsourcing Conundrum is based on understanding the purpose for why activities are being outsourced or re-outsourced through a bidding or sales process. The outsourcing opportunity may have been initiated by a business development professional within a service provider, or it could have been something the company decided made strategic sense. Suppliers would then have been sought to explore the opportunity. Typically I have found that most outsourcing opportunities have one thing in common—they are functions that are non-core to the buying company. In my experience, only a handful of outsourcing opportunities were for services that were core to the company doing the outsourcing. These services were in the form of production support and were critical to the company's production process.

In all cases, the company deciding to outsource has a business need that requires a solution. The company also typically believes at some level that outsourcing is the best option, although those closest to the actual service being considered for outsourcing may very well not share this opinion.

The first step in understanding purpose is defining the need. Define the Need is the step where a specific opportunity is investigated. The solution being sought by the customer typically falls under at least one of the following categories:

Financial

A need for financial relief is pretty much a constant for anyone considering buying a service from an outside supplier.

Many initial outsourcing opportunities involve companies that are outsourcing non-core activities currently being performed by their own employees. Over time, the costs for employees doing these activities often put the company in a non-competitive condition.

Performance

The work is just not getting done, resulting in a negative impact on the company's core business. Typically a company that outsources a service looks for improvement in the area of performance. The key is to define what that performance standard looks like.

Quality

The standard for the required level of quality is not being met, leading to a negative impact on the end product. The key is to define what quality needs are associated with the opportunity. Misinterpretation of how quality

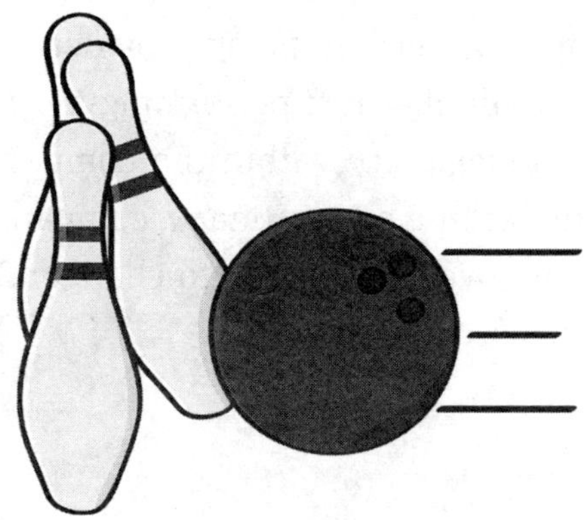

is defined can result in over- or under-pricing a service. The cost of a craftsman does not have to be built in, for example, if a contract requires only a general laborer, but companies go poor pretty quickly if they price for a general laborer but really need a higher level of expertise.

Risk Avoidance

This reason to outsource has grown over the past decade. It is where companies identify activities that have an uncomfortable level of risk associated with them, so the activities are tendered for outsourcing. The level of risk impacts what a company is willing to pay for the service. The higher the risk usually means both a higher perceived value for that service and a higher-profit price tag for the IOSP.

The downside for any supplier when risk is identified as a primary reason for outsourcing is having to evaluate fully the cost of the risk over the long term.

Culture

From my perspective, opportunities associated with a need for culture change are the most desirable. Contracts are often awarded on the merits of the supplier's management systems and teams. These opportunities also lend themselves to becoming partnerships more quickly, as solutions are being provided to a business problem, as opposed to the supplier just performing a list of activities.

Flexibility within the company's labor force is also becoming an important part of many companies' cultures, including how quickly employees can adapt to change. Outsourcing very often fills a need in this area.

Perceived as Non-Core

This is also an area of high growth in outsourcing, where companies declare openly they are no longer going to manage certain aspects of their business.

Over the years I have experienced numerous contracts that failed due to suppliers and buyers not adhering to the basic principle of really fishing to find and define a company's true need, and to fully understand the purpose for why a specific opportunity was being outsourced. The table below gives examples of misunderstood business cases.

In each of these examples, the outsourced service is defined, as well as assumptions made about the purpose, and then the reality of the actual purpose is revealed. It usually took a few months to a year to get to the bottom of an issue that began with a misunderstood purpose. The financial costs to both supplier and buyer were typically extreme.

BUSINESSES PURPOSE TABLE

1. Automotive Maintenance 1970s

Outsourced Service: High-pressure cleaning of an automotive paint shop exhaust system over shutdown.	
Assumed Purpose: Customer required skilled support to complete project over shutdown period.	**Actual Purpose:** The scope of work was deemed too dangerous for completion by customer's employees.
Required Adjustments: safety concerns, value pricing, schedule.	

2. Automotive Production 2005

Outsourced Service: Provide labor and management to run production for off-line door assembly.	
Assumed Purpose: Partner with plant to reduce production cost by outsourcing less skilled production function.	**Actual Purpose:** Transfer safety ergonomic risk from customer to supplier.
Required Adjustments: safety concerns, job rotation, process engineering.	

3. Plastics 1990s

Outsourced Service: Paint Shop Cleaning Services	
Assumed Purpose: Complete cleaning activities as outlined in the prepared Scope of Services.	**Actual Purpose:** Assume ownership for the readiness of the paint shop for day-to-day painting production.
Required Adjustments: scope, caliber of management, number of resources, value pricing.	

4. Weld Line Maintenance 2004

Outsourced Service: Weld line cell and robot cleaning, and minor maintenance.	
Assumed Purpose: Utilization of a skilled supplier to perform non-core cleaning and maintenance activities.	**Actual Purpose**: Transfer downtime issues/blame associated with a poorly designed system to a supplier.
Required Adjustments: caliber of management, schedule, value pricing.	

5. Production Painting 2008

Outsourced Service: Provide production support to paint over-road truck axles.	
Assumed Purpose: Provide motivated skilled painters to offset high production demands.	**Actual Purpose:** Remove customer's employees from an unsafe work environment.
Required Adjustments: choice of customer, safety, work environment.	

6. Managed Services

Outsourced Service: Provide management team to directly supervise customer's employees.	
Assumed Purpose: Implement proven management systems to engage and improve employee productivity.	**Actual Purpose:** Right size labor force, remove customer's management team from line of fire.
Required Adjustments: caliber of management, access to senior management, scope, value pricing.	

Many new business opportunities for inside-outsourcing providers are brought forward by well intentioned, gifted sales people who can make every sale sound like the opportunity of a lifetime. In the table above, all of the contracts are actual examples where we did not adhere to our rule of properly defining the need and fully investigating new business opportunities. All led to extraordinarily bad results, including:

- Loss of limbs
- Major financial losses
- Loss of customer / branding issues
- Management turnover
- Labor conflict and assault
- Loss of growth opportunities

In early 2000, our teams were introduced to the Heiman Miller approach to large account management. In this management process, each customer service opportunity was ranked for its value on the buy/sell hierarchy. At the bottom of the hierarchy, you are a provider of commodity services and at the top you are a valued provider of business solutions. In the middle you are a provider of valued services. Our ability to define the need, versus just listing the activities within each new sales opportunity, gave us the chance to be viewed by our customer in the upper rankings as opposed to being viewed as a commodity. Without a lot of explanation, it is safe to say that suppliers need to avoid being branded/labeled a commodity on the bottom.

IT DOES WORK

In the early '90s, we were given the opportunity to provide services for a Canadian transplant automotive company. (The term transplant is applied to those foreign automotive assembly plants who have moved their manufacturing to North America. Honda, Toyota, Subaru, Hyundai, BMW, Mercedes would be labelled as transplants.) This company made its purpose very transparent, and went overboard when it came to helping us understand its business needs. They were looking for a service-provider partner who would be willing to grow with them over the course of the next decade and more. What started out as a small $250,000 per year opportunity moved to a $10,000,000 opportunity within five years, and a $20,000,000 opportunity over 15 years. If the math is extrapolated over the life of the contract, it has been worth in the neighborhood of $250,000,000. When we started this contract back in the early '90s, we replaced a service provider who could not, or would not, understand that they needed to align themselves with the purpose of their customer. Within a 10-year period of starting at this one location with this customer, our ability to align our people with the purpose of this customer resulted in our being awarded the majority of their business throughout North America.

BEST IN CLASS

Most of the examples used in this book are based on experiences stemming from time spent working with and around manufacturers. I am also going to talk, however, about an extraordinary company I had the privilege to partner with as both a customer and a facilitator.

The company is Team Trek, an Arkansas-based privately-held company that specializes in leadership development and giving leaders tools to help them to re-direct their culture.

Team Trek does not agree to any engagement with any new customer if they cannot clearly understand the business need, why the company is seeking to outsource a project to Team Trek, as well as the desired business outcome expected from the engagement.

This exploration is not done via any complex program or system. It is accomplished simply by Team Trek owners sitting down with the leadership of the customer's company and having an open and direct discussion around purpose.

My first interaction with Team Trek was back in 1998. At that time they were unknown to us other than by reputation, and we were unknown to them. Our conversation was based around some very simple but probing questions:

- Why are you in business?
- What is your vision?
- What are your core values?
- Do you have operating norms?
- What are your immediate challenges?

- What challenges do you feel you will face in the next three to five years?
- Why do you feel we (Team Trek) can do this better than you?
- What are your expectations from this engagement?
- Tell us about your leadership style.
- Who is the target team for this engagement?

In an afternoon of discussion, we aligned ourselves with, and understood, our new partner, Team Trek. This relationship spanned a decade. I will touch on how the company lives the disciplines of *The Outsourcing Conundrum* in many chapters of the book as we move forward.

IMPLEMENTING DEFINE THE NEED

First, accept the notion that the profitability of your new business opportunity can be seriously impacted by the ignorance of one of your competitors. If the wrong supplier makes it through the audition process and performs poorly, everyone loses.

Second, accept that the reason why the work is being done is not the same reason why the work is being outsourced. It is that gap that needs to be defined.

Third, accept that all outsourced opportunities need to be viewed on a business-cycle basis, meaning they will be around for multiple years. There can be far-reaching positive and or negative consequences

Go Fish for the Big Needs - Don't base a contract around the small needs.

associated with each opportunity as a result of the time invested in this relationship.

An open discussion around the questions listed in the table below allows both buyer and supplier the time to ensure that the outsourcing opportunity fits both companies.

Key Questions	
BUYER	SUPPLIER
Financial What is the current economic condition of your company? Which services are the most profitable; which are the least? What metrics do you use to draw this conclusion?	**Financial** What are the economic drivers of this outsourcing opportunity? Who is the customer for this opportunity? What metrics do you use to draw this conclusion?
Performance What performance issues do you anticipate you will face with this outsourcing opportunity? What counter-measures will be put in place to limit our risk? What metrics will you use to monitor these conclusions?	**Performance** What current performance-related issues are being faced with this outsourcing opportunity? Are you looking for improved performance? What metrics do you use to draw this conclusion?
Quality What quality-related issues will you face with this outsourcing opportunity? What counter-measures will be put in place to limit our risk? What metrics will you use to monitor these conclusions?	**Quality** What current quality-related issues are being faced with this outsourcing opportunity? What metrics do you use to draw this conclusion?
Culture How does outsourcing this opportunity align or enhance your culture? Why do you feel you are uniquely aligned with our company? Who will you hire? What metrics will you use to monitor these conclusions?	**Culture** How does outsourcing this opportunity align or enhance your culture? Why are you choosing this particular time to outsource this opportunity? What metrics do you use to draw these conclusions?
Risk What risks will you be taking by performing this outsourcing opportunity? What counter-measures will be put in place to limit your risk? What metrics will you use to monitor these conclusions?	**Risk** What risks are you taking by outsourcing this opportunity? Do we eliminate risk for you? If so what? What metrics do you use to draw this conclusion?
Non-Core/Core What is your core business? Do you deem this opportunity to be core to your business? Why or why not? What are you currently investing in?	**Non-Core/Core** What is your core business? Do you deem this opportunity to be core to your business? Why or why not?

It would be beneficial during this discussion to have a good understanding of what you value in a new customer, or a new customer opportunity. It is also important for the buyers to have an agreed-to understanding of what they value in a supplier beyond, "Can you do the job?"

QUICK STORY

Two brothers owned a plant that painted mirrors for several automotive OEMs. I responded to an emergency call that went out because their current supplier refused to work over the weekend, and they were only hours away from shutting down a major assembly plant. One brother made a great case for needing a "quality partner" to grow with them. The other let it slip that they had not paid their existing supplier for six months. This was back when you were supposed to be paid in thirty days. Gee! Hmm! No wonder the supplier decided to stop working. I figured we'd pass on being their partner as they needed a bank, not a supplier.

TAKEAWAYS:

- Real contract need is not readily transparent—it must be fished out.
- Real need will only become transparent through discussion.
- No one can own a problem they do not understand.

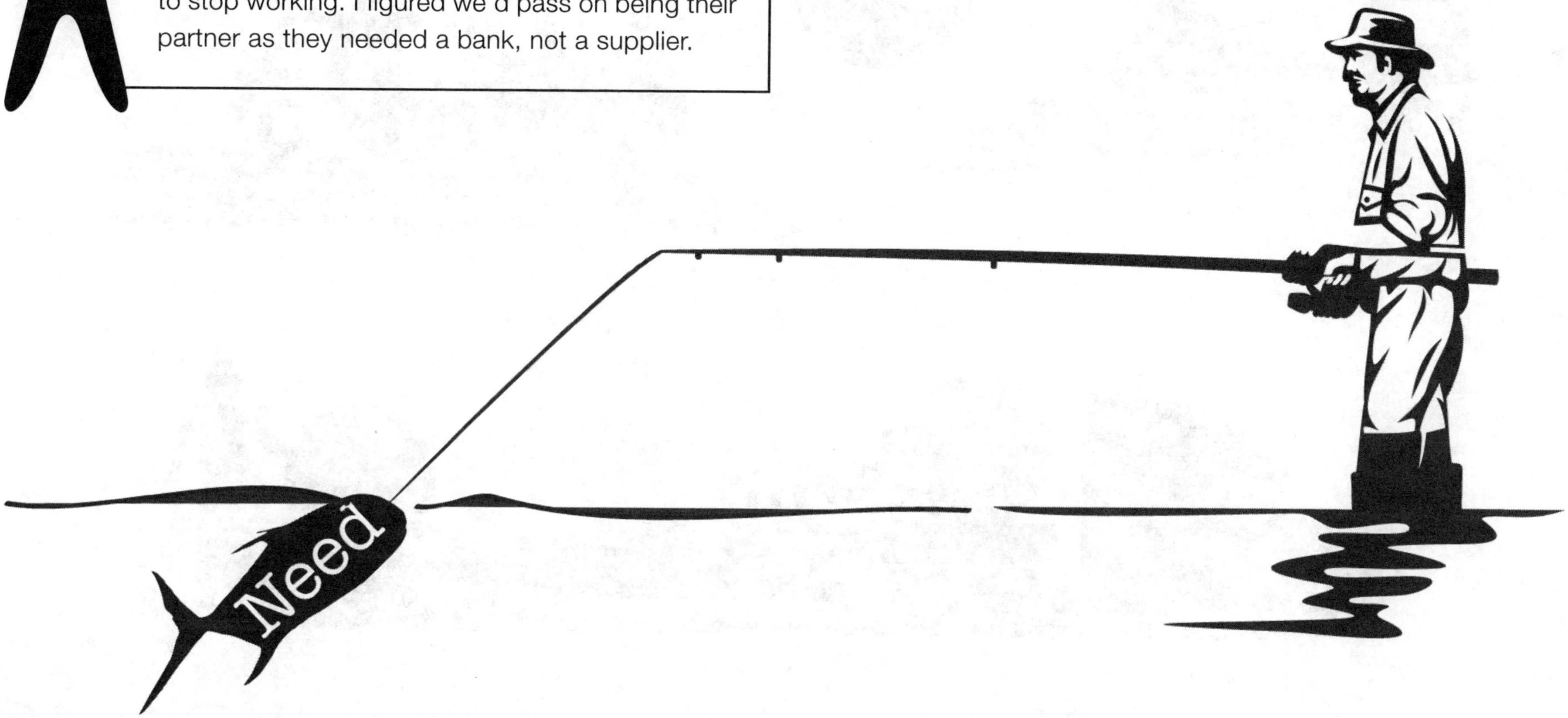

PURPOSE

Define the Need
Define the Scope
Define Expectations
Define Value
Re-Define the Need
The Outsourcing Conundrum

"All things are created twice: first mentally, then physically. The key to creativity is to begin with the end in mind, with a vision and a blueprint of the desired result."

Stephen Covey
The 7 Habits of Highly Effective People

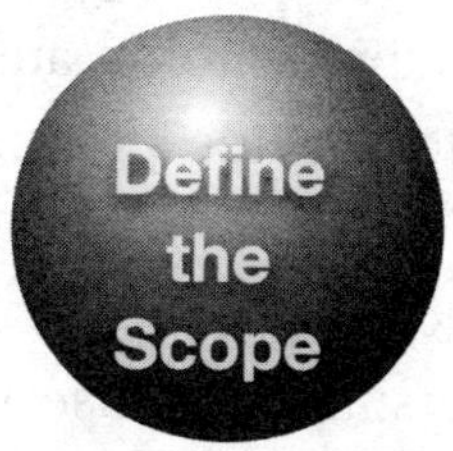

Throughout my career, I cannot point to one area that has caused more damage to delivering a service promise than a poorly defined scope of work. A scope of work is foundational to almost everything else that follows, as it defines what, how, and the environment of the service being provided. Failure in this area creates a catastrophic degree of misalignment to every other component in *The Outsourcing Conundrum*.

In 2005 we were awarded a service contract at a new automotive facility in Texas. Three well-seasoned members of our team had the responsibility to estimate and evaluate:

- what it was going to take
- how we would deliver
- the manufacturing environment

for this new service opportunity. The management team at this assembly plant were not as aligned with their parent company's purpose as we had experienced with this customer in the past. They became uncharacteristically vocal about "cost," "benchmarking other plants," and "how they were perceived by their superiors."

Models like TPS, GMS, Lean . . . and this one in *The Outsourcing Conundrum* exist to maintain consistency in conditions that are not inherently consistent. They provide framework, guidance, and direction on how to consistently deliver an expected level of performance and quality. Our team, instead of adhering to our model, succumbed to the pressure of getting the sale and meeting the requirements of local management directives. The result was a contract that experienced employee turnover within our company in excess of 300%, a financial loss in the first year of almost a million dollars, damage to our reputation for quality and performance that lasted for nearly a decade, and allocation of countless resources to try to correct the bad situation. In the end, we lost just under two million dollars on the operating line before we gracefully bowed out of the opportunity and handed it over to a competitor. Would we not have been better off to just evaluate the scope and accurately outline "What it would take and the best way to deliver on it?" Most definitely. I would rather have been in the position of our competitor who received the contract due to our failure than to have been first up to bat.

As I was researching and preparing for this book, I read about several very well-known misaligned projects with catastrophic results, and was reminded of the Montreal Olympic Stadium. Because I am Canadian and lived through that fiasco as it unravelled in the media, it caught my attention. The "Big Owe," as it is nicknamed, is a monument to a poorly defined scope that resulted in an initial building budget of $134 million becoming an actual cost of around $1.47

billion. An originally estimated finish date of 1972 was pushed out to 2006. By any measurement, this project was a disaster that affected a lot of suppliers and eventually the tax payers who were left with the ticket. Although my Texas example does not rival the Big Owe, the basis for the failure is still the same—an ill-defined scope resulting in a misaligned team between ourselves and our customer.

WHAT IS SCOPE?

Early in the '90s, I was privileged to deliver service to one of the transplant automotive companies who introduced me to the term "Gemba." During the late '70s I worked for a man who would repeatedly ask me, "Did you go and see it for yourself?" As it turns out, they both mean the same thing. Gemba, as I came to understand, is a practice of going and seeing so you understand and subsequently learn. It is much more poetic than the old "get off your butt and go look" that I originally grew up with, but, as stated, they both get you to the same place—where the action is—and that is key to understanding scope.

Scope outlines the work that needs to be accomplished, including the specific features and benefits, to deliver on the service opportunity. Scope is the first of three building blocks the service provider needs in order to construct the foundation that will provide the customer with what they need. This first building block, scope, evaluates the requirements of the customer.

The service provider needs to work closely with the customer to define the problems the customer is trying to solve, to weigh the options, and to choose a path forward for the service. Critical in understanding scope is determining the degree to which the scope will be outcome-based or activity-based. Any scope that is outcome-based will need to be very fluid and dynamic in its delivery.

Around 2004, we were provided the opportunity of developing a solution for a tier-one part supplier to an automotive plant in Tijuana, Mexico. Our scope was to provide production support by painting a part for a high-production small truck. As you might imagine, the details of the scope of work were very complex and involved, but extremely simple to understand because it was primarily outcome-based. Our service responsibility was to paint the number of parts required by the assembly plant, at the level of quality required, to meet their production schedule. There were many other aspects to the scope, involving the design engineering of the paint system, procurement of paint, application systems, system maintenance, reporting, etc., but none of that compared in importance to the primary outcome of the scope—under no circumstance were we to be responsible for shutting down the assembly plant. As you also might guess, it was very easy to communicate to everyone involved what we had to do, or, better stated, what we could not afford to do—shut down the assembly plant. Our customer had one question every day, "Will you meet the production schedule?"

An outcome-based scope tends to put much more ownership on the shoulders of the service provider. With ownership comes value and risk. An outcome-based scope is less debatable and defendable than an activity-based scope because either the desired outcome is achieved, or it is not.

An activity-based scope has a level of required results tied to successful completion of stated, agreed-to activities. The customer often displays a heightened sensitivity around how the work is executed. The results as monitored by the customer often take this sensitivity into account. Questions surrounding coverage, training, safety, etc., require documentation and reporting. Completely outcome-based service scopes internally monitor those same components, as that is a good business practice but not because it is demanded by the customer.

Activity-based scopes pretty much dominated the industry during the '90s. We had numerous contracts in automotive paint shops providing industrial cleaning and light maintenance services contracts. Every morning the customer would show up for an inspection of the completed activities from the night before. Each one was inspected and checked off as complete. Once the check mark hit the piece of paper everyone could go home and relax, job well done. An activity-based scope does not have the same degree of ownership as an outcome-based scope, the value is more difficult to assess, and the risk is less.

The discussion surrounding outcome-based vs. activity-based scope really just sets the stage for the team performing an evaluation to dig deep and be able to answer three questions:

- What are they buying?
- What are we selling?
- Do they align?

Scope has a tremendous ripple effect on how service delivery will be performed and who will perform it. We discussed earlier in the book

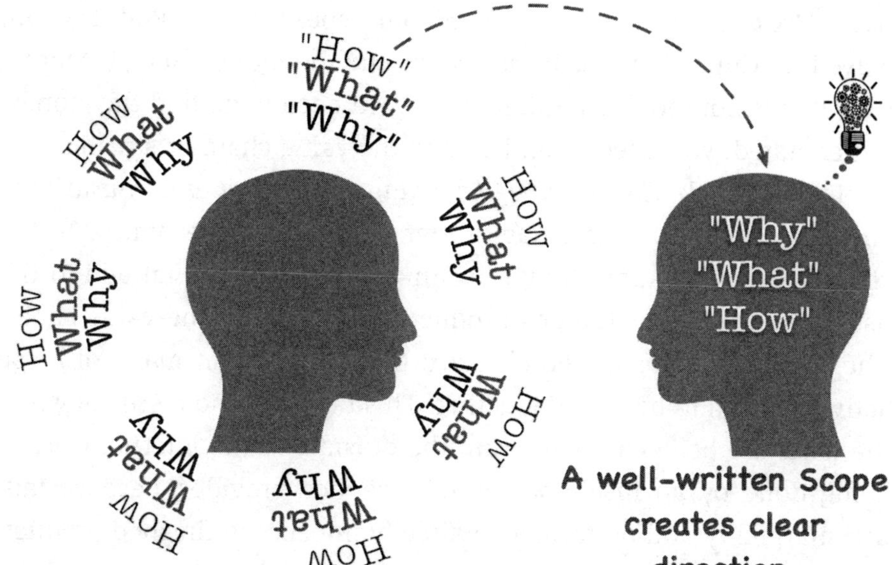

A well-written Scope creates clear direction.

how important it is to be able to communicate **why** a service is being outsourced and what **needs** the service must fulfill. Defining the scope communicates **what** services are required and **how** those services will be delivered. Great services are composed of thousands of minutes spent on thousands of activities and tasks that are all aligned to provide value for the customer.

SCOPE AND VALUE

When defining the scope, there are lots of areas to consider. Before we get into those mechanics, there is one very soft area that easily gets missed during the enthusiasm of getting the scope survey and estimation completed. This is value.

Every aspect of defining the scope requires a certain level of investigation and digging, but nothing rivals mining for value. In the movie

Jerry McGuire, the phrase shouted out repeatedly by Rod Tidwell, played by Cuba Gooding Jr., is, "Show me the money, Jerry!" Mining for value is not too much different, as you need to go find the money. Better stated, you need to understand the value chain or stream.

In his book *Competitive Advantage: Creating and Sustaining Superior Performance*, Michael Porter popularized the phrase "value chain." He spoke about how the sum of all activities that add to the usefulness of the customer's product are all part of the value chain. The word chain for me emphasizes the concept that many of these activities need to be linked together. This becomes more critical when the parts are being supplied from the outside, or the internal work is being done by an inside-outsourcing service provider, because failures in quality and performance directly impact the finished product. Porter goes on to discuss that coordination and optimization of the links enhance or detract from the value of the chain. If a company outsources a service to a service provider and those activities are validated as being integral to producing a best-in-class product, but the service provider is not allotted the time in the system to complete those required activities, then this service is not linked closely enough to the value chain and will detract from the quality of the product.

If a manufacturer's competitor (let's call them Company B) can locate a service provider that can provide a service to Company B better than the manufacturer (Company A) is able to perform that service themselves, then Company A is at a competitive disadvantage. This also speaks to why it is important that service providers chosen for outsourcing opportunities are able to prove they add value.

A competent IOSP should be able to demonstrate to the customer their ability to perform these services at a level far superior than the customer is able to perform or their competitors are able to perform. The customer must be convinced that the proposed service is a core competency to the IOSP and they can demonstrate they invest in this service offering. The IOSP should be knowledgeable of the impact of this service up and down the value chain. Let's look at two examples, one of a company who did this poorly and another who did it in an exemplary fashion.

In 2013, a major domestic auto manufacturer decided to put out for tender the facility's light maintenance, primarily technical cleaning work, at their US mid-west assembly plant. This was the third time this scope of work had been put on the market due to performance and quality issues with current and past service providers. Each service provider had lost money in the execution of this contract, to the point where they could no longer afford the opportunity. The auto manufacturer sent out the usual bid packages to those service providers who had been qualified for this opportunity. Each was given instructions to bring only one or two people to the walk-through, and they were told they would be given access to the multi-million square foot plant for less than one day. The chosen service providers very quickly branded this opportunity as a risk. The best a service provider would be able to do is what I classify as a "**me too**" scope, it's a carbon copy of what is already being done because there is not sufficient time to compile an alternative.

Each of the service providers quickly figures out how many people the current service provider (who is losing money) is using, they assess that against other sites in their portfolio, they find out what the incumbent feels they would need to be successful, and build their case based on these faulty assumptions. This plant was also ramping up production from a two-shift to a three-shift operation, making the existing conditions for completing the work even more taxing. In this situation, a service provider must ask, "How do we accurately define the scope?" and "Where is the value?" The two service providers who had failed at this location were both successfully performing similar services at other plants, but for some reason could not perform well at this location. To my way of thinking, if you do not have the time on the front end to assess the value you bring to an opportunity, you will never find time once the action starts and you are under the gun to deliver. This contract was awarded on cost, and the service provider receiving the award scrambled to hire the previous supplier's team. It just didn't add up to a formula for success.

In 2013 on the US east coast, a European transplant decided to bid out their lightweight maintenance work. This company contacted a group of service providers known for successfully providing this type of service. Each service provider was invited to visit to understand what the opportunity entailed, to decide if the opportunity was a good fit for them and if they felt they could add value if given the opportunity. The service providers made repeated visits to the plant for discussions with the OEM to determine fit and ability to provide value. These discussions allowed each of the service providers to explain both how they would add value and how they would differentiate themselves from their competition. The award was based on value plus cost.

One mistake that we often made throughout years of acquiring and launching new business was to confuse value with pain. There is an old saying, "sell to pain," meaning you identify the pain the customer is currently experiencing, and focus your energies on relieving that pain point. Resolving a customer's immediate pain is great in the short run but, once relieved, the underlying value must be understood. Identifying pain is important and should be a point of focus, but not at the cost of missing or not identifying the real value of the service offering.

Generating value can be achieved only by being able to go and see what is required, as well as how it is currently being executed.

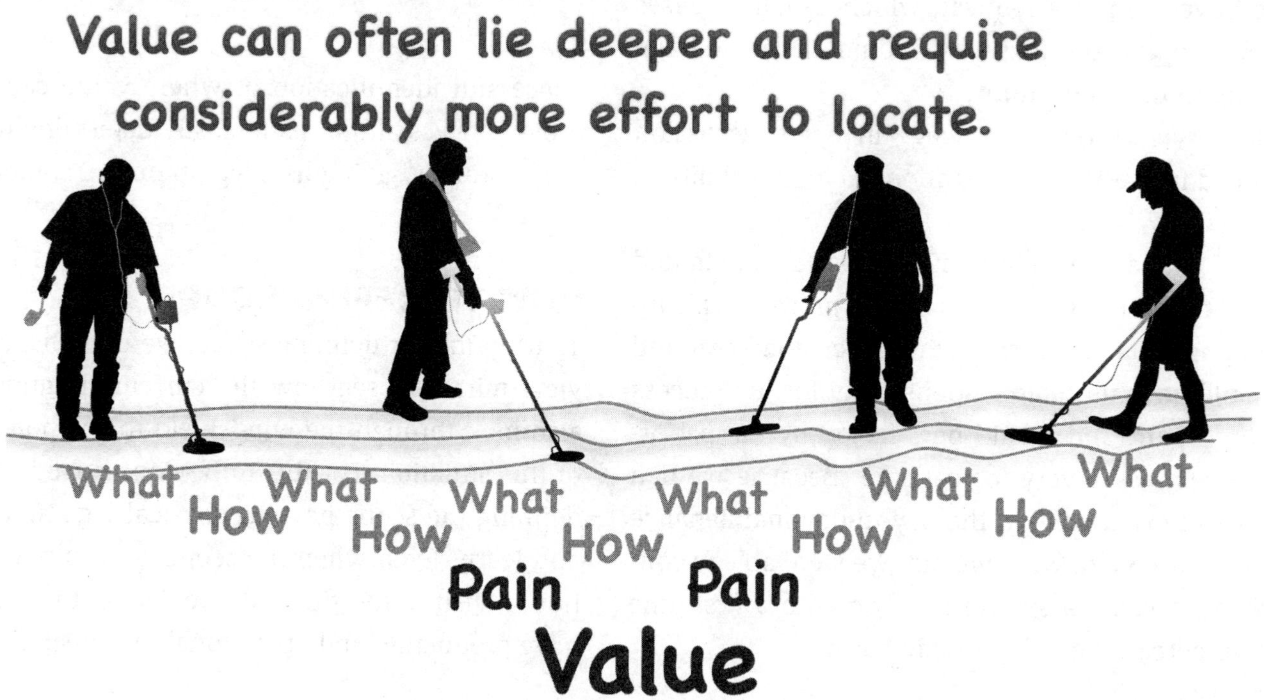

In 2009, we had the opportunity to launch half-a-dozen light-maintenance sites throughout the mid-west. The pain the customer was experiencing was that the current list of activities was not consistently being completed. The value the customer was seeking from the new engagement was to determine what activities, at what frequencies, using what methods, would optimize their production capability. During the initial launch, the focus was on "pain relief" to ensure completion of the previously listed activities. Once the launch was finished, the focus turned to analyzing and assessing what scope of work would optimize production.

The Value Generation Table at right outlines five core attributes a service provider can use to generate value for their customer. Great service providers are able to tackle any new opportunity with a degree of focus, expertise, technology, talent, and flexibility, better than their customers or their competition. Great service providers apply these attributes against the buyer's service request, which usually focuses on their immediate pain points, and focus on finding and identifying the value they will bring to this opportunity.

When buyers and service providers engage in open discussion around the areas outlined in the Value Generation Table, the ability to deliver value is enhanced.

At the operation in Tijuana, we were invited to participate in and contribute to the design and building of the painting process. This inclusion stemmed from our initial discussion with the customer around value. Because we would have ultimate responsibility for the process and cost allotted to each part, and would be affected by the performance of the process, this was a very logical step. Because we had thousands of man-years of experience in the day-to-day maintenance of paint shops, and this was core to what we did, we were able to contribute value that helped develop a system that ran with a first time through-put north of 98 percent on a day-to-day basis.

VALUE GENERATION TABLE

Focus	The required service is core or is an adjacent service to the service provider. The service provider focuses on mastering delivery of activities. The company's management systems are geared to service requirements.
Expertise	The service provider's team has extensive man-years of experience in this area, allowing for inclusion of "best practices" as to how services can be performed.
Technology	The service provider has spent years innovating better systems and methods to streamline delivery of service requirements.
Talent	The service provider's people are in the service business, and, by default, are accustomed to meeting the needs of a customer on a daily basis. Satisfying customer needs is paramount to what they do.
Flexible	The service provider is an expert at allocating resources and being flexible in the what, how, and when required services are delivered.

Successful identification of where value can be incorporated to improve process allows us to easily determine the value proposition for our customer, giving us a leg up on the competition.

HOW TO DEFINE SCOPE

To truly master defining scope, we must be able to look into the rear-view mirror to see how the current situation came to be. We must also look through the windshield to see potential for the future state of this situation. For this to be done effectively, those responsible for defining the scope have to physically go and see the situation—walk and learn. Even when the scope is for a new facility under construction, a visit to the site and a review of the blueprints with those who have production and operational responsibility is a requirement. If the scope includes maintenance, light or heavy, of any process or production equipment, a review of all the operation manuals is required.

According to the US Chamber of Commerce, 90 percent of the world's data have been created in the past two years. We are inundated with knowledge, and it is very often at our fingertips. Today, our ability to dig deeper is greater and easier than ever before, so there are fewer and fewer excuses for service providers not to be able to outline fully a scope of work.

I have read numerous books that outline effective project management techniques. I found many of the principles very important when it came to planning and executing the launch of a new service, but not overly helpful when defining a scope. A project by its definition is finite, whereas the contracts that are explored in this book are not approached in that manner. Some of the best outsourcing opportunities have spanned almost 30 years. Their starting points often cannot be remembered nor identified down the road because the scope has changed and evolved so much over time.

Below are three tables containing questions focused around three key elements of fully defining a scope of work. The Activity Definition Table focuses on what is included in the scope and how that scope will be completed. The Cultural Attributes Table focuses on identifying the environment in which the work will be performed. The Outcome Table focuses on questions used to identify required results. These tables appear quite formal and absolute, but that is not the case. The point is to put on the table some of the questions that must get asked while fully defining a scope of work.

ACTIVITY DEFINITION TABLE

	Current	Future
Tasks	What activities are required by the service definition and by location?	Are any of these activities unnecessary? What adjustments are required?
Frequency	What are the required frequencies for each activity? Shift patterns? Annual, monthly, weekly, 1st shift, 2nd, weekends?	Are the frequencies sufficient? What adjustments are required?
How	What methods will be used to perform each activity?	Are current methods efficient? What adjustments are required?
Quality	Is the required level of quality adequate? Is it being met?	What adjustments are required to improve the level of quality?
Performance	Is the required work being performed?	What adjustments are required to improve the level of performance?
Management Systems	What management systems are currently being used?	What management systems are required?
People	Is there a team currently performing the services? What is planned for this team? Should we plan to absorb the team?	What training will be required to build a team able to meet requirements?
Equipment	What equipment is currently being used to perform required services?	What changes need to be made to the equipment line-up to better perform services?

	Current	Future
Areas of Influence	Are there areas in the scope where more control is required?	What changes need to be made to achieve the correct level of control to optimize results?
Partners	Are any components of required services being outsourced to more than one sub-contractor?	What partnerships will be required? Are there benefits to sub-contracting more? Less?
Location	Where are these services required? Country, site location, area or department, plant, shop...	Are any location's required services drastically different from a sister location? What adjustments are required?

A good definition of the scope will quickly let you know if the required service requests by the customer fit with the skills and capabilities of your organization. Equally as important, as we discussed earlier, is that you continue to dig and make sure there is cultural alignment and "FIT."

Many of the aspects of *The Outsourcing Conundrum* were developed from experiences, some good, some bad and some pretty ugly. In 1992, I made a visit to a new site located in the Grand Rapids, Michigan, area that was a tier-one supplier of painted plastic parts to a few assembly plants in the state. As part of the visit, I sat down with the paint shop production manager. He informed me that if they did not start running significantly better, he would reach across the table and punch me in the face. I quickly explained, as any normal person would, that I did not wish to be punched, and asked how he thought we could help him to run better. After a very strange meeting, I met with our onsite team and conveyed his ultimatum. They informed me that as part of a daily routine, he would unload on the crew at the end of shift—a real morale killer. It was not long after that meeting that two things occurred: we fired the customer, and introduced the Cultural Attributes Table.

CULTURAL ATTRIBUTES TABLE

Process Orientation	Does the customer have a disciplined approach to process, and process controls?
Management Style	How does the customer manage its service providers? Its own team? By consensus, collaboration, partnership, fear?
Safety	Is safety a priority for this customer?
Innovation	Is innovation important to the customer? Can we see evidence of it?
Change	Is the customer open to change? Can we see evidence of it?
Accountability	Are all the players on the customer's team equally held accountable, including service providers?
Communication	Is information shared openly? Are dashboard or reporting boards visible? Are they regularly updated?
Strategic Impact	How will the proposed change, as outlined by the service requirement, impact the working environment and existing workforce?

The last step in defining the scope is to identify and document the outcomes required from the service. Most service providers agree it is rare to have only one customer within the buyer's organization. More often than not, they find themselves with a dozen or more customers in a single location, distinguished by department, title, function, etc. The outcome may vary slightly by customer, but the primary and dominant outcomes associated with delivering value should be common to all customers at the location.

OUTCOME TABLE

Safety	Is there a specific safety target? What safety impact does the required service have on the customer's employees? Can the service negatively impact safety?
Pain	What are the short-term pain points that need addressing?
Quality	Will quality be judged by how well the activity met standard, or by the impact of the activity on the product? How will a measure be determined?
Delivery/ Performance	Will delivery and performance be measured against what is contractually required, or by impact on the yield of finished product?
Cost	Will cost be assessed as meeting budget, or how the completed activities have positively affected the total cost of the product being produced?
Environment/ Waste stream	Does the required service impact the environment or the waste stream? How is it measured? Any current violations, limits?
Core/Non-Core	Is the customer's goal to exit and no longer perform work identified by the required service? What measurements will be used to assess that the service provider has taken ownership of the responsibility?

ENHANCE THE CHANCES FOR SUCCESS

These three tables help to achieve an appropriate level of focus on the customer's service priorities, and to probe for the value you can add for the customer in the engagement. The combined results from these three tables allow for development of a scope of work that will serve as a strong foundation for a successful service opportunity. The organizational structure required to complete the scope will hinge on the strength of the documented scope of work.

Organization and Scope

There is no service without people, great service relies on the caliber of the teams assembled to perform those services.

The scope dictates skills required by the team who will perform the services. If the scope is predominantly a maintenance function, it is safe to assume that the organization will be composed of technicians with varying degrees of skill to perform the work. As outlined in one of my quick stories, if the scope requires "better trained monkeys," then you can assign your best monkeys to the job, if you are so inclined.

The key here is that by completing the full definition of the scope, you will be able to build what the service team or on-site organization must look like to complete the scope successfully and meet the customer's desired outcomes.

During this stage, it is typical to have discussions around items like manpower leveling, skill requirements, on-site support staff, additional corporate staff if necessary, any specialty skills, partners or sub-contractors, union or non-union employees, shift patterns, etc.

The balancing of the defined scope and the required organizational structure to deliver on the scope is a key ingredient in the next stage of *The Outsourcing Conundrum*, Define the Cost.

BEST IN CLASS

Early in 1996, I met with Team Trek to discuss a scope of services we were going to require. As mentioned earlier, we had chosen to partner with Team Trek for leadership development programs for our management teams.

Because we had an open relationship with Team Trek and were familiar with a variety of service models, we were leaning very heavily towards an outcome-based scope of work. We were far more interested in the outcomes we would achieve than in the actual details surrounding hours in a class, or in course outlines, and so on. We had a few issues that needed improvement, and we did not have the level of expertise, or the focus or talent to do it for ourselves.

As we had sites throughout North America and were starting to penetrate Europe, it was becoming increasingly important for our site managers, our local leaders, to open lines of communication amongst themselves, as well as for them to accept 100 percent responsibility for the management of their sites in accordance with our company's operating methodology.

We were beginning to notice an uncomfortable level of finger-pointing between the sites and corporate, and between the sites and their customers. Neither of these situations was acceptable, and neither was characteristic of a great service provider. We were also growing much larger and taking on more sites, so it was becoming increasingly important that our sites communicate effectively and leverage our size as opposed to being negatively impacted by it.

This training and development had a pretty steep sticker price, but we also believed lack of responsibility and lack of open communication among our site leaders had a much steeper price.

Team Trek submitted a proposal outlining an experiential training program that would achieve three goals or outcomes:

- 100 percent responsibility
- Self-leadership
- Mutual respect

We discussed how we would measure these outcomes compared to how our team was currently functioning on their own without the training. We agreed with Team Trek that as we saw the results, we would continue the investment in the service. We were amazed at the number of calls we received before any of the participants had even boarded planes home, telling us that the training was one of the best uses of their time that they had ever experienced. In a series of follow-up meetings, it was evident that the desired outcomes were being realized. We started to experience a much higher level of e-mail traffic between sites, as well as interplant site visits. The turnover of frontline supervisors also started to trend in a more positive direction as site managers showed positive leadership skills.

As stated, the cost of the Team Trek training program was substantial, but when we reviewed our year-end results, it appeared we had achieved a good return on our investment. The sites were more likely to meet or exceed their targets on a percentage basis. Needless to say, we continued the program.

We will talk more about Team Trek as we move into different chapters of *The Outsourcing Conundrum*, and you will get a flavor for how they were able to achieve the outcomes specified in their scope.

SCOPE CREEP

There is one area that cannot be overlooked when discussing scope and that is scope creep. Scope creep is really expansion—the incremental expansion of activities that were not initially included, or deemed as not included, in the original scope submission.

Scope creep is very often associated with pleasing a customer, and its intent is very often well meaning. The issue is that scope creep that goes unchecked can lead to an overuse of resources, or an over-stretching of resources, that results in quality, delivery and budgetary issues. In some cases, scope creep can be directly tied to safety issues and violations because desire to please can outweigh the need to be safe.

Scope is in many ways just like life. It is always changing, and, just as how we deal with life changes can identify us as a person, how we deal with scope demands can identify how we are branded as a service provider. It is not unheard of to have documented proof that every line item on the scope was complete, on time and to standard, but then to hear from the customer that you are not meeting their expectations.

Changes in scope must be understood as a reality, and they must be welcomed, but controls have to be put in place to monitor "the creep." In my experience, scope creep, or the misalignment of resources, is on average about 10 percent on an activity-based scope of work. To put that another way, the time estimated for completion of activities was either 10 percent over or under, allowing for some give and take and realignment of scope. The scope must remain fluid, transparent, and continually adjusted to reflect improvements in the process, but contractually keep the scope of work well defined and balanced at all times.

We will discuss this much more as we move forward with building The Outsourcing Conundrum Model.

QUICK STORY

In the late '70s we had a project to chemically clean a home on Queen Street in Toronto, Ontario. The scope of work outlined that we had to complete the cleaning of the front and side of this two-story home on Queen Street East. We arrived, set up the scaffolding, carried out the entire cleaning project, but didn't have the opportunity to meet the homeowner. We called in the job as complete, and commented on how very pleased we were with how well this once-filthy red brick had been restored. The estimator was pleased, but commented that he thought the house would have actually turned out to be yellow brick. Oh, well. Red or yellow brick—the house was clean and looked great.

The next day the estimator was dismayed to hear from the homeowner about how dissatisfied he was with the cleaning. He went so far as to say it looked to him like nothing had been done. After receiving the call, I went to the house on Queen Street East, to find no-one home once again, but a neighbor was heading out so I inquired if he knew if the homeowner would be home soon. He said they were away for spring break, and he thought their house looked like brand new.

As it turns out, the scope for the project should have read Queen Street West, not Queen Street East. Upon arriving at the Queen Street West home, sure enough there was a home-owner with a filthy yellow-brick house. We were reminded that the littlest detail in defining the scope matters.

As you wrap up defining the scope, you should be partly starting to answer the question, "What do your service offerings bring that outweigh your customer's ability to do these services in-house themselves, or your competitor's ability?" If you have not made any gain in answering this question, you are moving yourself down the buy/sell hierarchy towards being a commodity provider. I suggest you revisit your scope, and do not let it go until you have some sense of how you can differentiate yourself from your competition.

TAKEAWAYS:

- Define Value when you are defining scope.
- Locate all pain points.
- Determine if the scope is activity-based or outcome-based.
- Organization = Scope
- Value Proposition = Defined Value plus pain points

PURPOSE

Define the Need
Define the Scope
Define Value
Define Expectations
Re-Define the Need
The Outsourcing Conundrum

"The value chain is the sum of all activities that add utility to the customer. Parts of the value chain will be internal to the company, while others will come from suppliers, distributors, and other channel partners. A linkage occurs whenever one activity affects other activities in the chain. To optimize a value chain, the linkages must be well coordinated."

Michael E. Porter (1985), *Competitive Advantage: Creating and Sustaining Superior Performance*

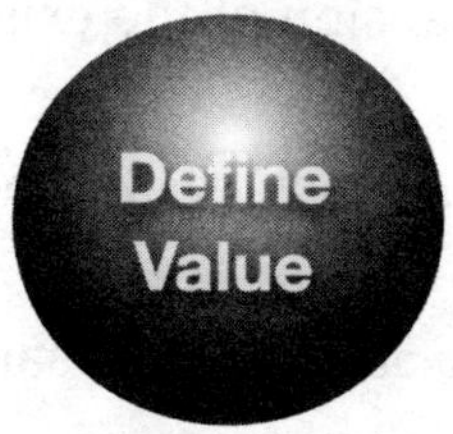

In this phase of *The Outsourcing Conundrum*, the potential for a great sale can turn into a disaster, and what looks like a mediocre sale can turn into a great opportunity. Every service provider requires some level of profitability in order for it to stay in business. Even if a new sale is labelled as strategic, and the level of profitability is minimal, the degree of the potential loss of profit must be known and understood.

Profit is a symptom of the price charged to the customer. Price should be a symptom of the value the service brings to the customer, plus the cost to deliver. Price is not cost times mark-up. Price is total cost to deliver plus value.

In this chapter we will discuss:

- Cost
- Customer Relationships
- Price
- Risk

and the role they each play in defining value so the ISOP can determine the right price.

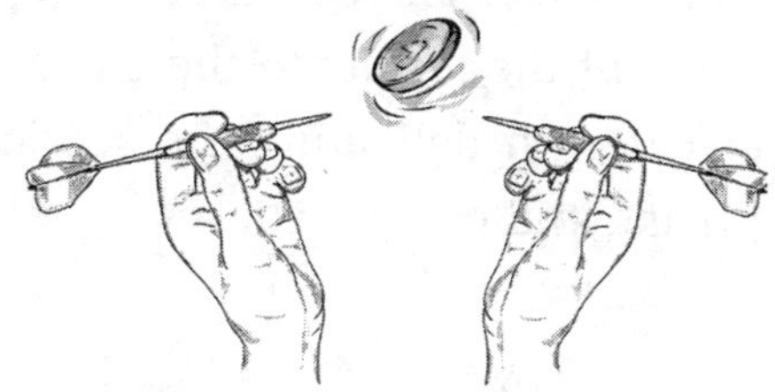

Success in this phase of *The Outsourcing Conundrum* relies upon how well we performed in Defining the Need and the Scope. Any shortcuts taken in the prior two phases will wreak havoc when you start to Define the Value, and subsequently determine the price charged to the customer. Too many times today the IOSP ends up diluting their brand and pricing themselves as a commodity because they fail to define value.

The inside-outsourcing service provider (IOSP) is a link in the overall value chain of the company for whom the service is being provided. The degree to which that value is critical is dependent upon the role or position the IOSP plays in the company that is its customer.

VALUE FOR THE MONEY

It is notably harder to sell a potential customer on the value you can add for them when an opportunity is being presented via an RFQ (Request for Quotation), and many service providers have fallen into the trap of allowing the process to become simply a numbers exercise. Business development teams exist for a purpose, and it is *not* to make their company a low-cost provider. You do not need a sales force to give work away at cheap prices. You need a sales force to sell the value of your company regardless, and if it were easy, everyone would be doing it.

Any business that is contemplating IOS should continue down that path only if it improves their value and not just cuts costs. As IOS continues to grow, and suppliers become increasingly important members of the value chain, the understanding and identification of value is key. The cost associated with delivering the service, plus the value of the results to the customer, equals the price. The cost associated with delivering the service plus mark-up, equals commodity pricing and everyone loses.

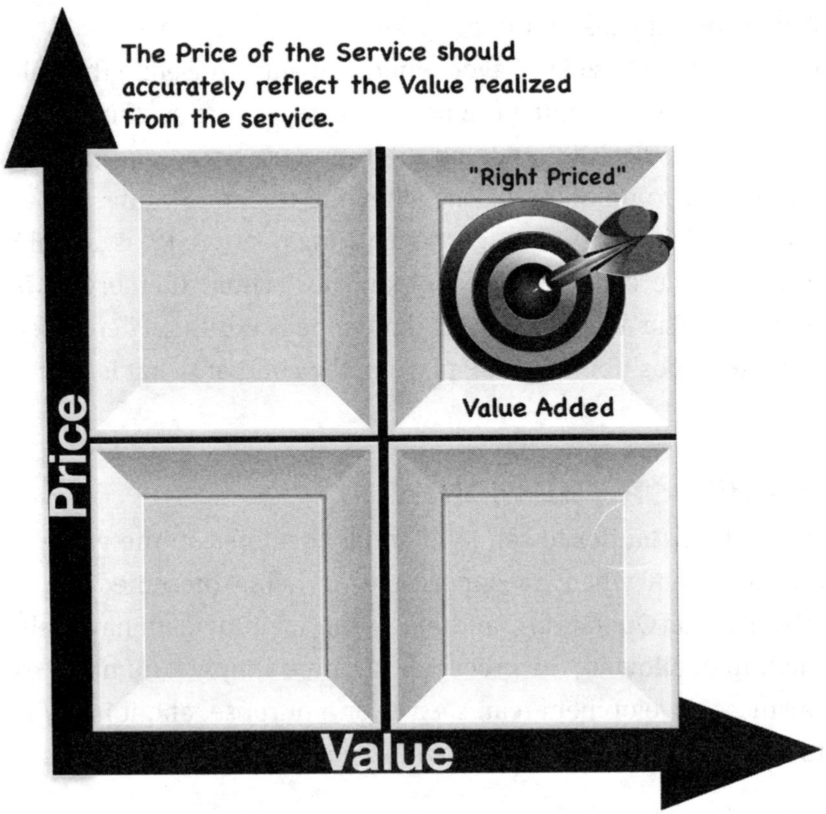

I once outsold a competitor by promising the customer a production uptime guarantee. The offer was for a five percent improvement, which equated to $250,000 a year. My price was $100,000 more a year than my next competitor. With the inclusion of a performance clause, my customer purchased the service at a $100,000 premium to save themselves a net $150,000 in downtime. We sold value versus lowering our price to meet the competitor.

Value can be viewed as a two-headed coin because value must be realized by both parties on every flip. The customer must realize value, which we will discuss in detail, but the IOS provider must also realize value.

Value for the service provider can easily be summed up by three Rs:

- **R**etention
  - Longevity and expansion of the existing service.
- **R**eferral
  - The level of influence achieved to help attract new sales.
- **R**elated Sales
  - The opportunity to add adjacent sales to the existing bundle of services. It is far more cost effective to sell to existing customers than to start fresh with a new customer.

One of the graphics I speak about on numerous occasions with management groups is the Business Life Cycle. The three Rs listed above are a delicate balance that requires constant care. Just as a farmer plants, harvests, and ploughs back under, a service provider must also constantly strive to grow anew.

Just like the farmer, the IOSP must continually search out opportunities to sow the right seeds that will give them a chance to grow their existing business. The graph depicts that without this mindset, over time the current opportunity will start to decline.

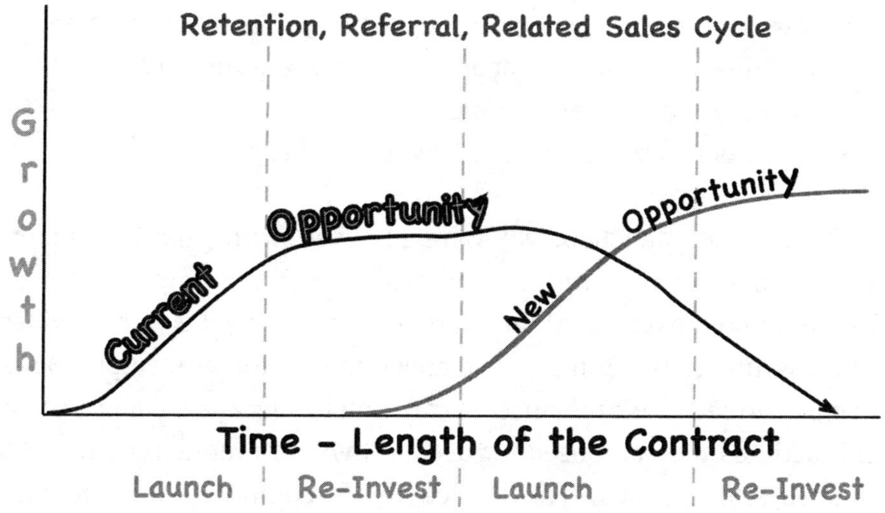

One of the greatest success stories I have witnessed was an engagement with an auto-manufacturer in Tennessee. The project began in 1990, and continues to the present day. It is a 24-year-plus contract with a strategically bundled set of services that grows year after year. The addition and bundling of two dozen services over the same number of years allowed us to achieve great retention, the complexity of the scope became a flagship that led to several referrals, and our success allowed us to be favored for related opportunities with new clients that stretched our capabilities. The combination of the three made this location extremely valuable to us as a reference site with other potential clients around the world. After much discussion at the outset of this opportunity surrounding the vast number of activities to be included in the service as it progressed, we identified the value. The one thing this customer was really looking for above all else was a "one-stop shop," the ability to go to one provider, with one management team, who would be dedicated to the continual improvement of these services year after year.

In 1955, Ken Annakin directed a British comedy called *Value for the Money*. The story was about a wealthy young Yorkshireman who met a girl, who on the surface seemed very attractive, but subsequently took him for every penny he had.

Sadly, many purchasing groups look at service providers with that same view, which makes the need to prove value all the more important.

With customers demanding new and enhanced service offerings through a variety of delivery options, we need to find robust ways of determining what constitutes value for the money. Identifying this value is particularly difficult if we do not have a good grasp of the existing cost or benefit associated with how the services are currently provided. On occasion the customer does not know the true cost either.

An IOS provider cannot provide value if they do not have the capability to deliver, we will discuss this more in Part Two of *The Outsourcing Conundrum*. To truly provide value, the capability has to be unmatched, it must be efficient and effective.

Any semblance of a "me too" product changes the landscape from a "value buy" to a "commodity buy," which, in the words of J. Palmisano, CEO of IBM, "is just hell."

Back in the day when I listened to AM radio, it was inevitable to hear the same song over and over again. Now, in meetings with prospective customers, the one song that I imagine hearing over and over again, just like on AM, is a little tune I like to call, "What makes you unique?" by the Commodities.

Many think that by switching service providers, all they did was switch letterhead. Sadly, on many occasions, with many IOS providers, that is accurate. Why? The service provider did not have the tenacity to challenge its team to figure out what made them and their service unique. Instead they defaulted to becoming a low-cost provider of mediocre services.

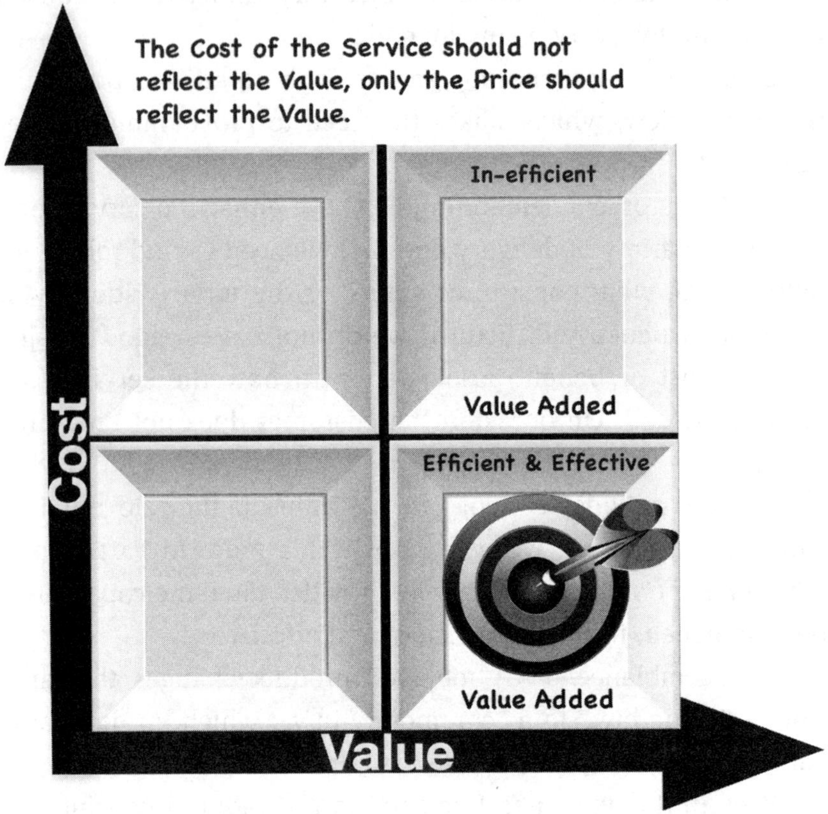

When our team had done its work in defining and understanding need and scope for a potential customer, we were able to identify value by discussing a few key questions:

- What pain are they in?
- How are we unique for being able to resolve their current and future issues?
- How do our services look through the eyes of this customer?
- How does our talent compare to those doing the service currently? To our competitors?
- Where is technology going? How can we use it?

In the mid-'90s to 2000, we were involved with an IOS initiative called Management Services. It was used by many large companies that could no longer corral their indirect labor costs. Service providers were essentially being hired to manage the customer's employees as they performed work they had been doing for decades, using systems and methods they had used for decades, with a productivity rate that declined year after year. The IOS activity the companies were purchasing was the management of their own labor forces. So, if you had a mind to, you as a service provider could simply look at the size of the management team required to cover the shifts, establish a compensation package, mark it up, and present your proposal. *If* you had a mind to. We chose a different path, and developed a pilot to be implemented at one of the most difficult sites. The pilot was successful, and we proved what a competent management system of accountability could produce.

We were subsequently awarded more than a dozen locations to repeat the success realized at the initial site, which resulted in annual customer savings of up to $75 million in re-allocated labor costs. The savings dwarfed the price of the service paid by the customer—a value-priced service, supported by a strong capable process, reaping huge savings back to the customer. We identified the value to the customer of right sizing the labor force to match the activities that needed to be performed. This was the true need of the customer.

COSTING STRATEGY

"Without the discipline of the model to guide them, most people do not connect the external realities with internal activities."

Confronting Reality

Larry Bossidy and Ram Charan, 2004

Over the years, I have had the luxury of being a piece on every box of the costing game board. I played the sales guy, the estimator, the launcher, the operator, the "final say" guy, and, the most stressful role, the "buck stops here" guy. Regardless of the role, it was always a battle to establish the right mix.

The battle ground was made up of three intertwined, yet competing components:

- Financial Targets
- Internal Competencies
- External Realities

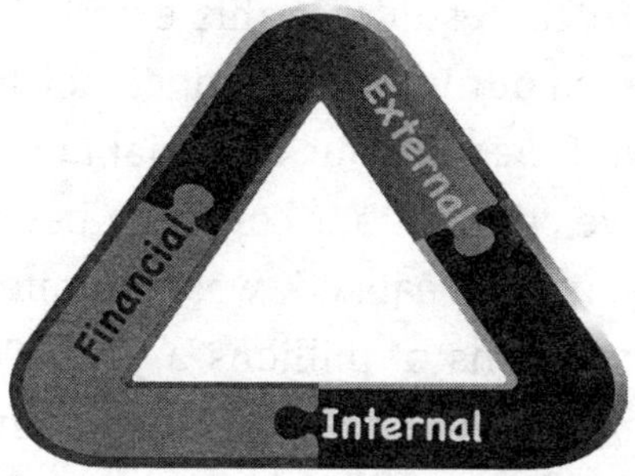

With every new opportunity, these three intertwined components have to be resolved to the mutual satisfaction of all involved.

Does the opportunity fit our required financial targets?

This question was much easier to answer in the early years as a small company, when the question was simply, "Will we make a profit?" As we experienced growth, our financial targets became more complex and dealt with:

- Cash flow
- Overhead
- Return on investment and employed capital
- Risk
- Vertical growth

Does the opportunity fit our internal competencies? Do we possess the capability and skills to absorb this opportunity into our portfolio of business?

In the early years, again, all of this was simple. Contracts were simple and risk was reasonable. As we grew, new questions surrounding fit needed to be answered, such as:

- Strategic alignment
- Brand recognition—do we see ourselves in this opportunity?
- Operation system capability
- People
- Organization

Does the opportunity stack up well against external realities?

External realities are things outside of our control that we must pay attention to when moving forward with a new opportunity. Even as a small company, this area received a lot of attention and intensified with growth. There is an ongoing debate as to whether a business makes a market or a market makes a business. Personally I fall into the camp of the latter. A market will make or break a business, so certain questions need to be answered:

- Brand recognition—does our customer base see us in this opportunity?
- The financial history and health of the customer we are exploring
- Condition of the market our potential customer is serving
- Regulatory conditions surrounding the opportunity
- Size of inside-outsourcing market with this customer?
- Will we bring VALUE to the equation?

Back in 2006, we had an opportunity to look at providing IOS to an automotive parts manufacturer on the east coast. We conducted several meetings and gained a clear understanding of their needs, including why they were choosing to outsource this scope of work.

For years they had been augmenting their full-time workforce with a pretty substantial amount of temporary labor. Over the years, this strategy had gotten to the point where it made sense for them to bring in a company that could not only provide the labor force to perform necessary activities, but also implement management systems and take full ownership of areas where activities were being performed. This seemed like a perfect fit for us. A well-rounded group was convened to explore the opportunity and fully define the scope. As we gained more knowledge and information, we naturally moved into defining value, and started dialogue surrounding financial, internal and external components.

It appeared the **financial** components were solid. The company was not looking to buy cheap, they sought value, payment terms were in line, the need for capital was low, and risk associated with performing the work was reasonable and within our parameters.

The **internal** competencies required for the opportunity fell within our boundaries, and would also give us a push to become more innovative in our reporting systems. The opportunity fell into our strategic plan of moving into more technical service offerings. With a few additions our existing management systems would fit well, our global reach allowed us access to people resources, and organizationally we were in solid shape to add the opportunity.

The **external** realities did not fare as well. The addition of this opportunity would definitely enhance our brand in the marketplace. The addition of this new customer enhanced our value. It was a solid company that had been around for decades and treated its suppliers well. All of those elements were good. However, we stumbled upon two issues that started the battle of the three intertwined components: **financial, internal and external**. The first was a clause that if you worked for this company, you could not work for any of its competitors. After much dialogue and debate, we agreed this opportunity and future opportunities with this customer would offset that issue. The second issue became the show stopper: unlimited liability. Even though the work we would perform had minimal risk to us, we would be performing production support activities which affected the quality and reliability of the product. After countless meetings with the customer and the insurance companies, we were not able to put a cap on our exposure.

The result was this external reality, as imposed by the customer, defied our internal competency to absorb it, and thus put us in jeopardy of meeting our financial targets. The magnitude of a failure would have crippled our company beyond its ability to recover, as the liability, if ever realized, was unlimited. This opportunity would have been worth tens of millions a year. The initial contract was for five years, so in essence we walked away from an over $100 million-plus opportunity. We also moved away from a multi-hundred-million-dollar risk we could not cover.

Over the years, as the companies I was associated with grew, their tolerance to "gamble" became less. Sometimes I wonder if we became too strict, but with growth came responsibility. Many people relied on us to make correct decisions as their livelihood depended upon it.

CUSTOMER BASE

The service provider has two extremely valuable assets, which are both relationship based: the people who serve the customer, and the customer base itself. As customer base is one of the most precious assets to service providers, it is critical for IOS providers to ask themselves these key questions on a regular basis:

- What can be done to deepen our relationship and enhance our position by taking the time to understand our customers' markets and business issues?
- What steps move us into being a partner and full solutions provider?

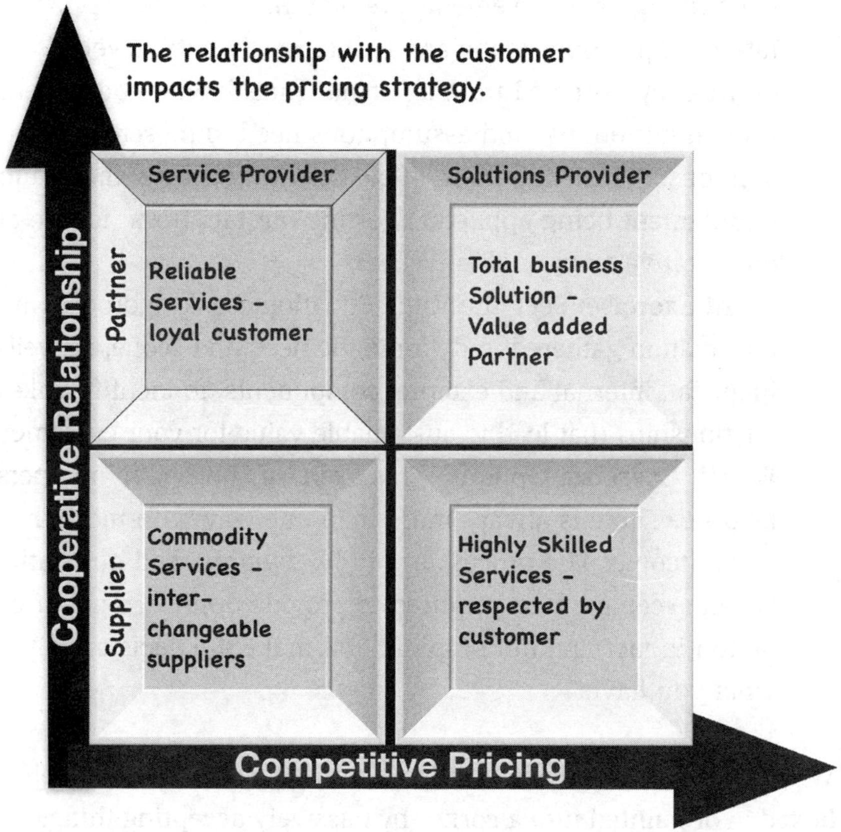

As a service provider, if you do not take the time as an organization to ask yourself these questions, you will inevitably start to erode your differentiator—the uniqueness that impacts your price.

Along with this discussion, it is beneficial to sharply define your customer base. We call this our "targeted customers." For each targeted customer, we would have discussion surrounding:

- How can we sell more of what we have to the customers we are serving?
- How can we sell new services to the customers we are serving?
- How can we add more of our existing customers' locations to our portfolio?
- How can we attract "new" customers who are not currently in our portfolio?

These discussions allowed us to focus on a set of target customers, to better understand their perception of quality, to better understand their issues, and to tailor our services to offset their pain points and provide value.

J. Palmisano, CEO of IBM, made a statement, *"Either you innovate or you're in commodity hell."* After 40 years, I firmly believe you cannot be a commodity service provider. By its nature, service requires you to provide a positive experience for your customer. You can choose to be a commodity provider of activities. but then you are not truly in the service business anymore. Service by its nature must find value in what it is providing, or it is just bundling activities to be sold by the pound. My career involved a tremendous amount of travel, and I ended up being one of those million-miler flyers—you know the ones—they get to sit up front. Even though I am a huge user of the airline industry, I find the experience is terrible. There are a handful of exceptions, which we have all heard about, but the majority are pitiful. In a recent article, I read that airlines were finally making money again, and the story walked through the reasons. The not-so-funny thing is, the sources of their profit were all the things that ticked me off as a customer: pay for baggage, pay for exit aisle, buy your own snacks, pay to change or re-arrange your flight, and so on. Bad profit from bad service.

Attitudes of procurement groups and their purchasing philosophy and methodology need to be discussed as you view your customer base, to establish whether a customer is a good or bad fit. A purchasing group who is committed to a balance between competitive pricing and cooperative solutions will tend to build a stronger partnership than one that is committed to the lowest price for delivery of specified activities.

THE HEAD GAME

Costing strategy can become a real "head game" where members of the team rally for position and point of view, all with good intentions of "winning" the business. This was, and is, typically a great dynamic as long as sight of the end game is not lost—value for money. I adopted a mental exercise program for use during cost strategy sessions, and I would move from exercise to exercise, trying not to become emotionally attached to any one opportunity, and forcing objectivity and realism.

- **First Exercise:** I get started with a good general sense of my company's required financial targets or what I want to achieve. From my experience, the targets can be labelled as hopeful rather than realistic, but it's important to start with them as they serve as a benchmark. The benchmark is important as a line against which analysis is conducted.
- **Second Exercise:** The costing model should not be mechanistic. Even though some elements are quantitative, like the pay rate for a position, many are qualitative, like the level of proficiency expected from a person. Facts have to be screened from assumptions, and assumptions need to be screened from opinions. A true definition of cost cannot occur without a lot of judgment being applied to sorting out fact from fiction, and quantitative from qualitative.
- **Third Exercise:** Seek the Value Equation. Look rigorously at information gathered in defining the need and scope, as well as financial, internal and external components, to identify links and relationships that lead to sustainable value for your customer.
- **Fourth Exercise:** Options? This exercise is probably my personal favorite. There is always more than one way with more than one outcome. The process has to be dynamic and not static. Several scenarios are required to provide options. Anchor each option in fact and not opinion, and make the decision with what you have.

When doing the analysis it helps if you do not allow yourself to get boxed in or painted into a corner by passively accepting things as they are. The words "battle ground" are not chosen by accident. To come up with the best answer is a battle. If it was a walk in the park, every competitor would be able to do it.

It's helpful in the fourth exercise also to ask, and seek a factual answer to, the question, "How do we stack up against the competition on this opportunity?"

In 2009, I was reviewing a bid for submission to a customer in Ontario for light maintenance. The customer had a service provider on-site who had been performing the work for several years, but they were experiencing performance issues, which resulted in the customer conducting a market test. We had recently hired an eager beaver sales guy who had mined this opportunity. During one of our war room sessions as we were conveniently convincing ourselves of our chances of success, the question was asked, "How do we stack up against the competition?"

Mr. Eager Beaver hopped on to his soap box and began to revel in how dissatisfied the customer was with our competitor's performance, and how eager they were to get us on board. We knew this competitor very well and it was not branded as a poor performer, which led to a couple more questions, "Why is this niche player struggling at this location but not at other locations? What is unique about this location?"

To an IOS provider, the number-one cost is labor and everything associated with labor. As we started to delve into proposal details, questions arose surrounding current wages vs. our proposed wage structure. Our eager sales guy stated that the current supplier was making a "killing" at this site, and it was ripe for competition.

Question: How do you draw that assumption?
Response: From the prevailing wage in the area.

Question: Were you able to obtain payroll records?
Response: No.

Question: How is their turnover?
Response: The customer said it was very high.

The dialogue proceeded for a good hour or so until we flushed out the facts. The current supplier was underperforming because their turnover was over 30 percent a month. Where the site was located did not have an abundance of available labor, and the current service supplier had been slowly increasing starting wages to attract potential labor. Over the past year, starting wages had increased about 25 percent.

The suggested plan of attack by our eager sales guy was to provide value by presenting a bid lower than our competitor by using a lower wage starting point. He felt the customer would not buy a higher price.

Our solution: present a bid outlining the value we would bring to the facility, via the engagement of our teams and our process, to achieve employee engagement and lower the turnover rate significantly. We would not lower the cost point as we could not engage if we could not hire, and we could not hire if we did not have the appropriate starting wage. We did not get the contract.

Several years after we counted ourselves lucky not to have been awarded that business, I was able to find out more relevant facts associated with the opportunity. It turned out we made the right decision. If we had gone in with a lower price, we would have realized an estimated loss of over $500,000 a year.

The four exercises are beneficial to keeping the Eager Beavers in check, and ensuring cost analysis is challenged every step of the way. The goal is not to win the business. The goal is to win profitable business. Commodity bids are a sucker's choice, even for purchasers of IOS.

KEY QUALITIES TO WIN THE HEAD GAME

If you find yourself in the position in your company to approve the final price submitted to the customer, there are a few qualities I feel are key for keeping a strong sense of realism:

- Inquisitive mind
- Intense curiosity
- Intellect to sort the complex into the simple
- Persuasion
- Courage
- Emotional tenacity

The final is worth expanding upon. You cannot consider yourself as complete until your entire team, including you, have exhausted your thinking. Every service provider today has to battle being competitive with providing value, and it takes a lot of pushing and pulling to get to the answers.

I have always liked to rock the boat, I have a fundamental belief that if I am not willing to disrupt what we do or how we do it, then someone else, like a competitor, will do it for me, or, better said, "to" me. I'm the type of person who would rather do it to myself than have it done to me. The sales guys usually forget me at Christmas and on my birthday, but everyone has a role on a team and no one made me VP of Harmony. Conflict and a healthy degree of disharmony make for better discussion in a war room. It is important not to associate disharmony with distrust. While hashing things out, we always have a tremendous amount of trust for each other, but we also need to identify the true cost to deliver if we have any hope of accurately pricing the value we bring to a customer.

A good costing strategy is also reliant upon having good tools. Just as the IOS industry has evolved, so have the tools. In the very early years the tool was more often than not a bar napkin. Today the tools are sophisticated databases that provide updated costs associated with labor, and provide for input from several members of the estimating team. Whether or not the tool you use is a simple spreadsheet or a sophisticated database program, the deliverable is the same: true, honest and accurate costing information. The disciplined use of a costing process and tool will give you the power to view a new opportunity as it is and not as you wish it to be, and to do what needs to be done versus what you would like to do.

VALUE COSTING

Over the years I became very accustomed to the term "Cost Build Up." It served me well for many decades. In the past few years, I've replaced the old term with a new one, "Value Costing." Let's look at a few definitions to see if you think the term "Value Costing" has merit.

- Cost = All of the charges associated with the delivery of the services.

- Price = What you will charge your customer for delivery of the service. What is someone willing to pay?
- Profit and Loss = The difference between the cost and price.
- Profit Percentage = The Value perceived by the customer, and your target.

Price should never be determined without reconciling the **risk** this opportunity presents. I am a huge believer that profit is a symptom. Really great service companies do not chase profit. They chase value, running on a very solid **cost/risk** foundation.

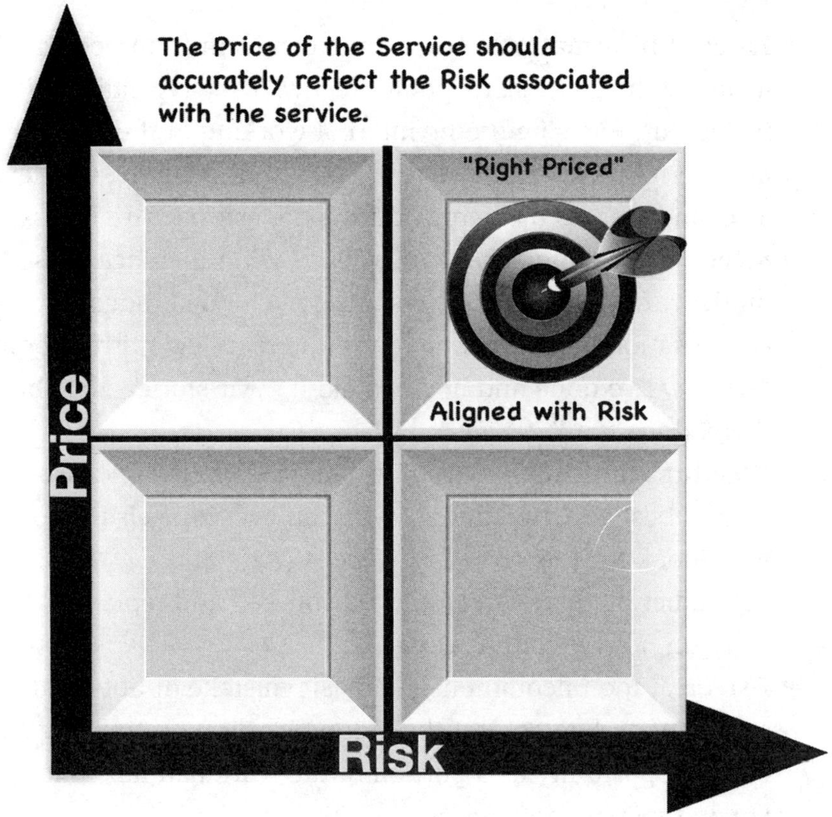

I have sat in numerous war room meetings where we had premature discussions about profit percentage of a new sales opportunity. Discussion was premature because we had not nailed down the cost to deliver the service as outlined in the scope. The conversation was meaningless as it lacked foundation.

Recently I visited a quaint candy store located in a small town along the Ohio River. On the counter was a jar of jelly beans, and in front of the jar a card outlined a challenge: How many red jelly beans were in the jar? You were required to be within 25 in order to win the prize, a bag of jelly beans.

As most know, you calculate what is visible to assess the remaining volume of the jar, and through averaging conclude the number. Unfortunately, I am not Rain Man and I was off by more than the allowed 25. It was a fun and harmless thing to do, and all I had at stake was a ¼ pound bag of jelly beans.

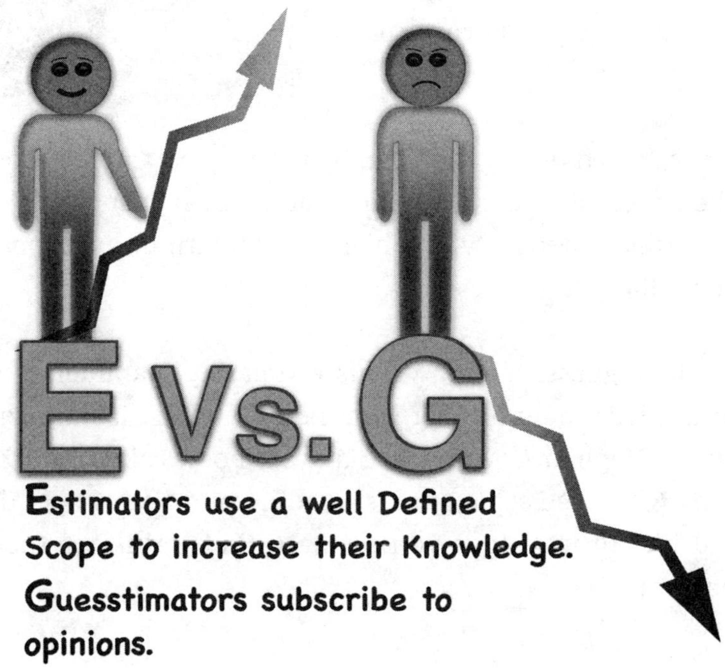

When estimating a service for a customer, however, we cannot apply the principles of the jelly bean jar. We must fully define and evaluate cost drivers that need to be figured into the estimation. In service there is always a level of assumption and, as the term estimation implies, it is a calculation based on the best data available at the time.

There is also another term, "guesstimate," which is far more informal than estimate, and, if used, increases the level of risk linked to a new sales opportunity.

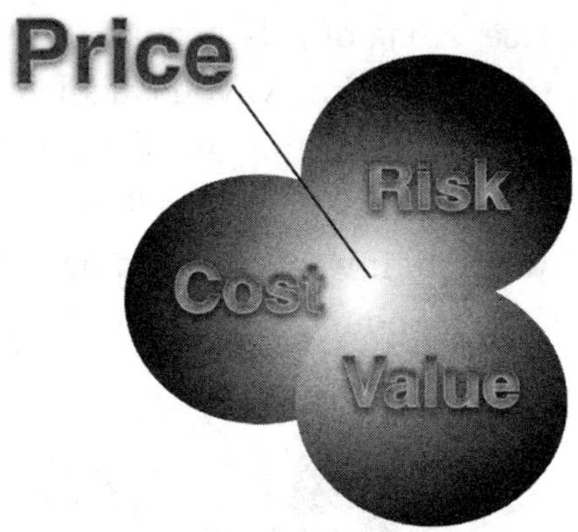

Define Need is the foundation for understanding value. An ill-defined need results in a poorly constructed price.

Define Scope is the factual foundation to assess cost. An ill-defined scope results in a poorly constructed cost.

Risk is evaluated during the defining of the need and the scope. Risk must be balanced against cost and value. The higher the risk associated with the opportunity, the higher the return on investment, and the higher the price.

To minimize guesstimating versus estimating, parameters need to be put in place to strain fact from fiction, otherwise known as assumption. Stephen Covey wrote a great book called *The 7 Habits of Highly Effective People*, a must read if you have not yet done so. I would like to introduce you to the **6 Bad Habits of Ineffective Estimation:**

- **Filtered Information:** Information comes in from people who all share the exact same point of view. They typically look inside-out, focusing on the internal working of the company vs. outside-in, focused on the reality at hand, resulting in a level of arrogance that is dangerous during the estimation process.
- **Selective Hearing:** The team screens what they hear based on their own experiences, resulting in clouded judgment. The conversation tends to hang out in the rearview mirror about "what we've done and how we did it" war stories, the "been there, done that" crowd.
- **Wishful Thinking:** If I want it to happen it will because we are the best and we know better than everyone else. Another great book for this crowd is, *Hope is Not a Strategy*. Facts that contradict the hope are quickly dismissed and replaced with a story on how we did it when....
- **Fear:** Not too uncommon—the basic mistake of not wanting to stand out and go against the group. Fear is akin to being scared of the opportunity as a portion of the workload falls onto your lap and you are anxious.

- **Emotionally Over-invested:** We have too much time invested in this to turn back at this stage. The group becomes blind to reality.
- **Unrealistic Expectations:** The sense that for some miraculous reason we will achieve levels of performance for this opportunity that we've never achieved up to this point. I like to call this one "Clark Kent" syndrome—the need for superman.

In 2012, I headed to Atlanta to visit a small site that was owned by one of our key customers. The current supplier was failing miserably, and the plant was missing every key performance indicator. We broke into groups and toured through the facility to identify and define the scope of the opportunity. After several hours, we re-convened and met with the sales group that had been discussing the site's "needs" with the plant manager and his team. It was a pretty interesting meeting. The group who had met with the plant manager and his team were all hyped up about the opportunity, and those of us who had walked the facility were looking for the door to run down the street and get as far away from this plant as possible. During that 30-minute meeting I would say each of the six bad habits was in play, but luckily, and reflective of the caliber of the group, we politely reconvened with the plant management team and stated we were not in a position to aid them at this time due to serious safety concerns we had about the facility. It was the agreed opinion of our team that the risk could not be offset by any price we would charge the customer.

Earlier I spoke about the "Big Owe," the nickname given to Olympic Stadium, located in Montreal, Quebec, and the tremendous cost overrun incurred by that project. There are a few other examples to help lay the foundation for understanding cost drivers. The Suez Canal cost 20 times its original estimate. The Sydney Opera House cost 15 times its original estimate. The Concorde jet ended up 12 times its original estimate, and the Channel tunnel between England and France, 80 times its original estimate. Each one of these examples was estimated by smart, intelligent companies who got it wrong. As big and noteworthy as these examples are, the cost overrun that affected me the most was a new site in Texas.

As with many other projects that experience a cost overrun, our team assigned to the Texas opportunity were an experienced, intelligent group. We had principles, tools, procedures, and enough experience to bid for this opportunity correctly. Due to a lack of adherence to our own guidelines and a misguided desire to land this business at any cost, we missed the mark on several of the key cost elements associated with this site. The impact of these errors during estimation was compounded by realization of several of the cost drivers, such as the lack of industrial labor in general. This was a multi-million-dollar mishap born out of an unrealistic sense of how cost effective we could be. True cost effectiveness is the optimal use of all resources to achieve the intended outcomes.

While we were busy correcting and evaluating the Texas mishap, we concluded that three key components impact cost effectiveness:

1. **E**conomy: Balance the cost of resources required without impacting quality. In Texas, we misread prevailing labor wages for our services.
2. **E**fficiency: Alignment and performance of resources required to produce outputs. In Texas, we built in levels of performance only realized at our most seasoned locations.

3. Effectiveness: How accurately targets are set and met. Due to an unrealistic perspective on the economy and efficiency, we became very ineffective, which increased the customer's demands and produced a "death spiral."

The service business has a handful of cost elements that require a very high level of attention to detail during any estimation. These cost elements are best served by fact—solid quantitative information. If for some reason that is not available, the only second choice is qualitative information and well-founded assumptions. This is not the place for opinion or best guess.

- Hours required to complete activities outlined in the scope.
- Management hours required to govern the group performing activities outlined in the scope.
- Management support required to meet the needs of the customer.
- Cost of labor, including labor burden.
- Cost of capital.
- Cost to maintain capital.
- Cost of materials/supplies.
- Cost of obtaining and implementing management systems.

Each of these elements can be impacted by cost drivers—factors that will drive costs either up or down, but usually up. Greater discipline in identifying and managing cost drivers is necessary with longer-term contracts, when the need to predict the cost drivers becomes critical.

Capturing cost drivers allows for a much better "what if" analysis, and not just a "what is" analysis. Although the latter will dominate the value costing to evaluate the current situation, it will not allow for a healthy discussion around the probability of various cost scenarios in the future. Estimation on one level is a form of basic mathematics, but on another level it is the art of deciphering reality and probability in the search for value to decide price.

SERVICE COST DRIVERS

Driver	Description	Examples
Geography	Costs associated with the location of the facility relative to the customer.	Prevailing wages Availability of talent Weather Demographics
Facility	Costs related to the size and age of the facility, equipment and technology.	Horizontal vs. vertical architecture Use of automation Past maintenance
Operation	Costs that differentiate a well-run facility vs. a poorly run facility.	Labor productivity Labor harmony Rejection rates Production planning Facility utilization
Culture	Cost impacted by a bad working environment.	Safety-related issues Absenteeism/turnover Sabotage Attitude toward quality
Regulations	Costs impacted by a change in regulatory conditions	Wage rates Benefits Unionization Legacy-related costs, such as severance
Service Level	Cost impacted by adjustments made to the level of service. A change in product or leadership can quickly affect this cost driver.	New plant manager with higher expectations New product demanding a higher level of service New corporate ownership

Typically a new sales opportunity unfolds over many years. The first year or so allows time for the service provider to confirm with facts each of the cost elements bid upon during the initial contract process, but it also allows time for cost drivers to gain momentum and to affect those costs as time passes. As correct as your estimates might have been when you bid for the business, those assumptions can quickly change as cost drivers kick in, changing costs on the fly. Cost overruns can be attributed to a handful of areas that can go awry if not paid attention to during the life span of a contract, including:

- Technical components of the contract.
- Inadequate data used to assemble the original bid.
- Scope Creep.
- Politics, both on site and at the company's corporate level.
- Economics, where the tide can turn against you or your company.
- Change in customer leadership, which is usually outside of the service provider's circle of influence, but still needs to be acted upon and monitored.

A strong focus on the cost drivers during the estimation process can minimize their impact as the engagement unfolds.

In 2011 when a tsunami hit in the Asia-Pacific, it wiped out several plants that were an integral part of the value chain for many of our service contract plants. As a service provider, there was little outside of prayer that could be done to offset the impact of the tsunami at the local level. As a value-added supplier, however, we quickly ascertained from our customers the expected impact to facilities where we were providing services, and put together a plan to re-adjust our costs on a proactive basis, limiting the impact of a cost over-run.

We undoubtedly experienced a loss of revenue and profit, but we positioned ourselves to control our costs ahead of the impact.

LAUNCH COSTS

When a new opportunity has been awarded to the IOSP, that work must be transitioned. More often than not this is simply called a "launch." There are no free throws when it comes to a new sales launch, it cannot fail. Failure costs time and money, and affects the entire psyche of both organizations. I am a believer that as a service provider you rarely bounce back from a bad launch of a new service, and the customer, even after 10 years of great service, will never forget whether you did or did not launch well.

The costs associated with the launch must be captured even if they are viewed as an investment and are not going to be passed onto the customer.

Launch is one area of value I would say is universal throughout every customer and every new service opportunity. The cost to perform this well needs to be clearly outlined and understood. Whether or not these costs are passed onto the customer or absorbed as part of the investment in this customer, the cost to seamlessly deliver the launch or start up plan must be visible.

COSTING MODELS DRIVE BEHAVIOR

Excellent service, good service, mediocre service, and poor service all have one common denominator: the service rating is dependent upon the people who deliver the service. How the service is experienced by the customer is dependent upon how those people working for the service provider behave. Behavior is usually something discussed in

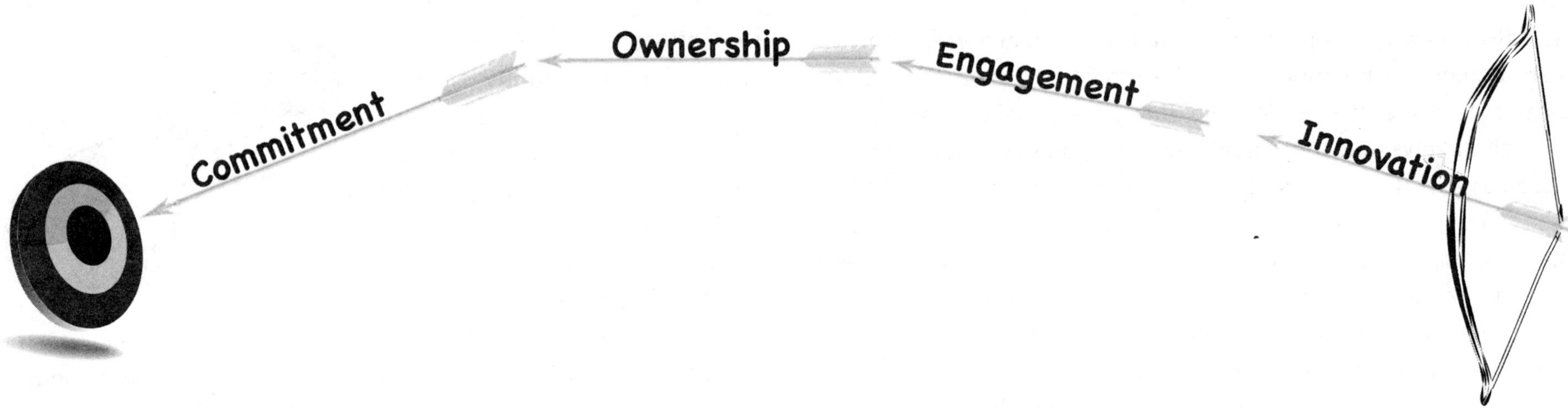

books when you are looking at hiring, team development, team performance, and so on.

We will discuss behavior in great detail at those points in *The Outsourcing Conundrum* as well, but it is important to understand that behavior is fundamental to the success of a service provider. The commercial terms set in place are a root that feeds the attitude of the team, and drives their subsequent behaviors.

Earlier in the book, I told a quick story about a meeting where the plant manager was looking for "better trained monkeys." It is not difficult to conclude quickly that this potential customer was looking for a very low-cost service provider. He did not even have the basic understanding that if you treat people like animals, they will act like animals. An IOS provider suckered into this type of arrangement will be branded as one that does not deliver value.

I usually quickly sort opportunities into two buckets—Low-Cost Service Providers and Best-Cost Service Providers—because I personally cannot bring myself to be branded as a low-cost service provider. Like most things, these buckets have degrees. There is always a middle ground that is more often than not larger in scale than either of the two extremities. But for simplicity's sake, breaking service providers down into two buckets allows me to demonstrate how behaviors experienced by the customer are birthed during this phase of *The Outsourcing Conundrum*.

TYPES OF SERVICE PROVIDERS

Low-Cost Service Providers	Best-Cost Service Providers
Very basic customer service	Enhanced service focused on value
Perform to minimal accepted standard	Performance driven to enhance customer quality
High employee turnover	Employee turnover low
Low employee engagement	High employee engagement
Minimal resources assigned to activities	Approriate resources assigned to activities
Service team exhibits low self esteem	Service team exhibits pride
Minimal alignment with customer targets	Maximum alignment with customer targets

As you read down the column of low-cost service providers, imagine how an employee would behave who is trained and managed to do only the basic job, is expected to meet the lowest standard possible for inspection, continually sees new people coming and going on each shift, perceives his opinion as meaningless, has neither the tools nor the appropriate number of people to complete assigned tasks, notices the morale of the group is low, and does not have a clue as to why the activities he is doing are important.

Can anyone explain to me:

- Why you would want to own a business like this?
- Why any company would award business to a company like this?
- Why purchasing groups have manipulated suppliers to end up like this?
- Why companies who choose this route are confused as to why their value supply chain lacks value?

As stated, this scenario is extreme, but I bet that some of you reading can relate very quickly to this type of service provider, even if it is not to this extreme.

The best-cost service provider is not the most expensive. They are the most aligned with customer needs, and represent the best value for the money being spent. I have a friend in the high-end home restoration business who periodically shares interesting client stories with me. He called one day with a, "You are not going to believe this" story. "Probably not," I replied, "What's up?" My friend went on to tell me he was delivering four—yep, four—accent sofa pillows to a client, and he wanted me to guess how much the customer was paying for the four—yep, four—pillows. "Not a clue," I stated. He urged me again to guess, and I said, having an idea of where he was going, "Two thousand dollars—$500.00 per pillow." He told me I wasn't even close. "Try $12,000.00 total—$3,000.00 per pillow!" I could not believe it. Value for the money? Highly unlikely. Possibly stroking one's ego? Much more likely. That is not being a best-cost service provider. Best-cost service is the service solution that best aligns with the customer to improve the customer's competitive advantage by enhancing the value in the value supply chain.

As you read down the best-cost service provider column, you should picture a very different employee. He is probably not actually an employee, but more of a team member or associate, committed to the best level of customer service. This is an individual engaged in improving performance and quality because he can see his role in the product the customer is delivering to the marketplace. A team member like this is upbeat and enjoys working with his teammates because they have the resources to do their jobs, and people are listening to what they have to say to improve their jobs.

These are the choices surrounding the commercial arrangement made by companies that are considering IOS and by service providers who are considering delivering on those services. Plant the seeds for the type of service experience that will follow.

My experience with a Japanese transplant is probably one of the best on a large scale where the company made the decision to inside-outsource a large degree of light maintenance work. They did what was typical in specifying activities to be outsourced, and setting up suppliers to interview/review to assess their capability. Not as typical was that they also delved into the people culture of the supplier, wanting to know how their people were treated, rewarded, incentivized, etc. The actual business model used with service providers was designed to ensure people delivering services were well treated and engaged. Of all the meetings I had with this key customer over the years, I can safely say that over 95 percent of them involved what we were doing to motivate our team and what they could do to help. This customer got more of our discretionary effort than any other customer we serviced.

Each of the two service buckets, whether it is a low-cost or best-cost strategy, has a series of costing models to choose from in terms of how the contract is set up. Almost all IOS contracts follow one of the following five pricing models:

- Lump Sum
- Time and Material
- Price Per Activity
- Piece Work
- Management Fee

In the table on the right, I have expanded on each one with a brief description and the primary behavior it will promote. In many cases, I have found that any given opportunity can have two or more of these models working alongside each other at a given location.

All costing strategy types and models respond to "What" and "How" the service will be approached, delivered, and inspected. The choice, or the combination of choices, will impact how the service provider behaves. Each one of these models can have a risk-reward component associated with it, whereby the service provider can realize a financial upside or downside depending upon their ability to meet set expectations. We will discuss expectations in much greater detail in the next chapter.

Personally, I like models that result in the best alignment with the customer and in-depth knowledge surrounding the opportunity. If the risk is great, or the information surrounding the opportunity vague, then I lean toward a time and material contract for a period. If the risk is known and/or reasonable, and the information well understood, I tend to move toward a model that drives the highest level of performance possible, like lump sum or price per activity. Piece work is usually associated with sub-assembly service opportunities where we have been contracted to complete only a part of the production process at a fixed price.

COSTING MODELS

Model	Description	Dominant Behavior
Lump Sum	The price to complete the scope of work is fixed.	Drives work effectiveness, and efficiency.
Time and Material	The price for the work is determined by how many hours, people, tools, material and other resources are used.	Drives a strong sense of adaptability and customer orientation.
Price per Activity	The cost to complete the work is tied to each activity, and the price paid for the service is dependent upon the volume of activities completed.	Drives high degree of scheduling efficiency and task completion/ inspection.
Piece Work	The price charged is dependent upon the successful completion and inspection of parts. Usually tied to sub-assembly services.	Drives high degree of scheduling efficiency, task completion/inspection, and a high need for structure.
Management Fee	The price is associated with overall management of the service. This is very typically attached to one of the other models.	Drives accountability, and a sense of leadership.

Two key attitudes I have always tried to build into the model to force us to become the best service provider possible are:

- Profit is a symptom.
- Paycheck is a symptom.

If you look at profit not as something you are entitled to, but rather as a symptom of providing value for the money through a well-oiled delivery mechanism, then you are better positioned to stay sharp and not become complacent. The second attitude is very similar but trickles down to your management team. The paycheck is also a symptom of the value of the work you do and not an entitlement. The combination of both, tied to a well thought out commercial arrangement, is a perfect setting for a service opportunity.

A CONTRACT OR SERVICE AGREEMENT

Simply stated, a contract or service agreement is a document that outlines the obligations of the IOS provider and the customer. It is very often referred to as the commercial terms, or terms and conditions, of the project. The commercial terms outline the rules of engagement that both parties will adhere to in order to ensure compliance. From my experience, and probably why this particular subject is at the end of the chapter, although the terms and conditions can affect whether you would or would not engage with a customer, they rarely, if ever, add value to the engagement. Determining where the value is in the opportunity, and applying the appropriate costing models will do far more to determine employee behavior and the eventual success/outcomes of the IOS engagement. Nonetheless, the following terms of the contract are important and essential to include.They are must-haves required to produce a lawful contract, and not much more than that, although many lawyers might disagree.

A service contract or agreement will typically cover issues surrounding:

- Contract Acceptance
- Billing and Shipping
- Delivery to Schedule
- Quality Standards
- Force Majeure—delays
- Warranties
- Termination—non-performance and convenience
- Intellectual Property
- Indemnification
- Insurance
- Recoupment
- Relationship of Parties
- Non-assignment
- Jurisdiction
- Payment Terms

This is a pretty normal list, which you can expect to be present in most agreements. We have run into agreements in which the list is far more extensive, and tries to establish a legal footing for just about everything that can go wrong.

QUICK STORY

In the mid '80s, in Oshawa, Ontario, dealing with the high-pressure water blasting of exhaust stacks for an auto manufacturing plant, I was introduced to a very unique way to price new work. As the project commenced, the engineers were able to see the condition of the entire paint system, and decided to expand the scope. The purchase order was based on a price per stack basis. There was no ceiling on the number of stacks the purchase order covered, so the engineer decided to take the additional required work and calculate the additional scope as if they were adding stacks.

For example, as they moved the scope to include cleaning air make-up houses and exhaust chambers, they would say that an air house was worth two stacks, and an exhaust chamber was worth five stacks. It worked out well. All of the work got done, and the currency used for the project was based on dollars per stack. In reality there were only about

50 stacks total, but the final invoice submitted stated 175 stacks were cleaned.

The funny part was that the following year, that same plant sent out a request again to clean the stacks, all 175 stacks. Even more funny, one engineer was assigned to find the missing 125 stacks that had been cleaned the previous year.

BEST PRACTICE

My partners in Arkansas, Team Trek, who deliver leadership training for us, have a philosophy they call 100 percent responsibility. It means that we are all 100 percent responsible for our actions, no excuses. If you spend time with any of the TT team, you will quickly realize just how well this is branded into their belief system.

When it came to obtaining pricing from TT for their services, this concept of 100 percent responsibility was paramount. They spent time to build a relationship with us, thus becoming a partner and solutions provider that added value. They were able to articulate our pain clearly, as well as their plan to correct the pain efficiently and effectively. They made it clear that if for any reason any one of the participants felt a lack of value or growth from the program, they would step in and repeat the process or conduct follow-up coaching. Yep, 100 percent responsibility. I will buy that every day and be willing to pay a bit more for it.

TAKEAWAYS:

- Profit is a symptom and not an entitlement.
- Price is related to value and not cost.
- Costs are founded on fact and not opinion.
- Bad estimating habits produce bad opportunities.
- Value is price minus cost.

PURPOSE

Define the Need
Define Scope
Define Value
Define Expectations
Re-Define the Need
The Outsourcing Conundrum

> "Measurement creates focus for the future because the measures chosen by the managers communicate to the organization what is important. To take full advantage of this power, measurement should be integrated into a management system."
>
> *The Strategic Focused Organization*
> Robert S. Kaplan, David P. Norton

The Outsourcing Conundrum has evolved and morphed into what is being presented in this book by necessity and many degrees earned in the school of hard knocks over the years. It would be refreshing to be able to convey that I had tremendous foresight which allowed me to see the consequences of my mistakes before they were made, but that is not the case. I was, however, given the gift of "why."

Although this gift would often show up late to the party and sometimes after the party concluded, it did allow me to learn from my mistakes. Define Expectations and what is contained in this chapter is no different. Each component of the model is a result of lessons learned.

In 1987, I was in Montreal, Quebec, restoring an old hotel into a boutique shopping and office complex. Our role in this project was to clean the exterior of the building from a blackened, dark structure to reveal the yellow brick underneath. This building had stood at its location for more than 100 years, exposed to rain, city pollution, the residue from a city using coal to heat homes, etc., and our job was to clean it. The word "clean" seems so simple and easy for everyone to understand: the building is now black; when we are finished performing the duties of our contract, it will be yellow and, therefore, "clean."

As with all projects like this, a sample cleaning of a section of the building can be performed to determine what the brick will look like upon completion, as well as to help formulate the dilution rate of chemicals. Our completed sample, framed by the surrounding dirty black brick, was spectacular. It looked so good, our sales person used the statement, "Looks like new." The general contractor and building owners agreed, and complimented the sales person. He felt so good, he thought it would be a great selling point to include in the proposal two very small words he thought would clinch the deal, "Like new."

Well, those two words clinched the sale for sure, and also removed any semblance of profit from the project. The funny thing was that as we started to "clean" large portions of the building, say 150 feet wide by 150 feet high, the difference between the old and the newly cleaned became less and less distinct.

The owners showed up weekly for what was known back then as a "polaroid" tour. They would walk the building, and take pictures of everything that did not meet their satisfaction. As the building cleaning progressed, the euphoria over the initial sample diminished to "you call yourselves a restoration company?" in a few short weeks.

In the follow-up clarification meeting with the general contractors, owners, and our onsite project leader, our sales person argued his point of a "clean building," and presented numerous pictures to prove his point. He concluded by clearly stating how much cleaner the "old hotel" was than when we started. Even the homeless guys who hung out by the coffee shop on the corner told us it looked great. The owners, however, kept repeating two words from the agreed-to proposal, "like new." "Like new" was not achievable, but due to those two words a crew stayed at the building for a solid year scrubbing all of the bricks until the owner, due to time constraints, had to let it go. They also kept the last 10 percent of the contract. What a lesson learned. All we should have done was put in the proposal that the building would be cleaned "like the sample" as opposed to "like new." We would have been off to the races, or at least heading home from Montreal many months earlier.

I would be remiss not to point out that both the owners and general contractors in this case had character flaws that cannot be described using Webster's Dictionary, but it is a mistake as a service provider to ever blame your customer because you did not do your job and Define the Expectations surrounding a new or expanded service offering.

As a service provider, you have to accept the brutal reality of a myriad expectations. As an IOS provider, that reality is greatly enhanced. In most cases you find yourself delivering services at customers' locations for clients who report up to corporate offices at other locations. This creates many layers of management, many expectations, and many customers to serve.

On several occasions during discussions with corporate-level customers, they would express that as long as the management team in the plant was happy, they were happy. This could not be further from the truth. If and when plant management teams are not meeting expectations, IOS providers are drawn into performance issues by association. Very rarely have I heard a plant management team state "the service provider is doing a great job, but we are not." This is pretty much human nature, and underscores the need for clear communication surrounding service expectations both up and down the food chain.

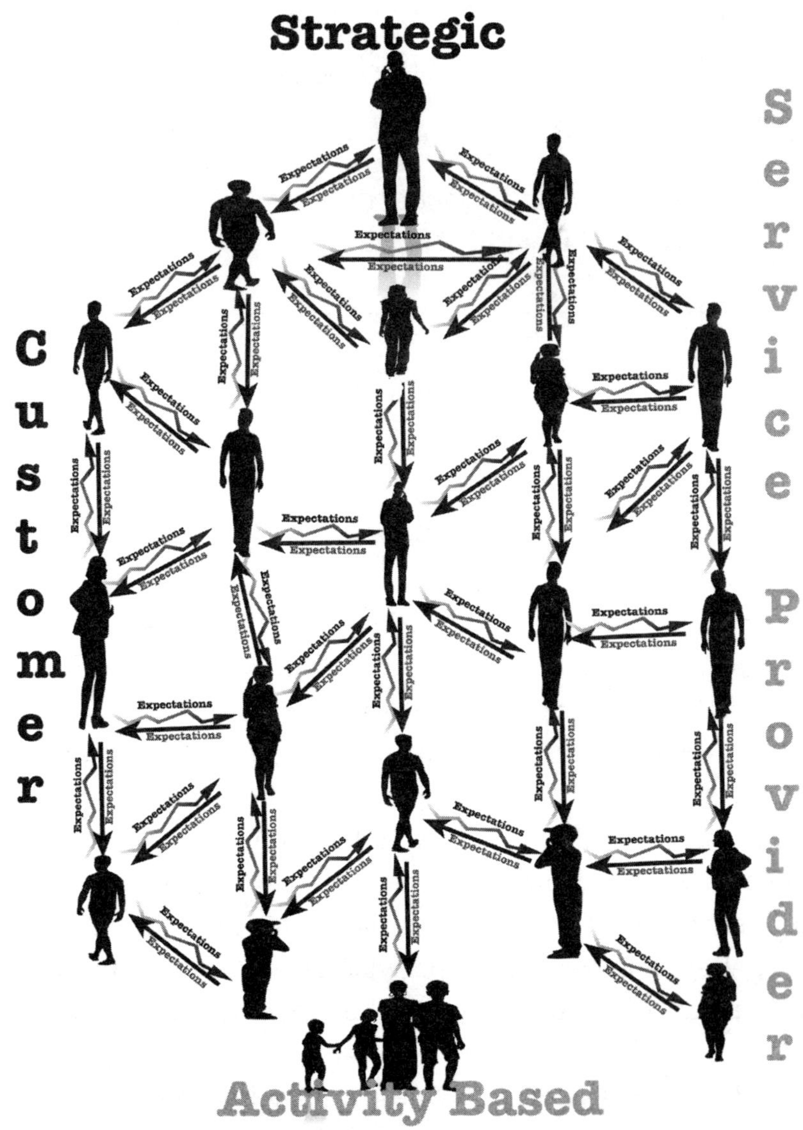

PCV VALVE

PCV Valve - Noun, a valve used to control and direct flow (associated with automotive gases). A valve, as we know, is a device for halting or controlling flow of material through a designed passage. It has an inlet and outlet. I would like to introduce you to the "IOS - PCV Valve" that is designed to halt and control the flow of myriad expectations surrounding the addition of a new or expanded IOS offering.

Three components make up the valve and allow for a smooth flow of expectations, increasing the likelihood of success by both buyers and service providers. The inlet to the valve is the Proposal. The metering within the valve is the Clarification. The outlet, or required outcomes, from the valve is Validation, to confirm "what was bought" and "what was sold" are on equal footing, and to clarify how outcomes will be measured.

- **Proposal**: Noun, the act of offering or suggesting something for acceptance, adoption, or performance.
- **Clarification**: Noun, the act of making an idea, statement, proposal, clear or intelligible, free from ambiguity.
- **Validation**: Noun, the act of substantiating and confirming suspicions and assumptions.

Proposal

In my career, I have seen proposals for services on as little as 3½" × 3½" bar napkins, up to binders that were 3½" thick. Both of these extremes have landed their fair share of new services. So, how do IOS providers choose which format to use to pursue a new opportunity?

Choose by clearly understanding your customer, as well as what it is going to take for two very important points to be clearly outlined:

- You understand the customer's Need, Scope and the Value they seek.
- You are uniquely positioned above all other competitors in this race to deliver on the Value required at a competitive price.

The proposal pulls together in a succinct fashion the answers to these two critical questions and starts the process of defining the expectations. The proposal is a source of how you and your company will be perceived. In a world of Six-Sigma, LEAN, TPS, TQM, etc., you cannot expect to be taken seriously if you cannot put forth a proposal that makes your two key points, that you understand the customer and you are uniquely positioned to deliver on the expectations, without re-writing *War and Peace*.

If you have a strong relationship with the customer, it is often a great practice to bounce a draft of your proposal off of them to gain a better understanding from them if you have truly captured the full expectation in the proposal.

One practice that we used to convey our understanding was to outline our proposals in a manner that followed our operating process. The table of contents would look similar to the table of contents you see in this book. It showed the customer that we operated to a methodology that was customer focused and targeted to meet the desired expectations.

Let me share one other practice that we terminated pretty quickly after it proved to provide little to no value. I had the unfortunate experience back in the late '80s of working for a man who, as part of his job, would review proposals going out to new customers. He would take the binder that housed the proposal, and, based solely upon its weight, decide if it was good enough to send. I used to joke that he was the only man I knew who sold services by the pound. He had what I came to call "boilerplate cancer," throwing crap into binders to make someone think he spent way more time on something than he actually did. Newsflash: it doesn't work, it never worked, and it's never going to work. Be respectful of your customer's time and our national forests, and use only the amount of paper it takes for you to clearly make your two key points.

If your proposal is being delivered via PowerPoint, Prezzi, or any other media, the same rules apply. It doesn't matter how cool your presentation is, how well you can transition slides, insert movie clips, or prove you are a clip art aficionado or a Steven Spielberg wanna be. Human beings in general only dedicate a limited amount of time to reading or listening to or watching your proposal. The more extraneous stuff you include in the proposal, the greater chance there is that your real message will get lost in all the fluff. Even when I started out in this business, and more so today, you have a very short amount of time and attention to make your two points clearly. Don't waste it.

In the mid '80s to late '90s, many manufacturers were starting to follow the trend of using Tier One and Tier Two suppliers for inside-outsourcing light maintenance and technical cleaning activities. Many of these companies lacked the sophistication on how to buy IOS services. It became pretty obvious these services were not core to them, and as such they had not paid much attention to or invested in them. This resulted in poorer and poorer product quality, and customers started to complain.

Faced with an unsophisticated purchasing process and an inability of customers to specify a scope, we chose to take our service offerings and package them as a program. The program was an earlier version of the Outsourcing Conundrum Model. By doing this, we were able to dictate scope requirements, and sell the value of a program versus a list of activities. Our customers loved the convenience of the program, and rewarded us with multi-millions of dollars of new business in dozens of new sites. The concept of the program allowed us to better outline the expectations and gain our customer buy-in to those expectations. It also gave us a leg up on the competition for a period of time.

Clarification

During clarification, the goal is to remove as much ambiguity as possible from the proposed service offering. Said another way, you use this time to table and document any assumptions that might be built into your proposal. These could be little things, such as: I assume you will be in business next month, I assume you are going to pay me for the work I do, I assume you will not harass my people, and I assume you will be a good and fair customer. Clarification should flesh out and gain agreement around the strengths you are bringing to the customer, and any known weaknesses where you will need support from the customer.

In San Luis, Mexico, we were bidding on facility services. Our company had a great brand, and we were noted as being an employer of choice in the local area. We treated our teams well, and word had spread. The issue was the customer's facility was located many miles outside of bus routes. We did not have the means to get team members to the facility. Through clarification, we were able to offset this weakness by using a bus-line structure installed by the customer, for a nominal fee.

Clarification is also a good time to discuss any opportunities that can be taken to improve the success of this new service. During the site survey and scope preparation, there are often conditions that can be corrected to provide improvement for both the customer and service provider. You may also have uncovered threats that lie outside of your circle of influence that will need to be addressed.

As I write this book, the US is facing the implementation of what is being called "Obama Care." The impact of this legislation on medical costs for employers is still up for debate, and it hinders accuracy of the estimation process. As an employer, we must comply with these new regulations but we are not in a position to influence the outcome of the regulations. Areas like Obama Care are seen as threats to business opportunities, and should be discussed.

During clarification, we also find it helpful to discuss the management team we have assigned to launch, and the strengths each team member brings to the project. We also use this time to make clear where we are weak and where we need support from the customer. On many occasions what we need is often best described as "tribal knowledge," such as who are the "go to" people in the plant that can make things happen and who are not. In my experience, customers appreciate the level of candor during these discussions. This process of clarification also helps draw customers into the success of projects as stakeholders.

A simple SWOT discussion at this stage of the relationship can very often avoid the need for an emergency SWAT team to be called in a few months down the road. SWOT is a very common model to frame a discussion around Strengths, Weaknesses, Opportunities, and Threats. I think we have all seen enough TV to understand SWAT!

In later years, as with many components of The Outsourcing Conundrum Model, we became much better at clarification, and developed tools to help the integrity of the process. The Customer Clarification Check-Up Table on the next page is a pretty informal way to determine quickly what further level of discussion might be required with the customer.

This is a simple pass/fail analysis to allow the group to determine objectively what adjustments need to be made to the proposal so it is foundational to the success of the opportunity and not a potential source of failure. "Like new" versus "as per sample." During clarification, compromises of various degrees are inevitable. A Clarification Check-Up helps keep the team honest, and confirms if any of the compromises discussed impact our ability to provide value.

The goal at this point is to further translate expectations into mutually understood and measurable terms that can be used to assess and determine success. These terms are applied to the operating plan in the validation process.

In 2010 I was working with a large auto manufacturer that was in the process of replacing their current service provider with a new service provider. The proposed project affected numerous manufacturing locations throughout the US. In preparation, we spent a lot of time in discussion with the customer clarifying their true need. As part of investigation and research, we invited customer reps to visit some of our existing locations. This allowed them to witness our services first hand, and to interact with our local team. The reps were impressed with what they observed and by the culture exhibited by our team. Upon returning to corporate, they made it clear that what our company was delivering was what their company needed.

CUSTOMER CLARIFICATION CHECK-UP TABLE

Value Assessment			
Our value promise is aligned with customer needs.	+	–	Our customer does not recognize our value proposition.
We differentiated ourselves from our competitors.	+	–	We are selling a "me too" product.
Cost / Price Assessment			
Revenue stream is predictable.	+	–	Revenues are unpredictable.
Costs are predictable.	+	–	Costs are unpredictable.
Our price and value are well matched.	+	–	Our costing has left too much money on the table.
We realize cost and revenue within an acceptable range.	+	–	Our receivable terms put our cost structure at risk.
Resources Assessment			
We have properly identified the caliber and skill of the team.	+	–	We fell short in our analysis of what the team needs to be successful.
We have appropriate costs assigned to our resources.	+	–	Our resource costs are mis-aligned against the opportunity.
Levels of additional support are accurate and available.	+	–	We fall short in additional required support.
Management Systems Assessment			
Our management systems are adaptable to this opportunity.	+	–	Our management systems fall short of the expectations.
Expectations for reporting are reasonable and within our scope.	+	–	Reporting expectations fall beyond our capacity.
Relationship Assessment			
Customer relationships are multiple and strong.	+	–	Relationship is singular.
We are known and respected for our service at the customer location.	+	–	Customer location is not aware of who we are.
Customer location is open and willing to change.	+	–	Customer location is resistant to change.
A method for conflict management and resolution was reviewed.	+	–	The customer uses fear to resolve conflict.
Customer respects management team assigned to project.	+	–	Customer has not met management team assigned to project.
Delivery Assessment			
We are capable and able to deliver services in the time frame specified.	+	–	The time frame does not match level of activities to be completed.
We have the necessary skill to complete activities safely.	+	–	We fall short of being able to complete activities safely.

The hurdle we ran into surrounded the definition of Scope. As you may recall from the previous chapter on scope, it is critical to determine total manpower and level of manpower required on a shift-by-shift basis. The purchasing group's technical advisors could not let go of the idea of "wiggle room." They were determined not to specify all activities or frequencies associated with services so they could have services on demand. The misalignment happened when they opted for a lump sum model which requires a very well-documented scope. We opted to make the necessary adjustment to our pricing structure to place ourselves just out of the reach of being accepted. It was a very tough decision as we had spent a long time nurturing the opportunity, but in the long run it was the right answer. Their need for wiggle room made the next component, Validation, nearly impossible to nail down.

Validation

Validation not only validates (through measurement) the strategic purpose of what has already been agreed to, but it also surfaces evolving needs and acts as a tool for continuous improvement of the services provided, and of the customer/IOS provider relationship.

During validation a strategic site operating plan is assembled with the IOSP management team and input from the customer. This tool is the birthplace of accountability and it helps to ensure what was agreed to during the clarification meetings is transposed to an operating document. As per the previous example, one area of measure revolves around contractual obligation to complete specified scope within the required time frame.

Every CEO, company president, or operations leader I have ever had the opportunity to interact with shares one common problem, regardless of their industry, market or geography: the inability of their teams to execute on promises made. As a service provider whose pride and brand are rooted in doing what they say they are going to do, we have always made accountability a critical priority.

At a retreat back in the mid-'90s, I handed out money clips to all of our site management team members. On the face of the clip was, "WWAOD." What Would An Owner Do? Our goal was to start a push toward very strong site-level accountability. As you will recall from some of the earlier reading, we also engaged Team Trek to help push what became known as 100 Percent Responsibility, No Excuses.

DWYSYAGTDWYSYAGTDI

Okay, so that's a mouthful. Do what you say you are going to do, when you say you are going to do it. Pretty old-school stuff, but it is the essence of good service and cannot be achieved if your teams are not aware of the expectations of them that were agreed to during finalization of the sales process.

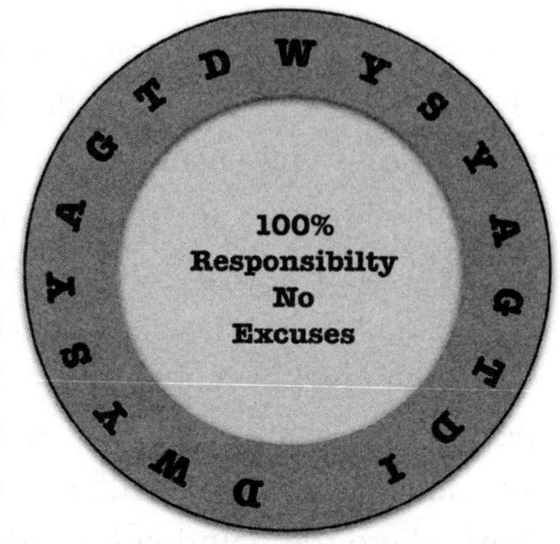

Validation, through measurement, becomes the proof that the strategic purposes for outsourcing any service are being met. Very often visible numbers, sometimes referred to as lag indicators, are not the answer and not the indicator of strategic success. A visible number to the service provider is profit, whereas a visible number to the customer is on, or better than, budget as it relates to cost. Chasing one visible number could actually impact the other. A set of lead indicators that are mutually beneficial are often better metrics. Cost savings per team member will lead to improved profit and better budget results, pleasing both the IOSP and the customer.

Sales teams are experts at smoke and mirror tactics to highlight their unique sales message and to position their company ahead of the competition, as well as solidifying margins, getting through the purchasing process, and getting the go-ahead nod. After the sale is complete, they are also masters of re-visiting the deal to get back whatever was given up during the negotiation and clarification process. Validation helps keep everyone focused on the end game: the strategic purpose for why the service was outsourced in the first place. In scenarios where there is IOS, customers are in many ways giving up or losing some level of control to service providers. It becomes increasingly important for customers to ensure service providers have management systems in place along with the necessary data to ensure processes are operating within allotted parameters.

Service providers are going to innovate, invest in R&D, train people and modify systems, all in an effort to be successful. The creation of the right measures will ensure all those efforts head in the strategic direction required to meet the purpose for an inside-outsourcing initiative.

Previously I spoke about a project in Tijuana where we provided painting operation services. This was a critical process that mandated a very high level of reporting to assure plant management that every aspect of the painting process was operating within set parameters. Eventually this led to installation of flat screens in plant management offices where the painting operation and key performance indicators could be viewed and monitored in real time. This micro level of detail fed into our strategic site operating plan, and provided direction for our onsite team to continually meet the strategic needs of the customer.

In 2011, I attended a meeting at an auto plant in Ontario with plant leadership, where we were complimented on our participation in the launch of a new model. They were most pleased with the alignment of our teams in meeting the plant's strategic goals. From day one with this customer, we were aligned to their strategic goal by a tool called a Hoshin.

Over the course of my career, many different tools with various names and formats have been used to establish alignment. At one point, I took on the futile exercise of trying to standardize the name and format of the tool. In the last half-decade I am more concerned that the tool, regardless of its name, accomplishes the goal of validating that our services are aligned with the strategic needs of our customers.

A TOOL OF MANY NAMES

In his 1996 book entitled *What is Strategy?,* Michael Porter discusses the "foundation of strategy as the activities in which an organization elects to excel. Ultimately all differences between companies in cost or price derive from the hundreds of activities used to create products or services. Differentiation arises from both the choice of activities and how they are performed."

In 2006 we had the opportunity to partner with a customer who received the Shingo prize, an honor awarded to exemplary manufacturers that meet specific criteria. Our customer invited us on stage during the ceremony to participate in the receipt of the award. Our services for this customer were made up of facilities maintenance, production maintenance, and environmental services. From day one of our formal relationship with this customer, we were aligned to their strategic goal by a tool called the Balanced Scorecard.

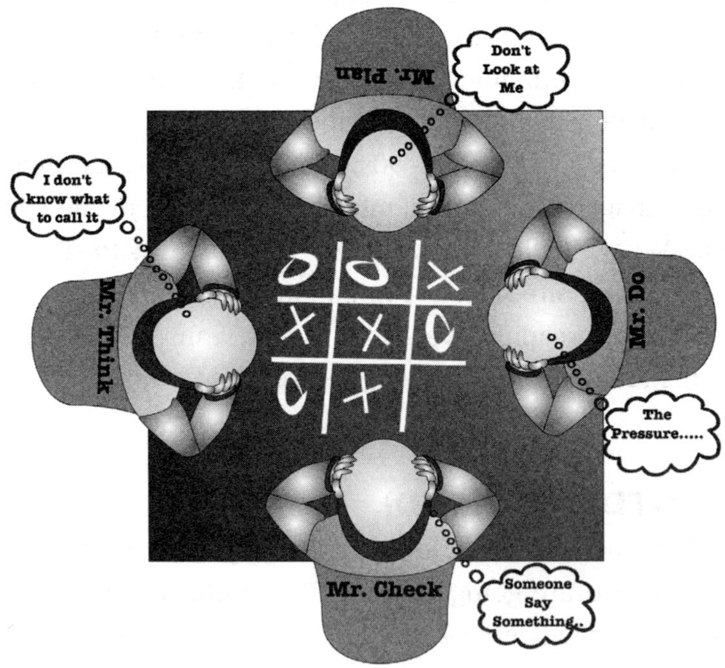

Regardless of the name—Scorecard, Balanced Scorecard, Hoshin, Strategic Operating Plan, Business Plan, CUBE—it is essential that the measurement tool accomplish two goals:

- The tool drives forward thinking (strategic thinking) by allowing management teams the ability to communicate strategy in a manner that can be understood and acted upon.
- The tool drives focus, in fact creates unwavering focus, by clearly communicating the direction the team needs to navigate. Every resource and activity is aligned to the strategy and mission at hand.

Depending on the size and complexity of the service engagement being undertaken, the tools may need to be able to cascade down through several levels within your organization and also that of your customers. The tool is pretty much useless if the information contained in it is not relevant to the user. For it to be relevant, it must be meaningful. For it to be meaningful, content has to relate to the users' day-to-day activities.

In order for the tool to work and meet the two goals, independent of its name and format, it should at a minimum identify:

- Key Strategic Drivers: Vital areas that require unwavering focus and that cannot be overlooked, such as safety, quality, productivity, morale, cost, waste, and innovation.
- Performance Indicator(s) for each driver: What lead measurements will tell you that you are on track to achieve your goal? These include incident rates, percentage of first-time pass, hours per activity, suggestions per team member, and percentage of reduction in operating costs.
- Strategic Objectives or Outcomes: What objectives are you looking to accomplish with each key driver, such as employee engagement, employee turnover, re-work reduction, etc.?
- Initiatives or Projects to Positively Impact Results: What will be implemented by the team to positively impact strategic objectives, such as a better hiring plan, improved safety program, improved training and specific activities, better visual display of operational data, etc.?
- Grading Mechanism: a means of accountability to rate and communicate results.

As with all tools, with use they become smarter and the management team becomes smarter. As the team evolves and the management team becomes more sophisticated in its use of the chosen tool, there are a few additions to the tool that can enhance its ability to create direction:

- Benchmark data
- Trends and cyclical analysis
- Very defined "cause and effect" relationship between the strategic drivers

Strategic management tools contain input from the leadership who are required to deliver on the services, and from the customer who will be receiving the services. There should be an understanding that if the plan is working and trending in the right direction at an agreed-to pace, then the services being provided are aligned and performing to everyone's expectations.

In 1986 Mary Walton wrote a book called *The Deming Management Method*. Dr. Deming was known for saying to the US Agency for International Development, "Export anything to a friendly country except American management." Dr. Deming believed that American management suffered from a series of diseases and obstacles that hindered the opportunity for success. In summary, these are:

- A lack of purpose—the inability for long-term planning
- Too much emphasis on short-term profit

- Running the business on only the visible numbers
- A belief that our problems are unique

In short, from reading Mary Walton's book and several others that outline Dr. Deming's management methods and tools, I drew one conclusion:

"Do not proceed without a plan."

We live in a very knowledge-based environment with knowledge-based workers who need to know why their work is important. The plan, therefore, cannot be static. It must be dynamic. The management team must keep their antenna up or, probably more fitting for today, keep their WiFi "hot," to stay tuned to changes in the customer's business environments and the needs of IOSP team.

A site SOP (Strategic Operating Plan) has to be linked directly to the operating budget for the location. The plan needs to be an important topic of conversation with the customer during budget setting or contract renewal. The plan should also be used much more regularly with your customer, for example, as a monthly scorecard to discuss your progress. Thus the SOP enables you to continuously validate your customer's expectations and adjust as needs and conditions change in the engagement.

The strategic operating plan is a means for driving required change so you can continually meet your customers' growing expectations. It is not a metrics game or numbers game. The plan is a foundation for continual improvement and effective execution of your services. Nothing can be executed if it is not understood. It cannot be understood if it is not described.

MISFIRE DURING LAUNCH

"You sold and I bought, so what is going wrong?" A misfire during launch is when the service is not transitioning according to plan and set targets are being missed. You cannot bounce back from a bad launch. There are several contributors to a misfire:

- Inability to overcome local resistance to change.
- Trying to execute a plan that conflicts with the existing power and structure.
- Inadequate buy-in and information sharing.
- Unclear accountability or responsibility, resulting in a lack of ownership.
- Lack of upper management support or resources on the side of the service provider and/or the customer.
- Ramping up too quickly with no realization of the consequences.
- Hurdles:
  - Financial: bad estimate.
  - Expertise: misread scope, misaligned resources.
  - People: misread capacity and availability.

The disciplined use of the IOS-PCV Valve can control and halt a misfire before the cartridge has been loaded. Each one of the above-mentioned bullets had two results: the onsite team blamed someone else, often the customer; and the cost of doing business went up. Human nature drives people to blame others when things go wrong, but no one wins the blame game. Some service providers have allowed this game to become commonplace and accepted when things go awry.

By using the IOS-PCV valve to instill a level of accountability for meeting everyone's expectations, the time and energy wasted on blame can be redirected to focusing on forward thinking.

A solid management tool used to align service strategically with a customer's strategy offsets a misfire if the tool is transparent to the customer. In the examples I cited, customers would participate in joint meetings with our local management teams to review our progress, provide input, and help mold the strategic management tool. From my experience, when we were disciplined in the use of the tool, our partnership with our customer grew. Our value also grew, and we experienced nice levels of vertical growth.

QUICK STORY

I do not remember where I first heard the phrase "fall forward," but it sure describes much of my life. It really describes my relationship with this particular chapter as I sit here and think about which of many stories to share, where I failed to Define the Expectation, where I neglected to clarify the situation fully before jumping in head first.

Back in the mid '80s we were contracted to clean out a group of very large holding tanks at a manufacturer of electric cable. At this time I was a crew boss, so I was very hands-on with the work being done. One of the crew called in sick, so I picked up his job as water blaster. The idea was simply to perform the "annual" cleaning of the pits that collected sludge from the manufacturing process.

Anyone who has ever done this type of work knows that one of the key questions to ask the customer is, "When was the last time this was cleaned?" Followed by, "What exactly is in the pit?" to give you some bearing on what you are heading

into. Remember this was the mid-'80s so those questions are very lax by today's standards. But as simple as they were, we didn't ask them at the outset of the project, so we didn't get the answers or the clarification we needed. By the time we cleaned the first pit out of five, we had consumed all of the time dedicated to the entire project. As we attempted to adjust the contract to reflect the time it was going to take more accurately, the customer pointed out that we must not be as efficient as the company who performed the cleaning the previous year.

"Really," I said. "So last year, ABC company cleaned all of the five pits down to bare metal?"
"Sure did."
"And you inspected all five of them?" I responded.
"Sure did."
"Did you notice the park bench?" I inquired.
"Park bench!" he snorted.
"Yes, sir. In the bottom on the third tank we found a park bench from a local park."

As it turned out the pits had not been cleaned for 20-plus years, and this solid citizen was lying through his teeth. Oh, yeah, the park bench was put in by the guys who installed the tanks as the tanks were used for their break room during the construction of the production line some 25 years earlier. Clarify, Clarify, Clarify....

BEST PRACTICE

Earlier in Part 1, I spoke about a not-for-profit kids' camp located in southern Ohio. The camp provides programs for children with special needs, school groups, and leadership programs. The business model required that the school programs run at break even and the leadership programs make a profit, to provide for investment in the special needs programs. I worked on a focused basis with this camp for three years to implement an earlier version of The Outsourcing Conundrum Model.

The camp was running in the red overall and could not locate the source of the loss. After several months of analysis, we determined the major source of loss was the school programs. These outdoor experiential programs serviced primary schools from Cincinnati, Columbus, Dayton, and Indianapolis. This program was in high demand and served more than 10,000 children a year. The cost to deliver the program was running in the neighborhood of $25 per student more than the camp charged for each child. The program charged each child roughly $100 per week, but the cost needed to be around $125 per week. Percentage-wise, that is a big jump.

We identified the problem in January, just ahead of the annual renewal for all the schools. At the time, I was working with an extraordinary woman who knew the value of her programming. She knew and respected her customers, and had a phenomenal staff of instructors.

She took the time to call every school and all the teachers involved to outline the situation. For the camp, this communication was critical, as it had to either raise the price or exit that business to stop the red ink. She was honest and upfront. She outlined the surveys of her programming over the past decade, the program innovations to appeal to upcoming generations, and the dedication and caliber of her team.

This data-driven, honest approach allowed the camp to raise its price and retain over 90 percent of its customer base. Also during conversations, she was able to validate where the teachers saw value versus other camps. You see, there were several other camps in the area that provided similar programs at a much lower price, but not of an equal value. When it was time to choose, customers chose value at a reasonable price.

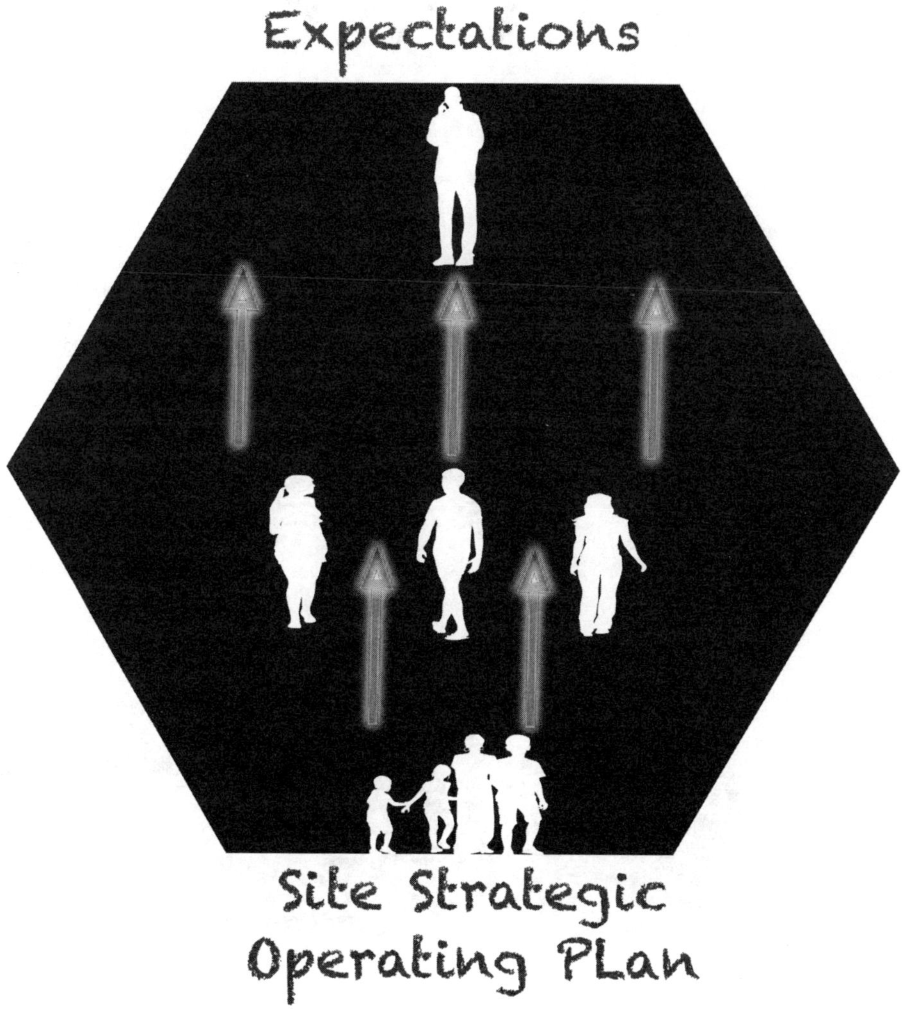

TAKEAWAYS:

- A myriad expectations need to be funneled into a single management tool.
- The IOS-PCV valve is regulated to produce a successful contract.
- No one will forget a poor launch.
- You cannot move forward without a strategic operating plan.

PURPOSE

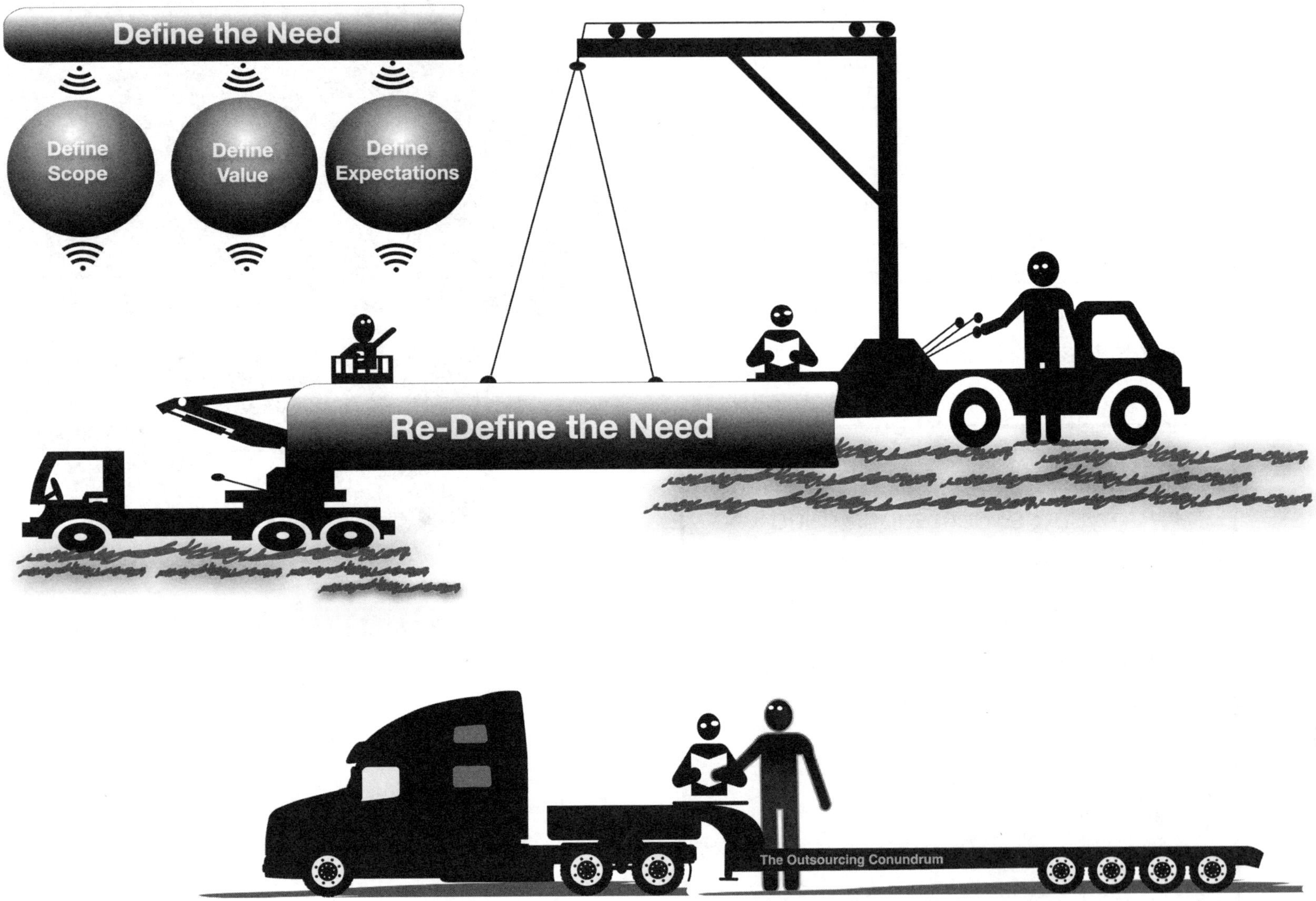
Define the Need
Define Scope
Define Value
Define Expectations
Re-Define the Need
The Outsourcing Conundrum

When you get what you want in your struggles for self and the world makes you king for a day,

Just go to a mirror and look at yourself and see what that man has to say.

For it isn't your father or mother or wife whose judgment upon you must pass,

The fellow whose verdict counts most in your life is the one staring back from the glass.

Some people might think you're a straight-shooting chum and call you a wonderful guy.

But the man in the glass says you're only a bum if you can't look him straight in the eye.

He's the fellow to please, never mind all the rest for he's with you clear to the end

And you've passed your most dangerous test If the guy in the glass is your friend.

You may fool the whole world down the pathway of years and get pats on the back as you pass

But your final reward will be heartache and tears
If you've cheated the man in the glass.

"Man in the Glass"
Author Unknown

Re-Define the Need

I was first introduced to this poem back in 1992 when I moved to Cincinnati and met a man who was fondly referred to as the "chief." The chief, otherwise known as Mel, was the owner of the company I had joined, and this poem served as his creed. Mel was one of a handful of people who crossed my path over the years whom I adopted as a mentor. Mel was about 20 years my senior and, with the support of his sons, had built several companies that were incredibly successful because they were built on the humble foundation of being customer focused.

One of Mel's mantras was, "Who signs your paycheck?" His point wasn't that he signed it, but that the customer signed it. He lived the belief that as a person or as a company you had to bring value to the equation. Without value, the foundation for your existence or the company's existence was weak.

In an earlier chapter, Define Value, I make two points that are foundational to this chapter on Re-Define the Need:

- Profit is a symptom.
- Paycheck is a symptom.

In the service business, both profit and paychecks are symptomatic of the value of service being provided to a customer, and that value is based on how well the service is meeting customer needs.

What we have discussed to date with Defining Need, Defining Scope, Defining Value, and Defining Expectations, adds up to a fair bit of work and disciplined focus to do it right. Sadly, it is not a one-time event. Determining Purpose is a continual cycle of self-analysis required to produce sustainable profit and subsequent employment opportunities for the IOSP team.

Jim Collins, in his book *How the Mighty Fall*, speaks of hubris born of success. Mel made the same point in his own way by asking the question, "Who signs your paycheck?" Complacency is the kiss of death to an IOS provider. As a service provider, if you are not relentless in Re-Defining the Need, or in continually assessing why you have the opportunity to service your customer, you will fall victim to your competition, as they are looking at your customer base and trying to come up with ways to provide better value and bump you. Don't fall victim to your competition. Set your own bar and your own pace, and keep raising it and beating it.

I mentioned earlier that every component of the Outsourcing Conundrum Model evolved and morphed over years of lessons learned. Re-Define the Need is no different, but the lessons at this stage of the process can be very costly. Consider a service contract that is awarded for three or five years. You do an amazing job initially by fully defining what the customer defines as value and why, and then you stop. Three years down the road you are providing services to solve a problem or need that is three or five years old. You might even be lucky and go 10 years, but inevitably the changing needs of the customer will catch up with your initial service offering if you do not stay on top of it and continually Re-Define the Need.

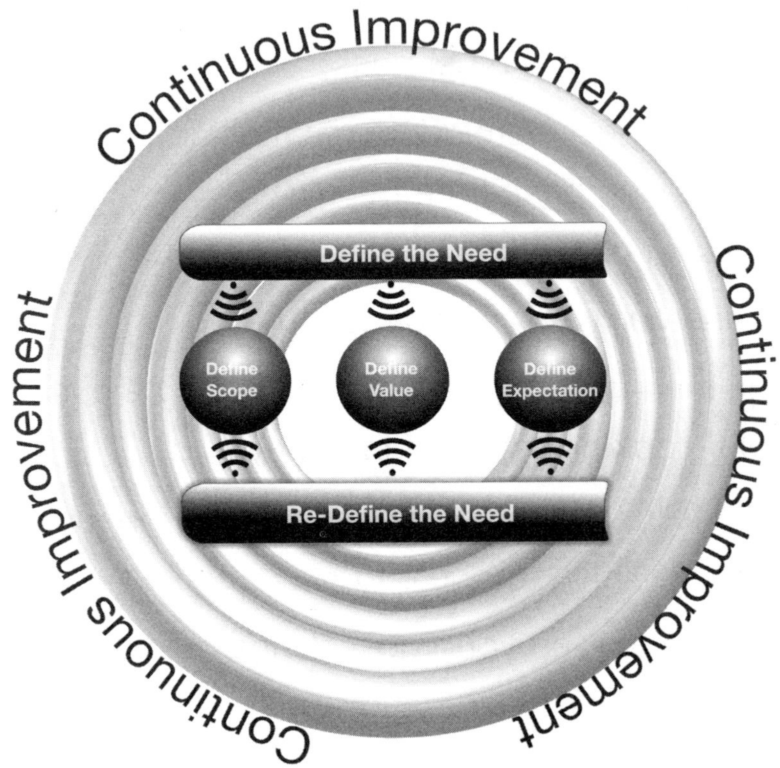

The Outsourcing Conundrum Model is a continuous improvement cycle and Re-Defining the Need is the driving force to ensure the IOSP does not lose sight of the customer's needs. Re-defining the need is what allows you to keep getting better and better, growing with your customer, and fulfilling their ever-evolving needs.

I have learned this lesson more than once, but probably the biggest lesson came from a customer who was actually one of our first. The customer had embarked on a new way of doing business through a joint venture. Two major auto manufacturers created a joint venture to produce a competitively profitable small car. We engaged with the customer at the very start of the project in the early '80s, and continued with them until the plant closed some 25 years later.

During that time we received numerous supplier awards for our contributions to the success of the project. We were doing great. If you asked us, we would tell you we were doing great. If you asked the team on site, they would say they were doing great. If you spoke to the customers with whom we interacted each day, they would say we were doing great. So what happened?

This plant became a huge success story within the auto industry, and received numerous accolades for "this is how you do it." It was written about, talked about, and had tons of tours to show the world its success. As an IOS provider at this plant, we were part of this success. But, as with all great business ideas and success stories, the rest of the world started to catch up. Year after year, doing business on the west coast became more and more costly. As the plant experienced these struggles, new demands were placed on management teams and subsequently on suppliers. As an IOS provider, we needed to step up to the plate and push ourselves to new levels of efficiency and effectiveness. Ironically we knew we were not performing at our best, but the account was profitable, we were getting awards, and our customer "friends" at the plant told us we were great.

Then it happened. One year we didn't get the award. Why? What happened? Weren't we great? After much dialogue with plant upper management, it became apparent we had stopped listening to what they needed. We were behind, viewed as mediocre, and not so great.

We ended up investing a lot of resources back into the plant to initiate change and get back on track. The hardest thing, from my experience in this business, is to try and "right side" a ship once it has started to take on vast amounts of water. To turn around a site in trouble, you need to adjust the behaviors of the team performing the work, and that is neither an easy nor a quick task. This team had been in place for a couple of decades and still thought they were "great."

We ended up losing half the business to a competitor before we were able to convince our onsite team and local union management of the need to change. Once we lost half the business, we got everyone on board and were able to re-position ourselves as a value-added supplier to this customer.

From the day we were informed of our shortfall to the day we were notified that we were back on track, 36 months passed, and we lost millions of dollars and half of our ongoing revenue and profit.

Mel's creed of "The Man in the Glass" basically warns you as an individual or as a company to stay grounded, live in the reality of your current situation, and continually seek out ways to improve. Re-Define the Need is a critical step that service providers need to take to stay abreast of changes in the business climate. Ignoring this step could result in the demise of your contract, your customer relationship, and/or your brand.

HOW OFTEN DO YOU RE-DEFINE THE NEED?

In the chapter Define Value, when we talked about value for the money, we discussed the business life cycle—an appropriate point of discussion and graphic for evaluating the frequency of Re-Defining the Need. The IOS provider site leadership has to look at the current opportunity with a very open mind and ask themselves, "Can anyone else do it better?" "Are we 100 percent efficient and effective?" "Are we drinking our own Kool-Aid?" "When was our last great idea?" "When was our last new opportunity?"

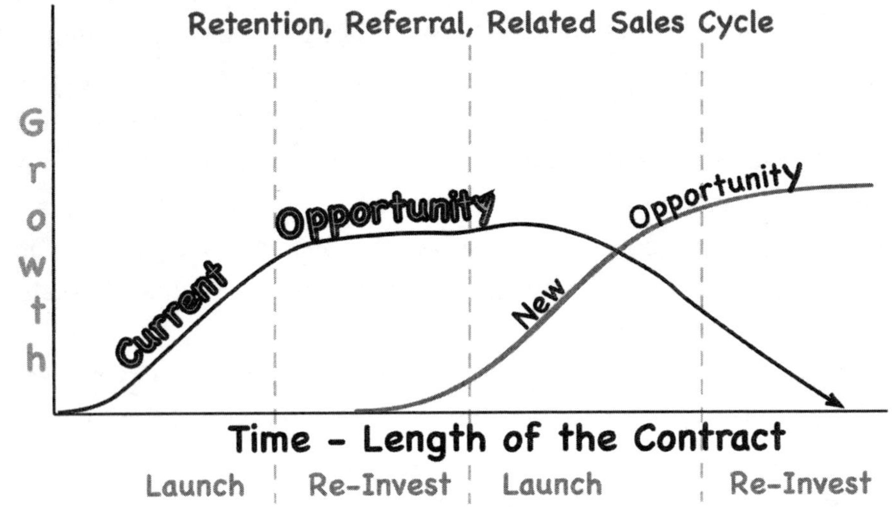

As the graphic depicts, an IOSP must continually be looking to re-invest in the customer relationship and build new opportunities. The current opportunity has a life span and you do not want to wait till it is on its death bed before you investigate a new one. Evaluate the relationship and your performance while performing the current opportunity. That way you can head problems off at the pass, make adjustments as you go, and keep renewing and improving the relationship with your customer by always being in tune with their needs and meeting their expectations.

We used to have an old saying that is still very relevant today: "You are only as good as your last shift," meaning your customer's evaluation of you is based on the caliber of work just completed. This is similar to a restaurant that could say their reputation is only as good as the last meal served.

We go, or should go, to our doctor once a year and make sure our vitals are within the parameters for someone our age, build and gender. If we have concerns, we may go more frequently until our vitals are back within acceptable parameters. My experience is that if you can take the pulse, blood pressure, and heart rate of your customer at all levels, formally, once a year, and truly act on what you are told, then you will probably avoid the situation in the example I shared with you earlier. At different levels in the customer's organization you will get a different perspective. The C-level view will be drastically different from that of the customer's front-line supervisor. But both are important and both need to be understood.

When you initially take over a contract, it may be in absolutely terrible shape. You may perform miracles in the first year or two and get a lot of pats on the back, but over time the customer forgets "what it was like," and focuses on "what it's like now" or "what it's not like." Over time, customer needs change, and your contract must be realigned to meet those evolving needs. Your team cannot become complacent thinking about "what we have done." They need to engage around "what we are doing" and "what we are planning to do."

STRATEGIC OPERATING PLAN

The Strategic Operating Plan (SOP) discussed in Define Expectations became a critical tool for us to promote forward thinking. This tool was the source of communication between our onsite management, our customer, and our hourly team as to where we needed to focus.

The discipline surrounding the use, alignment, and updating of this SOP tool allowed us to stay one step ahead of the competition, and

realize multiple opportunities for renewals and growth. The reverse, as described earlier, was also true. When we lacked discipline, we lost business and growth opportunities.

An SOP should be viewed as a long-range tool that, over the course of several years, positions you as a strong partner with your customer. Each year you need to add more and more value to that end, and each year it will not get any easier.

Customer Voice

The SOP will be worthless if the customer's viewpoint for improvement is not captured. You must go ask the customer for their ideas and opinions on improvement and not assume you know what they are. Over the years, we've embarked on several initiatives to gain a clearer understanding of the voice of the customer. Some were very formal, some informal, some long, some short. At the end of the day, we came to the conclusion that you just had to do it. It was best done when that was the sole purpose for a meeting, and the dialogue was open and focused on, "What can we do to help?"

Two programs that we became acquainted with and used as best practices were:

- Voice of the Customer
- Net Promoter Score

Both of these use structured, open-ended questions that force the customer to think about, and provide information on, what we could do to add value. The responses from both programs require that you take the time and categorize the information so it can be used in a SOP. You are looking for themes and patterns that can help you better understand what your customer values, so you can proactively act on it.

Some major directional examples concluded from discussion with a customer fell into strategic drivers, like:

- **Ownership:** The customer looked for us to take full ownership of an area, and be responsible for its results.
- **Engagement:** The customer looked for a higher level of engagement from our team by providing ideas and solutions on how to re-engineer parts of their production process.
- **Technology:** The customer wanted a much greater level of transparency through the use of real live data.

- **Skills, Capabilities and Capacity:** The customer looked for us to increase our level of expertise in order to take on additional service, allowing them to streamline their service providers.

RIPPLE EFFECT

Re-Define the Need has a ripple effect throughout the entire Outsourcing Conundrum Model. Once the need has been re-defined, then a recalibration is required for each of the three P's:

- **Purpose:** you may need to update the scope, your costing model, the metrics that determine success
- **Process:** it is very likely that upgrades will need to be made to your delivery process.
- **People:** the team will need to be realigned and adjust to this new direction.

This can be very minor with minute changes, or extreme with major changes. The People calibration involved in the turnaround I described earlier was immense, and resulted in many management personnel being replaced. We had left it so long that the team was not able or willing to change. Without their change, no other change would occur. It also impacted our Processes in some of the areas we will discuss in Part 2, but they were minor in comparison to having to adjust our culture.

END GAME

The statement made by J. Palmisano, CEO of IBM, "Either you innovate or you're in commodity hell," really sums up what success from Re-Defining the Need looks like. As an IOS provider, your goal is to be a valued partner in the company's value supply chain. You will not accomplish this goal as a commodity supplier of "whatnots." You will achieve this goal only if you are able to move yourself up the ladder to being a business solutions provider.

The discipline surrounding continually Re-Defining the Need keeps you one step ahead of the competition, and it keeps your team continually sharpening the saw, and not becoming complacent or taking their position for granted.

In the table on the right, Re-Defining the Need Questions, are questions that can be posed to the customer to solicit ideas and direction on how to move your service offering to the next level. In each case, with each question you are looking for what improvement can be made by you to improve your position with the customer. You are not looking for them to tell you what to do or how to do it. You are seeking to understand from them the areas of value they need and that they feel are absent or in need of improvement.

It is important to ask these questions at multiple levels with the customer, executive management, middle management and front line management, including the customer teams you interact with on a daily basis. You are seeking ways to add value and subsequently profit. If you do not seek ways to add value, then your profits will head in only one direction.

RE-DEFINING THE NEED QUESTIONS

Questions to the Customer		Improvement
Are we meeting your current expectations in the areas of Delivery, Quality, Cost,...?	+/–	
If we continue on our current path, will we still be meeting your needs next year, year after...?	+/–	
What are your areas of concern, and what role could we play to assist you?	+/–	
Are there any departments or areas within your facility that are negatively impacting your bottom line? What role could we play to assist you?	+/–	
Are there any risks to your business that we need to be made aware of? What role could we play to offset these risks?	+/–	

The questions in the following table, Re-Defining the Need Challenges, can be posed internally to keep the saw sharp and to convey to the customer that you are on your game and ready to move to the next level.

RE-DEFINING THE NEED CHALLENGES

Internal Challenges		Improvement
Is there any area where we are self-performing activities that would be better served by being outsourced?	+/–	
Are there any areas where we outsource that we may be better served by self-performing?	+/–	
Could we use less costly resources and obtain the same or better result?	+/–	
Which of our resources are under-utilized?	+/–	
Do we have the appropriate level of flexibility with all our resources?	+/–	

There is no business or business opportunity that is immune to the business life cycle. If there is one, please reach out to me and let me know. Well, I guess you could debate a funeral home might be exempt. I will have to ponder that one further. As far as I know, for the IOS provider, there are no exceptions. Success breeds hubris, and the cost of complacency is substantial.

An IOS provider is in a relationship. It is a business relationship, but nevertheless it is a relationship. I do not know of any relationship that grows and prospers if left unattended for any length of time or if the relationship is taken for granted.

IOSP relationships take years to develop and days to destroy. Re-Defining the Need will keep your relationship fresh, your team motivated and your profit margins heading in an acceptable direction.

Mel's creed, "The Man In The Glass," served our company extremely well for over two decades of double-digit growth. That simple poem drove a mindset to stay one step ahead of the customer at all times, putting us in the position of greatest potential. As we grew, the importance of Re-Defining the Need grew as well, as did the tools and processes we used. As I have shared, the cost of missing this step is substantial.

TAKEAWAYS:

- You have to honestly reflect on the true value you are providing.
- Becoming complacent becomes expensive.
- You must know your customer's voice.
- Incorporate an annual strategic operating plan to capture your customer's needs.

PURPOSE

Define the Need
Define Scope
Define Value
Define Expectations
Re-Define the Need
The Outsourcing Conundrum
The Outsourcing Conundrum

PART 2
PROCESS

PROCESS OVERVIEW

"The problem is not that there are problems. The problem is expecting otherwise and thinking that having problems is a problem."

Theodore Rubin

"Expect problems and eat them for breakfast."

"Intellectuals solve problems, geniuses prevent them."

"We can't solve problems using the same kind of thinking we used when we created them."

Albert Einstein

In the Introduction, I spoke about an incident that occurred in 1974, the night I started in the service business. The story touched on a very bad accident that happened my first night on the job. In Part 1, I spoke in detail about how critical it is to an IOSP to fully understand the purpose for any IOS opportunity. In Part 2, I will focus on the importance of having a delivery process that meets or exceeds the capability and complexity demanded by the purpose of the service opportunity.

That night in 1974 at the automotive plant in Scarborough, Ontario, was the start of a 20-year relationship with this customer. The plant initially opened in 1952. In 1993, the last product rolled off its line, and the plant was decommissioned shortly thereafter. During its tenure, it was one of a handful of manufacturing plants that embraced the idea of IOS very early on in the evolution of that practice. It was symbolic to me, as it became the sandbox where I played with concepts and ideas to ensure that the unsafe operating conditions and inefficiencies symptomatic to the service industry at that time were eliminated.

In 1974, the plant spent in the neighborhood of a million dollars per year to have its paint production system restored through the use of high-pressure water blasting. This service was performed four times a year, required 30,000 man-hours, a half-dozen pieces of high-pressure equipment, miles of high-pressure hose, and a couple of dozen part-time recruits. Inevitably during each of these projects, someone got hurt.

In 1993 when the plant closed, that work was completed for roughly $300,000, and required only three people full time. Equipment was reduced to one piece, and it was located in proximity to where the work was to be done. It required less than 500 feet of hose, and no one was hurt at the site for a decade. The net result was a 75 percent improvement by every metric: cost, productivity, turnover, safety, utilization of capital, and customer satisfaction.

For me, the period between the mid '70s and mid '90s solidified what I labeled as the process portion, Part 2 of *The Outsourcing Conundrum*. Since the mid '90s, the process has continued to evolve, but the main roots have not altered. They have become more complex, more critical, more challenging, and definitely more computerized, and, therefore, more transparent.

If we rewind to 1974, no-one took the time to train new recruits like I was then on how to do the work. The tools we used were not aligned with the work and activities to be done. None of us knew what good work looked like versus bad work, as quality was not high in our vocabulary at that time. The awareness for preventing safety incidents was not overly prevalent, and when accidents did happen, they were viewed by the degree of severity. A cut, scrape, or minor laceration was something that you just pushed through and kept going. Even the catastrophic accident I related during the Introduction only halted work for the hour it took to get the guy off the roof; then it was back to blasting. Activities given to the team to complete were not aligned to their skills, but rather to their availability to complete the activity. For example, guys weighing more than 200 pounds tried to fit into openings designed for much smaller people, and much smaller people tried to perform work that outreached their capacity and capabilities.

Each shift started with a roll call, followed by supervisors heading to phones to call their aunts, uncles, brothers, sisters, cousins, neighbors or any other warm body willing to take the place of whoever didn't show up for that shift. Based on who showed up, the volume of work to be done was set for the shift. From what I have described thus far, you can only begin to imagine the condition of the equipment and the lack of operating uptime. On an average night in 1974, we were lucky if two out of six pieces of equipment operated for the full shift.

So how do you move from a scenario as described in 1974 to the much-improved situation in 1993 when the contract was over due to the plant closing?

It's pretty simple really—you implement a proactive process to deliver results. Back when I started in the outsourcing industry in the 1970s, operational methods were reactive, and resulted in a high volume of man-hours dedicated to redoing activities because they fell short of required quality expectations. The whole concept of a plan was completely absent. The model was 100 percent reactive and zero percent proactive. Our first step in developing a process was to ensure that every project at least had a plan. The second step was to check the work as it was completed, and not rely on mass inspection at the project's end.

Between 1975 and 1985, we improved the process significantly by incorporating planning and checking into our day-to-day thinking. Let me elaborate by giving you a quick glimpse of the project and activities involved. The activities consisted of high-pressure cleaning and the performance of light maintenance on 75 paint stacks located on the roof of the plant, 75 elimination sections and three spray booths located on the second floor of the plant, and three spray booths and a waste treatment area located in the basement. It took a good 15 minutes to walk from the paint stacks to the waste treatment area, and the better part of an hour to walk all areas involved in the scope of work. This should give you a flavor for how easy it was to lose a team member in the plant, how much effort was needed to relocate hoses to different areas, how much walking a supervisor needed to do to check on work, and how much time was lost if someone forgot to take something with them in order to complete their assigned activity.

The first thing we did to incorporate planning and a consistent process into our operational method was simply to sketch out on a piece of paper all areas within the scope, and then decide the best place to locate equipment. The second thing we did was to make note of tools required in each area to complete the work efficiently. As simple as this sounds today, it was a big deal and a big change back in the mid '70s.

We focused energy on recruiting past workers who were noted performers for upcoming projects. New recruits were brought into the project in advance to go through an orientation process, which described and demonstrated how work was to be done, what good quality looked like, and how to identify bad quality.

Another big step we took was allowing team members to walk with the customer when completed work was inspected at the end of each shift, which resulted in the team members being able to view quality through the eyes of the customer. We continued with improvements year after year, which resulted in our being able to retain the same part-time workers, get work completed on time and safely, and, as you might guess, more profitably. The extra money we invested on the front end, in planning more carefully and extensively, netted a considerable improvement in our profit.

PROCESS DELIVERY

In 1986 at a customer dinner, I stumbled upon a book titled *Kaizen* by Masaaki Imai. I have read *Kaizen* at least a dozen times, and have drawn upon portions of the book more times than I can count. It discusses topics like profit planning, total quality management, suggestion systems, just in time delivery, cross-functional management, quality deployment, total productive maintenance, standardized work, corporate culture, customer satisfaction, supplier relations, problem solving, and the PDCA cycle.

When I first read it, most of these concepts were totally foreign and way over my head, but the one thing that took root initially was the concept of PDCA. I am hopeful that I am completely stating the obvious by explaining that PDCA is an acronym that stands for the continual improvement cycle known as Plan, Do, Check, and Act. It was originally called the Schewhart Cycle after its owner, and over the years has been altered by others to suit their needs. In our attempts to improve service, we had stumbled on two of the key components on our own: plan and check. The revelation of a proven, existing model gave merit to our direction and way of thinking, and intrigued me beyond words. I became a huge disciple of *Kaizen*, and for many years it was on the license plate of my car. Because we had already stumbled our way into some of the components contained in the book *Kaizen* and saw the value of them, we did not hesitate to put in place the balance of the PDCA cycle. Over the course of the next few years, the content of the book that was initially over my head made more and more sense, and we began to professionalize our IOS delivery process.

I crossed a threshold in 1986, when I began to understand fully the importance of a formal delivery process—a path forward we could follow for our business. Part 2 of *The Outsourcing Conundrum* outlines how we performed that implementation. If you have not heard of or read *Kaizen*, I strongly suggest you entertain adding it to your library as its principles are timeless.

MECHANICS OF PROCESS DELIVERY

From the mid '70s to mid '90s, it was apparent to me that the process for delivering service excellence had to be mechanical. It needed to be made up of cogs and gears, just like a machine, that can be adjusted to suit the specific demands and complexity of a service opportunity. It also became crystal clear that the people who performed the actual IOS activities were a lot happier, more productive, and safer as this process evolved. By the late '80s, we were realizing some very large benefits, including less turnover, fewer safety issues, and increased profit, all as a result of having a consistent and predictable delivery process understood by the team who performed IOS activities.

I described earlier that much of the work done at the plant in Scarborough required team members to climb into very close quarters with pretty dangerous equipment. By the end of the '80s, over 50 percent of those activities were completed by automated methods that required service operators to monitor equipment doing the work versus actually performing the activities with their own hands.

All of the ideas that led to these innovative improvements arose from the team clearly understanding the mechanics of processes, which allowed them to drive how work could be and should be completed.

As I came to appreciate fully the consistent, mechanical nature of the delivery process, I also started to give more thought to the idea of the delivery process being the engine that drives IOS excellence to deliver **customer satisfaction**.

From Part 1, Purpose, we know the customer needs, as well as the results being sought. The Outsourcing Conundrum delivery process must provide expected results. Another way to express this is to say that Purpose defines the inputs and outputs of the delivery process. By performing Part 1 well, we clearly understand **why** we were given the opportunity and what **results** are required for us to retain the opportunity. Inputs and outputs. The delivery process is the machine where inputs, **why**, enter and outputs, **results**, exit.

By the early '90s, I was able to conclude two other points:

- The lack of a service delivery process caused us about 85 percent of our problems.
- When we put good people into a bad process, situation, or poorly planned project, we lose them.

Now that we have a clear picture of a delivery process being the engine that processes inputs to produce outputs, we need to understand fully the mechanics of that engine:

- The engine must fit the complexity of the opportunity.
- The size of the engine must be engineered and aligned to the desired output.
- The work to be done must be scheduled.
- How the work is to be done must be standardized.
- The work must be completed to the standard at the scheduled time.
- The level of quality must be established and monitored during the process.
- All variations, both positive and negative, to the plan must be reviewed or corrected for inclusion in the cycle of continuous improvement.

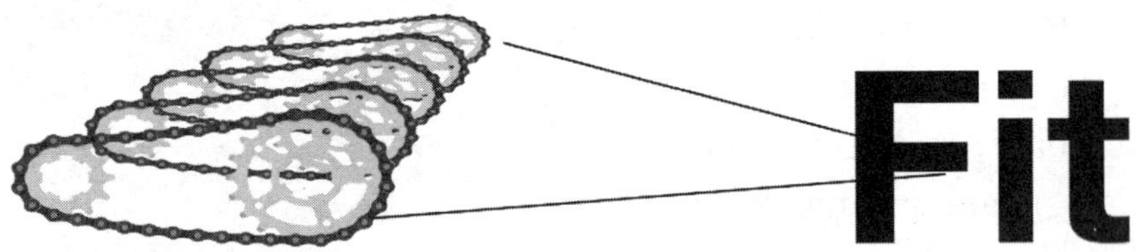

By design, a process can be set on a course for success or failure. Whether it succeeds or fails is based on how well the process "fits" both the service opportunity and the team delivering the service opportunity. A sledge hammer is not needed to drive home a penny nail.

Success	Failure
Understandable	Confusing
User friendly	Cumbersome / Overkill
Linked / Aligned	Fragmented
Visual / Transparent	Hidden / Creates Suspicion
Empowers	Alienates
Intelligent	Lacks Common Sense

PROCESS-ORIENTED MANAGEMENT

Back in the '70s and '80s, the fire alarm sounded, we grabbed our Dalmatian, slid down the pole, pulled on our boots, hopped on the truck, hit the siren, and headed for the latest fire created by poor service delivery. The introduction of the Outsourcing Conundrum delivery process told us our management style required change.

A process-oriented manager is more like a fire marshall than a fire fighter. Instead of rushing in to help fight the fire, the marshall is concerned with the bigger-picture things that help to reduce the number of fires there are to fight, and with improving the fire-fighting process. It is safe to say that the better a fire marshall does his job of enacting codes, laws, procedures, and increasing awareness of fire prevention, the fewer fires there are. Back in the '70s and '80s, the bigger your cape and the faster you could react, the better you were viewed. However, by the 1990s, as our strategy for implementation of the Outsourcing Conundrum model was realized, the better you could empower and be proactive, the better you were viewed. These are two very different ways to manage, and they do not co-exist very well together.

A process-oriented manager doesn't run into the customer's location and start performing activities that are part of the process, they are more concerned with designing and improving the process itself to achieve the customer's goals as efficiently and as profitably as possible. A process-oriented manager is concerned with:

- A disciplined approach
- Continuous improvement/problem solving
- Time management and allocation
- Skill/capacity development
- Participation and involvement
- Morale
- Communication
- Customer satisfaction

The process-oriented manager improves the process first to obtain desired results or outputs. Their people-oriented style of management stimulates efforts to improve how people do their activities. On the other hand, the results-oriented manager chases outputs at the expense of process and people. This does not mean the process-oriented manager is not committed to the goal or output at hand; they just understand that results are symptomatic of putting good people in good processes.

A process-oriented management team understands that adherence to process builds a team's overall capability. A good process drives out fear because the team knows what, how, when, where, why, and by whom something needs to be done. Under a process-oriented management style, team members focus their energy on more critical issues such as innovating and improving delivery of the service versus bailing out a poor service delivery as we did back in the '70s.

You will see the word improvement numerous times throughout the book, and, like many words, there are several ways it can be defined. Improvement, by my own definition, and how it is used in this book, is a mindset—a way of developing a standard and making it better over time. Improvement drives innovation, and improvement cannot take place in the absence of a standard. You cannot improve on something if you do not know its current status. It is somewhat like the concept of improving one's own health. The first step is determining current conditions and agreeing on required standards. There is not much sense in setting a weight-loss goal to be 200 pounds if you are already 198 pounds. To improve, current conditions must be known, and, for the purposes of the Outsourcing Conundrum delivery process, that condition is outlined as standardized work.

NO PROBLEM

IOSPs must be addicted to solving problems, and never allow themselves to become the problem they were hired to solve. An IOSP only has an opportunity because the customer has a problem. An IOSP must get to the very root of why there is a problem, what the underlying need is, and what the solution needs to be. An IOSP must be a provider of a solution, and it must be an ongoing solution that never becomes complacent. If the customer did not have a problem, there would be no need for an IOSP.

Another very obvious statement is that service is reliant on people and, for an IOSP, the people must be able to deliver an ongoing solution to the customer. For this to happen, the delivery process has to enable the team to solve the customer's existing and future problems. The characteristics of a great problem solver are critical to becoming a valued solution provider.

Alex Lowy wrote a book called *No Problem* in 2007. In his book, he breaks problems down into three categories:

- Decisions: Where options exist, Path A or Path B, all you have to do is choose.
- Problems: Where the issue can be solved but the answer is not apparent and needs investigation.
- Dilemmas: Where a troubling condition flies in the face of a solution.

A solid, mechanical delivery process can go a long way toward helping the team with decisions and problems. Dilemmas represent challenges that will often conflict with the morals or values of a company and its brand, and are usually tagged for resolution higher up in the organization. The key to decisions and problems is self-knowledge, and the ability to put that knowledge in the hands of those performing activities and interacting with the customer on a day-to-day basis.

If too little knowledge is combined with a strong emphasis to solve problems, the team may overreact. If there is too much knowledge and no emphasis on the team to solve problems, paralysis may result.

There are two resident enemies to a team becoming proficient problem solvers. One is uncertainty and one is complexity. Uncertainty and complexity feed off each other. The presence of one, empowers the other. If I am unsure, an issue feels very complex. If I allow the issue to become complex, I become more unsure and less confident about making a decision. In my 1974 example, when the guy got hurt on the roof we were powerless to make a decision, never mind solve a problem. It was two o'clock in the morning. The roof was pitch black.

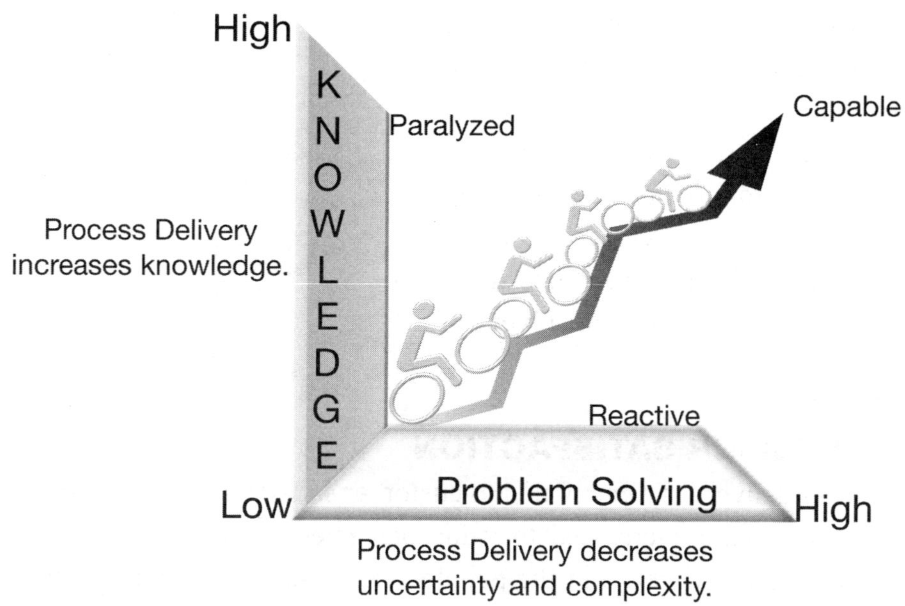

No-one knew how to get from the roof to find a phone, or how to get the elevator to respond, or, worst of all, how to find a supervisor. I cannot imagine a world like that today. The implementation of a delivery process puts knowledge in the hands of those doing the work so decisions can be made.

To allow and empower a team to operate and pedal the process with a good level of certainty and simplicity, a delivery process must explain:

- **Who** is supposed to do the work, and who else could do the work.
- **What** work needs to be done, and what work should be done.
- **Where** to do the work, and where else the work could be done.
- **When** to do the work, and when else the work could be done.
- **Why** the work needs to be done in the outlined manner.
- **How** to do the work, and how else the work could be done.

As we continue in *The Outsourcing Conundrum*, we will address how to implement a service delivery process that reduces levels of uncertainty for team members by providing this knowledge, enabling them to make informed decisions and be valuable problem solvers.

CUSTOMER SATISFACTION

Process delivery is directly tied to customer satisfaction, and customer satisfaction is directly tied to value perceived by the customer. The driver is the process, and the people are the source of momentum to keep the gears moving and driving customer satisfaction.

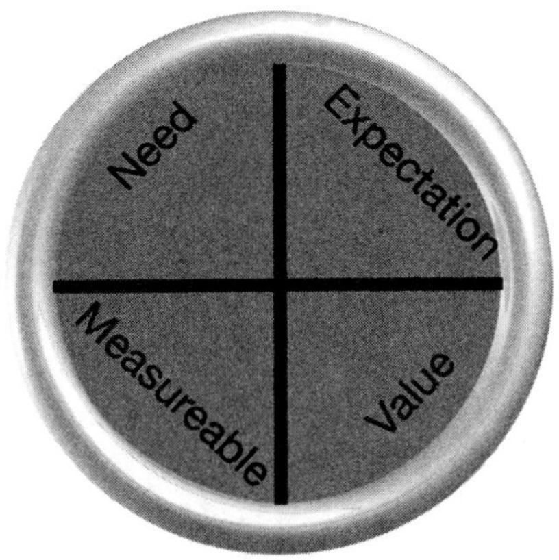

A well-oiled service delivery process in turn drives work design, job design, decision-making latitude, resource allocation, adequate tools, and adequate information. The continual cranking of this process delivers customer loyalty, retention, brand recognition, reliability, and profitability. The rigidity and structure of the process is a balance. The balance is one of flexibility between a process rigid enough to have integrity and enough structure to empower but not overwhelm those using it. This scale must weigh the complexity of the contract with the skills and capability of those servicing the contract. It is important not to over- or under-engineer or over- or under-design the delivery process. A process that is too strict dilutes the ability of the team to think, and one that is too vague does not provide necessary information for the team to make decisions. Both of these conditions retard customer value.

Naturally, the process requirements demanded by services where we could potentially shut down production, or where there are high-risk activities, are much more stringent than those where we provide lawn care or office cleaning. The cogs and gears foundational to the process are the same, but the amount of teeth of each cog is relative to the complexity of the service being provided. The process must also evolve as the onsite team evolves, as it continues to drive change to the process to meet the customer's ongoing demand for value. If the process is too restrictive, the onsite team may adopt the

- "I did what I was told,"
- "It's not my job,"
- "Talk to the boss,"

attitude that is detrimental to the ongoing provision of value to the customer.

In Part 3 we will elaborate on engagement and empowerment of the team delivering the process and performing the work, but for now let me make one very critical point. The Process must be designed to be aligned with the Purpose, and with a level of complexity that aligns with the caliber of the team members who will drive it forward. Good people in a bad process will not provide value, but an excellent, well-aligned process can help a mediocre team become great.

QUICK STORY

During a scheduled night-shift visit to a site in southern Alabama with 30-plus team members, I received a valuable education. We had recently made some changes in our HR benefit process to improve the ability for folks in the corporate office to enroll in our retirement program. The 401(k) enrollment was moved online, and team members were automatically enrolled unless they went online and altered their status.

During the site meeting, a team member brought up the issue and fairly quickly two-thirds of the room jumped on board and wondered why we were taking money out of their paychecks. After what I thought was an outstanding job of explaining how this worked and how easy it was to go online and make changes, the floor was re-opened for questions.

There was a quiet spell, and then an elderly woman put her hand up and asked, "Where do I find the web?" I stood there for a moment, and surveyed the body language in the room. She was not the only person still looking for the web. In our attempts to improve a process, we over-engineered it. It was too complex for many of our onsite team members to grasp, which created a huge morale issue for us. Point well taken—establish processes that meet the skills and capabilities of those who will be using them.

BEST IN CLASS

In the very early 1990s, we implemented a scorecard process. It was a simple, single piece of paper that contained our Values, Mission, and Strategic Objectives. The ideas of strategy maps and balanced scorecards were not yet mainstream or household concepts.

Each year we spent two days in discussion that ultimately populated this single piece of paper that was then distributed throughout all of our sites. When we started, distribution was easy as there were only five sites. By the time I left, distribution was 200 sites in several languages for communication around the world.

Each year the scorecard contained about six strategic objectives. For example:

- Be a great place to work.
- Improve our safety performance.
- Deliver operational excellence.
- Strengthen customer relationships.
- Pursue technology and innovation.
- Grow profitably.

Each of these strategic drivers was aligned with a few key deliverables. Each deliverable was a measurable objective designed to enhance our position as a service provider. During the first few years of the scorecard process, I struggled to see the value. After a few years, as we started to blow away competition, the value became apparent, and after a 20-plus-year run of double-digit growth, the process seems like genius. This simple piece of paper kept 6,000 people all rowing in the same strategic direction--not tactical, but strategic.

The one, simple piece of paper aligned all investment dollars and our people in a single direction, to meet the mission of:

"Developing long-term global partnerships with manufacturers by delivering key services that make a measurable improvement in customer quality, production uptime, and total cost."

From 1990 to 2011, not one year went by where our leadership team did not sit down and hash out the content of the scorecard. The amount the scorecard would change year to year was related to what we faced in the marketplace. If we were experiencing a year of minimal growth, our scorecard would focus more on improving our internal processes. If we were planning on a large amount of growth, our focus would be more externally focused on talent attraction. Upon its completion, the annual incentive program was aligned with successful completion of the annual scorecard.

Like all great processes, it took strong leadership and commitment to stick with the process until it found legs of its own. That process grew as business grew, but the root of the process as an alignment tool between our Values, Mission and Strategy never changed.

In the upcoming chapters, we are going to explore the roots that make up Process in the Outsourcing Conundrum Model.

TAKEAWAYS:

- Do not put good people into bad processes.
- All processes must be assembled, assessed, and aligned to meet the needs of the customer.
- Process must align with the skills and capabilities of the team.

PROCESS

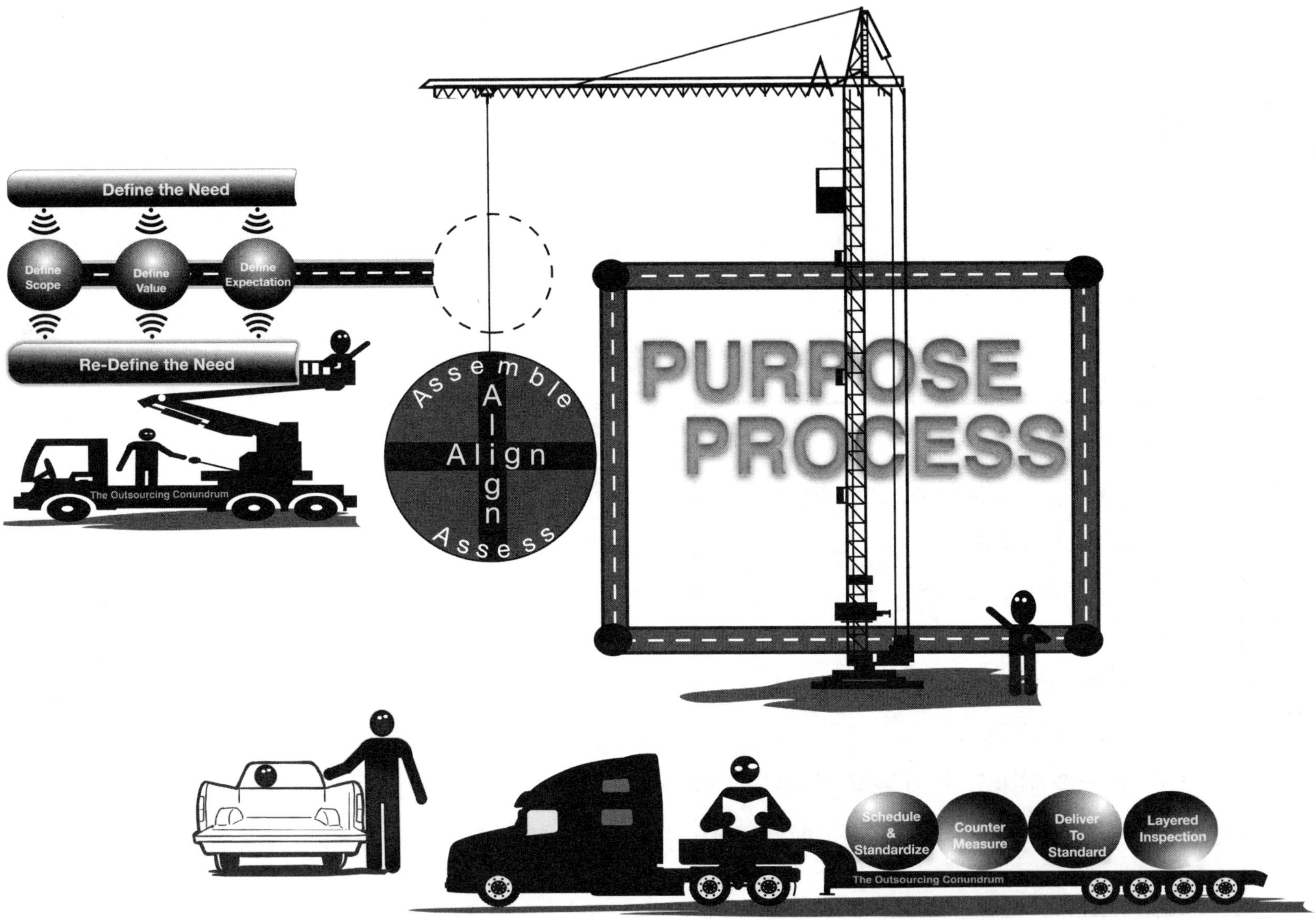
Define the Need
Define Scope
Define Value
Define Expectation
Re-Define the Need
The Outsourcing Conundrum
Assemble
Align
Align
Assess
PURPOSE
PROCESS
Schedule & Standardize
Counter Measure
Deliver To Standard
Layered Inspection
The Outsourcing Conundrum

"Would you tell me, please, which way I ought to go from here?"

"That depends a good deal on where you want to get to."

" I don't much care where...."

"Then it does not matter which way you go."

Lewis Carroll, *Alice in Wonderland*

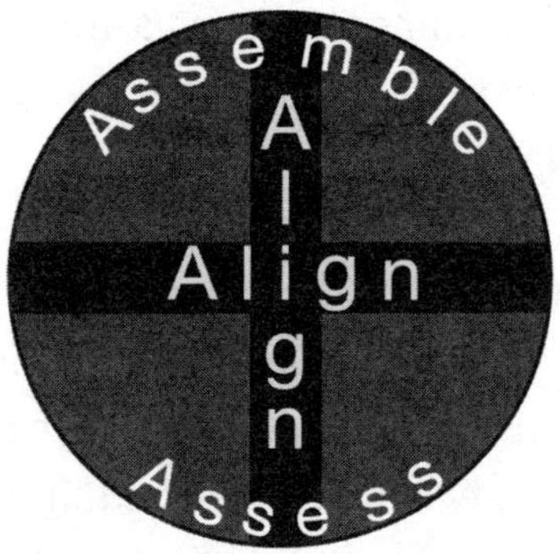

It is very difficult to plan for a journey if the destination is unclear or unknown. You have no idea of the climate, the environment, what activities await you, your mode of transportation to get there, and whom you will be interacting with upon your arrival. Just as difficult is to be given a destination with no idea of your departure point. A trip to New York is much easier to plan for if you live in Boston versus Los Angeles. If you live in Boston, you are more familiar with the climate, environment, and possible modes of transportation. If you live in Los Angeles, you are leaving a much different climate and environment for a destination that could be very foreign to your current experience.

New IOSP opportunities are no different. The destination must be crystal clear, and the current skills and capabilities of the IOSP must be known. In Purpose, specific steps are followed to ensure the destination is crystal clear: Define Need, Define Scope, Define Value, and Define Expectations. If this work is not properly executed, the journey forward will not be a safe and happy adventure.

This chapter, Assemble, Align and Assess Processes, is the crossroads that joins each of the three pieces of the Outsourcing Conundrum Model—Purpose, Process and People—together. I view it as the intersection where an IOSP opportunity must halt for a period while certain key components foundational to its success must be analyzed. It is, however, critical that the results from Part 1, Purpose, are in place before any practical decisions can be made for moving forward.

In this chapter, we are going to focus on moving through the intersection and into Process. We will discuss the assembly, alignment, and assessment of processes necessary for best-in-class service delivery. We will revisit this chapter again in Part 3, People, where we will discuss what steps are necessary to build a best-in-class service delivery team. In chapter 6, I discussed how a focus on implementing the ideas of Plan, Do, Check, and Act altered our outlook on service delivery. This focus started a strong shift towards evaluating new and better processes for delivering our services.

In 1984, ten years after the 1974 story I shared with you pertaining to the contract in Scarborough, Ontario, we were given an opportunity to look at a project in Lordstown, Ohio. The opportunity grew out of our reputation for service delivery in Scarborough being communicated to plant management in Lordstown. Both Scarborough and Lordstown were producing the same vehicle at this time, so management from both plants interacted frequently and shared ideas between the facilities. As part of this best-practice sharing, our name became known and we were granted an opportunity. For the previous 10 years, the IOS work in Lordstown was performed by a local contractor. The contractor was well known and very comfortable. Said another way, he was complacent. The needs of the plant evolved over those 10 years, but the contractor did not pay attention. One day in June of 1984, that contractor lost a half-million dollars worth of work to a company from Canada, of whom they had never even heard. The contract we were awarded was for the cleaning of about a mile of automotive curing ovens over an eight-day period. The plant was going through a model change, and timing was critical.

Our learning curve from 1974 to 1984 had taught us several valuable lessons that led to the ideas introduced here as this chapter's theme: the assembly, alignment, and assessment of the right process to ensure success. A mile of ovens in eight days requires a tremendous amount of coordination, well maintained equipment, and a full understanding by everyone of the schedule and quality standard.

If you recall the 1974 story and our capabilities at that time, you'd immediately realize that this opportunity would have been far from our reach back then. Due to the implementation of a simple PDCA cycle that produced a team approach to planning, scheduling, equipment placement, and engagement, we were able to tackle this 1984 project with a level of professionalism that this plant had not seen from their previous contractor. That level of professionalism does not hold a candle to the standards of today, but it was revolutionary for its time.

A key component in the success of the project was scheduling work inspection with our customer's plant personnel, and a system to pick up on any variances for immediate correction so we didn't have to backtrack. A second key component was the introduction of an innovative method to direct pressurized water through multiple hoses simultaneously, allowing for several people to work in concert with each other, increasing productivity five-fold.

The plant was very satisfied with the project and rewarded us most of their shutdown work over the next few years, while keeping their existing supplier on for other activities. Over time, the local contractor watched and learned, and within a couple of years were performing much better, but it had cost them several million dollars in revenue. That's a pretty expensive education for being complacent, and not understanding the need to take the time to fully assemble, align and assess the right process to meet customer expectations.

There are four foundational components that are essential for the success of any IOSP project: Schedule and Standardize, Deliver to Standard, Layered Inspection, and Counter Measures. We'll look at them in detail in each of the next four chapters.

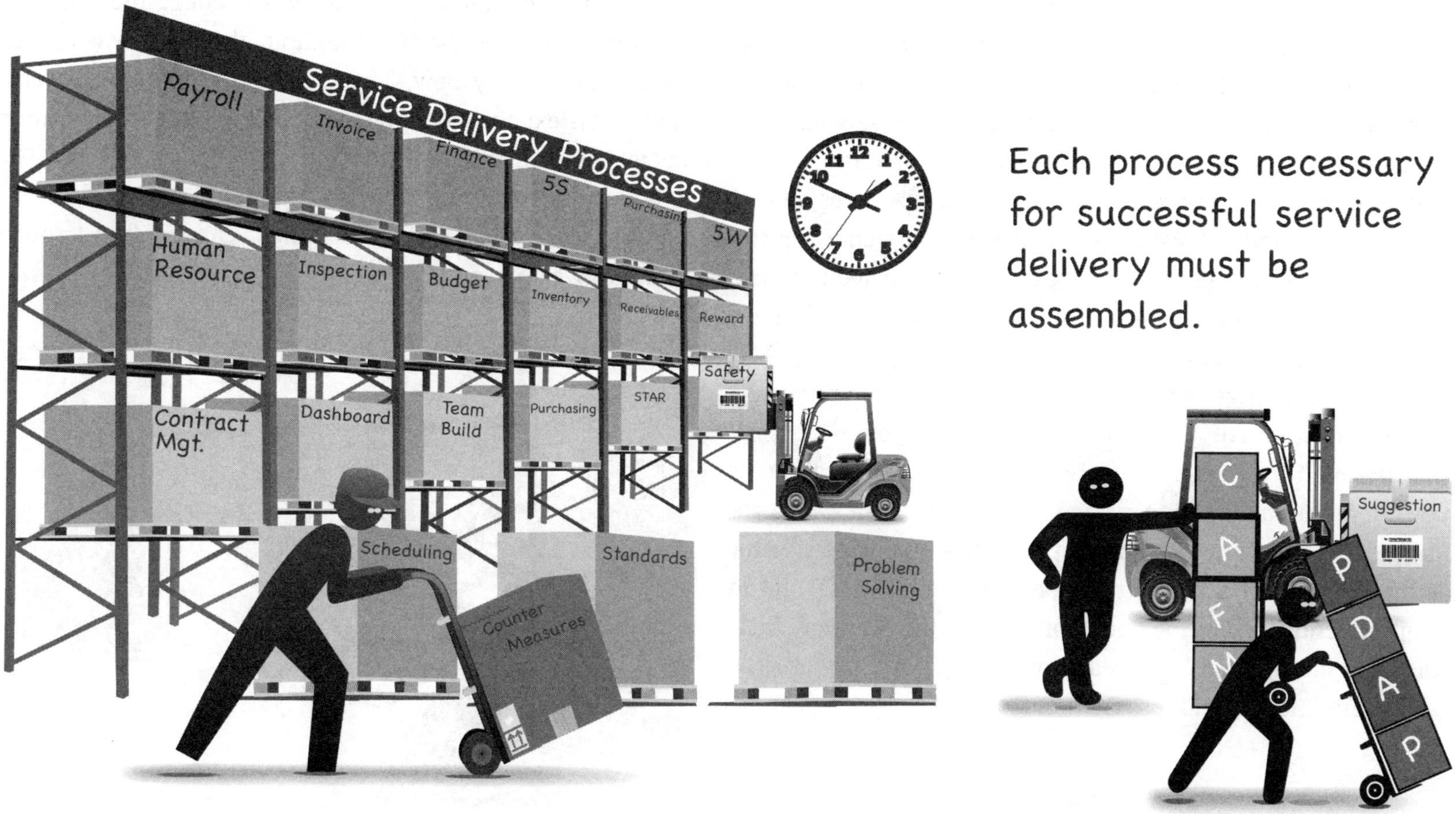

ASSEMBLE

Assemble what exactly? Let's take a look at what we know, and how we take that information to assemble required processes.

We understand the customer's problem. We understand "why" the customer is outsourcing the solution to an IOSP versus correcting the problem in house. We know what activities need to be done to correct the problem. We know the frequencies of each activity. We know the time it takes to complete each activity.

We know if we are going to sub-contract any of the work or self-perform all of the work. We know what equipment is required to complete the work. We know what maintenance is required on equipment to ensure its reliability. We know the safety concerns associated with all the activities and the equipment we will use. We know we are going to have to transfer knowledge and skills to those who must deliver the service. We know if any special expertise is required. We know what is included in the scope of services and our estimated cost to deliver those services. We know the price we are charging the customer. We know our margin percentage or value expected from the opportunity. We know the expectations of success from the customer, both short-term and long-term.

This bank of knowledge is used to assemble necessary processes for successful execution of the IOS opportunity. If you were self-performing, the list of required processes would be notably different than if you were sub-contracting to a partner. Self-performance requires a higher focus on human resource processes, whereas the latter requires a higher focus on sub-contract management processes. If the IOS is non-production related or does not directly impact a product, the training, scheduling, problem escalation, and reporting processes are typically more tolerant and less frequent.

We talked a little about 1974 and 1984. Let's jump to 2004, and look at a service contract with a power-train facility. This opportunity entailed housekeeping, facilities maintenance, production maintenance, power house maintenance, grounds maintenance, production equipment and tool re-calibration, training of production workers on immediate maintenance uptime techniques, as well as sub-contract management.

The list of required processes for successful completion of this contract far outstripped both of the previous examples from 1974 and 1984. Not only was the level of service far more complex, but a lot of focus had to be put into communication processes. A process for the use of handheld mobile devices was needed, and access to electronic schedules and standards throughout the plant was a necessity. Prior to the start of any new, large IOS opportunity, or a significant addition to an existing IOS engagement, our operations group—those of us responsible for the direct delivery of the services—convened in a war-room environment with functional support groups to discuss what processes had to be assembled. Our bank of knowledge on the contract was presented.

Our functional groups—Finance, Human Resources, Engineering Support, Information Technology and Business Systems—would be presented a summary of the new contract, outlining what processes were required for its successful execution. It was imperative for us to build a time line including the time required by each of the functional groups to be able to assemble the required processes. The forum for these meetings built the foundation for us to align our process, we will talk more about alignment in a minute.

The more complex the new contract, and if the new contract was unique in its design and expectations, the more critical the war-room pre-launch meeting became.

Each functional group leader was given time to question for clarification prior to committing to having the process assembled and ready for execution to meet the time line. If the opportunity required a specialized time tracking system, the IT guys used this meeting to understand fully the specifications and time line for installation. The meeting concluded with "speak now or forever hold your peace," as everyone had to assemble their processes on time and to the required specification.

Reporting

The reporting process, both internally back to corporate and externally to the customer, is an area I have seen grow the most over my 40 years in the IOS business. It also seems that this area of growth is not slowing down either, especially our own internal reporting, where engaged work teams have a much higher demand and need for knowledge to stay engaged. Reporting processes today must be far more integrated, visual and accessible. It is not a good idea to play catch-up with the processes, as they are foundational to trust, which is foundational to customer and employee satisfaction.

Another aspect of reporting that must be considered during the assembly phase is use of technical iDevices. This leads to discussion surrounding the value of information versus information for information's sake.

Need, Nice vs. Cute

As part of the assembly process, it is critical to perform a quick sort of the processes into three categories. Those that we need are the ones deemed absolutely necessary to meet the minimum requirements of the opportunity. The second group, nice, are those that will make the work more sane and enjoyable for the team. Years ago, the trend was to discard the nice-to-haves as they did not provide value. Today, with the ongoing need for IOSPs to improve morale and employee engagement—crucial to driving customer satisfaction—those nice processes are more important. The third group, cute, are a lot of features that provide no benefit or real value to either the team or the customer.

Processes that fall into the need category can and will directly create havoc with the service delivery if they are not put in place. Manpower leveling—in which the amount of resources for each day, shift, department, and activity are calculated—for example, is an absolute requirement for any service delivery. A process where that information can be accessed by the team is a very nice thing to have and builds better engagement. Spending time and money to put that information into an animated format is cute, but does not add value.

Another area where the need, nice, vs. cute discussion is very important is how information is communicated. The current trend of iDevices can falsely lead people to believe that if all team members walk around with a tablet strapped to their hip, information and reporting processes are effective and efficient. There are great uses for tablets, and we will discuss some of these in future chapters, but they must always be used in ways that meet customer needs, rather than for their own sake.

In the early years when standards were being written outlining correct steps on how to complete an activity, the "cute" factor often got in the way. Managers believed if they put everything they could think of on a single sheet of paper, a team member would have everything they needed to be successful. This was sometimes taken too far, however, and team members were given a printed copy of extensive instructions along with details of their work route. These poor folks walked around with three-inch legal binders. Cute idea, but very, very impractical. The sheer administrative maintenance of this process was not economically sustainable

Something I learned from Marcus Buckingham's book, *First Break All The Rules*, is that the key is to give employees the right amount of information and the right tools. Find out what they need and what will make their work enjoyable while providing an optimal level of customer satisfaction, and then stop. It is very possible to assemble too many processes and to unintentionally implement too many processes. In the chapter Deliver to Standard we talk about how you engage the team to continually improve the process with a focus on being customer- and employee-centric.

ALIGN

We aligned our processes to ensure they met customer needs, the capability of the team, and the complexity of the service being provided. An inventory process we used for years in our industrial cleaning services became seriously outdated when we embarked on production maintenance services. The service was far more complex, our customer needs were greater, and our team was far more capable. Our past process had to be upgraded to align with this need. Alignment creates balance.

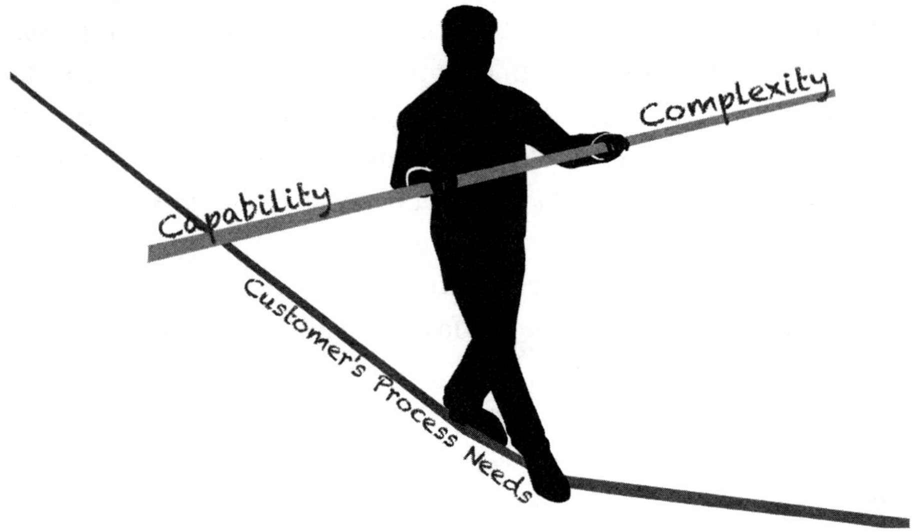

If we jump ahead another ten years to 2014 to another opportunity for providing production support services, we faced the need for an extremely elaborate payroll process. The production support services spanned over a couple of dozen business cells in the plant, who all operated with their own budgets. This meant each business cell was invoiced independently, resulting in the creation of 100-plus invoices a week, all specifically outlining levels of production support, hours per area, and cost per hour. To remove this potential bottleneck to service delivery at this plant, the time clock system needed to be upgraded and aligned to this unique circumstance.

Without the investment to automate the time clock process, the ability to complete billing activities on time and accurately was nearly impossible. Investment in a sophisticated, technically integrated system allowed us to align this process fully to meet our internal billing requirements, as well as provide our customer with manpower allocation reports at the touch of a button. This investment was well suited to this opportunity, but would be cost-prohibitive and simply not required at many of our other sites. Fact is, tracking time is integral to being a successful IOSP, but level of detail and reporting requirements must be aligned with each service opportunity.

Most sites where an IOSP delivers services have a stringent set of rules pertaining to employee conduct, safety, parking, access point to the plant and other subjects that require 100 percent alignment. We always found it extremely beneficial to meet with a plant's safety manager ahead of starting any new project to get a full debrief and establish process alignment.

Specialty Processes

A good IOSP always works hard to improve their position with their customers by becoming as invaluable as possible. Often while trying to gain this position and add new services, the IOSP is required to add services that are unique to a customer, industry, or department. Until the late '80s or early '90s, if you were providing industrial cleaning in the world's automotive painting facilities, all you needed to do was perform your daily activities on schedule and to standard. By the mid '90s, as the industry matured, you needed to understand the impact of your activities on paint defects seen on a car, as well as your impact on developing a clean-room environment. You started to hear phrases like "hospital clean," and the expectation of an IOSP was to lead the charge. In order for an IOSP to keep moving forward, it needed to develop specialty processes like paint defect analysis and clean-room programs to better align with their customers' new demands. These new specialty processes also required new tools like particle counters, microscopes, digital defect imaging, and more advanced problem identification and problem solving tools. Unlike many of the IOSP processes, the specialty processes were only applicable in specific customer service opportunities.

The alignment of a process to the complexity of a service and the capabilities of those who perform the service is mandatory. If you develop processes that require a higher caliber of talent than your costing model permits, you engineer yourself to be unprofitable. The reverse is also true if you under-engineer and do not meet the needs of your team and your customers' expectations. To prevent this from happening, we performed assessments of our processes to keep them in alignment.

Identifying what processes need better alignment and how to best align processes becomes the ongoing job of the management team as they interact with the team members on the delivery of the services. We will discuss this more in the upcoming chapters.

ASSESS

In 2006, we met to discuss the addition of a large piece of business with a key customer. The opportunity was exciting as it met many of our strategic objectives for organic growth, market penetration, and diversity of our profile. Our issue was that this volume of growth would stretch our company in many ways, including our processes. To understand fully how this growth would impact our organization, we created a Process Matrix to assess the capacity of our internal processes to handle the new, increased demand from our customer. These were processes that we used day to day in our operations, but their efficiency and effectiveness tended to decline very slowly over time if they were neglected rather than being continually assessed or improved. In many cases, the fact that we had a problem with some of these processes was not recognized unless there was a failure.

To correct this issue, each of our key, critical processes in question was listed and its ability to meet the increased volume of new business was assessed:

- Payroll Administration
- Hiring / On-boarding
- Labor Negotiations
- Purchasing
- Time Tracking
- Manpower Leveling

Our first step was to make note of the current condition of our processes. If any currently showed stress cracks, the cracks would be further compounded by more demand. We discussed all of the processes, and broke them down by who owned each, who relied on the process, who supported the process, and how visible the process was to the customer. Our payroll process, for example, which was owned by the finance group, was identified as experiencing stress cracks. It was supported by HR as the HR information system was the source of employee data. The payroll process was also supported by the IT group, as they were responsible for the program on the server. The operations group relied on the payroll process to pay all team members. The payroll process, however, was not directly visible to the customer. The Critical Processes Assessment Matrix clearly shows how this one process impacted much of our company, whereas the manpower allocation process did not impact as much of the company, but was very visible to the customer.

As we completed the Matrix, it painted a clear picture for us of where we needed to invest if we were going to align our processes with our new opportunity, to meet both customer needs and our own internal needs.

The very first time we conducted this exercise, it became very apparent that our IT department needed to understand more fully our issues in the field and get better connected with the field. We

Critical Processes Assessment Matrix

	Payroll	Hiring	Labor Negotiations	Time Tracking	Workforce Leveling	Purchasing
Condition						
Capable	Yes	Yes	Yes	No	Yes	Yes
Scalable	No	No	No	No	No	No
Department						
Human Resources	Support	Owner	Owner			
Finance	Owner					Owner
I.T.	Support	Support	Support	Support	Support	Support
Operations	User	User	User	Owner User	Owner User	User
Visibility to Customer	Low	High	High	High	High	Medium
Concerns						
Skills	No	Yes	No	No	Yes	Yes
Resource Issue	No	No	Yes	No	No	Yes
Software Issue	Yes	No	No	Yes	Yes	No
Hardware Issue	Yes	No	No	No	No	No

started discussion well in advance of requiring solutions to allow our department teams time to re-group and investigate solutions. The Matrix was updated as each group identified a solution and a plan for improvement.

This exercise proved very valuable, and resulted in the discipline of an annual evaluation of all key processes required to provide service delivery. We also started to see much better alignment between our corporate office, those who owned and managed many of the processes, and the people in the field who used the processes.

CRITICAL PROCESS VALIDATION TABLE

Criteria	Repeatable	In Control	Best Practice
Standardized	Much of the process is documented.	All of the process is well documented and documentation is followed.	Relationship to all sub-processes known and documented, regularly updated.
Metrics	Process measures are known.	Process measures targeted and met.	Process targets are continually updated and met.
Ownership	Ownership is known.	Owners are empowered to suggest improvement.	Owners are empowered to manage ongoing improvements.
Need for Improvement	Opportunities for improvement are known.	Plans for continuous improvement are known.	Process is benchmarked and targeted for future improvement.
Visibility to Customer	Requirements are known and understood.	Requirements are known, understood and met.	Process exceeds customer expectations.

As we became better disciplined and more comfortable with the need to assess our processes, the format for evaluation evolved. The long-term goal was to have all of our processes labeled as best practices, but realistically our three-year target was to achieve processes that were validated as repeatable and in control. As you can see in the Critical Process Validation Table below, we tightened up the criteria and held processes more accountable for meeting desired outcomes.

BEST PRACTICE

Team Trek mastered the concept of assembling, aligning, and assessing their delivery processes. If you recall from previous chapters, we partnered with Team Trek to help us build leadership capacity and 100 percent accountability within our management ranks. The group at Team Trek use an arsenal of programs, all designed to expose teams to patterns of behavior that positively or negatively impact their ability to take on roles of 100 percent responsibility and become strong leaders. Team Trek's magic is their ability to assemble the right processes, and put them into the best order of exposure. That is, a group would be exposed to a situation so the behaviors detrimental to their success became visible. If a group's leader was overly autocratic, for example, then Team Trek would design the order of the events to flush out that behavior so team members experience desired behavioral patterns.

Team Trek did a great job of understanding what we needed by fully exploiting all the steps in Part 1. They then assembled a series of processes from their arsenal that, when fully integrated, met our expectations. Eighty percent of the delivery of the processes did not change from one of our groups to the other, but 20 percent did. The key to success was the 20 percent. Before we arrived at Team Trek, we completed personality profiles that were assessed by the Team Trek group. The profiles provided insight into how individual group members currently worked together, and gave Team Trek the ammunition to tweak a process and dial it into the needs of our group.

One issue we faced as an organization was the need for our leaders and managers to understand they did not need to have all the answers, but they did need to be able to facilitate answers from the broader team. Team Trek saw our pattern of behavior and adjusted their programs, to emphasize how harmful this gap in our understanding was to the team. While participating in the various programs, managers faced the repercussions of this behavior repeatedly, and over the course of the week they were in large part able to let it go and draw on the entire team brain as opposed to just their own.

Because Team Trek customized 20 percent of their programming for the specific needs of our group, we were able to get far more from their training and facilitation processes than if they had been off-the-shelf products and the same for all their customers. They assessed our strengths and weaknesses, and then aligned their processes with our needs, assembling the right mix of programs for our team. As a result, the customer experience was outstanding for us and our level of satisfaction high.

QUICK STORY

For about ten years, we trained our supervisors on a program called "Focused Cleaning." The course was made up of classroom plus experiential exercises. The purpose of the class was to develop strong roots around the need to operate to a PDCA cycle. One of the experiential exercises required the group to dress up in full personal protective equipment, and use simple kitchen tools to scoop M&Ms from a big bucket into a small bucket. They then had to take the small buckets to a corner of the room to have them inspected. The guy we used for the inspector role was a very gruff person who said little, stared a lot, and did not provide too many answers.

For 10 years we conducted four classes a year with about 16 people per class. In every class, the team leader chosen by the groups to take their small bucket up for inspection returned and stated, "It did not pass." The balance of the team inevitably asked him why it didn't pass, and the team leader admitted he did not know. The team then completely re-did the exercise with no knowledge of what was wrong with their process. On average, the teams did and re-did this exercise five to six times until someone finally figured out that they better directly ask the inspector why the bucket did not pass and what changes needed to occur for it to pass. The inspector eventually told the group that he did not care for one of the colors in the bucket, usually red, which sent team members scurrying back to remove all red candies from their buckets.

The exercise was timed, and was designed to get teams in a very competitive mode and to act without thinking or taking time to analyze fully their delivery processes to meet customer expectations. This exercise—so simple, yet so effective—hit a home run, and led us into a great discussion about processes used in the field that had similar attributes to the exercise just completed.

TAKEAWAYS:

- Assemble only the processes that are needed and nice; avoid the cute.
- Align the customer need with the complexity of the processes and capabilities of those delivering the service.
- Assess all delivery processes annually.

PROCESS

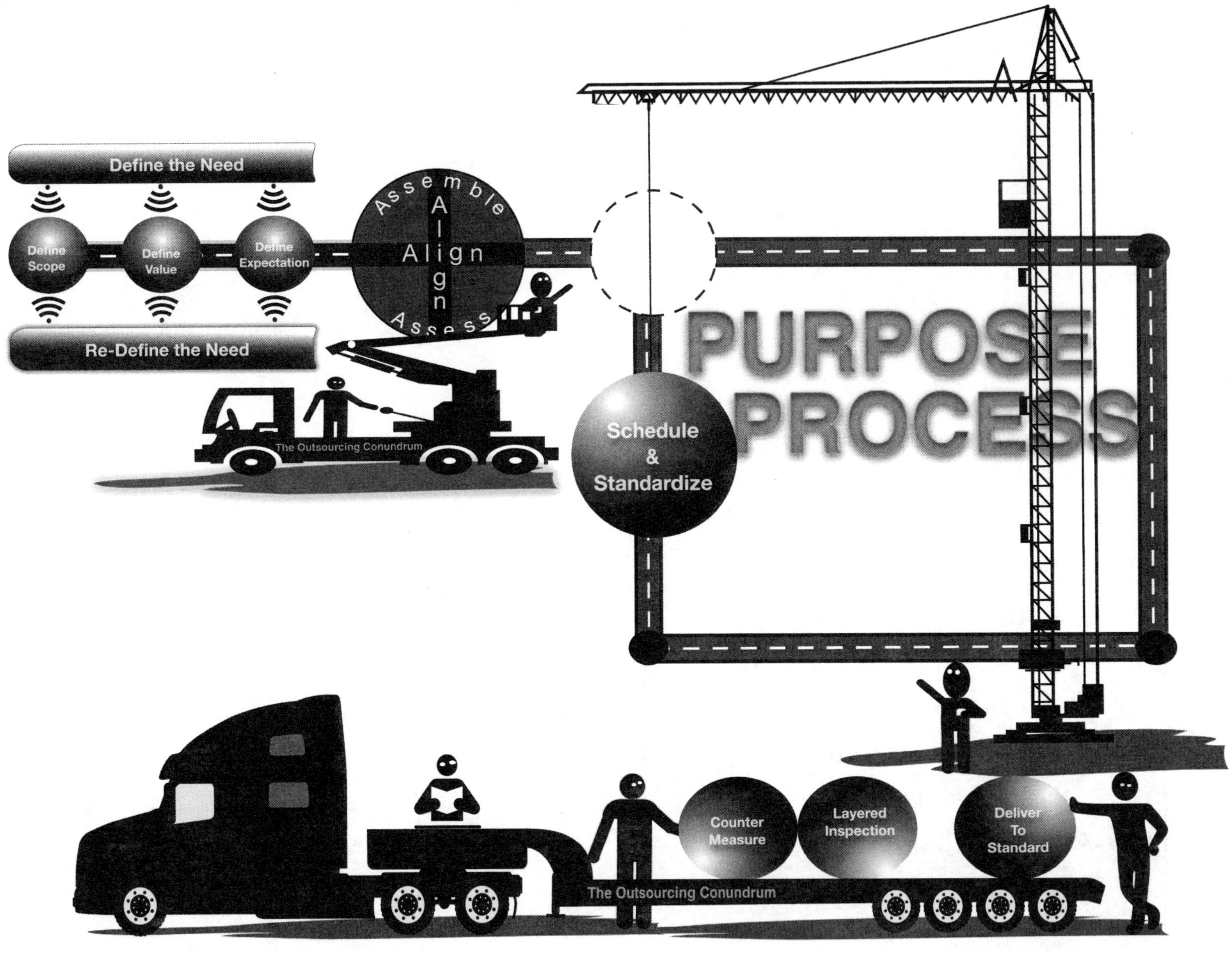
Define the Need
Define Scope
Define Value
Define Expectation
Assemble
Align
Align
Assess
Re-Define the Need
The Outsourcing Conundrum
PURPOSE
PROCESS
Schedule & Standardize
Counter Measure
Layered Inspection
Deliver To Standard
The Outsourcing Conundrum

"If you go to work on your goals, your goals will go to work on you. If you go to work on your plan, your plan will go to work on you. Whatever good things we build end up building us."

Jim Rohn, Author, Business Philosopher
7 Strategies for Wealth and Happiness

"Organized chaos" is a term I heard numerous times growing up as an IOSP. It was not very flattering, but in the early years extremely accurate.

The primary purpose of Schedule and Standardize is to turn chaos into a plan. If you have ever had the opportunity to be responsible for organizing 50 to 100 people in the delivery of several hundred activities, the complexity of this task will not escape you.

If the opportunity is new to you, let me briefly show you why there is a definite need for this step.

Take a simple situation where there are three activities and three team members (TM) capable of executing the activities. The result is six possible ways to allocate the three team members to three activities.

Option	TM A	TM B	TM C
1	Activity 1	Activity 2	Activity 3
2	Activity 1	Activity 3	Activity 2
3	Activity 2	Activity 1	Activity 3
4	Activity 2	Activity 3	Activity 1
5	Activity 3	Activity 1	Activity 2
6	Activity 3	Activity 2	Activity 1

Six possible scheduling options exist based on three people and three activities.

Okay, so that is not so bad. Six options. We can live with that. Let's increase the size of your crew to eight and give you four activities to complete. You now have 720 possible options. Is it starting to feel a bit like chaos?

We are also not taking into account at this point the possibility of there being more than one way of completing an activity. We are just discussing What activity and Who will do it.

If you are into math and have a crew numbering in the hundreds, the possibilities move into the trillion range, which you have to admit might be chaos, and again that is assuming there is only one way to deliver each activity. I do not know about you, but I find it both fascinating and mind-boggling. I thought it was tough scheduling a couple of dozen people to clean 75 stacks back in the '70s. The advantage back then versus now was the bar was pretty low, and a clipboard with graph paper got the job done.

As complex as this can be, it still boils itself down to two components: a schedule and standardized work. No matter your choice on how elaborately you design your process, it must include these two components.

SCHEDULE

The best way to describe this step is to call it the "pacemaker." The goal of a pacemaker is to control an irregular heartbeat by sending electrical impulses to the heart. Over time, an irregular heartbeat causes stress on the body, damaging other organs and even proving fatal. A pacemaker helps to ensure the entire body's health by allowing the heart to beat regularly and predictably. Schedule, acting as the pacemaker for a project does the same thing by setting a pace, a reliable sense of delivery and/or urgency, for all activities that must be executed. The schedule develops a predictable, consistent rhythm for service delivery.

In Part 1, Define the Scope, we outlined every activity associated with the service we must deliver, and in Define Value what our cost or budget would be to deliver on that scope. We also Defined Expectations, outlining the required results expected from the delivery of the IOSP to the customer. In order for us to deliver on this purpose, there are many activities that need to be put into a schedule. At an absolute minimum an effective schedule must:

- Ensure our contractual obligation is met.
- Level out the workforce required to deliver the service.
- Align and work around other conflicting activities, such as plant production or limited access to the facility.
- Produce work schedules for those responsible to deliver services.

In actuality, a schedule is a timeline that commits and communicates necessary resources to every minute aspect of IOS delivery. The schedule needs to accomplish this task while taking into account the many variables associated with resource planning that can truly escalate the complexity of this process, such as:

- Vacation time
- Absenteeism
- Customer requests
- Logistical constraints
- Worker skill and knowledge

On the front end of a schedule there are **Inputs**, and on the back end of a schedule **Outputs**. A seamless, integrated relationship between inputs and outputs produces a schedule that is both effective and efficient. It produces a scheduling management process. An effective and efficient scheduling management process is a tool used to establish the operating rhythm for the entire project. The accompanying table contains a list of input data a schedule requires to become a scheduling management process that develops an operational rhythm for the project.

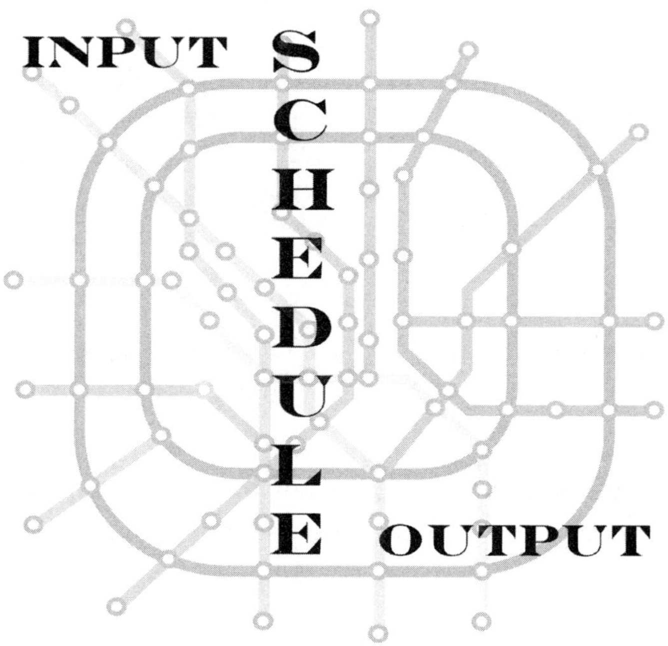

Input Data	Notes
What physical activity must be completed?	Perform routine maintenance on the Air Supply House.
Where will the physical activity be done?	Penthouse Level - Column H44.
When must the physical activity take place?	Date and frequency this activity occurs. 4-4-15, weekly.
Who will perform the physical activity?	Tech I or Tech II. John Smith.
What is the priority of each physical activity?	In case of any imposed time restraint, the minimum activities need to be known.
How much time will each activity take?	Usually displayed in minutes.
What value is given to the physical activity?	Is the activity busy work or does it provide actual value to the customer?
Completion Status	Date the work was completed and by whom.
Level of Risk	High, Medium or Low risk should be indicated. The level of risk is a lead indicator to safety, morale, quality, and cost concerns.
Quality Inspection Grade	Quality inspection data needs to be captured for analysis by the scheduling management system.
Employee Team Meetings	All necessary employee team meetings are captured in the schedule, such as: start of shift, best practice sharing, and town hall meetings.
Customer Meetings	Daily, weekly, monthly, and quarterly meetings are captured in the schedule.

Input Data	Notes
Training and Development	Updated information pertaining to the skills and knowledge of each team member must be integrated into the schedule.
Asset Maintenance	The necessary maintenance required for equipment and tools to deliver on the scope of work.
Supervision and Management	Supervisor and management meetings must be captured in the schedule.
Safety Observations	Times and frequencies for all safety walks must be scheduled.

There is an old saying, "What gets inspected gets done." Another saying, even more important, is, "What gets scheduled gets done," or at least stands a fighting chance of getting done. Too often an IOSP uses the schedule only to capture the physical activities that must be completed, and not to schedule peripheral activities as well, such as customer meetings, employee team meetings, dates reports are due, scheduled maintenance on their own equipment, and, most importantly, employee training. Planning for these peripheral activities is what changes an IOSP from being mediocre to being truly great.

A perfectly completed schedule represents every hour allocated to delivery of the scope of work. To meet this goal, the input data must be current and accurate, which is way easier said than done. During my 40 years, the projects that ran the best were in the upper 80th percentile of scheduling efficiency. For some reason, that last 10-plus percent was very difficult to achieve on a consistent basis.

Output Information	Notes
Actual hours scheduled by period	Hours by shift, day, week, month, quarter, year.
Manpower Leveling	The required resources by shift, day, week, month, quarter, year.
Hours by Activities and Area	Breakdown of hours to activities, departments, facilities, processes.
Capacity	Level of capacity and efficiency of the organization.
Work Schedules	Staff, team work schedules by shift, day, week, month.
Work Routes	Schedule outlining the sequence of activity completion.
Technical Versatility of the Team	Who is skilled and trained on what activities.
Scheduling Efficiency	What is scheduled versus completed within given time restraints.
Quality	The inspected level of quality by activity, area, facility, process. Level of rework.
Scope Hour Validation	Validate estimated hours, resources assessed in the scope versus actual.
Management Utilization	Time spent in meetings internal vs. external.
Training Resources	Time spent training the team.
Team Meetings	Time spent in team meetings.

It would be interesting to poll all of the IOSP companies to determine how many millions have been spent on home-grown scheduling programs. You can put me down for at least one million in wasted resources to produce an efficient and effective electronic scheduling tool. In the mid-1990s, after eight months of programming, we went to one of our largest sites and started the implementation process we called OMS. After a couple of weeks the scope of work and related peripheral data were loaded, and we hit the print button to produce our very first, comprehensive, all-inclusive monthly schedule. Two hours passed and we were still waiting; four hours, one day, then two and lo and behold the schedule printed. It consumed two full reams of paper and was by anyone's evaluation totally useless. Being a bit too resilient for our own good, we did not give up on that OMS program for a year but finally let it die a well deserved death. What we failed to do was to start the programming with the end user in mind and to solicit from the end user, the team leads, and supervisors, exactly what they needed in a schedule.

Our first real success with true scheduling management came when we implemented a Computer Aided Facility Management program (CAFM) purchased from a German vendor who specialized in scheduling tools. The vendor spent six weeks working with team leads and supervisors at one of our sites to understand their needs fully, and then went to work on customizing the program. Unlike our home-grown product, this tool was up and running at the pilot site within six months and received a tremendous amount of good press from the on-site team. We estimated the savings in labor previously associated with manipulating old scheduling spreadsheets paid for the new program and then some. It also provided a vast number of outputs not previously available to us.

We live in a fantastic age of digital data and unlimited options for the creation of very user-friendly scheduling management systems. An IOSP is given an opportunity because customers they serve lack the necessary expertise and/or desire to dedicate resources to what they are outsourcing. As IOSPs, we should have drunk from that cup as well and sought experts to build scheduling tools much sooner than we did. From my experience, this is a common flaw among many IOSPs. The key to outsourcing this process to an expert successfully is to complete an Input and Output Table accurately, in order to indicate clearly what is required by you and your customer.

Payroll versus Scheduling

We have used the term "effective and efficient" several times in this chapter relating to scheduling. One key metric to which every IOSP must pay very strict attention is hours scheduled to complete a block of the scope versus hours submitted to payroll. For example, if in the month of June the schedule indicated work to be done would consume 20,000 hours, but over 30,000 hours were submitted to payroll, you may have an issue. If you are becoming more efficient and effective as an IOSP, the time it takes to complete your scheduled scope of work should improve incrementally year after year. This single data point is critical to the longevity of an IOSP opportunity.

In the mid '90s we had the opportunity to implement a management services contract in a manufacturing complex in central Ohio. The contract was for management of the customer's workforce to perform a plant-wide scope of activities dealing with housekeeping, industrial cleaning and light maintenance.

When we first analyzed the schedule and the payroll records, it was evident the hours submitted to payroll were five times greater than the hours required to complete the scope of work. In essence, the labor force was 80 percent larger than what was required to complete the current scope of work. Following a disciplined approach to scheduling, man hours were cut in half during the first year and half again in the second year. The reductions were also done while the scheduled hours were increased to reflect the real scope of work required by the plant.

"Don't become the problem you were hired to solve." This statement was something we internally would say to each other to keep ourselves grounded and understand "why" we had jobs. The above noted story seems preposterous but in actuality it was only one of several. Over time, those contracts went from management services to projects where the IOSP self-performed activities with their own staff of people. We had to remind ourselves constantly to stay extremely disciplined with our scheduling management system to prove the effectiveness and efficiency of our team. Our livelihoods all depended on this discipline.

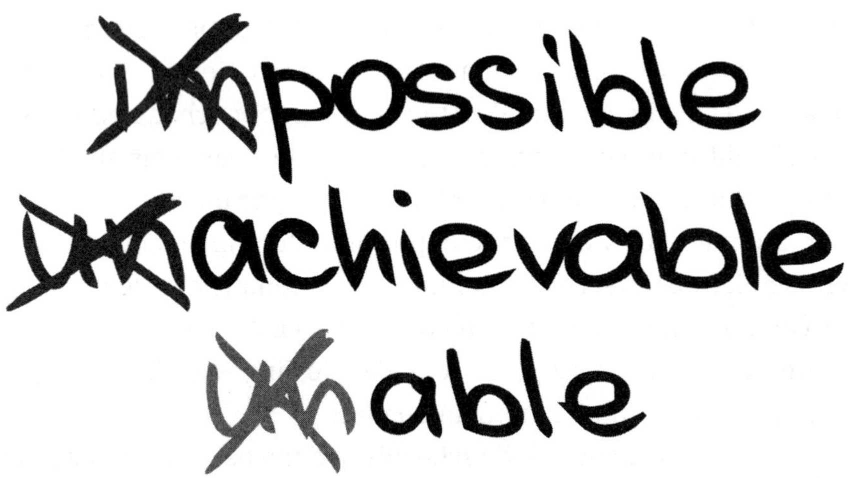

My career allowed me to work with, for, and alongside some amazing people. Many, many people through their diligence have moved the needle of IOSPs, making them much greater companies. They were able to make the impossible, possible, the unachievable, achievable and the unable, able.

A woman in Ontario is one of these individuals who moved the needle. She has been an IOSP for over 20 years, and started out as a team member on the floor in 1990. Throughout her career, she continually pushed her team to become extremely efficient and effective. Today she manages IOS for a manufacturer who produces a very high-end vehicle known for its level of quality. If the plant is producing this level of quality, it demands that level of quality from its IOSP. She implemented many ideas, but the one most notable to this chapter was the format of her weekend schedule. On the surface it seems extraordinarily simple. The genius of the idea is that it is.

The biggest problem she faced was successful completion of activities scheduled for weekends. The crew seemed always to miss one thing or another for a variety of reasons that boiled down to lack of a simple plan. After realizing the root cause of the issue, she spent years creating and then refining a simple schedule to be given to a team leader on a legal-sized sheet of paper. This tool gave the team leader everything they needed to know to complete the required scope of work successfully on the weekend.

The weekend schedule contains:

- Area: the manufacturing process area in which the activities are to be completed.
- Activity: list of activities to be completed.
- Standard: the ID code number for the standard work instruction for each activity.

- Shift/date: when the activity is to be done.
- Time: the time assessed to complete the activity.
- Risk assessment: notes on whether the activity has a high, medium or low risk.
- Risk management: what is critical to mitigate the risk, such as confined space procedures, fall arrest equipment, and awareness of open holes/spaces.
- Production requirements: what steps need to be taken by the customer for the safe execution of the activities, such as leaving lights on, or emptying the conveyor line of product.
- Plant contact info: customer contact for the scheduled time of the activity.
- Inspection: visual inspection requirements.
- Key requirements: any key step that must be taken not to impact production, such as opening a valve, clearing a photo lens, or removing a lock.

This tool was successful because the end user and the history of issues the team faced with poor scheduling completion were kept top of mind as the tool was being formatted. This tool took her team to a level of scheduling efficiency where she was measuring what percent of the one percent was not done. These were very impressive results due to the implementation of a very user-friendly tool. The programmers used this format when the weekend schedules were automated.

When you are considering an automated scheduling program, it is critical to keep in mind that one key output is the document, whether it is tablet driven or hard copy, that your team will receive. As shown, a well-formatted tool can achieve world-class results.

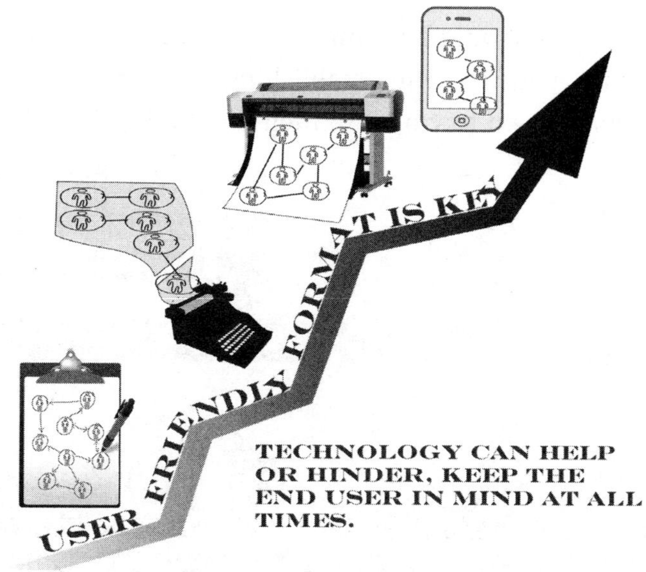

STANDARDIZATION

Standardization is a disciplined approach to continually trying to be a better IOSP. Create a standard, follow that standard, and then find a better way. Deploying standardization can be boiled down to four simple steps:

- Establish a best practice: Seek out the best possible method for delivering the activity for which you have responsibility.
- Document the practice: The practice will not become a standard until it has been documented. Base the level of detail in which to document the standard on the complexity of the task. A standard to clean a floor does not require the level of detail that repairing a paint robot requires.
- Gain clarity: Make sure the standard is understood, and establish a level of consensus on this way of doing the activity.
- Train to the standard: Instruct those responsible to deliver on the activity using this best practice.

Standardized work should be completed with the involvement of your team. Involving your team in establishing standards results in them taking ownership, and buying into their day-to-day use.

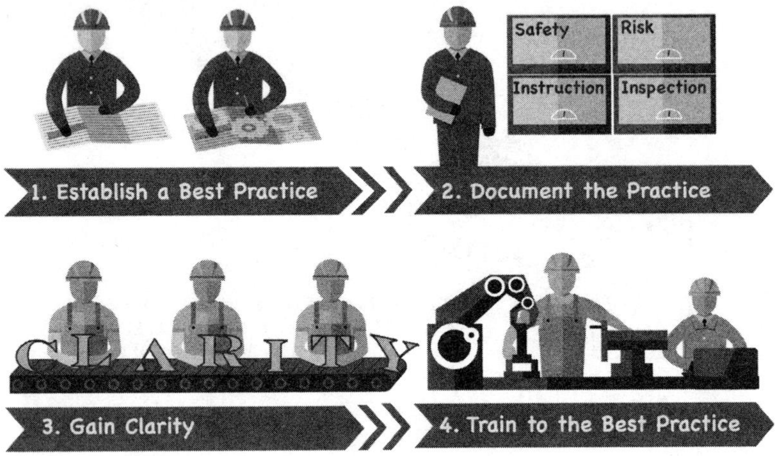

Standardized work has many, many labels and acronyms. The generic term is Standard Operating Procedures or SOPs. They are also known as:

- Work Instruction Sheets - WIS
- Standard Work Chart - SWC
- Current Best Practice - CBP
- Job Evaluation Standards - JES

This is the short list. Everyone has an opinion on what these should be called, as well as on what level of documentation is required on each. Regardless of the name, the intent of the tool is always the same:

- Safe completion of the activity.
- Timely completion of the activity.
- Completion meets the level of quality.
- Empowers the person performing the work.

To meet intent, a standard needs to define and provide instruction, including:

- What, if any, certification is required?
- Where will the activity be performed?
- What hazards are associated with the activity?
- How will the team member prepare to perform the activity?
- What are the safety requirements?
- What are the instructional steps for completion?
- How is the final inspection performed?

We typically referred to our standards as current best practices to avoid the mind-set sometimes associated with the word "standard" denoting there is only "one" right way. The purpose of a standard, as described and touched on in this section on scheduling, is to establish "a" way of performing an activity.

It is important that team members responsible for delivery of IOS feel their input is welcome, and that the way things are done can be challenged and improved upon. If they feel they cannot do this, any hope for becoming more efficient and effective just went out the window.

Every best practice should be forced to have its day in court, be challenged for its current value, and validated to determine that there is no room for improvement. The output from the schedule management system is critical to the management of standardized work. The scheduling management system will provide knowledge on standardized work activities that:

- Do not meet time budgeted time constraints.
- Result in safety issues.
- Promote absenteeism.
- Result in customer downtime.
- Result in customer complaints.

Standardized work is not just for hourly activities. There is considerable benefit to having physical activities standardized, but there is greater benefit to having management activities standardized.

The woman I spoke of earlier who had made tremendous gains through refinement of the weekend schedule also developed standards for start-of-shift meetings. Very often as team members are promoted to team leaders and front line supervisors, one critical area of development is their ability to stand up in front of a group. By developing standards for all team meetings, she was able to train and practice with her new team leaders and supervisors so that when they stood up for the first time, they felt respected, recognized, and empowered. She followed up with new management team members to solicit any ideas for improvement to the standards. A simple, yet very powerful discipline resulting in extraordinary results.

TEAM WORK

Marcus Buckingham, in his book *First Break all the Rules*, speaks to research proving what high-performing people and teams look for in their work. Marcus explains that performers need to understand what is expected of them, they need to have the right materials and tools to do their job, and their opinion needs to count for something. Schedules and standardized work are foundational to making this happen. Standardized work is the root of innovation. You cannot improve upon something that is unknown, and high performers like to innovate.

In Part 3 we will talk much more about teams and people, but the point that is critical to make here is that without scheduled and standardized work activities, you will never have a team. Think of any non-work-related team that works together, such as a sports team, where they are without scheduled and standardized work. They may call it something different, such as running a play, but if you break it down, where is the difference?

The companies I worked for were all good and some were great. The great ones put a tremendous amount of energy into Part 1, Purpose. But, let me make one point very clear: schedule and standardization is not about being good or being great. It is about being. If for some unknown reason you choose not to implement this component into your service delivery, you will not be great, good, or okay. You will quite frankly just be dead. These two elements are very basic and absolutely necessary for you even to take a breath in the service industry. My sincerest apologies if I just wrecked your day, but this chapter is the price for admission into the industry of being a IOSP.

BEST PRACTICE

It was a nice, sunny fall morning, and we were several miles into the trails at Team Trek. Our group of about a dozen was walking and talking when we heard the vague sound of a small plane in the area. A few of us looked up; the balance just continued with their conversations. Fifteen to 20 minutes later, a young man, out of breath, torn, bloody shirt, came out of the woods babbling and not making much sense. Startled, we tried to calm him down and understand what he was trying to say. The only bit we got was that his plane had crashed and he needed help. On a torn piece of paper he had roughly written some instructions for finding the plane. He said the plane was carrying medical supplies that needed to be put on ice.

We turned towards each other, and, as you can imagine, as a group started to try and process what was going on and if it was for real. We turned back within minutes to discover that our stranded pilot had disappeared into the woods with no visible sign of where he had gone, or from where he had come.

Hours later, after much orientation, we found the plane and were faced with a series of obstacles that helped us to refine and build our leadership skills and compatibility as a team. Coincidentally, when we did find the plane, our other group was also coming up on the same spot. It seemed our injured pilot made two stops that morning to set two groups on a collision course for learning and development.

This chapter is about scheduling and standardization and how important that is to flawless execution of IOS. What our groups experienced was a flawless execution of a Team Trek program. Due to their disciplined use of schedules and standards, the timing and delivery of each minute step in this event was amazing. It was so amazing, it took each of the groups several moments to actually get our heads around the fact that this scenario was not for real.

It does not matter if you are scheduling the cleaning of a building, the backing up of a server, the registration of a patient, or the maintenance of a machine, the execution will rely on how well you schedule the activities and how well you outline the required execution of those activities.

QUICK STORY

I am always fascinated when I see a different, very disciplined approach to an activity that on the surface looks spontaneous. The Best Practice story at Team Trek is one, but let me share another.

Have you every been to a Rolling Stones concert? Or seen the Stones on TV? If so, you have witnessed an extremely energetic group led on stage by Mick, who bounces all over the stage, engaging the stadium of fans who have come to see them perform.

In 1989 the Rolling Stones performed what was known as the Steel Wheels tour. It was a tremendous success, and beat out many records at that time for the revenue it generated. It was also captured on IMAX and was aired starting in 1991.

IMAX not only shot the concert from the front of the stage, but also from the back of the stage. So what was so fascinating?

That spontaneous demonstration put on by the group was fully orchestrated. As the camera pulled back from the stage towards the rear, you could see tape on the floor. The tape on the floor was used by Mick as a track outlining where on stage he could safely move in and out of the crowd. There were also areas taped off into a box where his security people were positioned to allow him closer access to the crowd. The security team was out of sight, just below him. The monitors that faced Mick instructed him what he should be singing at that time in the concert.

Again a flawless presentation, but only flawless because the basic disciplines of schedule and standards, associated with great service, were enacted.

TAKEAWAYS:

- Be very clear on desired outputs required from the scheduling management system.
- Output relies on input.
- Teamwork is dependent on scheduled and standardized work.
- No schedule, No standard…NO plan.

PROCESS

Define the Need
Define Scope
Define Value
Define Expectation
Re-Define the Need
Assemble
Align
Align
Assess
Schedule & Standardize
PURPOSE PROCESS
Deliver To Standard
Counter Measure
Layered Inspection
The Outsourcing Conundrum

"Quality has to be caused, not controlled."

Philip Crosby
Reflections on Quality

Deliver to Standard is where you must efficiently and effectively execute the plan you have put in place. As any seasoned veteran in the IOS business knows, it is critical that you execute your services seamlessly and flawlessly. Seasoned veterans also know that in itself is not enough, as execution to plan just scratches the surface of what needs to happen during the process of delivering services to standard. Delivering to Standard must also embrace continually improving how you deliver to standard.

It is amazing how a few words can almost stop your heart. Of the 40 years I've spent in the IOS industry, 75 percent were spent in heavy manufacturing, mainly automotive.

"We shut the plant down." These five words would totally disrupt my day and test the condition of my heart. These five words sent me running for my car or for a plane to get as quickly as I could to a customer location. Why?

Advanced Technology Services conducted a survey of 101 manufacturing executives whose companies had annual revenues between $10 million and five billion dollars. In this survey, respondents stated that the average cost of one minute of plant production downtime was somewhere between $22,000 and $50,000 per minute.

I don't know about you, but when I find out we shut a plant down and someone is tabulating a chargeback at the rate of $22,000 a minute, it tends to get my attention.

The only line of defense available to an IOSP is delivering in total compliance with each activity outlined in the scope of work to the documented standard, with absolutely no short cuts or compromises.

During my time in this business, I faced a dozen or so situations where our lack of compliance in delivering the standard resulted in a potential chargeback. Of those incidents, we were actually charged back six times. In each case, we had blatantly not adhered to the standard. In the other cases, we were able to point out clearly to the customer that some other circumstance also contributed to the failure.

In Purpose we spoke about understanding "why" your customer outsources services. Many of my customers over the years outsourced activities associated with their production equipment so they could hold someone accountable if the equipment was not ready for start of production. As this is the driving force for the outsourcing decision, being able to deliver the scope of work on time and to the desired level of quality was a given and fully expected.

Costs associated with failure are huge. Equally as big are the issues if you only deliver to standard. Don't get me wrong, you have to deliver to standard, but that is the minimum requirement; you also need to effectively and efficiently deliver to standard, which means you need to continually improve on the standard, if your goal is to keep a customer.

Many of the contracts we were awarded were set up over a multiple of years, and the contracted expectation was that the cost of the contract would either remain flat or would decrease year over year. Usually the required improvement factor was in the range of about three percent, which meant that each year the IOSP needed to perform its activities three percent more efficiently and effectively than they did the prior year. A multi-year contract was typically designed with a steady level of continual improvement.

As an example, let us look at a project at a customer site where the estimated time to complete annual activities outlined in the scope is 100,000 hours, which roughly equals 50 full-time team members. You now factor into this equation the required three percent year over year reduction, and you find out that each team member needs to become more effective and efficient by 60 hours a year. If you break it down further and look at it on a daily basis, it means a team member needs to identify 15 minutes of improved efficiency for every day they work. That is a pretty sizable challenge and totally unachievable if you do not start the process of continual improvement on Day One of your contract.

In the table below, you will see a contract outlining a five-year term that was originally based on 100,000 hours at a three percent cost reduction for each of the five years.

Contract Year	Annual hours	Reduction of 3%	Full-time TMs	Hours Reduced/ TM	Minutes / shift
Year 1	100,000	3,000	50	60	14
Year 2	97,000	2,910	49	60	14
Year 3	94,090	2,823	47	60	14
Year 4	91,267	2,738	46	60	14
Year 5	88,529	2,656	44	60	14

For each year of the contract, annual hours are reduced by three percent. The number of full-time team members (TMs) is also reduced to reflect total hour reduction. What is key to this table is what is not reduced: the number of hours that each team member must realize in efficiency gains over the course of the year. The numbers in the table are rounded to allow for an easier understanding of the key point, which is the level of continual improvement needed requires a mindset and habit that must be implemented right from Day One of the contract term.

There are, of course, a number of factors associated with improving the cost of running a project year over year, and it does not all hinge 100 percent on efficient utilization of allocated labor. But I would say for the record that in order for the IOSP to establish longevity with a customer, an unprecedented focus on efficient use of all human resources must exist.

I think it is safe to state that there is a common denominator associated with poor delivery to standard and inefficient delivery to standard. One impacts the IOSP quickly, and the other creeps up on the IOSP daily.

In the chapter Schedule and Standardize we discussed the importance of developing a plan whereby each activity's standard is based on best practices, and is delivered within a set time frame. Imagine the level of chaos if we fail to complete these requirements as outlined in that chapter. You just can't argue with the numbers!

To efficiently and effectively deliver to standard, there needs to be an unprecedented effort placed in four key areas:

- Management: setting the expectation.
- Customer Interaction: becoming customer-centric.
- Innovation: incremental improvements to the standard.
- Growth: development of the team and the opportunities.

MANAGEMENT

In 1954, Roger Bannister ran an amazing 1,760 yards to be the first person to break the four-minute-mile. Roger's time of 3:59.4 had never been accomplished. For years people had tried to break through that four-minute barrier. To attain his goal, Roger had to run at about 15 miles an hour, utterly amazing. Ironically, eight weeks later John Landy also ran the mile in under four minutes. Since 1954, many have broken the initial record to the point where it is no longer anything to talk about.

Roger made the impossible possible, and once it was possible others followed suit. Today there are records of people who beat Roger's world-class record by 18 percent. Imagine an 18 percent improvement over a world-class record on one single activity that people have been doing since the dawn of time.

In early 2000 I made a visit to one of our manufacturing customer's mid-west sites where our team had been delivering services since the mid-1990s. The motivation for the visit was that the site management team had a negative variance on every Key Performance Indicator, including safety, quality, delivery, cost, and morale. We were not delivering to standard, the standard of today. The management team had become fixated on the original standards which were now outdated, old practices. This multimillion-dollar project was now a break-even proposition. As per the table we discussed earlier, this group of over 100 team members had not achieved the goal of an annual three-percent, year-over-year improvement.

One of the first things a management team is responsible for is implementation of standards for the best practice for each activity outlined in the schedule. The next thing the management team must do is continually challenge their team to develop a more efficient and effective way to perform each activity for which they have responsibility. This site did a great job at first during the initial implementation, but they also turned team members into robots who were charged with carrying out an activity to the letter of the standard with no room for questions and, therefore, no room for improvement.

The site manager quoted an old saying that really summed up our problem, "If it were not for my employees and my customer, I would have a great business." Sadly this was actually how the manager felt. His mindset would never allow us to see success again at this facility. The mindset we needed was the polar opposite, "Because of my team members and my customer, I have the opportunity to have a great business."

Before mass industrialization, people who made things were often called craftsmen, who had a tremendous amount of pride in their skills. Mass production played havoc on this mindset, and the roles of craftsmen were replaced with the roles of production workers. In the IOS industry, if the mindset presented by a management group is that the team members who provide a service are disposable components, then that management team is well on its way to commoditizing their service offering. Management's job is to do the opposite, to convey to team members that they are unique individuals with thousands of ideas that need to be heard. Henry Ford said, "Why is it that I always get the whole person when what I really want is a pair of hands?" He could not have been more wrong.

C. William Pollard wrote a book called *The Soul of the Firm* while he was CEO of ServiceMaster, a very successful IOSP. In his book he outlines the people strategy that ServiceMaster used to achieve a level of unprecedented growth. We were acquired by ServiceMaster and worked under the leadership of Bill Pollard for a number of years. It was during this time that we solidified our "people approach" that became key to our ability to Deliver to Standard.

- Pay your people a fair and competitive wage.
- Give your people a cause to work towards.
- Properly define all tasks and activities.
- Empower your team and embrace mistakes.
- Establish a manager-worker relationship.

By simply embracing these five points, which were underscored to our management and supervision teams during all training and development sessions, our management–team member relationship began to grow. Team members who previously believed they were unable to make a difference began to feel they were able and expected to make a difference.

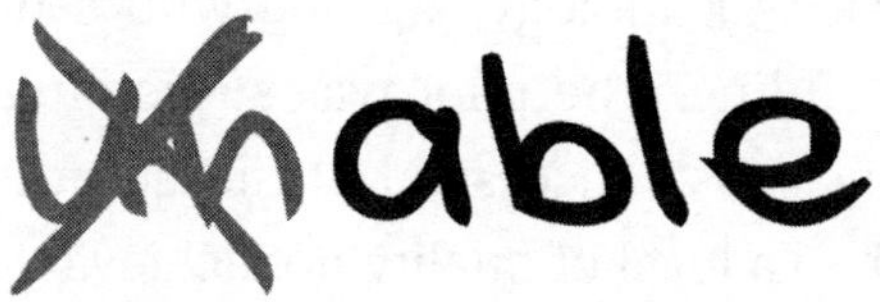

This growth led to improved prosperity that allowed us to invest in training and development on how to further empower our team members.

After some organizational changes were made at the mid-west site mentioned earlier, we started to apply our people strategy diligently, with a mindset that our team members deliver on our brand each and every day through efficient and effective completion of all tasks and activities.

This simple change in management mindset provided amazing results that were captured in our Key Performance Indicators.

- Our safety performance improved.
- Our productivity measures improved.
- Our employee engagement improved.
- Our gross margin improved.

In order for us to deliver efficiently and effectively to standard, our management team embraced our team members as being major contributors to help solve day-to-day issues. We took the approach that not only was it important to sell our brand to our customers, but it was equally as important to sell our brand internally to our team members. We used a simple transition from being labelled by a function—cleaner, housekeeper, maintenance technician, waste hauler—to being branded as a team of "Solutions Providers."

CUSTOMER INTERACTION

Our management promoted a mindset to our teams to partner with our customers as allies with a common goal and purpose. Everyone was encouraged to interact with the customer and seek out opportunities for improvement. The key was to establish increased touch points between our IOS teams and our customer teams.

In the book *The Human Sigma*, by John Fleming and Jim Asplund, the authors speak to the relationship between customer interaction and employee engagement. As one increases, so does the other, which results in a much higher level of perceived value by the customer and loyalty from team members. As an IOSP, it is very hard to argue with that formula.

Back at our site in the mid-west, as our team continued to improve on their ability to efficiently and effectively deliver to standard, they stumbled upon a great opportunity. (It is probably not fair to say "stumbled upon," because it was actually a direct result of increased customer interaction.) During a production start-up meeting, the customer's maintenance technician mentioned the number of times certain photo-eyes were dislodged during the cleaning process. Our team leader followed up with the maintenance technician, and over coffee discussed the problem. The team leader was also frustrated because in order to get the area cleaned in time for start-up the following morning, 13 people had to work side by side in pretty confined conditions. He explained to the maintenance technician that team members ended up stepping on each others' toes, and it was less than an ideal working environment. They both knew the activities had to be done, but the current standard wasn't efficient or effective.

They both agreed to meet to discuss the problem again after the next morning's production meeting, and to include the site and production managers. The level of customer interaction grew, and all parties were looking for a better way.

Clayton Christensen, a well known author and guru on the subject of innovation, points out in his work that if you are willing to put your customer in the center of what you do, you are six times more likely to grow. He feels that only about one in 10 companies will be able to sustain growth for more than a few years due to a lack of focus on being innovative.

INNOVATION

At the follow-up meeting from the story above, the site manager brought an "alert bulletin," an internal communication used to transfer new ideas from one site to another. This alert bulletin described a maintenance cleaning process known as dry-ice blasting. The technology was fairly new, and on the surface appeared to be extremely expensive.

The newly-formed improvement team agreed to explore the possibilities of the dry-ice technology, starting with a pilot on a piece of equipment located off-line. The pilot was successful, which led to an online pilot which was also successful. It turned out the new technology performed work to a level of quality not achievable through manual means. It was 40 to 50 times faster, and required only two people versus 13. Due to the reduction in required labor, the previous assumption of cost was offset and the overall process was very competitive. This newly-formed standard for performing the activities also resulted in areas that had previously been cleaned only once per year being cleaned upwards of five to six times per year. The increased frequency of cleaning resulted in an increase of production uptime of 17 percent.

Everyone won, although you are probably wondering how the 11 people who were no longer required to complete the task "won."

GROWTH

The team leader who commenced the dialogue with the maintenance technician was given the opportunity to become a supervisor as a result of his leadership during the implementation of the new process. The customer was so pleased with how well the team tackled the problem, and presented a viable solution and implementation for the solution, that he increased the scope of work, allowing the balance of the team to be deployed to a new opportunity with the hope they would work their"magic" in this area as well.

The biggest mistake we could have made would have been laying off the 11 team members who had all worked diligently to improve the standard effectively and efficiently.

The combination of a healthy management mindset that encouraged the highest possible level of customer interaction, and an open mind to pursue a "better way," led to growth for everyone, including our bottom line. It really proved the point made in the book *The Human Sigma*, that increased customer and employee engagement leads to a much higher level of service value, which translates into profit.

We have all heard the story of stone cutters who, when asked what they were doing, gave responses that spoke to their level of understanding of the reason behind their tasks. Each was asked, "What are you doing," and only one responded by saying, "building a cathedral" versus "just hammering a rock." In my travels to hundreds of sites, I judged management teams by responses team members made to a few questions:

- Do you know the standard and why it is important?
- Do you have the necessary tools to complete your activities?
- What is standing in your way of you being able to complete your activities?

Marcus Buckingham, in his book *First Break All The Rules*, discusses a study performed by the Gallup organization of what performers look for in their job. The first three of these questions are:

- Do I know what is expected of me at work?
- Do I have the materials and equipment needed to do my work?
- At work, do I have the opportunity every day to do what I do best?

The book describes a total of 12 questions that lead a team to the highest level of performance. If you have not read this book, I highly recommend it, as it sets the foundation for establishing a high level of performance within your team. You can easily survey against the responses and generate ideas to continually improve morale.

The responses I received to my three questions during site visits painted pictures for me of levels of employee engagement. As we've discussed, it is my firm belief that we cannot have a high level of customer interaction if we do not have a high level of employee engagement.

We will talk more about measuring employee engagement and customer interaction in the upcoming chapter on Layered Inspection.

Defining an activity properly and training on successful completion of that activity, regardless of how mundane, is the first step in providing a team member with dignity. The simple completion of the task builds confidence. That confidence can be molded through empowerment into ownership, and that ownership can result in the generation of thousands of ideas on how to improve or eliminate the activity. The IOSP needs a rainfall of ideas in order to continue to compete.

Ideas are typically very small, minor improvements to the standard. Innovation is not invention. Innovation is the continual improvement of the standard, but it cannot happen if there is no standard. One of the issues I faced while interacting with my site teams was the idea that new meant "wow." Although "wow" was sometimes very enticing, only a mindset towards small, incremental improvements would produce the level of reduction in labor hours required to compete.

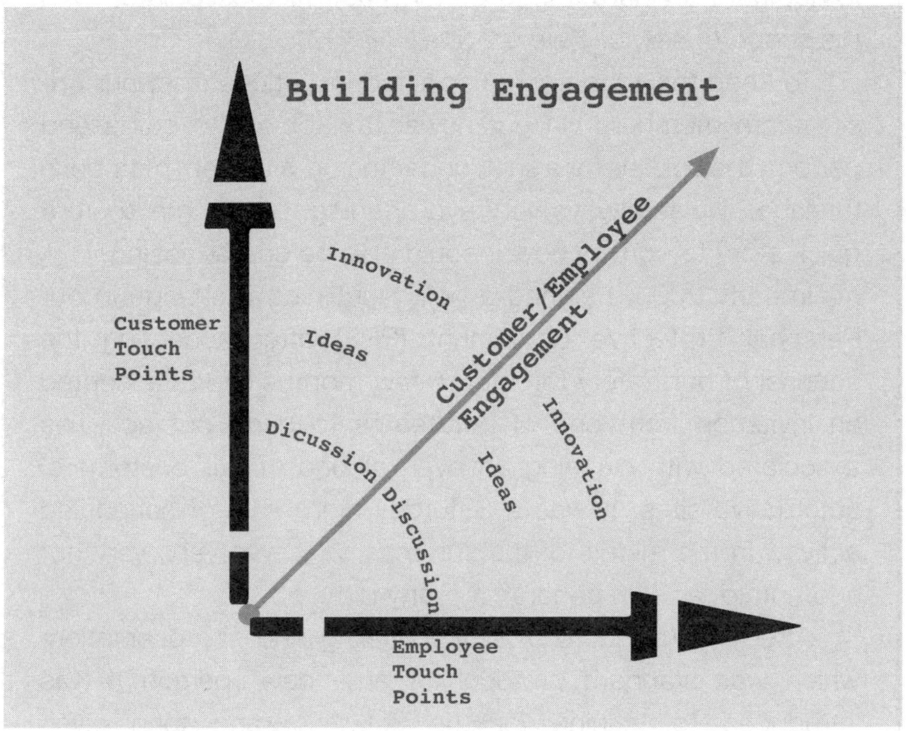

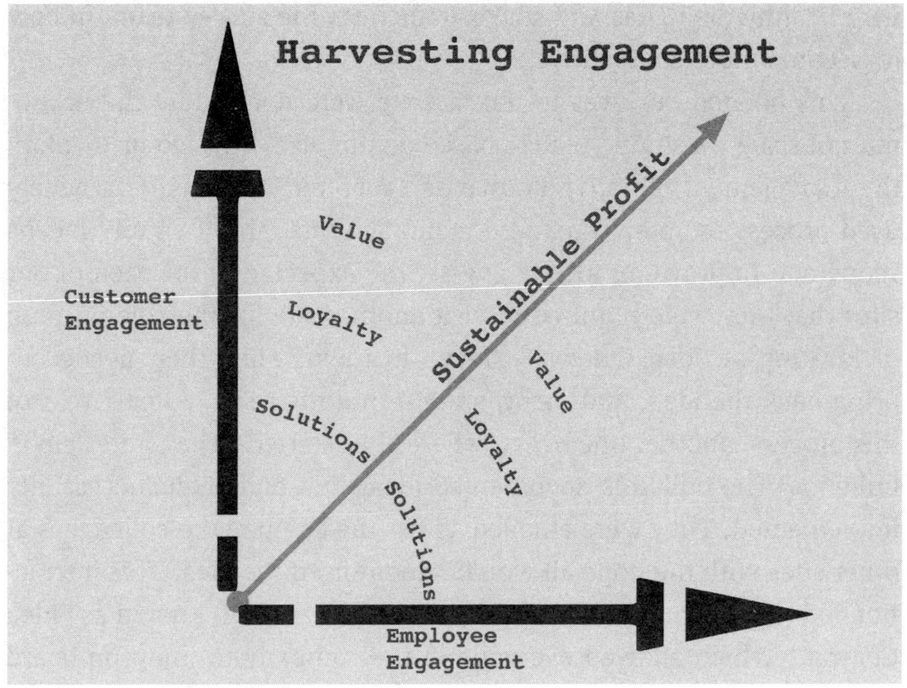

BEST PRACTICE

A practice we adopted was internal re-bid of selected sites. The purpose of this was to enable our onsite teams to internally learn from each other, rather than from the competition, what would be learned if we were put into a re-bid process. In a re-bid process, the contract is tendered. If the site is performing well, and the efficient and effective delivery of the standard is up to par, then chances are the customer is performing a market test. This is not an uncommon occurrence is the IOS business.

We assembled a survey team from other sites to go to the selected site, prepare documentation as outlined in Part 1 of The Outsourcing Conundrum Model, and perform a mock re-bid of the contract. This was initially done as a defensive technique, but it actually generated very healthy dialogues and suggestions from the survey team on how to become more competitive.

This opened our eyes to the fact we were not getting the economies of scale we should realize based on our size. This led us to adopt the management initiative known as "Yokoten." Yokoten is a widely used process by many Japanese manufacturers, and it simply means "copy and improve on ideas." We set the expectation for each of our sites that they were required to visit another site for the sole purpose of locating an idea that was "new" to them. They then needed to bring back the idea, and incorporate it into their site. After a year of this process, another one began where sites started to generate "alert" bulletins. The bulletins documented ideas that had been successfully implemented. They were emailed across the company to colleagues at other sites with the hope all would benefit from the idea. This interaction led to implementation of a virtual idea chat room known as "Idea Central," which allowed everyone in the company to jump on board and participate in company improvements.

What started out as a very isolated and selective improvement process, became a major level of engagement with reported participation in the 40 percentile range. Ideas that started out at a very tactical level grew and evolved into ideas of how to improve payroll, corporate communication, reporting, hiring, and so on.

In 2009, prior to our annual leadership conference, we asked all of our sites to submit an idea they felt was their absolute best, and maybe in fact the best idea generated that year by the company. The selected best ideas were to be presented at the conference by the teams who came up with them. As with all corporate requests, I was hoping to get a dozen or so ideas, and to pick a few to be presented.

Shockingly, we received just south of 50 responses from our sites, and it took two weeks to whittle them down to 16. The agenda originally set for the leadership conference had to be reworked to allow time for each team to present. It was an amazing opportunity to witness how proud the team members were to present and discuss their proven ideas.

QUICK STORY

I think I have shared enough stories for you to know that I grew up through the ranks of this business, starting out as an hourly laborer. Due to this exposure, and probably to my pride in being able to tell site teams I "have been there and done that," it is my solid belief you should never allow yourself to forget just how hard it is to perform activities associated with the scope of services we provide.

To keep this idea fresh, I solicited invitations from our on-site team members via our newsletter for me to come and perform their duties for a shift, under the on-site team member's tutelage. It was always very eye opening, but let me share a quick story to convey how it could also be embarrassing.

In early 2006, I signed a policy outlining a change in our Personal Protective Equipment (PPE) after accepting the counsel of our Safety Director. A few months later, I accepted an invitation from one of our teams to carry out activities associated with cleaning an oven at one of our customers' automotive sites. It was a Saturday night shift of scheduled activity, in the middle of the summer, so it was very, very hot and humid, and, in general, a pretty dirty job.

After several hours of safety briefing and site orientation, which was standard protocol for any "new" person, I was introduced to training for the activities, and then given responsibility for performing the activities. As stated, I had a purpose for taking the time to do this, but in just about every case those who did the inviting usually also had an agenda. This group was no different. In oven cleaning, there are a few reasonably "cushy" jobs that, although not easy, are not quite as difficult as others. As you can probably guess, I did not get the cushy activities. They put me in my PPE, and sent me into the oven ductwork where I spent the next six hours on my knees, butt, and back, making my way through the duct and cleaning every square inch. I have to be honest, by 2:30 in the morning if I could have snapped my fingers and disappeared, I would have. It was extremely hot, and the damned PPE was more of a hindrance than a help.

At lunch the next day, the team members were very accommodating and made me feel part of the group. They asked how I made out, and I responded that it was fine, except for fighting the PPE all night. They told me the new PPE was a real problem for all of them. I asked, "Whose stupid idea was it to make you wear all that needless stuff?" and they collectively replied, "Yours." I was dumbfounded. "Mine?" I asked. "Yes, yours," and they then presented me with a copy of the PPE document I had signed several months earlier, revising company PPE requirements.

On Monday when I got back to the office, I met with my Safety Director, and informed him that in three weeks he was scheduled to perform a "hands on" oven cleaning at that same site.

Needless to say, the PPE policy was amended. The site team worked together, was engaged, and collectively made their point. Once again I was reminded of implications sometimes associated with mass procedural changes, as was the Safety Director.

TAKEAWAYS:

- Deliver efficiently and effectively to standard.
- You need a thousand ideas if you are going to stay competitive.
- Employee engagement is the foundation of customer engagement.
- Management's mindset opens the door to innovation.

PROCESS

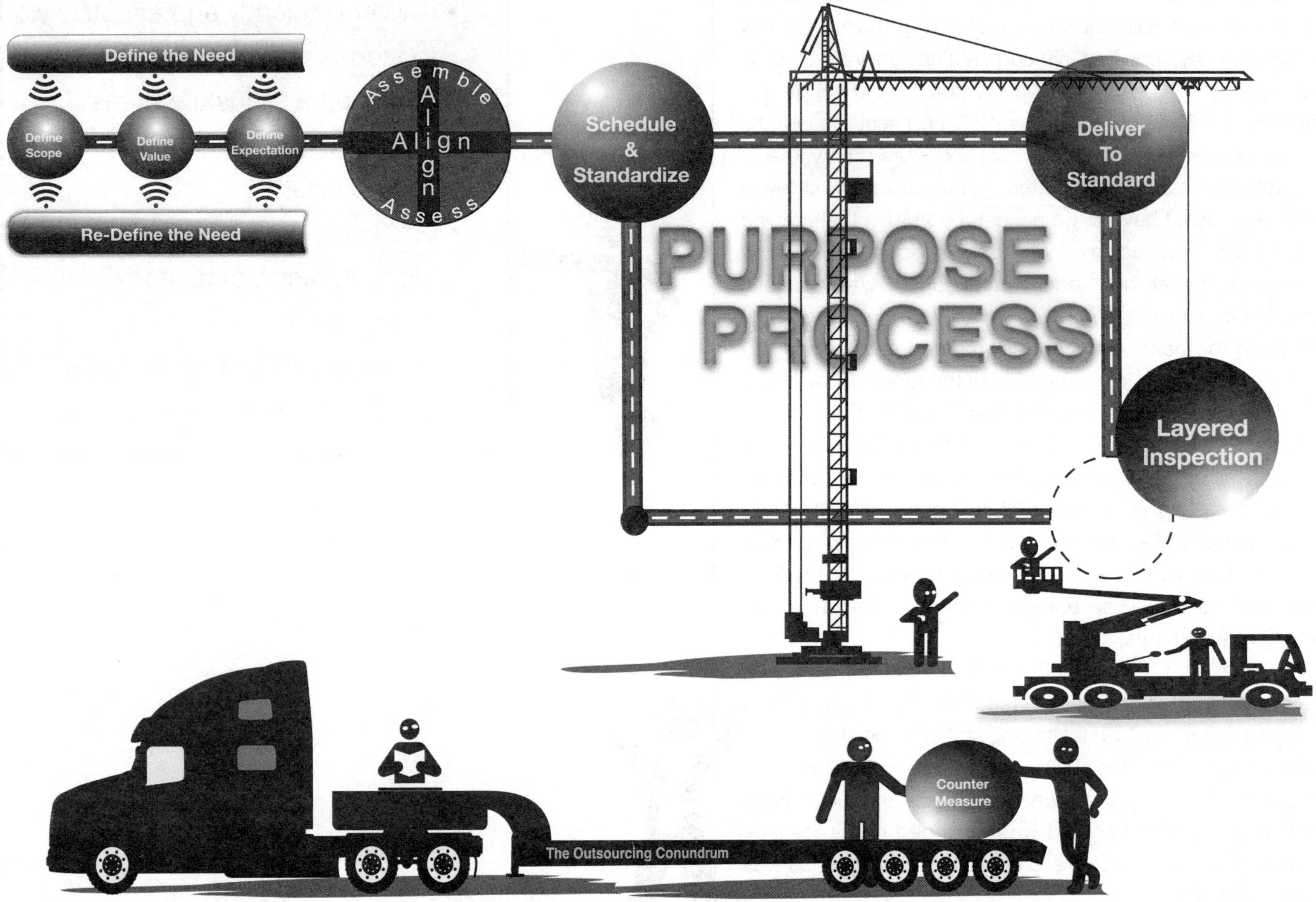
Define the Need
Define Scope
Define Value
Define Expectation
Re-Define the Need
Assemble
Align
Assess
Schedule & Standardize
Deliver To Standard
PURPOSE PROCESS
Layered Inspection
Counter Measure
The Outsourcing Conundrum

"I am your constant companion. I am your greatest helper or heaviest burden. I will push you onward or drag you down to failure. I am completely at your command. Half the things you do you might just as well turn over to me, and I will be able to do them quickly, correctly. I am easily managed—you must merely be firm with me. Show me exactly how you want something done, and after a few lessons I will do it automatically. I am at the service of all great people, and alas, of all failures as well. Those who are failures, I have made failures. I am not a machine, though I work with all the precision of a machine plus the intelligence of a human being. You may run me for a profit or turn me for ruin—it makes no difference to me. Take me, train me, be firm with me, and I will place the world at your feet. Be easy with me and I will destroy you.

"Who am I? I am habit."

Anonymous

Layered inspection is a habit that reflects your management principles, but how you perform layered inspection reflects your management style. The approach you choose for layered inspection will take you down a path of zero to incremental improvement, or a path of quantum improvement. Layered inspection is a skill that must become part of your character so it becomes a habit. This chapter will help you make it a good habit versus a bad habit.

The complexity, depth, level of detail, and risk associated with the IOS you are providing sets the stage for resources, training, tools, and systems required to complete layered inspection. Regardless of this, the attitude and state of mind with which you approach layered inspection are what will reap you benefit or give you heartache.

For years I have experimented with trying to play golf and, over the years, have taken the time to work with a trainer to improve my game. As any golfer knows, the key to improving your game is improving your swing. In 2006 I met a guy, Charlie, who did more to help me understand golf than any other trainer. He broke my swing down into a series of layers that align pretty well with what we are talking in this chapter, Layered Inspection. The first layer is to stand behind the ball, decide where you want your ball to go and put yourself into the mindset of delivering on that outcome. He called it the emotional side of golf. The second layer was the actual process of swinging the club, including gripping the club, your stance, position of your body, the path the club would take during your back swing and down swing, and the position of the face of the club when it strikes the ball. This process of swinging the club is an activity that is performed numerous times during a round of golf. One activity builds on the next to give you your score on a hole, and the score of each hole is tabulated to give you your score for the front nine, and the front nine and back nine are added together to give you your score for the round. Each score is an outcome leading to the final outcome, your score for the round.

Layered Inspection for the IOSP is not too much different than the golf analogy. The Layered Inspection, as we will discuss, goes through three layers:

- Emotional Layer – where we establish the right mind-set.
- Activity Layer – where we inspect the physical task/activity outlined in our scope of work.
- Outcome Layer – where we inspect the outcome at several levels.

Very similar to the golf analogy is the realization that if you do not perform all three layers with some level of competence you will spend much of your time in the rough delivering a mediocre service. If you master all three, you will live on the fairways and greens, delivering great service.

Layered inspection involves interaction through observation, by several levels of the team, on both the customer side and the employee side. The involvement of different team levels provides fresh perspectives on the quality of services being provided. In Part 1 we discussed the importance of transferring the service's purpose to those involved in delivering the service in order to engage the hands, head, and heart of those providing the service. To accomplish this goal, there are emotional layers that must be overcome.

In the fall of 2007, I received an invitation to perform the duties of one of our technicians for a day. As described earlier, we referred to these as "We Serve" days, whereby an hourly team member could invite someone from management to come and perform their activities for a day, under the supervision of that team member. This invite came in from Norm who was a "Tech 1," responsible for lubrication of all of the production machines at one of our power train sites in Michigan. Upon arriving at the site and going through the normal protocols, I was given to Norm for the balance of the day. Our scope of work was to perform several hundred lubrication checks on all of the production machines. There were over a half-dozen different oils and lubricants associated with every machine, and it was imperative that the fluid levels be within spec at all times. It was very apparent as I boarded the battery-operated flat bed that Norm was pretty passionate about his work.

Norm walked me through the standardized work, demonstrated what I had to do, and then watched me perform my first fluid check on a crank production machine. After checking the fluid level and surmising that fluid needed to be added, I grabbed a hose and started to connect it to top off the light oil tank. After a couple of minutes struggling with the connection, I asked Norm if there was a trick to connecting the hose. Very graciously he pointed out the hose I had in my hand was blue but the connecting hose was red. I quickly recalled the standardized work instruction, and remembered that all fluid delivery and receiving connectors were color coded. Norm went on to point out that not only were the connectors color coded, but each connector was specific to only one fluid. Basically the system was completely idiot-proof. You were not able to hook the wrong hose up to a machine mistakenly to add the wrong fluid to the wrong tank.

During lunch, I expressed how impressed I was by how well the standardized work instruction and tools had been set up, as well as how efficiently the route for performing the work had been laid out. Norm described for me the many levels of improvement that had been made to that specific standard work instruction. He said when he started the job, there was no flat-bed to transport the oil. It was moved around by hand-pushed dollies. None of the hoses were color coded, and one connector was used for all fluids. He pointed out that the job was not done efficiently or accurately. He took it upon himself to improve the way the job was done, to make it easier and reduce the chance of a mistake. He also stated that the work we performed that morning used to take almost two days to complete.

I was completely fascinated, and asked why he was so involved in trying to improve how he did his job. He said that from his first day on the job when Jim, his supervisor, followed up on him and inspected his work, he began to engage. Jim met with Norm, inspected his completed work, and stated it complied with the standard work instruction. Norm said Jim then asked if there was some way the activities could be made easier and more efficient. Norm had a couple of ideas. Jim listened, and helped Norm get them implemented. Norm said it just kept going from there until the process evolved into what I had seen today. He felt valued and appreciated. I expressed my gratitude for what he had done, and for making the execution of the activities perfect. Norm stated that it was still far from perfect, and he had a couple of other ideas involving the use of bar-coding and PDAs to really take the standardized work to a new level. Norm pointed out that improving how the work was done and always looking for a "better way" had just become a habit for him. I told him I hoped it was a habit he would not break.

On the drive home, I pondered my day and thought about the number of "Norms" I had interacted with over the years, and how each of them was fully engaged in continual improvement of standardized work. The common denominator was that management teams had all taken the time to inspect work, not only to make sure it was technically correct and up to the customer's specification, but also to use layered inspection to move through emotional layers of the work as well as the technical. Layered inspection closely examines the outcome of the work itself, but is also an opportunity to engage the hands, heads, and hearts of those doing the work by empowering them to improve how the work is done and find a "better way." Layered inspection allows you to make sure the work is done properly, and to improve how the work is done in the future.

As the name implies, layered inspection involves close scrutiny on several levels simultaneously, of both the work that has been done and the process used to do it. How deeply you choose to delve into these layers will directly affect your ability to engage employees and achieve continual improvement.

EMOTIONAL LAYER

To be able to get the most out of your team, the first inspection is the mindset of those doing the work. To accomplish this goal you need to inspect that the whole person is active and engaged and not just a part of the person.

Singular layer: The hands of team members performing services are engaged as activities are inspected for compliance to standards.

Secondary layer: The hands and heads of team members are engaged as activities are inspected for compliance while also discussing "is there a better way?"

Plural layer: The hands, heads, and hearts of team members are engaged as activities are inspected against revised standards, while discussing the improvement that resulted from input given by the people performing the activities.

This may sound like a lot, but, as described in Norm's example above, it is really nothing more than a few seconds of dialogue where individuals feel valued and respected for their ideas and input. Management teams that practice this style or habit of supervision, like Jim did with Norm, derive a great benefit of added value and lower operating costs from their teams.

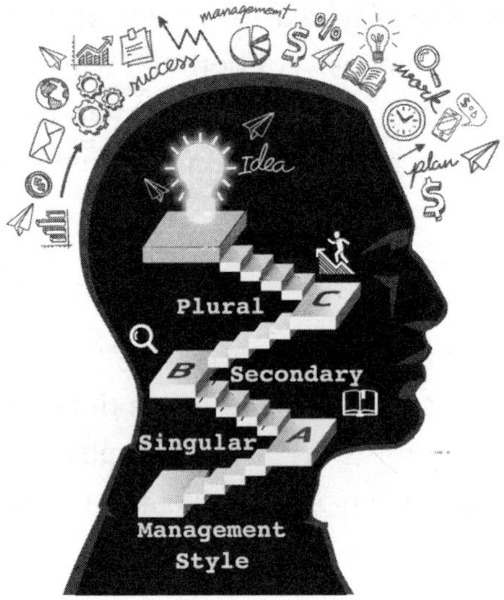

"The significant problems we face cannot be solved at the same level of thinking we were at when we created them."

Einstein

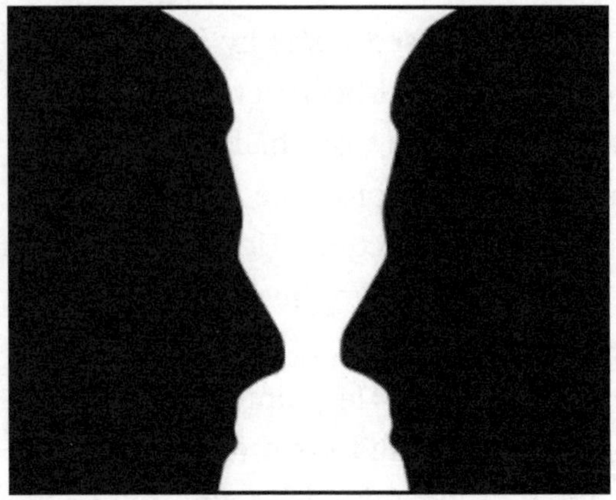

Is this a vase on a black background, or two silhouettes on a white background?

Is this an old woman or a young woman?

In both cases it could be either! Is the work completed to specification? Are both parties seeing the same end result? The focus on moving from the singular layer to the plural layer ensures a consistent, reliable perspective on the level of quality viewed by everyone.

ACTIVITY LAYER

In Chapter Two, Define Scope, we discuss activity-based scope versus outcome-based scope. In each case, activities associated with the scope, the actual physical work, must meet stringent requirements by complying with the documented standard for their safe and effective completion. Layered inspection can empower or demotivate based upon a management team's style and ability to move through the emotional layers. When this is done well, the team member owns the initial inspection or first layer of physical inspection. The team member inspects their completed activity to the written standard for compliance. The team leader inspects groupings of activities to ensure compliance with the broader process. The supervisor inspects compliance of the process with the needs of the production line or department. Site management inspects the production line or department for compliance with the needs of the project or site.

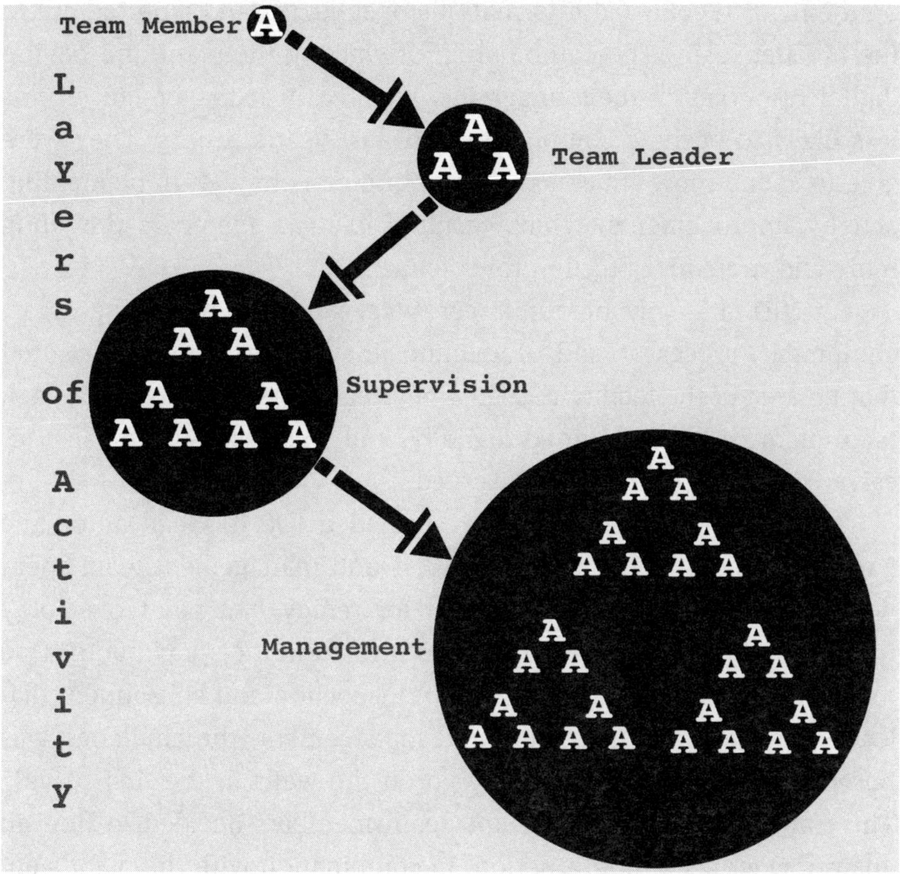

In the previous example, activities performed by Norm were specific and were performed on hundreds of individual machines along with other activities performed by other technicians. The combination of all these activities led to the overall effectiveness of the equipment. This is often referred to in manufacturing as the OEE, or Overall Equipment Effectiveness, the ability of a machine to run at optimal production and quality rates. The machines maintained by Norm and other team members were located on specific production lines that manufactured specific products, and the production lines were located in specific shops.

Another example is an IOSP who is a supplier to a hospital and has responsibility for cleaning of the facility. One team member may be responsible for general cleaning of a room, and another may be responsible for cleaning, stripping, and waxing the room's floors. The combination of these activities determines the level of quality for the room. A grouping of rooms leads to the level of satisfaction of the cleaning of a specific wing or floor.

Layered Activity inspection reduces the risk of human error often due to:

- Lack of training/instruction.
- Poor job design or ergonomics.
- Poor understanding of quality.
- Poor prioritization of activities.
- Misunderstanding of why the activity is important.

Layered Activity inspection provides several sustainable benefits:

- Reduces rework.
- Solves problems first time.
- Reduces mass inspection.
- Reduces waste.
- Improves quality.
- Improves delivery performance.
- Improves safety.
- Increases customer and team member satisfaction.
- Increases opportunities for growth.

LAYERED ACTIVITY INSPECTION

Old School	New School
Let me tell you why this is important.	Can you share with me why this activity is important?
Let me tell you what needs to be done.	Can you share with me what needs to be done?
Let me tell you how to perform that activity better.	Can you share with me how to perform that acitivy better?
Let me inspect your work.	Inspect your work for me and let me know if we can improve on what we are doing, how we are doing it, and why we are doing it. How can I help you make those improvements?
Take credit.	Give credit.
Seek respect.	Give respect.
Tell the team what's important.	Show the team who's important.

At Norm's plant, there were roughly 100 team members and a management staff of about 20. Each management team member was responsible for observing and inspecting a minimum of one activity per week while it was performed by a technician. Over the course of a year, this allowed every activity performed at the plant to be reviewed while being performed. The management team used this time to move through emotional layers, move activities from just being compliant, and have discussions around effectiveness and overall ideas for improvement.

Each of our facilities that achieved a high number of improvement contributions from team members all had management team members who spent most of their time on the floor walking rather than sitting behind their desks.

As the digital age progressed, our ability to provide our management teams with tools for layered activity inspection also grew. First, and most obviously, these digital tools reduced the amount of time associated with paper work. Beyond that, inspections could be done on the fly, and collected information consolidated and reported out to the broader team. The combination of walking the plant and having digital resources at their finger tips resulted in management groups less likely to become complacent with last year's results. They were able to spend more time assisting team members with implementing activity improvements, which resulted in team members providing more and more ideas for improvement.

By 2011 at many of our larger sites, we were barcoding areas, equipment, processes and production lines so we could be assured that no area of the facility missed a physical inspection. By 2013, each team member was identified digitally, and was assured they also received an opportunity to be observed.

At one of our sites, where we provided IOS to clean automatic paint spray booths, our team members and management team spent weeks improving a technique used for removal of paint overspray from walls, windows, and equipment located in the spray booth. Due to implementation of layered activity inspection and subsequent dialogue between team members and management, the challenge was posed, "Why does the overspray go on the walls in the first place?" The team leader, supervisor, and team members decided to find an answer. Over a six-month period, in combination with the plant's engineering group, an outside vendor, and support from our corporate engineering group, the team identified a solution that resulted in a two-thirds reduction in overspray, cutting the time spent on cleaning the walls by half. Results like these are possible only because the management team is active on the floor, inspecting and discussing the impact of how each activity affects the big picture. The spray booth improvement also led to an increase in the level of plant production and quality, which was highly valued by our customer.

The activity layer allows management opportunities to connect and interact with those who do the work, and to reaffirm alignment between the Purpose and Process. Using the right management mindset, an IOSP is able to communicate the standards directly to each team member as well as encourage improvement.

OUTCOME LAYER

The Outcome Layer is where you measure the impact of all the performed activities. Did we shoot par for the course? Unlike the activity layer, where the primary focus is the completion and improvement of the standards, the outcome layer measures the impact of the services against the expectations outlined by the customer in Chapter Four, Define the Expectations.

In Chapter Four, Define the Expectations, we established from our customer how they measure success. If the service agreement is primarily activity-based, those outcome measures will deal with issues such as the percent of work completed, absenteeism rates, employee turnover, work activities completed to standard and re-work. Very common in a contract where your customer is basically hiring you to supply people on a day-to-day, hour-to-hour basis. If, however, your contract is based more on how your service impacts your customer's ability to provide their product, then the measures are heightened.

Indicators of performance, customer satisfaction, impact on production quality and uptime often need to be broken down into smaller levels of detail. Each level is not useful to all layers of the organization. The downpour of information must be carefully regulated and funneled into content and a format that is relevant to a group or team. This is extremely important as you are commencing this process, because you can only achieve buy-in as the team more clearly understands what is being measured. Too much trivial information will hurt your cause.

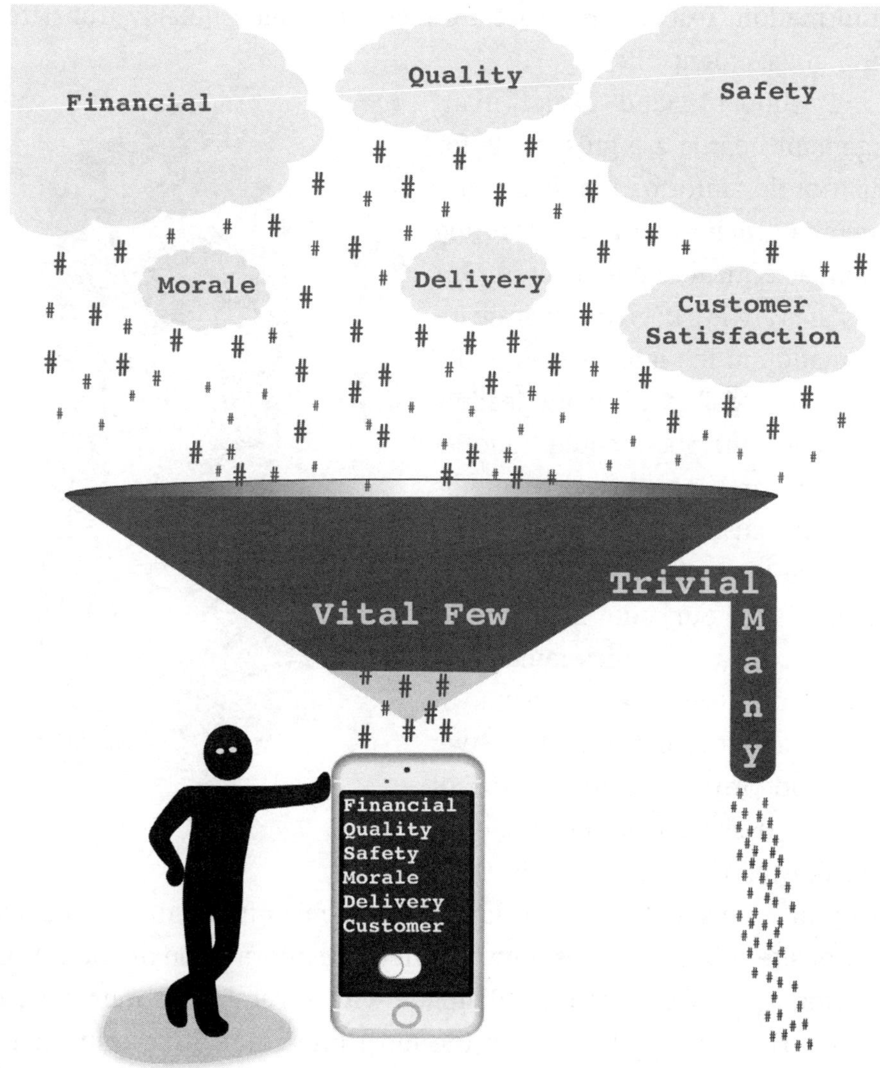

The most important layer in an organization is very often the most neglected layer: the team that actually performs the work. Engagement of the team is fostered by how well information relevant to the team is communicated. Everyone has an inherent need to be an important part of something outside of themselves. By communicating relevant information, respect and trust are fostered, which quickly translates into engagement.

Dashboards and visual management boards are great tools for distributing information to all team members on how we are performing in areas critical to our success. Our goal has always been to generate information in the most user-friendly manner possible so team leaders and team members could conduct effective and informative meetings with our customers.

One of the best visuals, implemented by our site manager in Buffalo, is a tool nicknamed the CUBE because of its design. It stands about four feet high by two feet wide, and is in the shape of a cube. It sits on top of four casters that allow it to be easily spun around from side to side. At the start of each shift and during breaks, the onsite shift team takes time to review the information on the CUBE. During a site visit and from dialogue with several team members, it was very apparent that one of the most important things our onsite team wanted to know was the status of implementation of their ideas. The CUBE is able to communicate visually the inspection results from all activities, as well as give each team member an understanding of how completion of each activity impacted site performance.

During my site visit I was able to witness a small group of team members engaging in a minor argument while they were rotating the CUBE from one side to the other. The team had just implemented a new cleaning procedure for one of the dirtier activities at the site, and were engaging in a discussion as to whether or not this improvement was showing any benefit and should be discontinued. The three people involved in this discussion each turned the CUBE to point to a different chart—safety, quality and absenteeism—to each make their point. I do not recall the decision by the team but I do recall walking out of the break room wishing every one of my several thousand team members would have such arguments during their breaks.

At several sites, we were able to attach an incentive related to performance of the team, which enhanced interest in outcomes even more. Even if a site did not have the ability to align an incentive to outcomes, it associated some form of celebration with outcomes, such as free lunch, coffee and donut breakfasts, family picnics, etc.

The onsite management team is the next most important layer when it comes to communicating outcomes. In Chapter Four, we discussed development of a Site Strategic Operating Plan (SSOP), which is designed to provide the status of the current operation as well as information pertaining to the continual forward momentum of the operation.

Unlike the CUBE that primarily deals with the impact of day-to-day operations of the business, the SSOP also deals with implementation of bigger initiatives and projects designed to move the business forward and drive competitiveness.

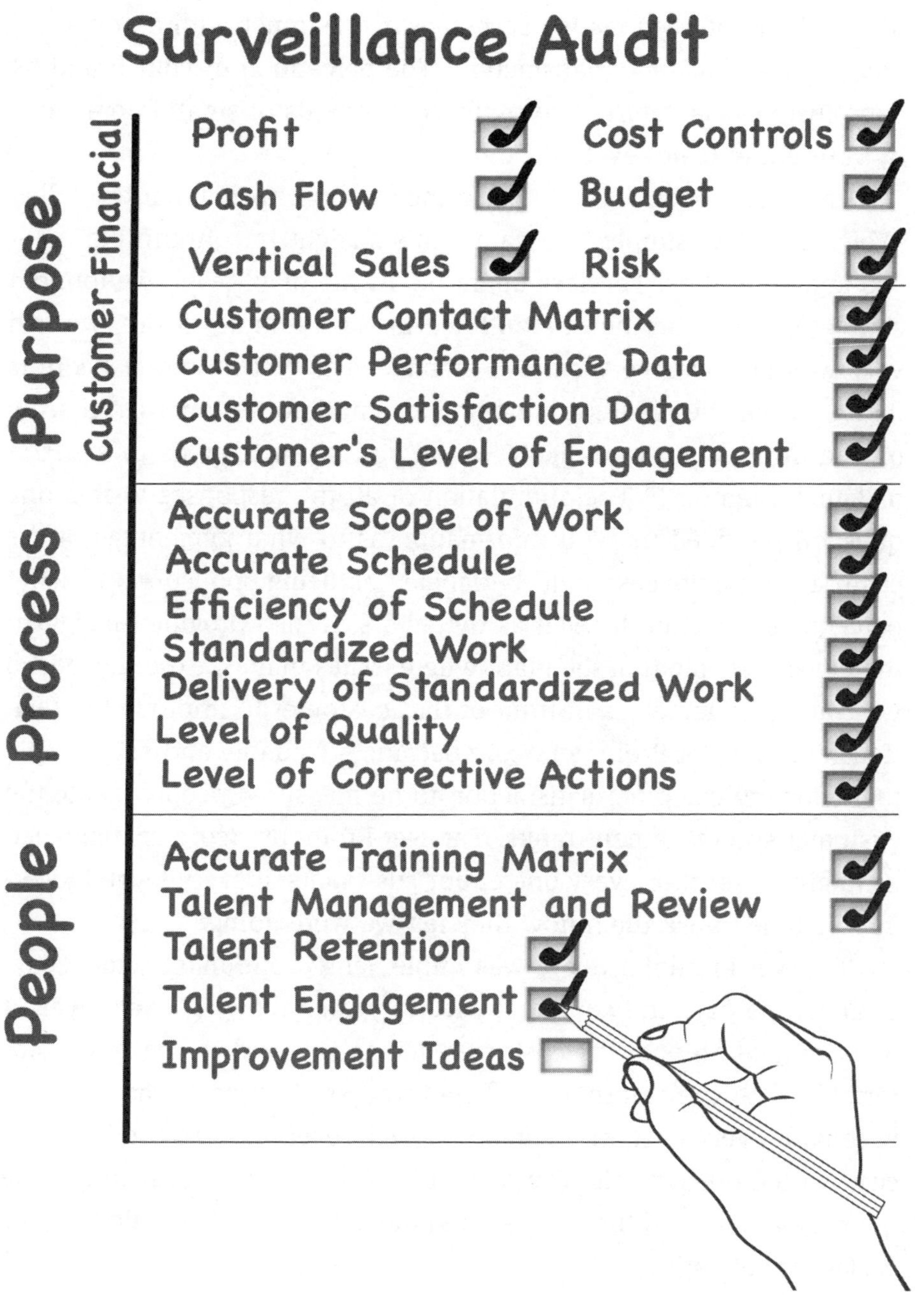

Everyone on one of our management teams had some form of incentive tied to successful completion of their SSOP. As stated in Chapter Four, SSOPs went by several names, including Scorecards, Hoshins, Key Performance Indicators, or Business Development Boards. Regardless of the name, they all contained strategic drivers and metrics designed to propel the site forward.

Looking back at Norm's plant that we discussed earlier, the SSOP for the site was broken down so that each shop and department knew exactly what they needed to accomplish to make a positive contribution to the SSOP. That level of transparency provided us a high level of engagement, which we measured by retention and attraction of key management personnel.

The final layer of inspection, and the least important, is the corporate layer. The corporate scoreboard is only as good as the players' ability to hit balls when they are pitched. If no one is hitting at the team level, there is not much use in spending time counting home runs. To ensure that our sites were hitting the ball and operations were delivering on our brand, we performed what was known as a Surveillance Audit.

Each year we would survey around 15 to 20 percent of our sites, or roughly two to three a month. The reason for the survey was to ensure each site was delivering services based around the three Ps: Purpose, Process and People. The survey of each site would take between one and two days, depending on the size and complexity of the services we provided. Consolidated data from all site surveys was reviewed each quarter, and survey data was given back to the entire company in each newsletter, keeping the information transparent. Each site survey included a tour of the facility, as well as engagement and discussion with team members who performed the activities. Areas deemed as needing improvement were documented for a follow-up visit within a 90-day period.

Earlier in the chapter we discussed emotional layers, and how important it is to move through the layers to engage the hands, heads, and hearts of team members. This doubly applies to a site management team when adopting any level of corporate involvement. An auditor's role, for example, is to help coach a team to success by providing support and resources to get the site back on target if deemed necessary, not simply to observe and record the outcomes while onsite. This process evolved tremendously over the years. It first started as more of a policing action, which reaped little benefit. When it morphed into a continuous improvement tool, with the emotional layers factored in, it reaped a lot more benefit and better sharing of best practices.

One of the benefits I received from surveillance audit data was that it gave me a clear picture of which sites to visit. I would visit a mix of sites that were in potential trouble to see what they needed to be successful. I also visited sites that were running well to say thanks, and to see if any of their reasons for success could be transplanted across the enterprise.

CUSTOMER LAYER

It is important for any IOSP to remember that a customer's experience must be inspected and measured. The level of customer engagement can be viewed in both the activity and outcome layers previously discussed, but an IOSP's number-one goal and source of value is customer satisfaction, so it's essential to measure it separately as well.

Customer satisfaction should be monitored at every accessible layer within a customer's organization. At every one of our sites we had our team members who interacted with the customer's team members, our team leaders interacted with the customer's team leaders, our supervisors interacted with our customer's supervisors. At each one of these interactions we accessed the customer with an opportunity to gauge customer satisfaction. The perception of your brand by your customer is determined by these hundreds of small interactions by your entire team, every day.

On several occasions we performed a more formal survey called "Voice of the Customer," to gain better insight into future plans for IOS and what those services might be. At the plant level, we found a simpler survey, like the one outlined in Net Promoter Score, worked very well and was very easy to manage. The Net Promoter Score is derived from the results of one single, simple question: "On a scale of one through 10, how likely would you be to refer us to a friend or family member?" The cumulation of all the responses to this one question provided us with information as to what percentage of the customer's employees could be labeled as being sponsors and what percentage could be labeled as detractors. It also provided insight if there was a segment of the plant where issues may be experienced, so we could put ourselves in front of that customer to improve the relationship. The Net Promoter Score became a valuable and very simple tool allowing customer satisfaction to be measured deeply inside the customer's management ranks. The Net Promoter Score also allowed us to give respect to every one of our customers at every level, by taking the time to ask them how they felt we were doing.

The Net Promoter Score was implemented one management layer at a time over the course of several years, allowing each layer of management on both the customer side and our side to become comfortable with the informality of the process. Our goal was to touch base with every customer contact at each level once a year. The process started out with the use of simple 5" x 8" index cards to ask the question and record the results, then moved into an iTool allowing for easier consolidation of the data.

Multiple levels of customer satisfaction are critical to the longevity of an IOSP contract, and an early warning sign if monitored regularly as to the onslaught of complacency. As we have discussed, complacency is like cancer to an IOSP.

BEST PRACTICE

Team Trek's success hinges on the experience of each individual participant and also on the experience of the collective team. It is critical for facilitators to have a constant pulse on the reactions and experience of individuals and teams as a group's leadership skills are developed and practiced.

To do this, facilitators take regular "time-outs" to allow the individuals to journal and to participate in well orchestrated discussions around key questions, to flush out if any member of the group is feeling inadequate for any reason. Information gathered from discussion is used by the facilitator to adjust the program on the fly to meet individual needs.

On one occasion, during an event involving a need to operate at great heights, one of our team who suffered from a fear of heights was acting a bit off. It turned out he had fallen more than 10 years earlier while working as an electrician, and never conquered his fear. Due to this fear, he made up excuses for not participating, but did not disclose the true reason. Team Trek operates to a philosophy of 100 percent responsibility, no excuses, as a foundational attribute for any leader. The facilitator was able to calmly flush out the issue, and adjust the upcoming event so the individual was comfortable in sharing his fear. Sharing gave this person a visible sign of relief, and by the end of the week he conquered his fear and rappelled down a cliff with the rest of his group.

Layered inspection comes in many varieties and sizes. The key is a constant habit of always looking at what has been done and asking, "How can this be done better?" This applies whether it is a physical task, building a relationship, the development of a new skill, or the adoption of a new behavior.

QUICK STORY

Old Man Murphy and his law.

- If anything can go wrong, it will.
- If there is a possibility of several things going wrong, the one that will cause the most damage will be the one to go wrong.
- If there is a possibility of several things going wrong, the one that will cause the most damage will be the *first* to go wrong.
- If anything just cannot go wrong, it will anyway.
- If you perceive that there are four possible ways in which something can go wrong, and circumvent these, then a fifth way, unprepared for, will promptly develop.
- Left to themselves, things tend to go from bad to worse.
- If everything seems to be going well, you have obviously overlooked something.

It is impossible to spend any large amount of time as an IOSP and not pay homage to "Old Man Murphy." He is the walking curse to those who do not adhere to the habit of Layered Inspection. Let me give you just one brief example.

In the early 1990s I was launching a new site in southern Illinois. We took over the site on a Friday, and had to have the

site ready for production of front and rear painted bumpers by Monday at 4:00 a.m. It was late Sunday, and we were wrapping up hundreds of activities and going through final activity inspections. The last inspection was the cure oven, and everything was looking good. The last, small item was to close all vent doors and latch them closed. Hello, Mr. Murphy.

At the end of the oven, we checked off the inspection sheet and sent two team members back in with the supervisor to close the doors. As I walked away, I thought to myself that I should have pointed out that the latches on the doors were very stiff, and for the team members to be sure they heard the latch "snap" shut. Did I mention we completed hundreds of activities that weekend to a level of performance that made us all proud?

Our Monday morning walkthrough with the customer was a tremendous success, and the plant fired up and started painting. A few hours later, around 7:30, I received a radio call to get to the inspection deck. Down the production line came hundreds of fire-engine red front and rear bumpers, all glistening in the light…except for a small scratch on the right side of every, yes, every bumper. Yep, a latch did not snap shut, the door dropped open, and christened every bumper that passed with a little kiss, turning it to scrap. By the time we fixed the issue, I was responsible for the destruction of about 1,000 bumpers. These types of stories—and I have several more—are why I adopted the concept of layered inspection, and why I pay homage to "Old Man Murphy."

Last night after a long day of writing, my wife and I decided to go out for dinner to one of our favorite restaurants here in Cincinnati, called Boca. This restaurant does a great job of delivering a consistent and reliable service experience at a value that matches the price. The restaurant has a very cool feature: if you want, you can get a seat at what is called the Kitchen Bar, where you overlook the kitchen and interact with the chefs. We chose to sit at the Kitchen Bar last night. As I sat there and observed, I was struck by why this restaurant is so consistent in the delivery of their service experience. Not one single piece of prepared food makes it to a table without being inspected by at least three sets of eyes. The person who prepared the dish inspects that it is cooked to the required standard. The next chef reviews it as he plates the meal, and then the kitchen chef reviews it prior to a server picking up the order to deliver to a customer.

Obviously a restaurant is not an IOSP, but they are most definitely in the service business. Our dining experience underscored one of the key messages I hope you take from this book: Great service is not an accident. It is a result of adherence to a well laid-out set of disciplines.

The Boca kitchen not only fully embraced the habit of layered inspection, but it also embraced the need for schedule, standardization and delivery to the standard.

Over the course of the two hours we spent at the Kitchen Bar, I noticed that at least two protein dishes were brought back to the chef in need of what we will be discussing in the upcoming chapter, Counter Measure.

TAKEAWAYS:

- Emotional layers are the first barrier to engagement and innovation.
- Continual inspection and continual improvement must become a habit.
- Data should be sorted with the user in mind.
- Survey your customer on a regular, constant basis.

PROCESS

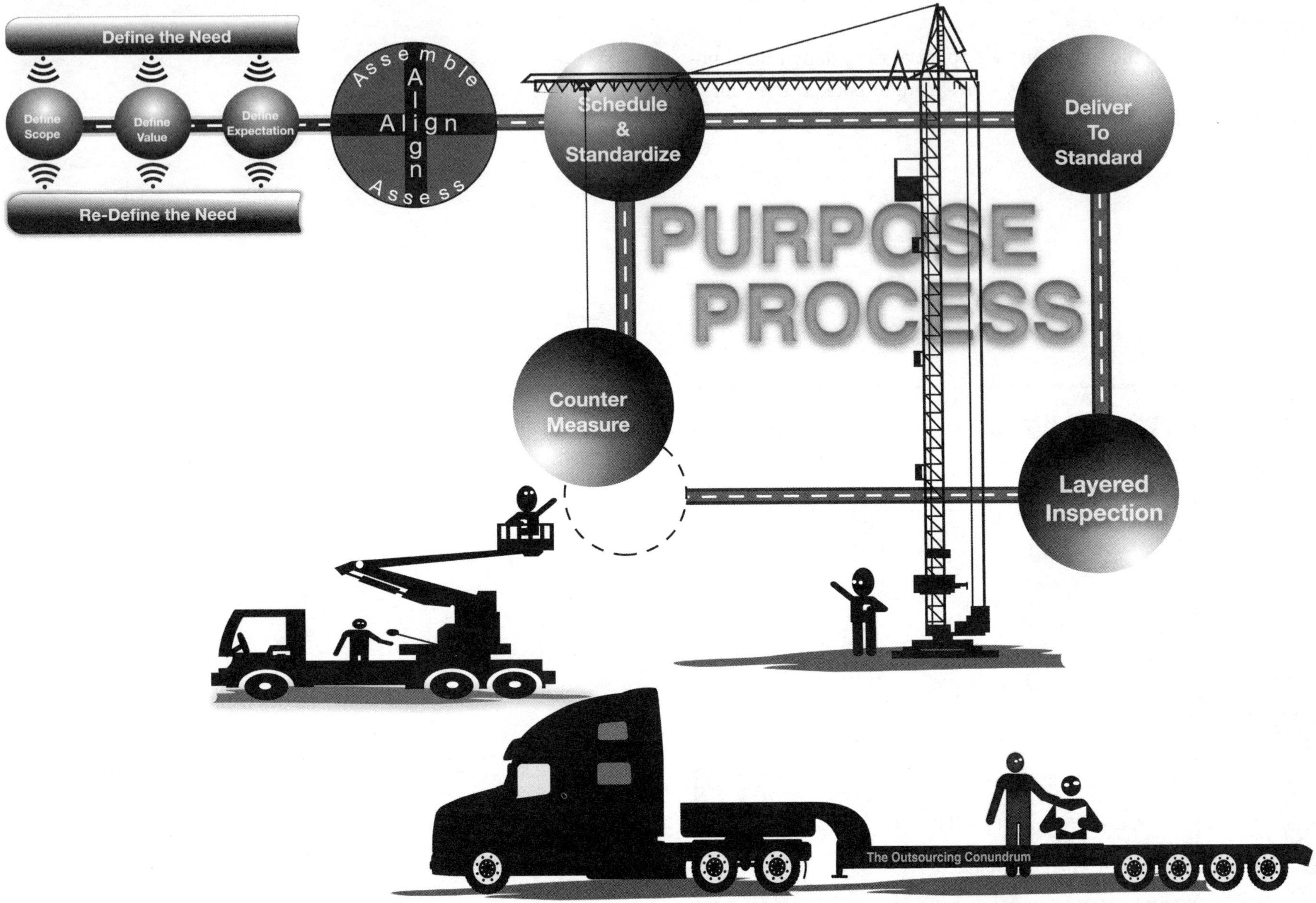

Define the Need
Define Scope
Define Value
Define Expectation
Re-Define the Need
Assemble
Align
Align
Assess
Schedule & Standardize
Deliver To Standard
PURPOSE PROCESS
Counter Measure
Layered Inspection
The Outsourcing Conundrum

"A business organization is like the human body. The human body contains autonomic nerves that work without regard to human wishes, and motor nerves that react to human command to control muscles.

"The spine of an older person does not bend easily and once bent it does not unbend quickly. This is definitely a phenomenon of aging. We observe the same phenomena in a business.

"A business should have reflexes that can respond instantly and smoothly to small changes in the plan without having to go to the brain."

Taichi Ohno

Counter measure, by my definition, and how it applies to the Outsourcing Conundrum Model, is a reflex. Academically, counter measure is most often defined as an action taken to counter or offset an undesirable outcome. I do not argue with the academic viewpoint, but add that for an IOSP to be truly great, the approach needs to be more proactive than the academic definition of counter measure implies. In order for this reflex to operate fully in a preventive manner versus a reactive manner, an IOSP must put themselves and their mindset in the place of greatest potential.

An IOSP management team will never accomplish the goal of developing the preventive reflex of counter measure if they manage from behind their desk, waiting to hear about an issue or problem. Their mindset needs to be one of continually seeking out the next problem, and their greatest potential to be able to view that next problem is on the floor, not behind their desk. In the first chapter of Part 2, Process Overview, we discuss the role of a fire marshall versus a fire fighter. A fire marshall's duties are to enact and enforce code. The purpose for the code is the prevention of fires and protection of lives. A marshall's secondary duty is to investigate fires to identify origins and root causes. A firefighter, on the other hand, reacts to the notification of a fire and, along with his teammates, heads in the direction of the smoke to extinguish the problem. It makes me cringe when I hear a management team reference their roles as "firefighting," another day another fire. Wrong attitude and wrong approach. A fire marshall views his day as an opportunity to identify a potential cause for fire and to recommend a way to avoid it in the future, in other words, to prevent or resolve a problem.

Throughout my years of working with and refining the Outsourcing Conundrum Model, I have given this counter measure step a variety of other labels:

- Act
- Adjust
- Corrective Action

None of these labels is wrong as they each speak to what is required at this step in the model, but they began to seem incomplete to me. Counter measure certainly includes the need for action, adjustment, and corrective action. However, the labels above seem more reactive than proactive. Counter measure as defined in *The Outsourcing Conundrum* applies data and trends to fight complacency and entitlement, two behaviors which turn great IOSPs into mediocre IOSPs.

In Chapter 9, Layered Inspection, I spoke about Charlie, my golf instructor, and his layered approach to teaching golf, using a disciplined process to go through the emotional, activity and outcome layers to help perfect my swing. My goal was to reduce my handicap, and there was no shortage of room for improvement. Actually, anyone passing by could probably offer me an idea that would help my game. But if I truly wanted to improve, I had to look at the overall data patterns to filter out those suggestions and prioritize them. How many holes did I par? How many tee shots made it to the fairway as planned? How many of my second shots stayed on the fairway? A simple, disciplined review of the data allowed me to provide Charlie with great insight on what we needed to work on at each subsequent instructional session. I truly appreciated all the free advice I received from other golfers, but if I listened and acted on all of it, I would have been chasing my tail. By performing counter measures based on data, my energies focused on maximizing results.

So, if we put it altogether, we define counter measure as a proactive reflex, responding to data, taken by an IOSP to prevent the undesirable outcome of becoming complacent, a has-been. In Chapter 8 we discussed the importance of soliciting ideas and suggestions from your team, as well as the concept that you need a thousand suggestions or new ideas if you are going to stay competitive.

Continual improvement suggestions and counter measures both require that the IOSP implement the levels of Layered Inspection outlined in Chapter 9. Counter measures and improvement ideas run parallel to each other by my definition. The big difference is that counter measures use the data available from the Layered Inspection to stay on course to the established target, whereas ideas or suggestions have a tendency to be more opinion-based. Let's take a look at a call to action, one through the lens of ideas or suggestions for improvement, and the other through the lens of a counter measure.

Idea for improvement or suggestion	"I think it would be easier for the team to use scaffolding as opposed to a stepladder to perform that activity."
Counter Measure	"Our observations and data conclude that many of our incidents are being caused by the use of stepladders for that activity. We need to discover a better and safer way."

Both recognize the use of step ladders as an issue. By using data, counter measure is able to put a level of scale to the problem that an idea for improvement often does not.

We found it easier to get a team to develop this attitude to service delivery if you make it very clear, in actions and in words, that you are open to new ideas and suggestions. In other words, the team member's opinions count; you are simply looking for that idea and suggestion to be further filtered through data to give it more merit. Counter measure becomes a reflex, responding to the patterns in your data that inform you action is required to correct the current direction of your service delivery. Counter measure is a disciplined approach to your service business that, with practice, becomes nothing more than a reflex to solve problems.

- I proactively seek out potential problems.
- I actively avoid problems.

If your organization does not embrace proactively looking for the next problem to solve, it will be condemned to continual, never-ending fire fighting.

This is not to say that even with counter measures in place you will not face "fires" while providing services, but the frequency of unknown problems and issues, "fires," will be greatly reduced. Because you have an attitude towards fire prevention, you will also by reflex adjust your plans to reduce recurrence of potential issues, again reducing the frequency of future fires.

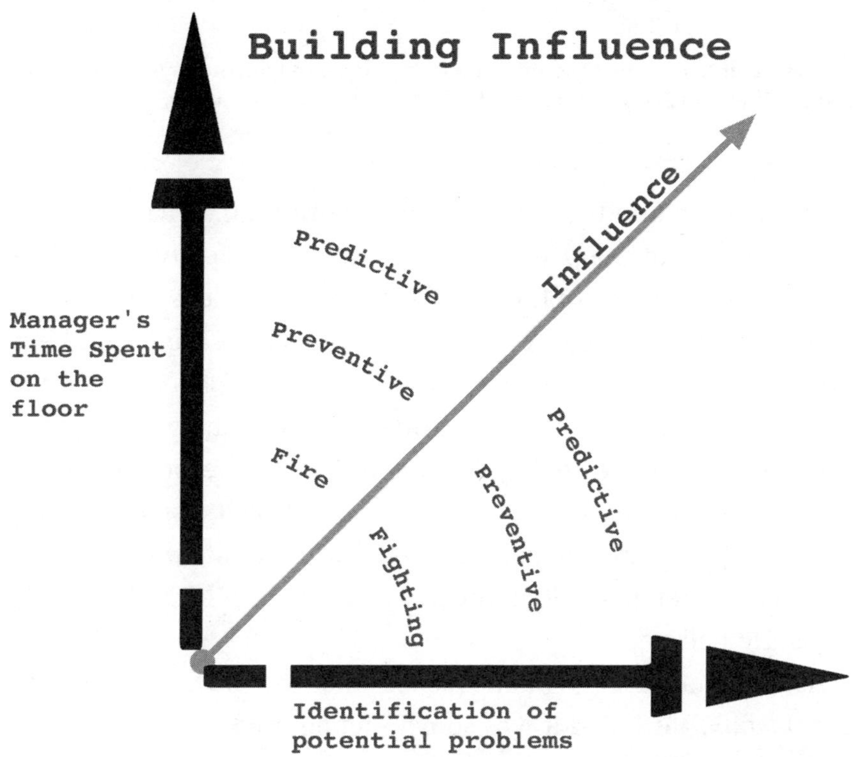

In the previous chapter, I discussed a local restaurant in Cincinnati called Boca, and how the head chef had returned a couple of dishes to the cooks to be re-done because of what they had seen during layered inspection. This action taken by the chefs was preventive. If the meals had made their way to a table only to be returned by the customer, the counter measure would have been very reactive, resulting in a negative impact to the restaurant's brand. They avoided a negative customer experience by inspecting and taking action before the problem could even impact the customer.

DEVELOPING THE REFLEX

In the late 1980s, I decided to get my small-plane pilot's license. About 24 months later I accomplished the goal, only to realize I probably did not belong piloting anything in the air. To be a truly good pilot, you must be able to stay in the cockpit mentally while flying. I had a tendency to daydream, which caused me enough wake-up calls to realize piloting was not for me. The venture, though, was a phenomenal learning experience that I applied to how we managed our operations. Before take off, you perform a pre-flight check because once you are in the air it's too late. Similarly, before you start to launch a new site or add a new customer, there are certain logical parts of the Outsourcing Conundrum Model, which we outlined in Part 1 (such as having the right scope of work, the right cost structure, and a detailed understanding of the expectations), that need to be in place.

The next thing that stuck with me from learning to fly was the use of the plane's trim tabs, located on the wings of the plane. A plane is actually a pretty easy thing to fly, but a pretty tricky thing to fly straight and on course (on target) if you do not continually adjust its trim tabs. The slightest adjustment to a trim tab adjusts the entire flight pattern of the plane, and over the course of a long journey that small adjustment could be the difference between landing at the desired location or missing it by miles. Stephen Covey discusses this in his book, *The 8th Habit: From Effectiveness to Greatness*. He talks about the people who inherently always adjust the trim tabs within an organization. He calls them "trim-tabbers," people who can exert their influence and move the direction of the organization.

It took me a while to get the hang of my plane's trim tabs. At first, adjustments were too slow, then too fast, too little or not enough, and the plane reacted accordingly. On early flights, I constantly asked the instructor if I should adjust the trim tab. He'd always say, "You're the pilot. Are you happy with the condition of your flight? If not, adjust accordingly." What he bestowed was an understanding of how I influenced my flight experiences with very small continual counter measures. With time and training, adjustment of the trim tabs became a reflex to the point where I did not consciously realize just how often I made small counter measures to align my flight path. Each adjustment was based on keeping the position of the plane on course, on target.

Similarly, counter measures for an IOSP also need to become a reflex. A reflex in the body is an involuntary movement in response to a stimulus. Similarly, with my experience of flying, I stopped thinking about whether I should or should not make a trim adjustment, or how much. I just did it. It was a reflex. By developing the reflex, I literally allowed my right hand to take initiative without gaining permission from my brain. I saw a concern, knew I could influence the outcome, and instinctively made a correction.

To develop this reflex of counter measures within an IOSP, the team has to understand what their circle of influence is, as well as how to expand their circle of influence.

In 2012 I had the opportunity to work with a site manager, Mike, who was facing some recent and growing challenges from his customer concerning their level of satisfaction with services being provided.

By developing the reflex of counter measures, you expand your influence, improve your initiative, and observe and counter your concerns.

The customer started the process of exploring other IOSP channels. On my first day at the plant, I walked the entire facility with Mike to gain an understanding of how he managed and his level of passion for the services he delivered. It was quick and easy to note that he was a very stand-up guy, really cared for his team and his customer, and could not understand why the customer was not happy. Everything in the scope of work was being done, and the team responded to every customer complaint within 24 hours. As we walked, I started to notice a pattern where someone had put their initials in different areas along with a date. After about 30 minutes, I asked Mike if he had noticed the initials. He had not.

As we continued to walk, I asked him how often he walked the entire facility. He stated it was something he tried to do every month. I stopped in the aisle and repeated, "Every *month*?" This should have been a daily activity; Mike was not "adjusting trim tabs" until he was told.

After completing the walk-though of the facility, we met with the customer's area manager to discuss and further understand his concerns. I asked him if would explain his issues. Before answering, the area manager inquired if we had walked the facility and what our observations had been. We reported that we felt the facility had met the contractual obligations outlined in the scope of work, but the facility did not look consistent area to area. The area manager agreed with the observation, and asked if we had noted anything else. I told him I had noticed someone's initials and a date in several areas of the facility. He said the initials were his, and the dates gave him a reference of how often our team, the IOSP, gave any attention to those areas. He went on to state that we had a great team who did a great job of what they were asked to do, but lacked the initiative to take service to the next level. He outlined that there was no dispute on whether or not we completed the scope of work and inspected our work. The issue was that the facility was looking for a partner to look out for their interests, and to take the initiative to move service to the next level. The area manager's needs were changing, and we were not adjusting accordingly.

We thanked him, and left with a promise to put a plan together to improve the level of initiative taken by our team. Mike and I grabbed a coffee, and I laid out a simple 90-day plan for him to follow. I asked him to observe how our team and our customer reacted to the plan. The plan was simple. Mike was to spend the first two hours of each day on the shop floor being inquisitive, nothing more.

In June of 2014, I visited the same plant to get some research material for this book. As usual, we went for a walk around the facility, and Mike discussed a new problem. He was getting bogged down with counter measures from his team, and was having a hard time processing all of them. Mike and I quickly agreed this was a great problem to have, and Mike and his team were working on effective ways to handle the volume of counter measures so as not to lose the momentum the team had achieved. Along with that, the customer was adding a large increase to the scope of work. We reflected on what a huge difference this was from where he was in 2012.

Mike fully implemented the plan we discussed in 2012—to be on the shop floor for two hours a day—and, as he spent more time on the floor, he found many areas for improvement. Following Mike's example, other management personnel also spent a lot more time on the shop floor and found many other areas for improvement. The 90-day plan of putting the management team on the shop floor became the new way they managed. By spending time on the shop floor with their customer and their team members, they increased their level of influence and were able to see and act on concerns that affected both the customer and the team members.

Over the course of a couple of years, the team moved out of the fire-fighting mode, waiting to be told what needed to be done, into the mode of being preventive, where data from layered inspection and time spent on the shop floor provided them confidence to take action to prevent something from happening. Our site manager now worked with the team to become predictive, to have the confidence to forecast that something was going to happen. The site manager told me the new business they were just awarded was a result of being predictive. They saw that sales of the plant's product were growing, and figured the plant was going to need to reallocate resources to offset the challenge, meaning additional maintenance work would need to be outsourced. Mike put himself and his team in the place of greatest potential to take advantage of the upcoming circumstance and offset the plant's concern.

Just like flying a plane, boxing, fencing, swimming, or any other activity that is reliant upon our reflexes, counter measure will become a well-tuned reflex only with the proper level and degree of training.

TRAINING THE REFLEX

So, is implementing the reflex of corrective measures as easy as going for a walk around your shop floor? Heck, no. But if you do not adopt the habit of walking in and around those who are delivering your services, then your odds of success greatly diminish. Why? Spending time with your customer and your team develops trust, and trust develops people's confidence for taking initiative. In my experience, people need to be invited out of their role and responsibility, and given the opportunity of helping to resolve, or even prevent, an issue or concern.

Familiarity with management and the customer breeds trust among team members. The best way to invite someone out of their perception of their role, and to invite them to use their hands, heads, and hearts, is to focus on moving through the emotional layers as outlined in Chapter 9, Layered Inspection.

Mike adhered to the 90-day plan, and practiced moving through the emotional layers daily:

- **Singular layer:** The hands of team members performing services are engaged as activities are inspected for compliance to standards.
- **Secondary layer:** The hands and heads of team members are engaged as activities are inspected for compliance, while also discussing "is there a better way?"
- **Plural layer:** The hands, heads, and hearts of team members are engaged as activities are inspected against revised standards, while discussing the improvement that resulted from input from the people performing the activities.

This quickly got Mike's team out of the mode of "It's not my job," and into understanding the need for improvement and the need for team members to provide input. The hurdle was to get his team not just to recognize a concern, but also to provide input to resolve the issue. Mike found it frustrating after the first several months when the team was basically asking him and his management team "What can *you* do?" when Mike was really looking for "What can *we* do?"

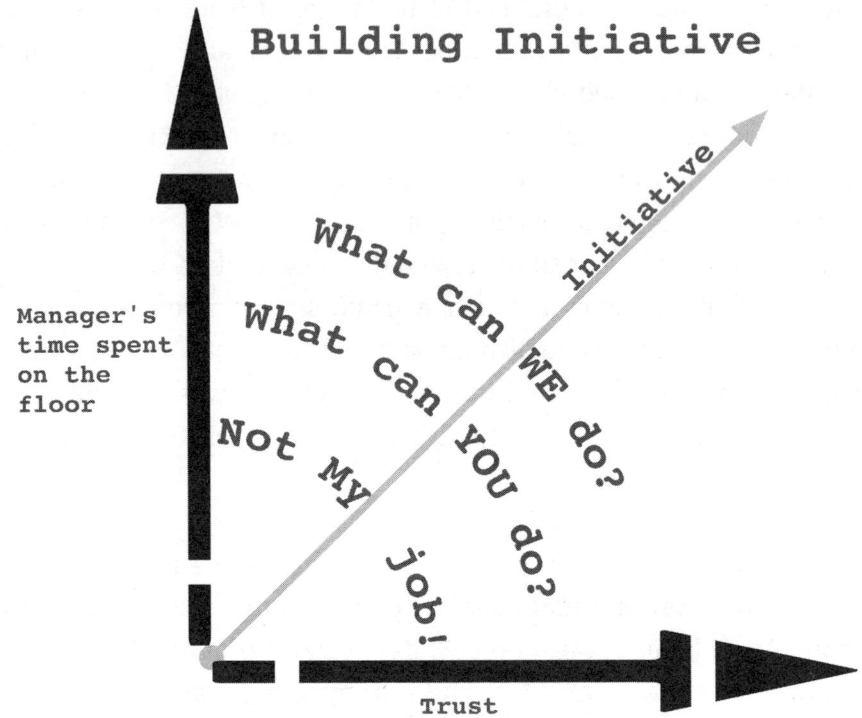

Mike's next step to train the reflex of counter measure was to become fully transparent with his team on how the team was measured, and how they were performing to those targets.

Mike learned from spending time on the floor that the more he was able to "touch" his team, the more he was trusted. He applied this mindset when it was time to inform his team on their targets. This was not going to be a one-time event, but rather a daily discussion. To achieve this goal, Mike developed a solutions room in the team room. The solutions room was a series of four-by-eight white boards that visually outlined how the group was performing. This solutions room communicated in a very transparent manner where the team excelled and where there was room for improvement. The solutions room performed the exact same purpose as the CUBE described in Chapter 9, Layered Inspection.

In order to give his team an initial jump start, Mike decided to create a theme by declaring war on waste:

- Waste of effort – energy spent on non-value add activities.
- Waste of inventory – too much stock resulting in inefficient store rooms.
- Waste of movement – too many steps being taken between value-added activities.
- Waste of re-work – activities having to be re-done due to poor standards or training.
- Waste of time – spending valuable time in non-productive activities, processes, or meetings.

The team was asked daily to look around the solutions room and, from their observations on the floor, identify potential areas of waste and develop a solution to get back on target or improve the target.

The solutions room, like the CUBE, accomplished the goal of providing team members with information, as well as acting as the stimulus and source for prioritization, for discussing what is acceptable, and what can *we* do to improve to become the best.

The team, through daily start-of-shift meetings in the solutions room, began to realize that by reducing waste through many different small counter measures, they were being rewarded with more and more opportunities to provide services to the customer, which for many meant better career opportunities.

The team also discovered that work became easier, methods were better, and tools more aligned. As the site improved, the team's ability to spend time on improvement projects also increased. As stated earlier, Mike and his team now faced a new problem: how to process the volume of improvement suggestions being provided by team members to reduce waste at *their* site, not *his* site.

> "Efficiency is simply a matter of doing work using the best methods known, not the worst."
>
> Henry Ford

As the team continued to train and practice around the reflex of counter measure, Mike pushed the team a bit further and introduced the idea of What If?

One of the biggest concerns Mike faced was the ability to hire really good people. As we all know, and as we will discuss in detail in Part 3, people will make or break you as an IOSP. Being open and transparent, the team began to understand some of the issues they faced as services continued to grow. At one team meeting the team asked, "What if we were involved in the hiring?"

Mike and his management team were ecstatic to have the team step up and present a counter measure to what was easily the most challenging problem they faced, the identification and attraction of good talent and the "right" talent.

This was a huge step forward, and it benchmarked for Mike and his management team that the disciplined training of the counter measure reflex was delivering better-than-expected initiative from the broader team.

In the previous chapter, we met Norm and discussed the levels of improvement his site had experienced. Similarly to Mike, Norm's site had set up a means to communicate visually and inform every team member of all information necessary to operate as a great IOSP. At Norm's plant, data pointed out that the group spent an undesirable amount of time and energy in maintenance activities associated with repairing the spindles used in production machinery. The energy and effort caused by these spindles distracted the team from being able to focus on other areas of the machines that also needed their attention. The team agreed a counter measure was needed to offset the growing number of hours spent fixing this one issue.

Our maintenance team, in alignment with the customer's engineering staff, researched options to improve the actual maintenance activities. They also went back to the original equipment manufacturer (OEM) to explore options for re-engineering the spindles. Over the course of several months and several trials, a new spindle constructed of different alloys was identified and installed into the production equipment. This new spindle was more tolerant of the stress associated with engine production, which resulted in improved machine uptime and reduced time spent on machine maintenance. This counter measure was viewed by the customer as a true value-add. It also enhanced the perception of our brand greatly, especially by the production workers who relied upon the production machine uptime to meet their production targets.

THE CHICAGO FIRE

This is the cow, at the O'Leary back gate,
Where she stood on the night of October the 8,
With her old crumpled horn and belligerent hoof,
Warning all "neighbor women" to keep well aloof.

Ah! this is the cow with the crumpled horn
That kicked over the lamp that set fire to the barn
That caused the Great Fire in Chicago!

Published by the *Insurance Monitor*

The Great Chicago Fire burned from Sunday, October 8, to early Tuesday, October 10, 1871. The fire killed approximately 300 people, and destroyed roughly three square miles of Chicago, leaving more than 100,000 residents homeless.

Absolutely no level of preventive or predictive counter measure would ever have been able to offset the published cause of the Great Chicago Fire, Bessie the cow, who some say knocked over a lantern in the barn of the O'Leary home. The cow was later deemed innocent as more facts became known about the fire.

The degree and level of major issues that an IOSP faces is in large part associated with the level of risk and the culture of the customer for whom you have chosen to work. There are situations where you do everything right, but you still face times when the cause is out of your control and the remedy is your direct responsibility. Thankfully I have not experienced anything to the degree of the Chicago Fire in my IOS career; however, over the decades there have been problems out of our control that nevertheless required us to take significant counter measures in order to provide a solution for the customer. These were the result of:

- Bankruptcy by our customer, like the one faced by the auto industry.
- Recalls of our customer's product, resulting in drastic changes to a plant's production schedule.
- A change in ownership where our customer was acquired by a new company with a different operating style or culture.
- A natural disaster, like the 2011 Tsunami, resulting in a disruption to the supply chain, which in turn affected production.
- Changes in customer's upper management.
- Loss of talent, where key personnel were no longer part of the team.
- Major safety violations resulting in loss of life or limb, or extended hospitalization.

Situations like these and others require a more formal approach to problem solving. There are a great many methods established for, and books dealing with, solving such problems; for example, *Managing to Learn, Using the A3 Management Process to Solve Problems, Gain Agreement, Mentor and Lead,* by John Shook, and Mike Cartner's book *The 8-Disciplines: Problem Solving Methodology*. Two of these (*Using the A3 Management Process to Solve Problems*, and *The 8-Disciplines*) provide great step-by-step approaches to problem solving, which became known as A3 and 8D. Over the years, I have spent time with both methodologies, and found them great resources and systems for getting to the root cause and solving a problem. Regardless of the chosen system, what I have learned over time is that it is imperative as an IOSP that you choose a problem-solving methodology for your organization and train your people in the use of it.

Situations like those described above have a set of common requirements that must be put in place to establish a resilient counter measure.

- You must clearly identify the problem you are trying to solve and not one of the problem's symptoms.
- You must develop a containment plan while the root cause is being sought.
- You must locate the root cause.
- You must choose your corrective actions.
- You must validate your choices.
- You must standardize what you have done so it can be repeated.

The continual use of a standardized problem-solving methodology develops a mindset or habit that can become a great reflex for counter measures. But beware, applying a full-blown problem-solving discipline to day-to-day smaller course corrections or counter measures can be overkill, and can inhibit many team members from participating in the process. We found it much better to use the tools as they best fit the needs. The bigger the issue, the more structured and disciplined the approach; the smaller the need, the lighter and more fluid the approach.

Over time we adopted the phrase "8D or A3 light," meaning a less structured approach to day-to-day problem solving, but using the general outlines of problem solving.

POINT OF NO RETURN

Over my years as an executive leader of an IOSP, there were a handful of times where the only counter measure to offset a series of concerns was "firing of the customer." We diligently abided by all of the steps we have discussed so far in *The Outsourcing Conundrum*, but, as I have stated and shown, we also made our fair share of mistakes. One of the most critical mistakes was to take on a customer who "used" an IOSP as a means to an end, a scapegoat, a customer with no moral compass in terms of what it meant to our people. On one occasion we were asked by a chemical company to clean its tank farm on a time and material basis, where the customer was charged for every hour it took the team to complete the task. As we were setting up the project, we noticed that foliage extending off one corner of the tank farm was very dead. The dead foliage actually formed a path down to Lake Ontario. After a discussion with a few of the farm's maintenance staff, we found out that the chemical company had ruined a batch of adhesive and the contents of the tanks were extremely hazardous. The data sheet supplied to us with the project omitted this information. This company's leadership was willing to put our team in harm's way to achieve their goal. Yes, we left.

The companies we fired typically had no regard for their environment, and were not above dumping waste into local streams. Some had little regard for the health and welfare of their employees, as they allowed a plant to be contaminated by vapors but were not willing to provide proper personal protective equipment, (PPE). Companies where plants operated at temperatures above a reasonable standard, and people collapsed from heat exhaustion and dehydration. Customer management teams who were hostile, abusive, and practiced forms of harassment. In these cases our only counter measure was to walk away. These customers today are very much the exception. I find more and more that many companies take the lead when it comes to setting good examples and being great corporate citizens.

The use of the Site Strategic Operation Plan (SSOP) is an annual counter measure to offset the risk of the customer having a point of no return and wishing to replace us as the IOSP. The SSOP is used as a strategic tool to align the service the IOSP is providing with the needs of the customer for the upcoming year. The tool outlines the measures for success inherent in providing great service, and outlines the initiatives requiring focus by the management team. Earlier in this chapter when Mike declared war on waste, he chose that area because waste reduction was one of the major strategic themes on his SSOP.

BEST PRACTICE

It was a chilly, rainy November morning down at Team Trek as a management group started an event in which they needed to transfer the entire team from a starting platform, across a hollow via several well-placed pylons, to a platform on the opposite side. The pylons were strategically positioned in their distance from one another so that there was only one safe path to cross the hollow. The team needed to identify the path and move each team member safely across the hollow.

It is very common to identify counter measures with production and manufacturing variances, but not so common when looking at counter measures to offset a management style or gap in leadership. At Team Trek, the goal is development of leaders, teams, and winning cultures. The group trying to cross the hollow was not experiencing success. They became increasingly frustrated and cold, and related negatively to their failure as this was their second so far that morning. The target for every group is that they grow as a team and are able to defeat the events. This team was not growing, and the root cause needed to be flushed out.

Instead of just moving the team forward in the program, we decided to take a time-out and challenge the team to flush out the root cause. To an observer of the group, the root cause was extremely evident. The boss, who was among the group, was not allowing the team's talents to come to the forefront during the events. He was very much the man with all the answers who took credit for their successes and quickly blamed others when they failed.

The group was taken inside, and, during an uncomfortable debrief, the boss's style was deemed the root cause. He was asked to step to one side and allow his team to perform.

Although they had just spent two frustrating hours in the rain trying to move their team across the hollow, the group asked to repeat the event. The team, absent the boss's counsel, developed a plan, appointed a team leader from within the group, and successfully completed the event in 11 minutes.

Two counter measures were enacted for the team to get back on course. The boss had to be told he was part of the problem as his style encouraged bad performance and sub-optimal performance. The team needed to repeat an event and get a success under their belt so they could rebuild their confidence and move on to much more demanding situations.

In a debrief that night, the team informed their boss that his management style, made very clear to him during the event, was the reason the team was missing their targets back at the office. Measure and counter measure.

QUICK STORY

In 2013 I visited one of our sites in Canada to meet with a newly appointed production area manager. He wanted to outline some observations of our service he had made in the few weeks since his new appointment.

He pointed out that although we were well regarded in the facility, he felt there was room for improvement. I shared with him that I could not agree more. As our goal was to be the best IOSP, we would never be happy, and must strive for year-over-year improvement.

During the discussion, I also shared with him our improvement over the past three years, and how the incremental gains our team had made related to improvements in his own production through-put. He stated that he knew of our success, but felt we wasted a lot of time. He went on to point out that he noticed our people walking the plant as they moved from one activity to another. Curious, I asked, "Were they being unsafe?" He stated no, just unproductive. He then asked me if I had ever considered giving the team dusters to put in both of their hands so as they walked, they would be able be more productive and clean as they moved through the plant.

I was sure he was joking so I said, "We could also connect mops to their shoes." Sadly, he was not joking. He thought adding mops to shoes was a good idea but might be a bit dangerous. He also said I should not give up on the idea; it just needed tweaking a bit. Seriously? How these guys get these positions I will never understand. Luckily, his stint in the role lasted only a year and he was moved on to bigger and better things. I wonder if his new group is wearing Nike-mops?

Counter measure, like layered inspection, is a great opportunity for an IOSP to truly engage its team and develop an enhanced level of competitiveness. This will never be the case if your team is not given the respect they deserve for what they do (or they are demeaned by turning them into walking mop-people).

In his book Navigating Change, Gary Gore speaks to the importance of identifying stopping points that represent missed marks when navigating the wilderness. He goes on to explain that the same rules apply to business. Missed business targets, like missed stopping points when you are orienteering, are symptomatic of being potentially lost. Both require that you take a counter measure.

We do not always have control of what takes us off course, but we can certainly control how well we correct our course and get ourselves and our team back on track and on target.

TAKEAWAYS:

- Counter measure is a reflex that prevents undesirable outcomes.
- To develop the reflex, the management team must operate from the floor, not their desk.
- To train the reflex, information must be prevalent and transparent.
- Everyone should understand how to solve a problem, everyone.

PART 3
PEOPLE

PEOPLE

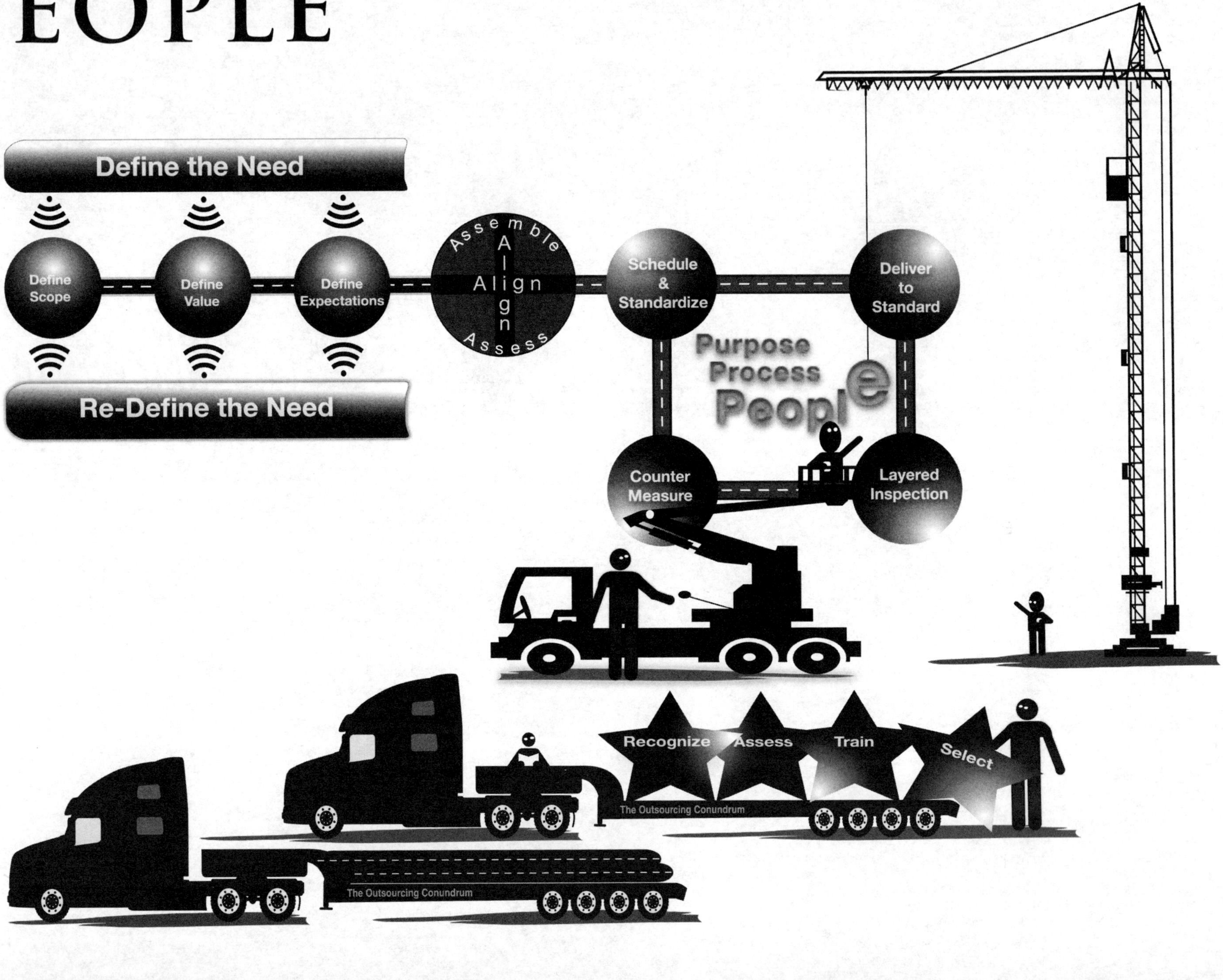

Define the Need
Define Scope
Define Value
Define Expectations
Assemble
Align
Align
Assess
Schedule & Standardize
Deliver to Standard
Purpose
Process
People
Counter Measure
Layered Inspection
Re-Define the Need
Recognize
Assess
Train
Select
The Outsourcing Conundrum
The Outsourcing Conundrum

Recently, I was sitting in a restaurant in Kansas City. A man about two tables away kept looking at me. I didn't recognize him. A few minutes into our meal he stood up and walked over to my table, looked down at me, pointed his finger in my face and said, "You're Captain Plumb."

I looked up and I said, "Yes sir, I'm Captain Plumb."

He said, "You flew jet fighters in Vietnam. You were on the aircraft carrier Kitty Hawk. You were shot down. You parachuted into enemy hands and spent six years as a prisoner of war."

I said, "How in the world did you know all that?"

He replied, "Because, I packed your parachute."

I was speechless. I staggered to my feet and held out a very grateful hand of thanks. This guy came up with just the proper words. He grabbed my hand, he pumped my arm and said, "I guess it worked."

"Yes sir, indeed it did," I said, "and I must tell you I've said a lot of prayers of thanks for your nimble fingers, but I never thought I'd have the opportunity to express my gratitude in person."

He said, "Were all the panels there?"

"Well sir, I must shoot straight with you," I said, "of the eighteen panels that were supposed to be in that parachute, I had fifteen good ones. Three were torn, but it wasn't your fault, it was mine. I jumped out of that jet fighter at a high rate of speed, close to the ground. That's what tore the panels in the chute. It wasn't the way you packed it."

"Let me ask you a question," I said, "Do you keep track of all the parachutes you pack?"

"No," he responded. "It's enough gratification for me just to know that I've served."

I didn't get much sleep that night. I kept thinking about that man. I kept wondering what he might have looked like in a Navy uniform – a Dixie cup hat, a bib in the back and bell bottom trousers. I wondered how many times I might have passed him on board the Kitty Hawk. I wondered how many times I might have seen him and not even said, "Good morning," "How are you," or anything because, you see, I was a fighter pilot and he was just a sailor. How many hours did he spend on that long wooden table in the bowels of that ship weaving the shrouds and folding the silks of those chutes? I could have cared less...until one day my parachute came along and he packed it for me.

So the philosophical question here is this: How's your parachute packing coming along? Who looks to you for strength in times of need? And perhaps, more importantly, who are the special people in your life who provide you the encouragement you need when the chips are down? Perhaps it's time right now to give those people a call and thank them for packing your chute.

Charlie Plumb,
Excerpt from Chapter 16, "Packing Parachutes," from
Insights into Excellence

We have discussed the importance of Purpose and Process, and the need for them to be aligned with customer needs. But beyond the need for that alignment, the service industry is completely reliant upon people, and, therefore, they must be aligned with your customers' needs as well. People are the roots that provide sustenance to the limbs to produce the result.

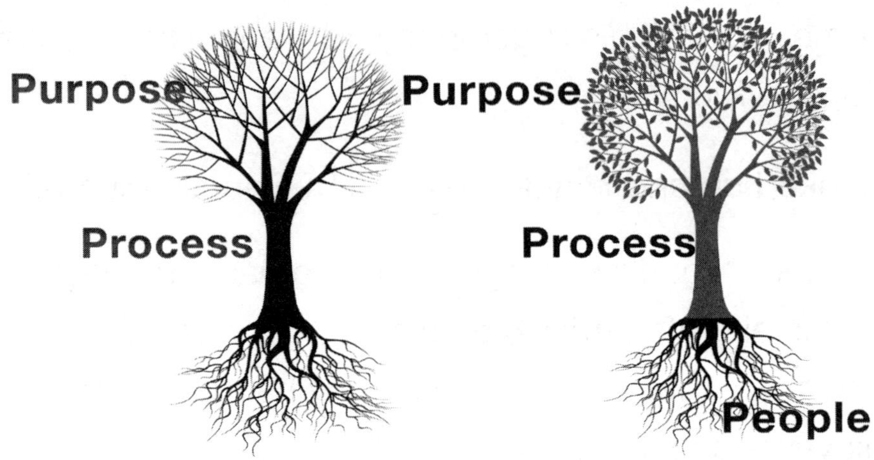

As Charlie Plumb puts it, very often we forget about the people who carry out mundane day-to-day tasks until we need them. We have a blow-up with a customer, and all of a sudden the person who did the work gets a whole bunch of attention. Does this parachute packer get any attention at any other time? Does this parachute packer have the equipment and tools he needs to do the job safely, effectively, and with dignity? Has this parachute packer received a "thank-you" for the countless number of tasks he has completed over the past months? Has anyone spoken to this parachute packer about what he may be able to do to grow and develop?

How an IOSP decides to behave towards the people who deliver the service inevitably creates the culture and brand perceived by the marketplace.

In an effort to grow our business and make a strategic move into Mexico, we acquired a small Mexican IOSP. It was a good, reputable company with good talent and a good customer base. The company utilized good processes, but lacked a strategic direction and an attitude to being people-centric. On a site visit with the management team of the company we had acquired, I noticed a very concerning trait. The management team would walk by team members performing the work and pay them no mind. They had not dialed into the fact that these people packed their parachute. At that time, the management team saw team members as interchangeable, disposable components of their business. Our culture was drastically different. We believed our people were the core to our success, and their engagement was critical to our long-term profitability.

In order to achieve the required cultural transformation, we spent time on joint strategic planning, which included defining our people as a core strength and differentiator. The Mexican management teams were enrolled into our management training sessions at Team Trek, which also emphasized the importance of Charlie Plumb's message of gratitude towards the parachute packer.

It was not a fast transformation and not everyone was able to make the transformation, but, regardless of geography, it was critical that how we viewed and respected our people was universal; it was our brand. Once we had clearly defined how we viewed our people, the next order of business was defining how we viewed our circumstance and our customer. Did we act as victims of our circumstance or leaders of our circumstance?

VICTIMS AND WARRIORS

Charlie Plumb, in his books and video, talks about another subject he calls "prison thinking." It is a state of mind that you allow yourself to fall into, thinking that everyone is out to get you, and nothing is your fault, and this is not your battle or your fight. In this state of mind, you give up your own personal control and your ability to cope. You no longer believe in the values of the company you work for, or the value of the services being provided. You are a victim.

The managers of our people needed to be excellent at day-to-day management, but they also needed to be good leaders. They needed the ability to be positive in order to improve their coping abilities and not to get trapped into the mindset of prison thinking, of being a victim.

In 2008 at one of our sites in Alabama, the plant went through a very large re-organization. Many of our customer's employees who had been our primary liaisons for the past five years moved on to new and different roles. This type of change within customer ranks can cause havoc for an IOSP. Our management team had spent years fine-tuning reports and inspections, and building rapport with this customer team. Now there were all sorts of new players. Our site manager made a choice. He arranged a meeting with the new customer liaisons to communicate how we currently performed our service and, more importantly, to understand from them what their "new" needs were. He then followed up with all of his team members at shift meetings, reconfirmed his gratitude to them for packing his parachute, and explained to them what changes would be needed as they moved forward. The entire scope of this exercise consumed a month of this manager's time, but it achieved two very important outcomes:

- He went to the front lines, and sought out his new challenge.
- He engaged his broader team in conquering the new challenge.

He made the choice not to be a victim, and he respected his team enough to engage them in the solution. He gave his team the choice to win or lose at their own hands, and not at the hands of others. As simple as this sounds, there are countless stories of on-site management teams working through customer changes who take a wait-and-see attitude. They become victims of their circumstance, and in turn let their team down.

Kim S. Cameron in his book, *Positive Leadership: Strategies for Extraordinary Performance*, talks about the need for a positive environment if a company wishes to achieve a positive result. He discusses how positive emotions need to outweigh negative emotions for a positive climate to exist. Acknowledgment of your team, and being a warrior, not a victim of your circumstance, are foundational to the development of a positive culture.

By building on these foundational blocks, an IOSP can begin to create a positive climate and set the stage for a high-performance culture.

CULTURE

A positive and high-performing culture is an extremely sensitive creature. I worked directly in three IOSP cultures over my 40 years, and each culture operated from a fundamentally different perspective: one focused primarily on their processes, one focused on their people, and one focused on using technology. Each focal point determined how they chose to differentiate themselves from the competition. Each company and culture had their share of success because, regardless of the vantage point they chose for directing their company, each of them picked their direction based on customer feedback. So many companies today make the mistake of spending countless hours discussing "who they are" and "how they do what they do," versus getting out into the marketplace and opening up dialogue with their key customers about what they want and need.

In the late '90s, we performed a process we called "Voice of the Customer." We spent time identifying our key customers – those with whom we wanted to do business, and those who valued what we did. We also sought to understand common needs, or threads, shared by all of our key customers. Feedback informed us that our customers were of one mind on several points:

- They looked for reliable and predictable services.
- They looked for our leadership and team members to be able to understand and deliver on their needs.
- They looked for "Cultural Fit."

As a result of these findings, dialogue with our key customers opened up a much bigger internal dialogue within our own organization. We needed to figure out what our culture was. How could we foster a people-centric culture, to continually meet the needs of our key customers? We knew from our years in business that if we lost sight of how to manage our culture to keep pace with our customers, it would take us years to bring it back.

We began to understand more clearly what "culture" meant and how powerful it was. What we did not fully understand were the ingredients that created and shaped one culture over another. What did we need to do to dial in and engineer our culture to align with a moving market and increasing customer demand?

It is important to note that an engineered cultural change, a positive change done on purpose and by design, will take much longer than a negative change done by accident. Kim S. Cameron, in his book, *Positive Leadership: Strategies for Extraordinary Performance*, speaks to how we are groomed from infancy to focus on negative events versus positive events. He outlines how from birth we are trained to pay attention to triggers on negative events, such as screeching car tires or sirens that put us into a default survival mode. Today's managers who face constant obstacles, threats to their business, and day-to-day problems, can quickly and easily slide down a negative path. A company's culture is a very sensitive creature, requiring constant care and attention to keep it positive, but how? How do you find or develop a people-centric culture, a culture that puts the people of your company smack in the middle of the cultural gear driving your business to meet the expectations of your customers?

In Part 3 I am going to show and explain how focusing on the selection, training, assessment and recognition of your people will allow you to engineer a culture that is aligned to your customers' and your own organization's needs.

In the 1990s I had the opportunity to attend the Ross Business School at the University of Michigan, where I met Dave Ulrich, a professor of business administration, who had written countless books discussing cultural alignment and the role of human resources. I was desperately looking for answers on how we could foster a people-centric culture, while facing explosive growth and increased customer demands.

Dave sat at the front of the class beside an overheard projector (remember, this was almost two decades ago), and as he taught, he would also doodle and sketch onto transparencies. As a visual learner, I put a lot of effort into capturing his doodles and sketches, and at the end of each day would process them into a series of notes.

Dave was great at taking questions during his class, and opening up the class to a free-flowing dialogue. In the class was an HR executive from a dominant retail chain, and he asked Dave a very good question: "What drives culture?"

Characteristically, Dave answered the question while doodling a sketch onto a transparency. I copied down the diagram while listening to the discussion. Dave began the discussion with several statements and questions: "Your strategy and promise to your customer is to be the lowest-cost provider of retail products. In order to do that, your company needs to be very capable at managing your company's costs?" The retail executive agreed, and Dave's doodle started to take shape, outlining the company's strategy based on the needs of the customer, which identified the key capabilities of the retail company. The first two boxes of the sketch, strategy and capability, outlined the desired culture – a company focused on being the lowest-cost provider by being expert at managing costs.

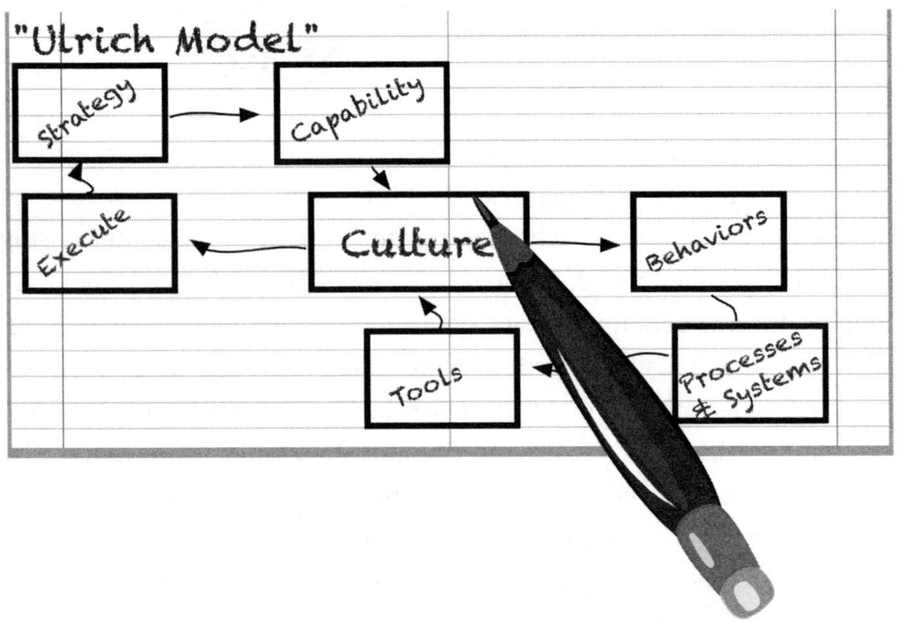

The HR retail executive agreed, and then asked, "What needs to be done to realize your desired culture? How do you shape a culture to execute on your strategy?" Dave moved on with his line of questioning, asking about how employees needed to behave to deliver the stated promise to the customer. What processes and tools were required and how would they be aligned to support the employees to deliver on promises to customers.

It became very clear during the discussion that if you promise to be the lowest-cost provider by expertly managing your costs, you cannot have an employee base behaving with no regard to how they use the company's resources. The company's behaviors must be aligned with the desired culture. You cannot expect desired behaviors to take root if the company's processes and tools are not effective and efficient at helping everyone manage cost. The adherence to this alignment of behavior, process, and tools builds the roots of the culture that will execute and implement your strategy.

The discussion that flowed from the question asked by the retail HR executive provided me with a simple model for how to manage and influence our culture. This sketch, which I came to call the "Ulrich Model," served me well. Like all models, it has evolved over the years, as has our understanding of, and knowledge about, managing and engineering our culture.

Part 3 will outline the steps we took to align, shape, create, and monitor a culture driven to meet the needs of our customers, focusing on small incremental changes and trying to avoid large disruptive time-consuming changes.

Culture is extremely important to every company, but, to those of us who are IOSPs, it's even more difficult to manage because we place teams of our people inside the culture of our customer's company, in addition to exposing them to our own culture. The school

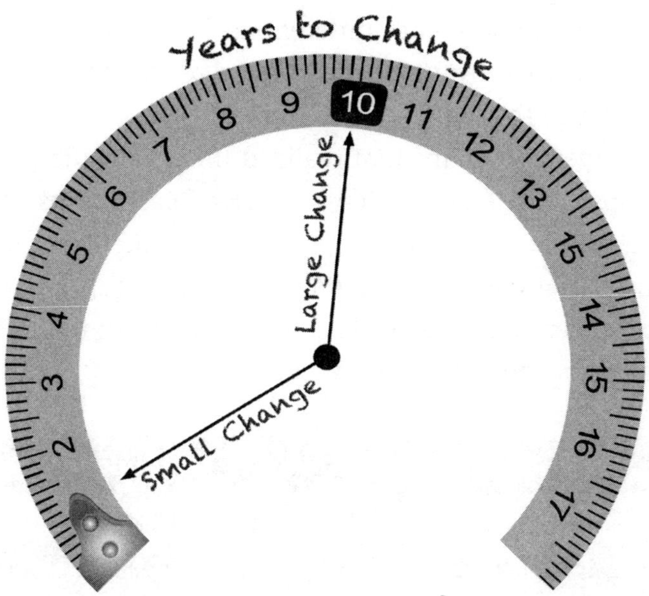

of hard knocks taught us a very valuable lesson about the importance of cultural fit with our customers. We had customers who were headquartered in Detroit, Tokyo, and Stuttgart, all of whom manufactured cars, but each of whom had very different cultures. Even within each customer organization the product lines varied from the high-end vehicle to the more economical vehicle, and the cultures of those individual plants were different. Furthermore, these customers also had plants operating in Canada, USA, Mexico, China, and Brazil, so geography also created some cultural challenges.

Our goal was to partner with our customers to deliver our services so that we could make measurable improvement in the quality, production uptime, and total cost for our customers. We delivered on this goal by adhering to our values to be the best, respect our people, satisfy our customers, and grow profitably. We would never have achieved this goal without a dedicated focus on the "fit" of our leadership, those who managed our customer site locations.

In 2005 we purchased a small company in Ontario that provided logistics service to an automotive assembly plant. The acquisition was done in alignment with our customer's need to consolidate suppliers who understood their philosophy and worked harmoniously within their culture. The company we acquired was small, about 30 to 40 people who loaded finished cars onto railway cars and trucks.

At the first meeting with this new team, the level of negativity and mistrust was evident. We first thought it was directed towards us, but quickly found out it was a lack of trust in their previous owner and they viewed this change of ownership as just one more negative step. The previous owner touted best-in-class service while providing minimal direction, poor processes and tools, and a continued lack of respect for the team. When we spoke about our values to be the best, respect our people, and satisfy the customer while growing profitably, we were met with a lot of resistance. In an open dialogue, we started to outline their concerns and set dates to review them and report back with corrective action plans. Our success with this acquisition relied on our capability to engage this team to meet the strategic needs of the customer.

One of the team members of our newly-acquired crew asked a jabbing question: "Which of the reserved parking spaces in front of the building are you going to use?" Our site manager gave him a puzzled look, and asked him to clarify his point. The team member said, “Let me show you.” He walked him out front, and pointed to 12 spots in front of the operations building, each posted with a “Reserved or Else” sign. The site manager did something that totally changed the tone of the meeting. He walked to the end of the row, took the first sign, shook the post until it came free, and dropped it on the ground. He proceeded to the next and the next. At the fourth post, he asked the team member, “What are you waiting for? Give me a hand.” in a matter of a few minutes, all of the signs were down. The manager turned to the team member and the many others who had followed them out and said, “Here you go, and they are all yours.”

That simple display of leadership changed the tone of the meeting, laying the foundation that would turn the team into warriors instead of victims, and giving them control over their own destiny. This choice of leader was a perfect fit for this project and this customer.

LEADERSHIP

No horse gets anywhere until he is harnessed.

No steam or gas ever drives anything until it is confined.

No Niagara is ever turned into light and power until it is tunneled.

No life ever grows great until it is focused, dedicated, disciplined.

Henry Emerson Fosdick

A common denominator that differentiated site locations where we realized great success from those where we realized mediocre success was the caliber of the management team on site.

The management teams that realized the greatest level of success were also those that demonstrated strong leadership traits. In the table, I contrast traits between leadership and management. A management team needs to possess all the traits within the group, but the person on top, the leader, needs to exhibit more of the traits under leadership than under management.

Leadership	Management
People	Activities, tasks
Empowerment, engagement	Control, structure
Principles	Practices
Direction	Pace, speed
Effectiveness	Efficiency
Value	Cost
Doing the right thing	Doing the thing right, on-time
Purpose	Process

As we continue into Part 3, we will discuss the steps we took to select, train, assess and recognize our management teams to ensure we had the right kind of leadership at the site level. It was critical to our success that our site leadership embodied our brand promise to our customer. If we failed at this level, and we did on occasion, the on-site culture failed and our service delivery failed. In other words, you have to get this cultural fit stuff right at the very top levels before you can hope to make it work among the employees on the floor.

BEST PRACTICE

In 2007 I read a book called *The Dream Manager*, by Matthew Kelly. The book talked about a fictitious company that struggled with employee disengagement, turnover, poor productivity, and low morale. Instead of throwing in the towel, this company investigated to find out what really drove their employees. They learned a very interesting fact: their employees were not necessarily motivated by the promise of a larger paycheck, but rather by the ability to achieve a personal goal or dream. The company created a new position they called a "Dream Manager." The role and responsibility for the "Dream Manager" was to interact with employee teams, and to work with them to fulfill their dreams.

As it turned out, the company referenced in Matthew Kelly's book is actually a real company located in Cincinnati. I had the opportunity to meet with the CEO, Mary, and discuss the concept of the "Dream Manager." Mary's company is a janitorial IOSP, so the wage scale is on the low end, with employees living from paycheck to paycheck in an industry notorious for high turnover and minimal loyalty. Mary believed that if she offered help and encouragement, she could help her people realize their dreams. She pointed out that if our personal dreams are not met, we live forever dissatisfied with our lives, our jobs, our careers.

With the incorporation of the "Dream Manager," one per every 300 employees, Mary found that about 35 percent of her team took advantage of the opportunity. Her productivity for square foot of area cleaned doubled. Her turnover shrank and customer satisfaction rose.

Mary believed that her company would become the best it could be only if her people could become the best at who they are. She pointed out that by creating value for her people, they created value for the customer, which in turn improved her profitability, allowing her to create a more positive culture for her people.

QUICK STORY

As I was preparing for this chapter and re-reading my notes on positive versus negative climates from Kim Cameron's book *Positive Leadership*, an old story popped into my mind.

It was a Friday morning, and I received a call from the administrative assistant of the plant manager for our customer site in Northern Ohio. She said that Tony requested I visit the plant at my earliest convenience. I drove up first thing Monday morning. Between receiving the call and driving up, I reached out to everyone involved at the site to try to get a handle on Tony's issue. No luck, and no information. Everything was apparently okay. I cannot tell you how many times I have heard those words.

Tony met me in his outer office and brought me into his office. "Coffee?" he asked. "Great. Black," I responded. "Please have a seat," he offered. I smiled and looked calm, but my guts were wrenching, waiting to hear about the issue and how bad it was.

"When I agreed to use your company, you promised me my facility would be in better shape." "I remember," I stated cautiously, holding the cup of black coffee. "Well, you have not met my expectations." Here it comes," I thought. "You have exceeded my expectations, and I wanted to meet you and tell you personally." Tony went on to explain why he felt that way, how his overall production uptime had been improving, and how his plant people were much happier.

As I drove home, I placed several calls to apologize to a few people. I had assumed this was going to be a negative experience, and because of that I assumed my team had dropped the ball and kept me in the dark, and I had told them as much before going to meet with Tony. Kim Cameron's message that feeling negative is more powerful than feeling positive rang very true, and, due to my assumption, I created a negative environment that actually hurt the good news we received. It also made me appreciate more what Mary had been able to accomplish through focusing her energy on the positive, on helping her people be the best at who they are.

PROCUREMENT

One of my responsibilities each and every month was the review of our operational metrics. One of those metrics was our profit-and-loss ratio. For the decades I reviewed our site locations, and for the hundreds of sites I reviewed on a monthly basis, one thing was always a constant. The people expense on the profit-and-loss statement represented no less than 90 percent of my operating cost.

Over the years I have met with dozens of leaders who shared a similar array of responsibilities, and all of these other leaders also ran businesses where the number-one operating cost was the people expense. Actually, we prefer to phrase it, "our number-one operating cost is our investment in people."

Based on this fact, procurement groups would do themselves a huge favor by spending far more time with their IOSPs to understand how an IOSP creates and shapes their own culture, and how they align that culture with their customers. If purchasing were to pay a few dollars more to hire a company like Mary's, would we all not be a lot better off?

In Part 3, you'll notice a new "Procurement" section like this at the end of each chapter. This section is addressed specifically to those companies who are hiring IOSPs to work with them, rather than to the IOSPs themselves. It's in this Part only because, as the customer of the IOSP, the easiest way to make a difference to the effectiveness of your partnership with an IOSP is to focus on the people aspects.

If you are going to start anywhere in attempting to maximize your investment in inside-outsourcing, start with the people. It's extremely important that you pay close attention to the people who are coming into your facility to work alongside your own company's employees. If you get the people piece right, all the other parts will fall into place more easily.

And while we're on the subject, a word of advice about the flip side of the coin. If you are an IOSP, you should be selling your customers and prospective customers on your people, how key they are to a successful partnership, and that you've got a model in place to make the fit between your people and the customer a good one.

Understanding the culture and environment you desire and how to shape your working climate is very important as you move onto Assembling, Aligning and Assessing your teams. Every step in Part 3 – People is designed to produce a team aligned to operating within your culture while meeting the needs of your customer.

TAKEAWAYS:

- As an IOSP, people are the roots to your success.
- Never allow your team to feel like victims of circumstance; turn them into warriors of opportunity.
- You can both create and shape a positive culture rather than simply react to a negative one.
- Continuous, small, incremental culture shifts take much less time than large shifts.
- Leadership, not management, is key to a great culture.

PEOPLE

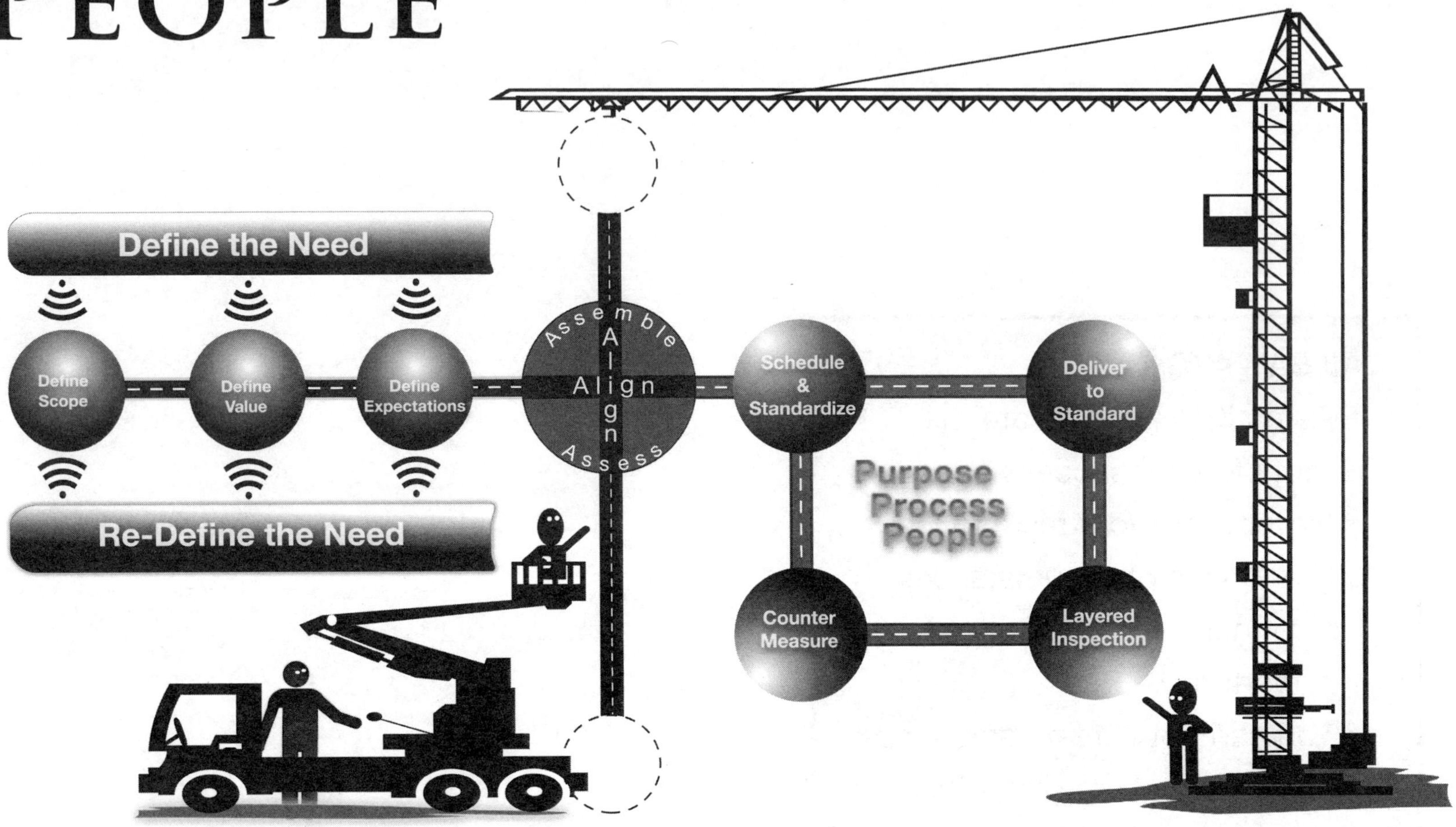
Define the Need
Define Scope
Define Value
Define Expectations
Assemble
Align
Assess
Re-Define the Need
Schedule & Standardize
Deliver to Standard
Purpose
Process
People
Counter Measure
Layered Inspection

Recognize
Assess
Train
Select
The Outsourcing Conundrum

"You cannot avoid a major catastrophe, but you can build an organization that is battle-ready, that has high morale, that knows how to behave, that trusts itself, and where people trust one another. In military training, the first rule is to instill soldiers with trust in their officers, because without trust they won't fight."

Managing the Non-Profit Organization: Principles and Practices,
Peter Drucker

In Part 3 of *The Outsourcing Conundrum*, we are going to discuss the drivers of inside-outsourcing, the people who deliver services via the processes, and ensure customer satisfaction. We already spoke about the need for a positive, forward-thinking culture and work climate necessary for the drivers, the parachute packers, to thrive and grow.

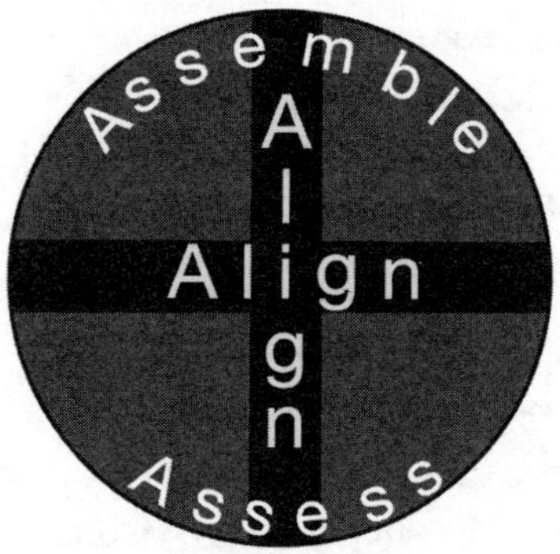

In Part 2, we discussed Assembling, Aligning and Assessing the required processes to be able to deliver to customers an inside-outsourcing service that aligns perfectly with their needs, gets done what needs to be done, and meets all expectations, the Purpose for why the service was outsourced in the first place.

In this chapter, Assemble, Align and Assess People, we are going to talk about what must first happen before we dash off and start hiring. In subsequent chapters in Part 3, we will delve into the Selection, Training, Assessment and Recognition (STAR) systems. First, however, we need to answer a few questions:

- ✔ Assemble to What?
- ✔ Align to What?
- ✔ Assess to What?

How do we want the group of people we are going to assemble, align, and assess to operate? Do we want a group of people, a crew of people, or a team of people?

How will we view them, identify them, relate to them? Will they be janitors, maintenance technicians, service workers, solution providers, team members, or painters, or will we first see them as people, people who by their nature are subject to all of the contradictions associated with being human?

Back in the very early 1990s, we made the conscious decision to be a people company. We believed that people were the strategic differentiator for us in the marketplace. Our company was designed to be a "great place to work," where performers could work with other performers in the fulfillment of a shared vision and strategy. We were not a group of people, or a crew of people. We were a very diverse team of people. We valued diversity where it matters most – diversity of thoughts, opinions, views, and perspectives.

Because we embraced the uniqueness each individual brought to the table, and were also committed to operating as a team where an individual's uniqueness, gifts, talents, and strengths, could make them more suitable to one position over another, we found it essential to establish a set of ground rules. Reflecting back on the previous chapter and the sketch of the Ulrich Model, we needed to agree on how we would behave as a team, something we came to call our Operating Norms, a shared mindset of how we would treat each other. The concept of the operating norms was the result of a training session at Team Trek. This simple one-page document created the foundation that enabled us to function as a high-performance team.

Operating Norms

I am 100% responsible for my actions, no excuses.
I am an attentive listener.
I seek to understand others' cultures, practices, and points of view before asking them to understand mine.
I speak my mind.
I commit to team decisions and directions even if I disagree.
I keep my commitments and agreements.
I abide by all ground rules.
I respect my teammates' time.
I respect my teammates' authority to do their jobs.
I treat my teammates as I want them to treat me.
I teach and learn everyday.
I balance family and work.
I celebrate victories with my team.

A second critical tool was our organization chart. We could not embrace the diversity of strength within the team and present it in a typical confining manner of boxes and straight lines. We decided to present how we organized ourselves in alignment with how we thought of ourselves, and with how we wanted to be known and identified in the marketplace, where our customers and people came first.

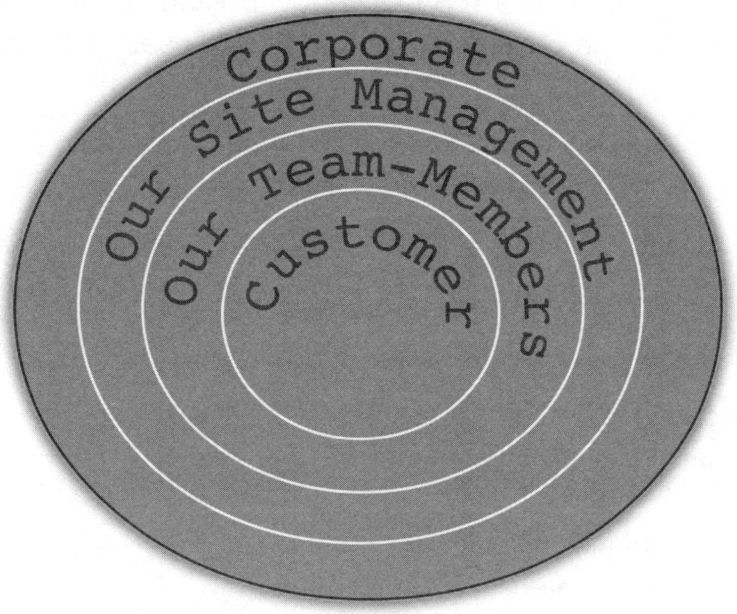

Our customer was at the center of what we did, our team members served our customers, our site management team served our team members, and the corporation served the site management team. Customer- and people-centric, we existed to serve, and we could only serve if all layers of the organization added value.

In the mid to late 1990s, a majority of our business was with one domestic car manufacturer that was experiencing some labor-related issues, resulting in a small strike at a component plant in Dayton, Ohio. So what was the big deal? Well, in a matter of weeks, just about every plant associated with this manufacturer halted production, as this one component was resident on most assembled vehicles. We had hundreds of employees at these plants, and if the plants were not in production, our services were not required. We did not have polices dealing with layoffs. We could not survive financially with this level of payroll and no ability to invoice our customer, so what did we do?

We spent several days coming up with a plan that would meet two primary goals:

- Not let our customer down.
- Not let our team members down.

We created a matrix of the employees, their capabilities, and their strengths. We asked employees to take their vacation time. We surveyed if any of the employees would like to take some time off. We solicited every other business unit in the company to find openings where people were on sick leave, taking vacation, or needed additional support. Through the combination of these strategies, we were able to place most of the team temporarily, allowing us to fire back up once the strike was over and cause a minimal amount of financial impact on our employees for the duration of the strike.

Abraham Maslow speaks to the hierarchy of needs, where all humans have certain needs that must be met. After we meet the most rudimentary needs of food, water, air and safety, we are met with the need to feel that we are a part of something. How we handled the situation in Dayton demonstrated to our team that they did belong to something, and that they were valued. Other IOSPs during that same time cut their teams loose on layoff and lost the respect of team members. We were fortunate enough to be able to hire some of those team members, due to our reputation, strengthening our own team even further.

CALCULATE VICTORY

As a team, we adhered to a set of unspoken rules, conditions, ideas, and beliefs that created the foundation of our culture. These beliefs were hard to describe or translate into tangible terms, but they amounted to the following:

- We believed in doing what was right for the customer and for our employees.
- We believed we had a job because our customer had a problem.
- We believed in being agile and being able to respond to our customer.
- We believed in not becoming the problem we were hired to solve.

As we started to grow, we adopted the idea of a Scorecard to help us to capture these intangible beliefs and translate them into tangible strategies that could be measured. In Part 1 – Purpose, we delved into each of these beliefs as we established and captured customer expectations and how our customer would measure success. Our Scorecard calculated and celebrated our victory, and was cast and re-cast each year depending on how our customer defined and redefined their needs for the upcoming fiscal year. Our Scorecard became the rudder of our boat. Every member of the team was privy to the Scorecard and each member of management was held accountable to its execution.

ASSEMBLE TO WHAT?

"Hire new people who embody the right mindset; promote those who live the mindset; remove those who do not."

Dave Ulrich and Norm Smallwood, "Building Intangible Value from the Outside In," in *Leader to Leader*, Spring 2003

If you hire people just because they can do the job, they will work for money, but if you can inspire them, they will give their all. This relates to both the employees chosen by the IOSP and also the IOSP chosen by procurement groups.

Assemble a team to a defined target.

The defined target is broken into two inter-related categories:

- Fit our brand and culture.
- Fit customer needs and expectations.

Before you start the hiring of individual team members, it is important to paint a picture of what the overall team needs to look like. Obviously, but very secondary, is the list of roles, responsibilities, duties, and titles of the team. First and foremost, you need to define how the team needs to act and interact with each other and the customer, a shared mindset towards delivering to the customer the level of service as outlined and promised in Part 1.

Defined Target Attributes	
Fit our brand and culture	**Fit customer needs and expectations**
Customer-Centric	Technically Competent
People-Centric	Adaptable
Service Oriented	Problem Solver
Team Oriented	Innovative
Learner	Teacher
Responsible	Accountable
Disciplined	Predictable
Strategic	Schedule Oriented
Tenacious	Dependable
Affordable	Value Oriented

Another important part of our success formula is the promotion of people into new roles and new opportunities. We set a target of two-thirds internal promotions to one-third external hires for our management teams. We find this formula allows us to grow our talent internally, while also allowing for new and fresh ideas to be brought in from the outside. This target was generally met when we were experiencing normal growth. In years of very high growth, however, the target was not met. As we will discuss, expansive growth can really test your people systems.

ALIGN TO WHAT?

"Keep one's orientation well matched to the real world during times of ambiguity, confusion, and rapid change, when the natural tendency is to become disoriented."

Certain To Win,
Chet Richards

Align a team to a defined target.

The defined target is broken into two inter-related categories:

- Our overall business strategy.
- Our Performance Indicators.

As was introduced and developed in Part 1 – Purpose, and inspected in Layered Inspection in Part 2, the Scorecard and Site Operating Plan are critical tools in the alignment of your inside-outsourcing service with your customer's needs. As such, they are also vital tools in the alignment of your teams with your overall business strategy.

Each member of our management team received a compensation package designed with a portion of their compensation at risk and dependent upon successful achievement of the Site Operating Plan and our overall corporate Scorecard. The Site Operating Plan and our Scorecard embody our business strategy, as such they are updated each fiscal year to represent the changes and challenges facing us at the site and in our market.

Over the years, we hired dozens and dozens of new people from our competitors. Our ability to align these new team members to our corporate and customer strategy was hailed as one of our primary reasons for success. It was extremely gratifying each year to pay out the incentive program to a very high percentage of all of the participants for a job well done and a strategy achieved.

The alignment of our day-to-day service delivery is achieved by the use of Key Performance Indicators. Each site is held accountable to meet and report on the key performance indicator targets, which are set annually to ensure the required level of service delivery is achieved. In Layered Inspection in Part 2, we talked about Outcome Layers and the need to align the day-to-day performance of the site to each of the teams and each of the team members. The teams can use tools like white boards, dashboards, and the CUBE, to visually display key performance indicators and to map out what is being done to meet the set targets.

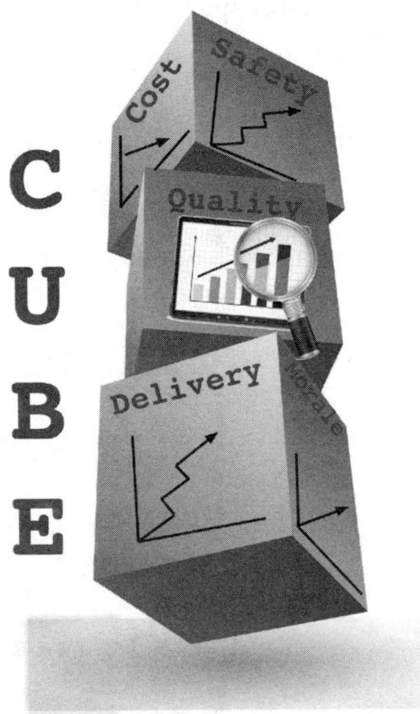

As part of the process to align the team, key performance indicators are peeled back to a point of absolute relevance to each member of the team to positively impact their behavior, resulting in improved performance.

Let's look at an example dealing with safety where the goal is to establish a level of alignment through six layers of the IOSP's organization.

Layered Safety Key Performance Indicator	
Level or Role	**Key Indicator**
Corporate / Division	Reduce consolidated lost time incident rate by 10%.
Site Manager	Reduce consolidated site level incident rate by 10%.
Area Manager	Reduce consolidated area level incident rate by 10%.
Shift Supervisor	Reduce consolidated shift level incident rate by 10%.
Team Leader	10% increase in the identification of near misses over previous year.
Team Member	Number of incidents / accidents

As the key indicators move down the organization, the characteristic of the indicator changes from being a lag, result-based indicator, to being a lead indicator of performance. The lead indicator is more appropriate for roles closer to the hands-on delivery of the service.

Let's look at another example dealing with the need to continually be competitive, and establish a lower cost point by seeking ways to improve day-to-day service delivery.

Layered Cost Savings Key Performance Indicator	
Level or Role	**Key Indicator**
Corporate / Division	Documented cost savings submitted to customer, 10% of annual revenue.
Site Manager	Documented cost savings submitted to customer, 10% of annual site revenue.
Area Manager	Documented cost savings submitted to customer, 10% of area revenue.
Shift Supervisor	% participation of shift in submission of improvement suggestions.
Team Leader	% participation of team in submission of improvement suggestions.
Team Member	# of improvement suggestions submitted.

Before starting to hire individual team members, it is critically important to paint the picture of what the overall team needs to deliver on a day-to-day basis.

As we will discuss in the upcoming chapter, Select, these metrics can be assigned to individual members of the team.

ASSESS TO WHAT?

"The new bottom line includes earning as well the confidence of investors, customers, and employees in the firm's ability to deliver in the future."

Dave Ulrich and Norm Smallwood, "Building Intangible Value from the Outside In," in *Leader to Leader*, Spring 2003

Assess a team to a defined target.

The defined target is broken into two inter-related categories:

- Performance – delivering the brand promise.
- Potential – ability to deliver on the customer's and our own future needs.

In an upcoming chapter, Assess, we will discuss the processes you can use to assess each individual member of the team against their Performance Map, allowing for them to be plotted onto the team assessment chart. The team assessment chart allows you to view the performance and potential of your team visually.

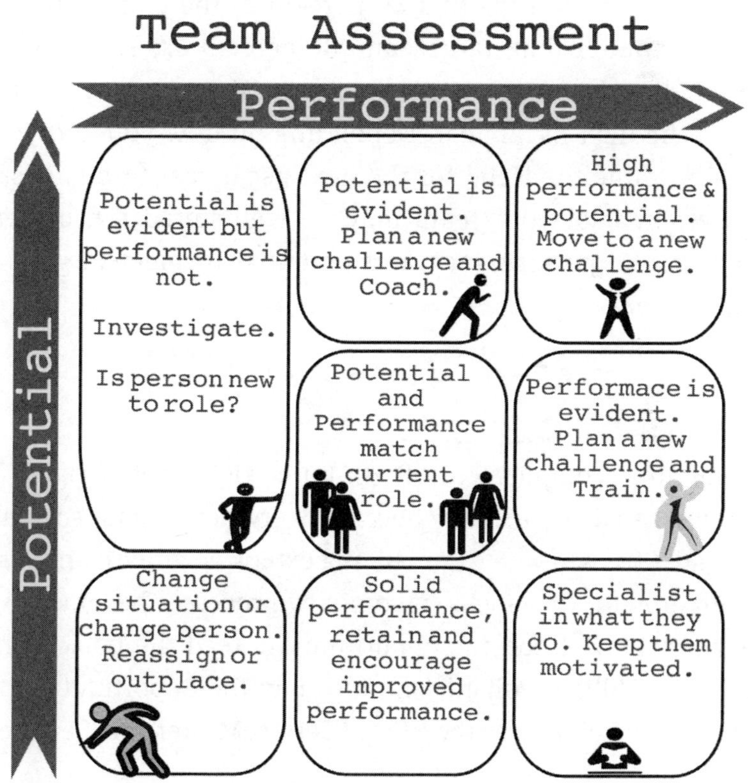

We adopted this process to plot our team about 10 years ago. This disciplined approach resulted in us being more proactive with selection of our training program curriculums, the identification of our high performers, and dealing with our low performers.

In the Team Assessment illustration of a 10-person team, 10 percent of the team is looking for an immediate new challenge; 20 percent should be ready for a new challenge within the year, with some training and coaching support; 40 percent of the team are well situated in their current role; 10 percent want to master their role with no desire to move up; 10 percent show potential but the cause of their shallow performance needs investigation; and 10 percent should be put on an immediate corrective plan or re-located to a new company.

Another viewpoint is that 80 percent of the team is performing at target or better than target, and 80 percent are showing average to better than average potential to meet the customer's and your needs in the next fiscal year. Depending on how you and your customer Re-Define the Need for the next fiscal year or business cycle, the assessment of your team may be well-suited for, or seriously lacking in, the performance and potential to meet targets for the upcoming year.

BEST PRACTICE

Is it really that complicated? "Right butts, right seats," right? Well, it was complicated and actually became overwhelming for several years. In the mid '90s, we were experiencing explosive growth and, as is typical with growth, the cracks in company processes become caverns.

Around 1997, I had the opportunity to read the book *Soul of the Firm*, by C. William Pollard, and also had the opportunity to engage with him. Bill Pollard was the CEO of ServiceMaster, and ServiceMaster made it clear to everyone that they were in the people business; as such they had a people system.

As stated earlier, we chose to differentiate ourselves through our people, and it was working well. It started to falter, however, and our growth demanded that we had to abandon our formula of filling open positions primarily via internal promotions and start hiring more people from the outside. Our formula of two-thirds internal versus one-third external was turning quickly in the opposite direction, two-thirds external and one-third internal. It also became very apparent that the culture we had taken for granted could very easily slip through our grasp.

During this time we fell into the trap of hiring people who could "do" the job, not necessarily those who believed in the company, shared our mindset and, most importantly, belonged in the service business. We hired based on skills and capability rather than hiring to build our team and enhance our brand.

To enhance our brand, we needed to hire people who understood our vision and also exhibited behaviors that aligned with how we wanted to be viewed.

Our growth meant we needed to formalize our process for bringing people onto the team where they would be given a cause to work towards versus just earning a living. We needed to establish a target so the people we selected met our needs. We needed a means to identify our training and development requirements. Our people needed to be able to be assessed and to assess themselves in a positive climate, and we needed to recognize and reward the "right" people and the "right" behaviors.

From C. William Pollard's book and our engagements with him, we adopted the STAR process, a very simple and easy-to-understand methodology to align your People with your Processes and your Purpose.

STAR Overview Table				
	S	T	A	R
Select	**Situation** Understanding the actual situation a candidate will be placed in.	**Task** Understanding the actual activities the candidate will need to perform.	**Action** Understanding how a candidate will need to behave.	**Results** Understanding what results will be required from the candidate.
Train	**Situation** Training, orienting teams to thrive in their situation.	**Technical** Training in the required technical skills for the activities to be completed.	**Attitude** Continually coaching the team on the required behaviors.	**Reality** Seeing the individual and their specific needs and developing accordingly.
Assess	**Situation** Evaluating how the team performs in their situation.	**Training** Evaluating the growth and development of the team.	**Action** Evaluating their attitude by their actions.	**Results** Evaluating the team's ability to meet the measurable targets.
Recognize	**Situation** Recognizing the team for their accomplishments in their situation.	**Team** Recognizing everyone for their ability to work and perform as a team.	**Above** Showing gratitude to the team for going above and beyond what is normally expected.	**Results** Recognizing the team for their measurable performance.

In the upcoming chapters,

- Select
- Train
- Assess
- Recognize

we will discuss each component of the STAR process in detail. The adaptation of this process allowed us to perform a course correction and put our people as core to our success and growth. Over the course of a decade the four-letter acronym STAR became our HR guiding strategy. In the STAR Overview Table the acronym STAR is broken down into each of the four areas of Select, Train, Assess and Recognize, to show further how this simple acronym is a good HR guiding strategy.

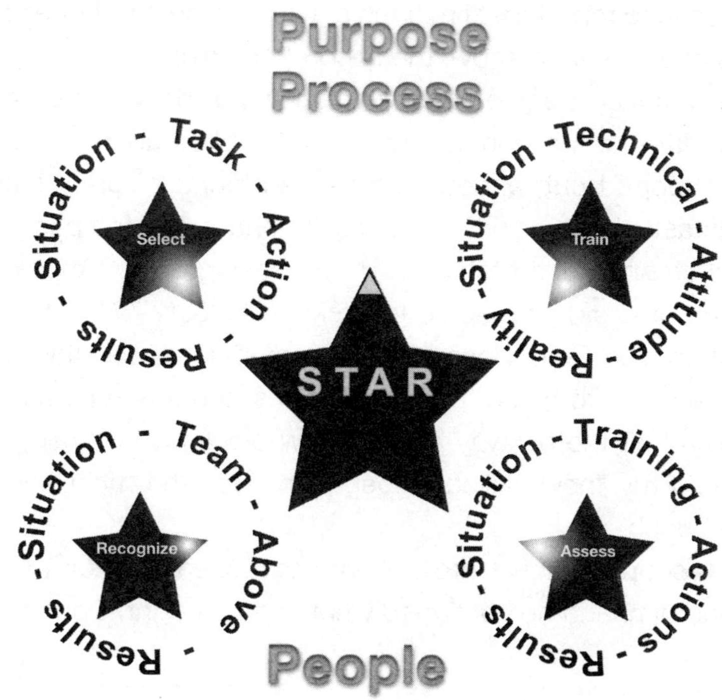

QUICK STORY

As a small company back in the '70s, we didn't always have the people we needed to complete our projects. Actually I think the entire company consisted of four people back then, and two of them were husband and wife. We took on a restoration job in downtown Toronto. The job was into its second week, and we needed to be completed by week three. The project entailed the chemical cleaning of the outside of an old three-story warehouse that was going to be restored into loft-like living spaces. It was a pretty simple project and the brick was cleaning up well. The only issue was operating the swing stage to move from floor to floor – it required two people, one on each side. After taking time to perform safety checks and allowing my part-time help a reasonable amount of tardiness, I called in to report that I needed a a new helper, as it looked like this one was a no show, the second one this week.

About an hour passed, enough time for a coffee, a few cigarettes and a donut, and my boss rolled up in his Riviera and hopped out, announcing he had found a "great helper." "Fantastic," I said fairly sarcastically, and out of the passenger side stepped this pretty run-down looking gent. "And where, dare I ask, did you locate this 'skilled helper?'" No reply was forthcoming, and since my boss needed to ask this man's name again to make the introductions, the answer was clear. He had hit the halfway house a few blocks over again, and I figured my "new skilled helper, Don" was the most sober of the bunch.

A couple of hours into the morning I asked Don how my boss found him, and he confirmed what I had thought. Don went on to tell me how he had been unfairly incarcerated for stabbing his brother-in-law several times in the chest. Hmm, I thought to myself, another winner. Why I asked the next question I will never know. "So what did your brother-in-law do to deserve his fate?" "He didn't get me a beer," he responded. "You know, he got a beer for everyone else, but completely disrespected me, so he got his." "Hmmm . . . I guess he learned his lesson," I said.

Don then asked me, "So when do we take a coffee break?"

"Whenever you say," I quickly responded, visualizing his brother-in-law on the floor with several chest wounds.

PROCUREMENT

It would behoove purchasers of inside-outsourcing services to acknowledge that the cost associated with people makes up the highest percentage of the expense associated with the price submitted by an IOSP. With that being the case, wouldn't it be worth spending quality time to explore how your IOSP is going to assemble, align, and assess their team in pursuit of meeting your expectations? An IOSP should also acknowledge that the largest category of cost to their contract is people, and be in a position to prove to purchasing how that cost can be the best investment they will make.

In the 40 years I have been an IOSP, there have been about a half-dozen situations where our customer requested we "take over" the entire team of a competitor lock, stock and barrel, and to do it overnight. Within 24 hours we on-boarded the competitor's entire workforce and performed their services. Why would they ask us to hire our competitor's workforce? If they did not like the competitor's service, would they not desire to change out the team? It's the team that delivers the service, is it not?

If you look at a team through the right lens, you see, for the most part, people who get up every day or night wanting to make some form of difference. All they need is an environment where they fit for them to be successful. That is what these customers changed by changing companies overnight. They changed the environment to one more dedicated to being positive and engaging the team, by aligning them and assessing them against a defined target of what needed to be done.

In each of these situations, not everyone made the adjustment. More often than not, senior managers did not make the change, but supervisors typically embraced it and so did the balance of the team. With a focused effort on the principles we have outlined so far, we typically witnessed a significant improvement in the morale of the team within 12 to 14 months, measured by their level of engagement, the number of ideas and suggestions they submitted for improvement, and our other key performance indicators.

By dedicating a bit more time, purchasing could better evaluate these IOSP cultures and choose one better aligned with their needs in the first place.

TAKEAWAYS:

- As an IOSP, your people display your brand.
- Without a formal people process, your brand is at risk.
- Before you begin to add people to your team, set a target of how the team must behave.
- People work for a cause. Make the mission clear and visible.

PEOPLE

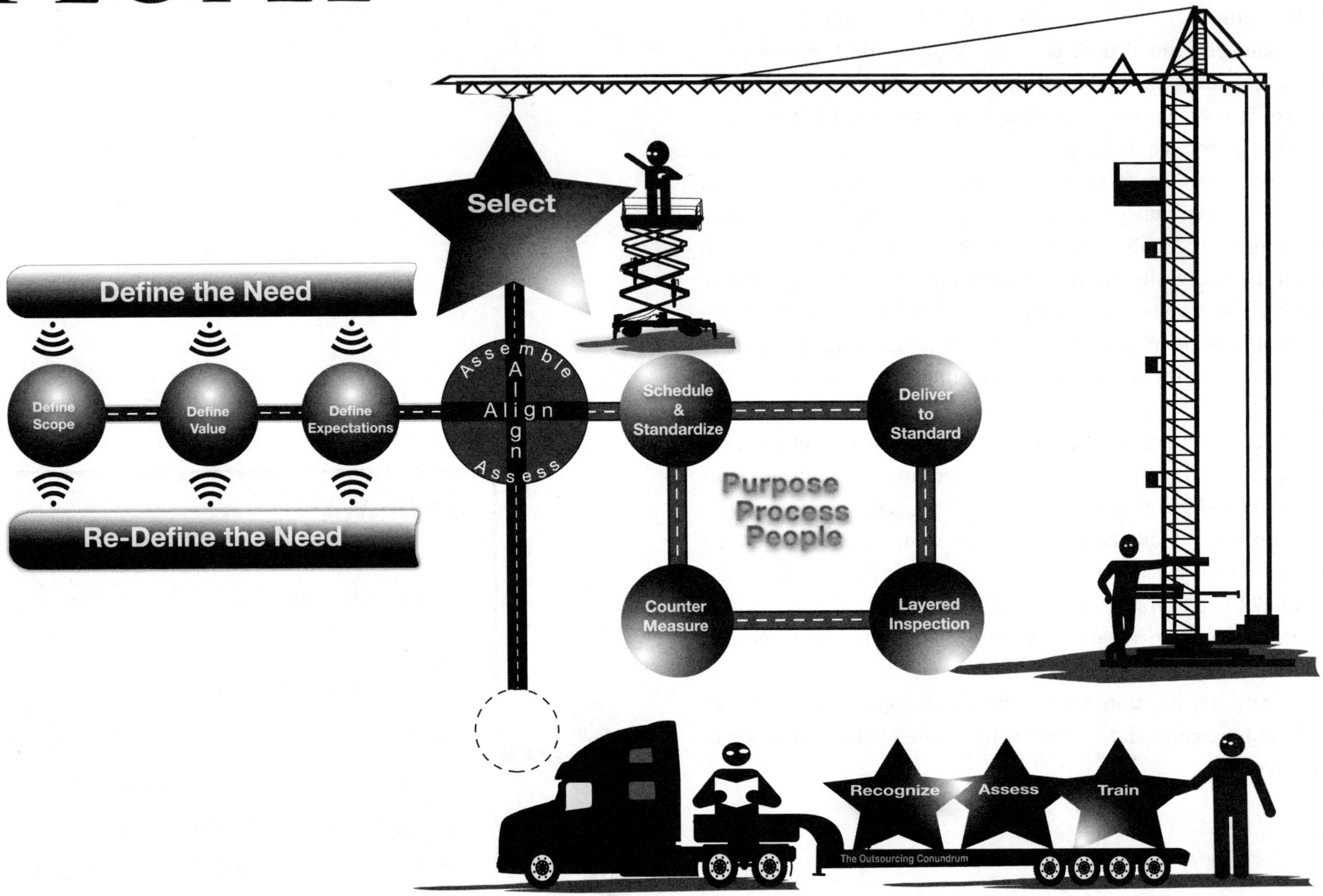
Select
Define the Need
Define Scope
Define Value
Define Expectations
Assemble
Align
Assess
Schedule & Standardize
Deliver to Standard
Purpose
Process
People
Counter Measure
Layered Inspection
Re-Define the Need
Recognize
Assess
Train
The Outsourcing Conundrum

"Nothing can stop a man with the right mental attitude from achieving his goal; nothing on earth can help the man with the wrong mental attitude."

Thomas Jefferson

"Our environment, the world in which we live and work, is a mirror of our attitudes and expectations."

Earl Nightingale

Throughout the 40 years I have been in the inside-outsourcing business as an IOSP, I would venture to say I have learned many lessons, many of them the hard way. While getting ready to write *The Outsourcing Conundrum*, I performed a mental exercise. Using a white board, I wrote down all of the reasons why a certain number of our accounts failed. Reviewing the list of failed accounts and reviewing the list of reasons, one reason stood out above all the rest: **"We Hired the Wrong People."**

Being honest with myself, a much better way to state that is, "I hired the right people for the wrong job." Most of the people I hired were very good people, just not the right ones for the situation we were heading into and the tasks we needed to complete.

While pondering the results of the white-board exercise, something else struck me: what I needed from a workforce had changed over the decades.

- Comply . . .
- Comply, think . . .
- Comply, think, engage . . .
- Comply, think, engage, own . . .

In the beginning, we just hired warm bodies to do the work. Then we wanted them also to think about what they did. Then we wanted them to engage in improving how we did it. Now we also look for them to take ownership of the work.

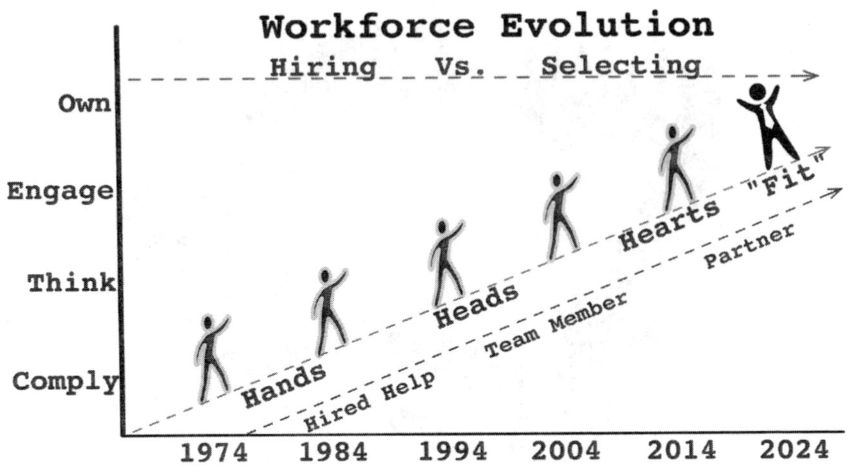

HIRE VERSUS SELECT

In the previous chapter, I told you about Don, the misunderstood gentleman who stabbed his brother-in-law. Don was hired help. In those days we referenced our human resource needs as helpers. By their definition they were hired to help someone else. It was a fall-back to the times when the skilled worker, like a bricklayer, had a helper. They were not hired to use their brains. They were just a set of hands to provide bricks, as the bricklayer needed them. Helpers were thought of as underlings and treated as such. The criteria for the job were extremely basic. Are you available? Can you walk upright without tripping over yourself? (And even this last one we sometimes let slide.)

As we moved forward a decade, we began to hear words like "team member," signifying that the help we needed was really a member of our team. Not only did we need to hire their hands, but we also needed them to think. Not only could they not trip over themselves, we looked for them to be a step ahead. As we discussed in Part 1, the need to know "why" started to become important, including for those employees at the lowest level of the organization.

The problem was the system we used to find competent hired help did not fare so well on this upgrade to recruiting a more evolved employee, the team member. It became clear that we needed to be able to select staff rather than just hire them. The early years of this change in mindset created what I fondly called "Cream of the Crap."

Cream of the Crap

Cream of the Crap was the people system where HR would post a job, usually in the local newspaper, gather a bunch of résumés, and then begin the interview process. HR would perform initial screenings and decide whom they liked for a position. The word "like" is important because this whole process used that vernacular.

- "Did you like them?"
- "I like A over B and C."
- "If you like them, I like them. Hire them."

As a candidate, your fortune was based on your luck of the draw. If you interviewed for a job with a pile of slugs and you were the least sluggish, congratulations, you were hired. Whether or not you "fit" the role, or were wired to do the role, became secondary to the fact you were looking for a job or you would not be there, and we were looking for help or you would not be there. Perfect marriage, no?

By the mid '90s our business growth became expansive, and our turnover in supervision and management started to increase. This is not a healthy combination of trends. It became extremely obvious that our old system of hiring and choosing our team was failing us. Our turnover was actually out of control as we experienced turnover in the upper thirtieth percentile. If this is how you are still recruiting today, please move on and select your people to a target.

SELECT TO A TARGET

The selection of a new person into an existing or new role, or the selection of which team member to promote into an existing or new role is crucial to the quality of services you provide. The development and discipline of a selection system that results in predictable returns of efficient and effective employees who enjoy their duties and responsibilities and seek out opportunities to continually improve their jobs, is critical to being a successful IOSP.

In the overview chapter of Part 3 – People, I mentioned that we needed warriors as opposed to victims. So all we need to hire are a bunch of warriors and we'll be fine? Not that simple, but we do need to understand how to select a warrior instead of a victim, and how to develop a selection target for warriors, allowing us to aim our hiring efforts in the right direction. More importantly, we need a selection target to hire against, that can alert us to, and deter us from, hiring victims. In life we typically develop a target for most big decisions: what car to buy, what house to purchase, whom to marry, where our kids will go to school. Hiring is no different: a target must be established to select and hire against. You establish that target by identifying the specific competencies and behaviors required to do the job.

Around 1997-98, I needed a change. I had been an operations leader for decades, and was craving a new challenge. After some dialogue with the president/owner of the company, we agreed that I would become the new Vice President of People Services, the name we chose for our HR group. My desire behind taking on this new challenge was to "fix" our people systems. I had little to no interest in the payroll, benefits, or generalist duties associated with a typical HR department. My interest was purely in the more strategic select, train, assess, and recognize aspects of HR, as those elements impacted our operations group the most. I was confident there had to be a solution out there somewhere.

As a condition of taking on the new role of VP of People Services, I agreed to engage a coach/mentor to help bridge the gap in my experience in the HR arena. After several weeks, I located a very seasoned HR executive who agreed to help me, by acting as a sounding board and being a valuable source of knowledge.

During lunch one day, Tom, my HR coach and mentor, told me about World War II bombers. Apparently during WWII, the US faced a huge problem: we were able to produce bomber aircraft much faster than we were able to train crews or replace those who were lost to enemy fire. It appeared this was an issue all the allies faced. Tom went on to describe how behaviors of successful bomber crews could be identified, as well as behaviors of those who were not successful. Those who were successful acted very differently under stress and pressure than those who were not successful. This identification and inventory of behaviors provided those responsible for recruiting new crews valuable insight into the make-up of individuals who would most likely be part of a successful bomber crew. As history has recorded, the outcome of WWII was very reliant on the skills and capabilities of those bomber crews and aircraft.

Tom asked, "What if you could apply this type of discipline to how you choose who is part of which team, and which teams are assigned to which accounts?" "Great idea," I answered, "but how do we locate those resources for basic civilian use?"

Tom explained that Dr. Donald W. Devine, a pre-eminent leader in the field of applied behavioral sciences, had developed a program to inventory behavior. Seeing that I was a tad skeptical, he went on to explain that Dr. Devine had studied in depth the work done by psychologists to prepare WWII bombers. He applied that knowledge to organizations like Xerox and Citicorp, as well as to Harvard's Advanced Management Program. Dr. Devine was intrigued by why some people succeed and some people fail at what they do. The clincher for me at that time was that the behavior inventory tool was available online and was affordable. As I understood it, with this tool we would be able to identify critical behaviors associated with being successful in our business. I was hooked. "What's the next step?" As we walked out of the restaurant, Tom stated that Marriott, a company well respected for being excellent at identifying the right talent for each of their positions, was using the Devine Inventory.

DEVELOP A TARGET

The discussion over lunch about the bomber pilots fully intrigued and consumed me for several weeks, and I believed we were on our way to a solution. If it was possible for the air force to predict success by understanding required behaviors for a role, why couldn't we?

We could and we did.

We reviewed the list of individuals in our management group, who numbered in the hundreds, and prioritized them by position and level of performance. From the lists, we selected groups of high performers and low performers in each position category. Each member of these groups was required to complete a Devine Inventory.

Trevor Wilson, in his book *The Human Equity Advantage*, speaks about a New York insurance company that hired a new CEO charged with doubling the revenue of the company. He, in turn, charged his HR department to identify the reason why some of his sales people outsold the others. He was looking for the "golden thread" that ran through the group. After dissecting the 100-member sales group and running them through a battery of psychological tests, HR found the thread, a strong trait that all of those who were successful shared. It was optimism. They were all optimistic. They worked in and around rejection each and every day, but that never prevented them from moving on to the next prospective customer.

As we completed our own reviews, we also tried to locate a common set of traits prevalent in successful management team members. The Devine Inventory profiles people to a set of competencies and a list of associated behaviors. Our goal was to identify the pattern of competencies, as well as behaviors associated with, and shared by, successful management groups, by position.

We found that successful management team members all shared strength in the following three competencies:

- **Customer Service Oriented:** Readily responding to meet the needs of others, either inside or outside the organization.
- **Adaptable:** Taking on new and additional tasks with comfort and ease, while responding to unexpected requirements inherent in such circumstances.
- **Team Builders:** Ability to relate to other people while drawing out their commitment and cooperation.

The results actually made a lot of sense to us, which made the whole idea behind the exercise easier to adopt. We were in the service business, operating as teams inside customer facilities, so it made sense that our management team members needed to be service oriented, adaptable to changes in their day-to-day environment, with the ability to gain commitment and cooperation of the team. It was even clearer that if the management team members did not share these competencies as strengths, their opportunities for success were impaired.

These three competencies became known as foundational capabilities the whole organization needed to master. This mindset is no different than a successful coffee chain that needs not only to make great coffee, but also to master creating a nice environment, pleasant and friendly servers, and timely and accurate delivery of products.

The competencies—customer service oriented, adaptable and team builders—really represented our corporate culture. From that point forward, everyone we hired had to "fit" into that culture, as that culture was our brand. We began to select and recruit to the target of team members who were service oriented, adaptable, team builders.

As we continued to dissect data from the Devine Inventory, we also identified certain strong behaviors shared by management team members that were associated with each of the above competencies. Successful management team members all tested with strength in the following behaviors:

- **Influence:** gains acceptance of ideas.
- **Self-Responsibility:** seeks accountability.
- **Conflict Management:** weighs in and resolves disagreements.
- **Emotional Composure:** acts professionally.
- **Decisiveness:** chooses a course of action.
- **Mobility:** flexible and willing to do whatever it takes.
- **Intimacy:** sensitive to the needs of others.
- **Sociability:** builds a network of relationships.
- **Instructiveness:** improves others' performance by sharing knowledge.
- **Self-Confidence:** establishes a strong presence among others, gaining respect.

This pattern of behaviors associated with our successful management team members surprised me. Typically we looked for people who exhibited an orientation to being planners and schedulers, who were organized in their day, detail- and goal-oriented. So the pattern of behaviors listed above (with more emphasis on emotional intelligence and demeanor) came as somewhat of a surprise, but it helped to explain why many of our latest new hires were struggling. They were overly focused on getting the job done, not on who did the job and for whom the job was being done.

As we continued to develop the target for successful management team members, we began to question the relevance of job descriptions and position descriptions. These antiquated documents had become static, useless pieces of paper. As described throughout this book, we were heavily engaged in using strategic tools like strategy maps, scorecards and such, so we brainstormed how to take that to an individual level. The result of the brainstorming was a tool we called a Performance Map. We also decided on the criteria for a Performance Map:

- **Motivation:** Why do we have the position? Why is the position important? We document our motivation for the position under the caption of Purpose. Purpose puts in writing the overall importance of the position far beyond the day-to-day requirements of the position. Purpose motivates the person to a higher level of being. Instead of being the bricklayer, they become the cathedral builder. Instead of the carpenter, they become the ship builder. Instead of being the day-to-day operations guy, they become the leader of a localized business.

- **Knowledge:** What skills and capabilities are needed to manage processes and complete tasks associated with the service delivery? As a result of the work completed in Define Expectations, we were able to align customer expectations to the numerical results required in delivery of services.
- **Behavior:** Which competency and behavior strengths are required for the position? Based on the work we completed with the Devine Group, we were in a position to document this requirement as part of the target for selection.

The Performance Map became the **target** used to determine whom we should select and hire for our team. This entire initiative to produce a target to select the "right" people to put onto our teams took about a year to complete, at the end of which we had performance maps for most key service operational roles:

- General Manager
- Site Manager
- Supervisor
- Team Leader

Over time, Performance Maps were created for every position in the company, including hourly team members. The management turnover issue we had faced faded away over the course of several years, and instead we eventually became the employer of choice within our niche. Our ability to attract and retain strong talent was no longer an obstacle to our growth.

To reinforce the competencies and behaviors we wanted to encourage at the team member level, we also decided to use Performance Maps for individual performance assessments.

Typically we had been accustomed to a job description that you saw once in your career on the day you were hired, and an assessment tool for individual performance that had very little resemblance to the job description. These documents and the process itself were very misaligned. We will elaborate more on the Performance Map as an assessment tool in the upcoming chapter, Assess.

There are several good tools in the marketplace to help determine and rate the behaviors required for a specific company. We chose the Devine because the logic behind the tool was academically supported. It was online, easy to use, and affordable. Some 20 years later, it is still in use. The tools have grown and developed immensely, as has our organization's knowledge of and comfort with them.

One huge benefit, or symptom, of our choice to use such a tool was that discussion about a person's behavior became commonplace. In the beginning, we faced a lot of resistance from people who did not like the idea of someone supposedly looking into their head, but over time it became the norm, and the behavior of an individual was openly discussed. The Performance Map acted as a catalyst to formalize and normalize that mindset.

INTERVIEW AND HIRE TO A TARGET

"It is not the employer who pays the wages. Employers only handle the money. It is the customer who pays the wages."

Henry Ford

The creation of the Performance Map, the target for the individual team member level, was a big step but it also required that we had to take one more. We needed to be able to interview to that target. The kinds of theoretical, leading questions we had traditionally asked in interviews allowed candidates to discuss:

- Would have done.
- Could have done.
- Should have done.

However, at the end of the day, those things do not really matter. What we need to know, and what you need to know to hire to the target for your own organization, are the following three things:

- Did do.
- Will do.
- Can do.

Just as in recruiting the WWII bombers, we need to be confident the person we put into the pilot's seat, or as a member of a team, will deliver in the situation they have been given. Bomber pilots today are trained using simulations. They are given situations, and their behaviors and actions are monitored. How do we apply that rationale, that way of thinking, to how we interview?

We met another great company called DDi, who listened to our issues and provided a solution they call "targeted selection." The name alone resonated with the work we had been doing, and the structure to their process made a lot of sense. Their interview approach is based on presenting questions to the candidate in a manner that forces the answer to be delivered using a real-life situation.

Old-style interview questions typically ask things such as, "Tell me how you are able to build teams?" The candidate then pontificates on his most recent readings of team building. The new, "real-life" approach cuts through much of that philosophical exchange by delivering a more focused question, such as, "Give me a specific situation when you had to build a team. What actions did you specifically take and what was the result?" If the candidate chooses to drift off and pontificate, you can politely stop them and repeat the question. The clarity gained by using this approach is amazing.

We knew from our history that our people needed to be able to respond in the right manner in the many situations they faced. As a result of the work we had completed with the Devine Inventory, we also knew the behaviors required to assure success.

We decided to use pre-determined, targeted behaviors outlined in our Performance Map as the basis for our interview questions. Adopting the DDi methodology, the questions followed a set structure, which forced the candidate to answer by describing a specific situation from his or her experience, the task being performed in the situation, the actions the candidate took, and the result. This interview methodology was also known as STAR:

- **S**ituation – or background involved.
- **T**ask – that was required to be completed.
- **A**ction – that was taken to complete the task.
- **R**esult – that occurred.

We found that adopting this interview style very quickly got the interview away from the candidate discussing what he would have done, could have done, and should have done, into what he actually can do, did do, and will do. As we were training with this new process, we used a few people in the office to play the role of a potential candidate. In one specific case, as we used this interview technique on an office worker who had been recently hired using the old-style interview technique, we found that we had been conned during the interview.

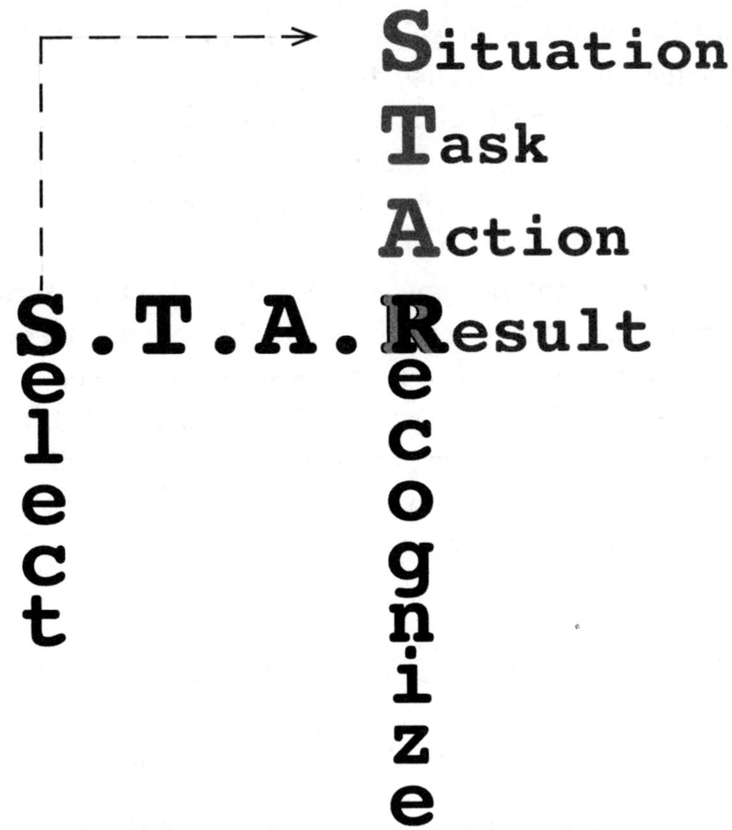

The acceptance of this new structure allowed us to produce Interview Guides for each position, which were designed to investigate a candidate's match to a target. The incorporation of the Devine Inventory, Performance Map, and Interview Guide, and following the STAR approach, provided our teams with tools to improve our "hit" ratio of successful hires. We chose to measure the success of the selection process by measuring the turnover of candidates in the first year of employment. We believed that if the candidate chose to leave within a year, we had failed the candidate and ourselves by not hiring the "right" person for the "right" job.

The idea shown in the illustration at left made sense to us: the STAR process enabled us to select the "right" person to fit the "right" situation, leading to the required results and allowing the person recognition. Situational questions forced candidates to reveal their potential for the position and "fit" for the company.

CHOOSE FROM A TARGET

"If everyone is moving forward together, then success takes care of itself."

Henry Ford

If you Google an address using only a zip code, you can be confident the property you are trying to locate will be somewhere on the street identified on the map generated by that zip code. You will have no reason to look in another zip code. Similarly, if you take the time to prepare your target for selecting team members, incorporate a behavioral assessment tool, and design an interview method, you will also find your candidate pool falls within the zip code, your target range. You will not need to look in other zip codes. The pool of candidates will be aligned to your needs. If you enter the interview process and the pool of candidates is from several different zip codes (that is, your candidate pool is all over the map), then your process is not being followed properly, or the target is poorly defined.

When it comes to making a choice on whom to hire from the candidate pool that falls into our targeted range, the "zip code" we are searching for, we weigh the following components:

- **Financial** – candidate has to fit into the financial parameter set for the role.
- **Motivation** – candidate must desire the job.
- **Behavior** – candidate's behaviors must "fit" those targeted.
- **Knowledge** – candidate must have the skill and abilities targeted.

Each component is assessed on a pass-fail basis, and failure in any one component disqualifies the candidate for the targeted position.

Adhering to the guidelines in this chapter will greatly improve the ability of an IOSP to develop and hire candidates targeted to match the culture, and who are more apt to fit the needs of your customer.

PROMOTE TO A TARGET

Besides running into an issue with hiring the wrong people during years of expansive growth, we also ran into a problem of promoting the wrong people—wrong in that they were not ready at the time of promotion, or wrong in that they did not have the capacity for the new role. We lost many good people to what is commonly know as the "Peter Principle."

The concept of the Peter Principle is credited to, and named after, Laurence J. Peter, who co-authored the book *The Peter Principle: Why Things Always Go Wrong*. The theory of the Peter Principle is that the selection of a candidate for a position is based on their performance in their current position rather than on their capacity to meet the challenges of the intended position. Basically, you take someone who is successful in their current position and promote him or her to a level where they are incompetent; they fail, it's their fault, and you fire them. Gee, thanks for the promotion?

Our organization, like many others, was guilty of promoting people according to the Peter Principle. On many occasions, well-intentioned managers believed the candidate would grow into the role, like they themselves had, but that didn't happen and the promotion did not work out. To avoid falling victim to the Peter Principle, we applied the same process to promotions that we had adopted for new hires. It was critical to our brand that those we promoted were successful. A bad promotion, just like a bad hire, impacted the person who was promoted, as well as the team who worked with and around the person, and our customer.

BEST PRACTICE

The IOSP faces many hiring challenges, and probably the most significant is who they select as their overall manager at a customer's site location, as that person sets the tone for the balance of the management and hourly team members. The long-term success of the site really stems from the ability of the site manager to establish a nice level of succession within the levels of his organization at the plant. This is even more important if his management team is ambitious and the company is growing, as his top talent may very well get swept away to a new site.

Unfortunately, the promotion from team member to team leader is very often overlooked and not deemed critical. But the next generation of supervision is rooted in those team leaders, so it is critical to get this succession path right. One of our sites in Southern Ontario took on this challenge, and developed an excellent program built around the concepts discussed in this chapter.

First, the targeted Performance Map for the job of team leader is posted, and those who are interested sign up, thus indicating their interest. This simple step signifies motivation. Those who are not motivated do not sign up. Second, past performance of those who signed up is reviewed, and the list of candidates is shortened based on that assessment. Third, candidates are interviewed with situational questions based on the Performance Map, meaning they are questioned for the new job, not on their old job. Their performance on the old job got them to this point, but only their future potential will get them to the next level. The list is shortened further, and the final list of candidates performs a 360-degree behavioral assessment based on behaviors outlined in the Performance Map.

The results are weighted and tabulated, and the choice is made. Does this take a substantial amount of time? Yes. But the gains made are worth the time investment.

Previously, few team members would apply for the position of team leader because most of the team leaders who had been in place before were victims of the Peter Principle. Therefore, the team-leader job was over their head, they weren't successful in the position, and the result was a general lack of respect for anyone in this position. Changing the process allowed us to fill the team-leader job with the right candidates, and thus make it a more attractive career aspiration in subsequent years.

This new selection process can be slow, but yields much better results, one of which is a higher caliber of team leaders who are respected and emulated. Filling the team leader positions with more suitable candidates is also starting to provide the additional benefit of producing a good selection of candidates for front-line supervisors, thus filling the succession pipeline at customer sites more effectively than in the past.

There is an old story about harvesting bamboo. The soil is prepared, and seeds are planted, fertilized and watered for years. Finally the bamboo grows tens of feet in just a few months. Did it really grow only in the last few months, or was it growing all along, but revealed its growth only in the last few months?

This promotion best practice reminds me of the bamboo story. This site runs extremely well, which has nothing to do with what was done just yesterday. It runs well because of what is done every day, paying attention to the team over a long period of time, resulting in a crop of loyal, customer-centric talent.

QUICK STORY

During the years when I was the Vice President of People Services, I wanted to add someone to provide support to our recruitment efforts. During this time, we were just starting to experiment with situational questioning around targeted behaviors. One of the targeted behaviors for this recruitment position was Learning, whereby someone would naturally learn from their mistakes and move on. We developed questions to investigate a candidate's strength in this behavior.

The candidate was a young, ambitious man who came to us from a job in HR at a regional airline where he recruited crews for passenger jets.

At his interview, I asked him, "In your own words, give me a situation where you made a mistake. Walk me through what you were doing, what actions you took, and what the results were."

Candidate: "I cannot think of an example, I have never made a mistake."

Hmm. Okay, let's try this again. "In the 10 years you have been working, think of a time where when you made a judgment error. Tell me the situation you were in, the tasks you were performing, the actions taken by you, and the result."

Candidate: "I just cannot think of any time I made an error in judgment."

I stood up, and reached out to shake his hand. "I'd like to thank you for coming in today. I wish you all the best. The interview is over."

Looking a bit dazed, he asked, "Was it something I said?"

"No," I replied, "I just can't afford to be the recipient of your first mistake."

Candidate: "Well, I have never made one."

I told him, "The good news is that on your next interview when you are asked if you have ever made a mistake, you can tell the story of this interview."

PROCUREMENT

When a procurement group is buying a part from a supplier that will be assembled onto their product, there are very stringent specifications written surrounding the composition of the raw materials for the part. This makes sense. As the product provided by an IOSP is its people, why are there usually no similar specifications? When purchasing chooses an IOSP, it is worth spending time on understanding how the IOSP selects the candidates for the project under consideration. It would also be worthwhile for the IOSP to inform purchasing on their process for selecting people. Keep in mind these new team members will be very visible operating inside the walls of your facility, so it is critical to learn how they are selected and hired.

In the late '90s, as we implemented the selection and interviewing structure outlined in this chapter, we faced a lot of internal challenges. As the management teams at our sites started to implement the criteria of the Performance Map target, we were very lucky if we could get 10 out of 100 people to the end zone for an interview. The good news was that the 10 were all competent candidates, and retention after hiring improved immensely because the candidate pool fit the jobs.

STAR Overview Table				
	S	T	A	R
Select	**Situation** Understanding the actual situation a candidate will be placed in.	**Task** Understanding the actual activities the candidate will need to perform.	**Action** Understanding how a candidate will need to behave.	**Results** Understanding what results will be required from the candidate.

We also were becoming well known as a great place to work. Word spread, so we had many talented people from our competitors sending us their résumés. Our customers also became a very valuable source of talent as the caliber of our management teams grew and improved over the years.

It truly is hard to measure return on investment in this process. The cost of a bad hire has been well documented by many, and I still find the numbers sobering. To me, the bigger intangible cost of a bad hire is the cost to the brand of the IOSP. Unlike the direct cost of a bad hire, the impact of that intangible cost can be felt for years. It is critical to get the right runner in the starting blocks, day one.

Select

TAKEAWAYS:

- The selection process has to move toward "right fit," which entails identifying the "right behaviors" for the company, the customer, and the position.
- Hire to a target and promote to a target.
- Identify a tool to determine objectively the behavioral patterns of your best performers, in all positions.
- Select and hire to where a position is going, not where it has been.

PEOPLE

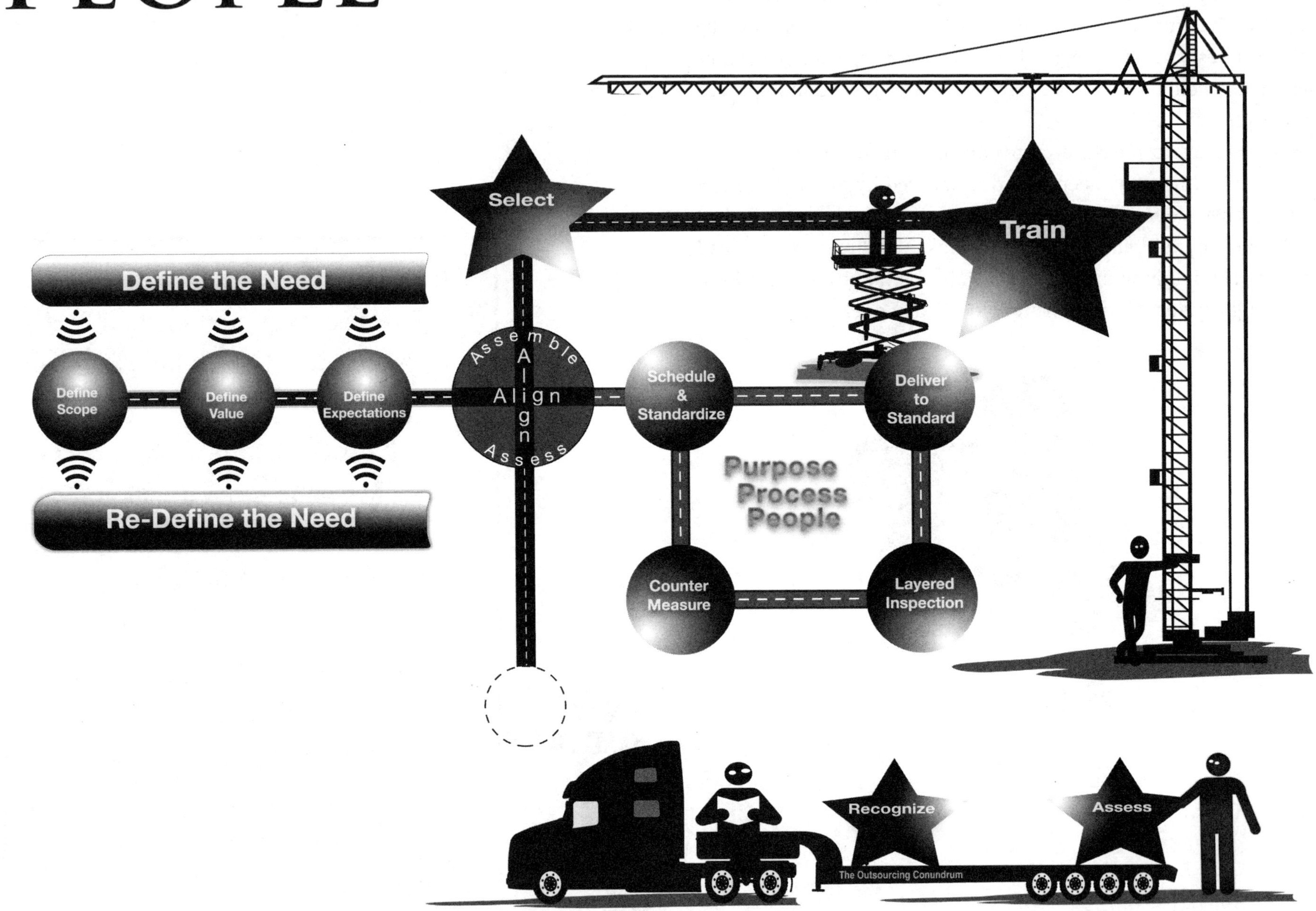

Select
Train
Define the Need
Define Scope
Define Value
Define Expectations
Assemble
Align
Assess
Schedule & Standardize
Deliver to Standard
Purpose
Process
People
Re-Define the Need
Counter Measure
Layered Inspection
Recognize
Assess
The Outsourcing Conundrum

"It never ceases to amaze me how much pain a human body can withstand and how much we adapt and live with the pain."

Dr. James Sammarco

The human body and an organization are more similar, to my way of thinking, than most people realize. When we begin our life, we are agile, limber, and open to new experiences, ideas, and knowledge. As we age, we become more rigid, structured in our thinking, set in our routines, and less open minded. Organizations follow a similar pattern, and very often an organization needs a jolt to wake up and change, just like people do.

On January 2, 1986, I participated in a martial arts event, competing against a handful of people. We were down to a tie between myself and another guy who had just successfully completed his second flying side kick. As I prepared for my third flying side kick, I could feel a strain in my left ankle due to a less-than-perfect landing from my second attempt. As I ran to the hurdles, went airborne, and positioned my body to move the four feet to the target ahead, I readied my left leg to perform the kick. As my left leg struck the target and my feet went to land on the floor, I heard a sound, a crack that I will never forget. As I lay on the floor with my ankle splintered and bones protruding through skin, the world stopped. "What the hell have I done? This cannot have happened. I am invincible." Yes, it did, and no, I am not. This single, significant, physical and emotional event changed not only my life, but also my view on life.

The surgery that followed was less than successful due to an allergy to the metal in the pins used to reconnect all of the bones. From 1986 to 1998, I limped along consuming Advil to get me through the day. By 1998 the pain had reached new heights and had become fairly intolerable, and that is when I met Dr. Sammarco, a surgeon well known for ankle restoration. In the years that followed, he was able, over the course of several surgeries, to restore my ankle to a point where I could live pain-free and I no longer limped.

After each surgery, I was on crutches for about 12 months. My biggest learning experience occurred when I accepted the reality that I needed to train myself to walk again each time, and could not fake it. I became very focused, and practiced daily to develop the habit of walking without a limp.

Successful organizations are similar in that they can't fake it, and they can't afford to limp along. In our case, our company was very successful, we were growing, our competition was getting stiffer, and we were facing a series of service-delivery issues that required our attention. In the mid- to late '90s, we performed what is known as a "Voice of the Customer" survey, to seek out new growth opportunities. What we heard from our customers' voices was, "You had better take care of what you have before we give you any more." We had been limping along, dealing with the day-to-day pain of outdated processes, developing shortcuts, but never taking the time out to perform the required surgery and fix what was broken once and for all. This awareness from our customer was the "jolt," the significant event dealing us a blow, that meant we needed to change.

To our credit, we were customer- and people-centric so we did not blow off what we heard from our customer. We also did not blow off what we learned when we interviewed and surveyed our teams. If you recall from the previous chapter, Select, we discussed that our expansive growth resulted in a fracture in our selection process (hiring and promoting). Combining what we learned from our customers and our teams, we realized we didn't have a single fracture but a compound fracture that needed addressing.

The reason I broke my leg was because I allowed my ego to talk me into doing something that was greater than my capability. I did not need to do that last jump. As an organization, we had outgrown our capability as well. We became victims of our own success.

As we discussed in the Select chapter, we took necessary steps to correct our ability to attract and retain our talent. Our next challenge was to train and develop our talent to keep pace with our growing market and customer demands.

TRAINING STARS

The initial action we took to fill our training void was less than perfect. We initially failed to understand the required alignment between the Purpose of our business, the Processes required to run our business, and the enhancement of our culture and brand through our People.

What we eventually discovered is that training and development, to be aligned with our needs, needs to be viewed from four areas:

- **Situational:** Training required to develop teams to be able to operate within our organization and within customer organizations.
- **Technical:** Skills and knowledge required by teams to complete the tasks outlined in our scope of services.
- **Attitude:** An awareness to develop and dial in the behaviors required to be successful.
- **Reality Based:** Individualized training and development based on a person's strengths and weaknesses.

Of the four areas, the first three—Situational, Technical, and Attitude—apply to many of our teams, resulting in a significant return on our training dollar investment. By developing each of these four strategic compartments for our training, we were able to ensure alignment between our People and the Processes in which they need to operate, and the Purpose for the service and needs of our customer.

STAR Overview Table				
	S	T	A	R
Train	**Situation** Training, orienting teams to thrive in their situation.	**Technical** Training the required technical skills for the activities to be completed.	**Attitude** Continually coaching the team on the required behaviors.	**Reality** Seeing the individual and their specific needs and developing accordingly.

Our team members were required to understand:

- Our market.
- Our brand promise.
- The fact that we operated as teams.
- The culture of our company.
- The culture of our customer.
- Every technical aspect of every activity or task required by our service.
- How we behaved and acted towards our customer and our people.
- The individual strengths and opportunities for improvement contained within each of us.

The STAR approach provided a simple model that met this need.

SITUATIONAL TRAINING AND DEVELOPMENT

I am going to walk through four different stories—each of which will outline a different situation we faced, and that may represent one you might be facing—and how we needed to develop our teams to cope with the demands of each unique situation. The training required in each scenario is different, not a cookie-cutter solution, but specific to the needs and circumstances of each situation. Similarly, you will have to be sensitive to the need for your training to be customized for the various situations you face in your business.

Situation One: Understanding our Business

The room was a healthy mix of corporate, advisory board, operational management, operational support, and one Harvard professor, Ben Shapiro. Ben led this diverse, seasoned group of 70-plus people in a discussion about our current situation and our dreams of a future situation. He used an architecture called the "Magic Matrix" to frame the discussion, analyzing the revenues and profits for our service offerings relative to our key customers. This two-day discussion painted a picture for everyone so we could understand where and why we made money, where we could realize our highest and lowest potentials for growth, and how we stacked up against our competition.

In the first few hours, as Ben introduced the work that lay ahead, many in the room whose normal day was made up of the daily grind of "getting the job done" were confused as to why they were here. By the end of the session, the feeling of the group was significantly different. They understood how their experience contributed to deciding the future direction of the company. They understood the challenges in the market outside of their day-to-day challenges. Ben's Magic Matrix created a means for everyone to visualize our business and their role in our business, and to buy into the agreed-upon direction.

Situation Two: Understanding the Customer's Perspective

As the production line fired up at a Japanese manufacturing plant, several members of our management team entered into a training room along with a dozen or so members of the customer's manufacturing team. This was the first of several days where this team of manufacturing, production, and service personnel would learn and discuss the "Toyota Way."

Although most of our customers in some way, shape, or form were involved in the transportation industry, each of them had a different philosophy on how they approached their business. In this situation at this plant, we needed to understand completely the manufacturing philosophy of this customer if we were fully to align our services to their needs. As time went on, books like *The Toyota Way*, by Jeff K. Liker, and *Gemba Walks*, by Jim Womack, made this far easier to accomplish and communicate down into the ranks of the organization.

Situation Three: Understanding the Team's Perspective

As Dale, our newly-hired director of training, finalized his paperwork, the discussion led to his first assignment: to report to work as a third-shift worker, providing paint shop cleaning services in one of our automotive assembly plants. "Say what?" If Dale was to understand our needs fully, he needed to be in the place of greatest potential, to see the world from the perspective of an hourly worker. In this situation, Dale witnessed first-hand what issues and concerns faced team members, and he was able to identify necessary steps to improve the situation. Dale spent the better part of a month in this role, performing the work, interacting with his team on the third shift, while working under the shift supervisor. This on-boarding technique removed any ambiguity about what we faced and what corrective actions were needed. The time Dale spent as a third-shift worker allowed him to witness first-hand what needed to be done to better develop our front-line supervision.

Situation Four: The School of Hard Knocks

It would be great if we possessed the insight back in the mid- to late 1990s to understand fully the need for situational training, but we did not. Many of the real lessons learned came from the school of hard knocks, and once learned were integrated into The Outsourcing Conundrum Model. Hindsight is truly 20/20. Our saving grace was due to our culture. Many vital discussions made it to the boardroom, and many became strategic initiatives with ownership.

Larry walked between the two huge pieces of production equipment, and suddenly felt a chill through his body he could not immediately explain. Seemingly out of nowhere, several gallons of pretty cold water were dumped on him. It was a perfect, well-rehearsed hit that thoroughly soaked Larry. He was stunned and dazed as he looked up to find the water's source. It was not to be found, but later in the shift Larry was informed, "You have been initiated. It is just part of the environment." Larry was a new supervisor working third shift at a manufacturing facility in northeastern Ohio. We had been awarded a management services contract, and our goal was to improve the effectiveness and efficiency of the current workforce, which was the source of the water.

Daniel was not quite as lucky as Larry. Instead of being bathed in water, he was drenched in purge solvent. The solvent burnt his skin and hair, and hospitalized Daniel for many months.

Neither Larry nor Daniel continued with their IOSP careers—Daniel for very obvious reasons, and Larry because deep down he did not wish to end up like Daniel. Both Larry and Daniel worked for an IOSP in the mid- to late '90s, a very difficult era for the industry, and very different than it is today. The types of situations they faced required people who were able to thrive in this very tough environment. Basically we needed some bad-asses, people wired to confront these types of situations and win. Fortunately, over the years since, we have evolved the IOSP working environment and the way in which we do things. Nowadays, with a defined "selection target" and the ability to hire to that target, we have managed to hire teams and train them to understand the situations in which they find themselves so they can, in turn, apply their skills and abilities to change the situation instead of simply reacting to it. In a matter of a couple of years, by training to rules of engagement and applying a strict set of disciplines, the workforce changed and became 50 to 60 percent more efficient and effective.

How Situations Teach and Train Us

Each of these four stories illustrates how people became more knowledgeable of their situation. With Ben, the team grew to learn about the strategy of the company and our marketplace. The Toyota Way informed our group of the manufacturing philosophy of the customer. Dale learned what was really going on on the front lines, giving him the insight to develop our long-term training strategy more effectively. Larry's and Daniel's situations exposed gaps in the target for selection, which we needed to hire against, and also the level of orientation required in that environment to achieve success.

A 2013 report of a study done on 230 organizations by the Aberdeen Group reveals their findings of best on-boarding practices to improve level of productivity, engagement, and retention of new hires. The most interesting point they found was the same as what we realized: 90 percent of all new hires make their decision to stay with the company long-term in the first year. It is not rocket science to conclude that Larry and Daniel, after their on-boarding experiences, would decide to pursue a different avenue for their long-term career. Similar to the findings in the Aberdeen report, we realized that our on-boarding and orientation processes needed to include our corporate strategy along with the technical requirements of the position. Retention relied on each new hire understanding the "why" behind our business as well as "what" the job entailed.

By 2005, our process to fully inform and train our new hires to adapt to their working environment and situation had improved greatly by introducing them to:

- The vision and values of our company.
- Our corporate strategy.
- The strategic operation plan for their specific location.
- Their individual Performance Map.

All new hires were assigned to a team that provided them with on-the-job instruction, safe levels of exposure to their working environment, and a sense of belonging.

In the years that followed, teams at each site became more involved in the selection process, which resulted in them becoming more invested in the success of each selected new hire. With the advancement of technology, our tools to help support the on-boarding and orientation process had improved greatly and allowed for all new hires at all sites in all countries to hear the same messages.

From the '70s, where we basically hired a pair of hands, to present day, where our competiveness relies on our ability to hire the whole person, we have learned that the on-boarding and orientation at a minimum must explain:

- Who we are and how we serve.
- Why we are in business.
- Who our customer is and why.
- The culture of our customer.
- What the customer needs from our service.
- The value of the tasks and activities we perform.

In order to remain continually dialed into our business and working situations, we continued to invite well-respected authors, business professionals, university professors, and customers to engage with our management teams. These engagements provided insight into new business thinking, marketplace challenges, customer challenges, and where we needed to be in the future.

We also found it very beneficial to examine the operating culture and environment of each new customer and site to ensure we were aligned and able to meet their needs. This examination resulted in declining to engage with some customers, as their values did not align with ours, especially in relation to how we treated our people.

Several times throughout this book, I mention the concept of "We Serve Days," where someone from our management team would visit a facility and perform the work of an hourly team-member. I also touched on an initiative where management teams were encouraged to visit other customer locations to engage, share, and swap ideas for improvement. We called each of these visits a "Yoketen." "Yoketen," simply stated, means copying and improving ideas that work, similar to best-practice sharing, but with an emphasis on improving the idea.

Our ability to understand the situations our team members worked in also provided us with keen insight into the technical training our teams needed to be successful.

TECHNICAL TRAINING AND DEVELOPMENT

Our technical training was designed and developed to improve our teams' skills, provide knowledge, and share/inform on best practices. Our technical training took many forms:

- On the job
- Classroom
- Online
- Gamification
- Simulation
- Experiential
- Books/Reading

In the very early years, our training was primarily classroom-based, and the main focus of our training was on our internal service delivery systems and processes. Our business was made up of hundreds of satellite locations, situated within customer facilities, and in many countries. One huge benefit we sought with our initial training was the interaction of our teams from around the world, discussing our processes, and sharing ideas for improvement.

One of the constant battles associated with face-to-face training in a classroom environment was the cost of getting people to the class. We could never fully tie our investment in face-to-face training to our bottom line. We knew the cost, but return on investment was always a debate. In the previous chapter, Select, we discussed some of our turnover issues. As we improved our hiring process, we began to monitor our training process as well. The combination of the two led to a dramatic improvement in our employee retention numbers. During site visits and discussion with our teams, and noticeable interaction between teams, we erred on the side of continuing to invest in face-to-face, classroom-type training.

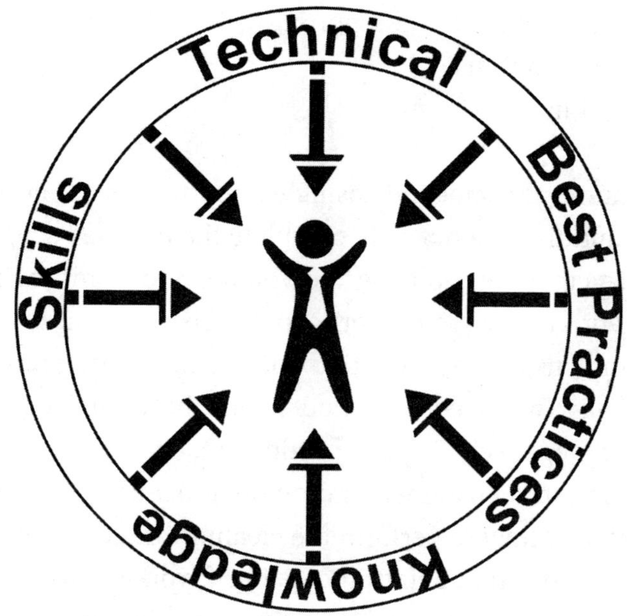

We also opened our training to our customers, and encouraged them to participate. There were many benefits to doing this. It allowed customers truly to understand who we were and what we were all about. It also allowed customers to participate in discussions about some of our issues and concerns.

During one of our training sessions attended by a customer, Jon, we were openly discussing the challenge of viewing our service from our customers' perspective. Jon posed the question, "Would you not be better aligned with us if you participated in our manufacturing and production systems training?" This dialogue and discussion led to Jon helping us formally enroll all of our management teams in the training classes at the plant to understand the customer's perspectives better on subjects like:

- Problem solving and escalation
- Visual management and reporting
- Root-cause analysis
- Continual improvement

Technical training became increasingly important as our customers began to demand that we not only complete the outlined scope of work, but also participate in reducing the volume and number of activities associated with the scope of work. To do this well, our teams needed to understand customer production and manufacturing processes better. Specifically, we needed to understand how our activities could positively or negatively impact production. For example, all of our teams working in a customer's automotive paint department needed to know not only how to perform the cleaning and maintenance tasks, but also how the actual paint process itself worked. With this knowledge, they could contribute to improving the painting process, thereby improving the value we brought to the customer.

Our Performance Maps, explained in the previous chapter, Select, also served as the source documents to identify what training was required by each position. Performance Maps were designed to be current with changes in responsibilities and expectations for each position, resulting in changes to the training and development matrix as the individual Performance Maps evolved.

Versatility Training Matrix

Course Name	Team Member	Team Leader	Supervisor	Manager
Level III				★
Level II			★	★
Level I		★	★	★
Process Skills	★	★	★	★
On-Job	★	★	★	★

At the site level with our team members, we incorporated a tool we called the "versatility training matrix." The purpose of this tool was to capture each team member's ability to perform the activities included in our scope of work. We followed an on-the-job, train-the-trainer methodology, with the goal of improving the versatility of our team members, resulting in a much more flexible workforce.

Not only does the content of your training need to be aligned with your organization's needs as well as the needs of your customers, but there also needs to be alignment between the content of your training and the mode of its delivery. That is, some training methods and environments are more suited to certain kinds of content than others.

We found, for example, that a classroom environment along with the use of simulations, became the option of choice for our management/

supervision and leadership skills training program. This training was typically divided into Levels I through III, as shown in the matrix. The curriculum for each level was revised annually to ensure alignment with the needs of our people and our customer. For a brief period, we explored the use of online training for some of our management/ supervision and leadership training, but face-to-face interaction between the teams was a critical part of the learning experience.

We found that online training was more appropriate when the transfer of knowledge was just one way. Required certification training for things like safety was very adaptable to forms of online training. Safety Management, though, was better suited for a classroom environment. Certain forms of technology training, like understanding how a production process works, were also well aligned for online training, which allowed us to transfer knowledge into the minds of thousands of our team members in a cost-effective way.

In the chapter Deliver to Standard, I speak about the use of "Alert Bulletins," a simple multi-page document used to capture and communicate best practices across all of our sites. A vast majority of the Alert Bulletins shared technical knowledge, which improved our ability to be efficient and effective in the delivery of activities for our customers. The Alert Bulletins became an informal training method, whereby team members from around the world could share, and train each other on, best practices.

In 2006 we made an investment in a tool called "Idea Central," which enabled us to have an online, virtual community in which to share and discuss new ideas. Idea Central allowed us to harness the collective wisdom of all our teams from across all our sites. Unlike the Alert Bulletins, Idea Central allowed not only the sharing of ideas but also a good forum for collaboration and developing the ideas around process improvements and other business challenges. One symptom with the development of the online virtual community was the promotion of collaboration and consensus building around new projects and initiatives.

In a previous chapter, Assemble, Align and Assess People, I introduced you to our Operating Norms. Our operating norms documented a commitment to how we would behave and treat each other as a team. One of those operating norms was, "I teach and learn every day." The use of Alert Bulletins and Idea Central were two ways that helped us live that creed.

ATTITUDE TRAINING AND DEVELOPMENT

"Hi Damian,

I stopped in and saw the pipe. I emptied the container while I was there too. I do suggest you have a plumber repair that piece asap, as it is under pressure and could release if the hole gets bigger."

Bob Weather, CAM
Maintenance Supervisor
Property Management Group

Sitting in my kitchen working on notes for this chapter, I felt a drop of water on my hand, then another, and another. Looking up, I noticed the ceiling drywall formed a pocket housing a lot more water. Great! After about an hour of demolition, I had a three-foot by three-foot opening in the drywall, exposing a leaking copper pipe with a pinhole leak nowhere close to any solder joint.

I live in a condominium that is managed by an IOSP providing property management services. I reached out to our in-house maintenance supervisor to inform him of the problem and obtain his advice. His response is captured in the quotation above. As I sat pondering how to introduce this part of the chapter, I realized his response was a perfect example to lead off the subject of attitude. Take a moment and re-read his email. Bob took time out of his day to tell me he saw the pipe, concluded it was leaking, and suggested I needed a plumber as soon as possible as the hole may get bigger. Gee, Bob, without your counsel, I could not have figured that out.

As an IOSP, what Bob totally missed was that my need was "WHY" was the pipe leaking, not "HOW" to fix it. The attitude with which you approach a customer's problem will make or break the quality of service experienced by your customer. Over the years I faced many situations like this one with Bob, where one of our site managers pointed out the obvious to the customer and did not represent us as what we branded ourselves to be, "a solutions provider."

There are many uses and definitions of the word attitude. In *The Outsourcing Conundrum*, attitude is defined as the way someone will act in, or react to, a circumstance. In the previous chapter, Select, I outlined necessary behaviors we sought in our new hires. These combined behaviors embodied our attitude towards our people and our customer. Our attitude of being people- and customer-focused is who we are. Our attitude represented our culture and our brand, and we did not take it lightly.

To instill our attitude, it was integrated it into every form of training. In 2008, we revised the training of our service delivery model into a board game that could be played during breaks by all of our team members. The use of gamification as a means of training underscored our need to behave consistently as a team. By playing the game, you had fun, were open minded, listened to your colleagues, shared experiences, sought out new ideas, communicated with others, acted socially, and were respectful of others' points of view.

Idea Central, as mentioned, promoted collaboration, building consensus, learning from one another, instructing others, influencing others, and having the confidence to reach out and speak out. During classroom training, we also paid a lot of attention to the attitude conveyed by our teams as they interacted to resolve issues during simulations.

You have read many stories about Team Trek throughout this book and how they contributed to helping us further develop our leadership skills. The training at Team Trek was a major contributor in promoting and refining our targeted attitude, to push through a situation and not become a victim of a situation.

None of what I have described would be remotely possible if we did not first and foremost make the conscious decision on what our targeted attitude needed to be, and then document our desired attitude in the form of competencies and behaviors in our Performance Maps. The right attitude can allow people to pole vault over amazing heights.

Earlier in this chapter, in the section on Situational Training, I spoke about our need to hire "bad asses" in order to be able to enact change in a very difficult situation. What labeled these management teams as "bad asses" was their disciplined use of the rules to establish order in the management of customer employees. By 2005 this situation began to change, and hourly positions held by customer employees were being transferred to our own employees. We would no longer manage our customers' people, but instead they would be our people. The seasoned management team who had performed so well in the previous situation of training a whole bunch of "old dogs, new tricks," now needed to change again and adapt to engaging a whole bunch of "new dogs," now our own people, in the delivery of our service. In order to initiate the required attitudinal adjustment, we engaged the University of Michigan and enrolled members of our upper management team in courses designed to develop positive leadership skills, to enable them to engage our teams. It was imperative for our long-term survival that our people be engaged in initiatives like Alert Bulletins, Idea Central, and suggestions for improvements. Without engagement of the whole team, we would not be able to be competitive.

We held an annual conference, attended by all site managers, to participate in a discussion around our strategic operating plan for the upcoming year. As part of the annual meeting agenda, we also invited our high-performing/high-potential supervisors to present to their colleagues. The topic of the presentations was typically geared to sharing a proven best practice. We found this exposure, in a safe environment, allowed these high-potentials the opportunity to hone their presentation skills for future use with our customers. The real benefit from these presentations was the difference in their attitude afterwards. They felt very valued and respected, and that attitude was taken back to their sites.

Even though we embraced and invested in the development of our teams, we knew that each of these teams was made up of individuals, and their individuality needed to be understood and valued. To do this, we also invested in training and development rooted in the basic reality of each individual.

REALITY-BASED TRAINING AND DEVELOPMENT

Reality-based training takes into account people's desires. Some people just want to come to work, do their job, and go home. Others want to grow and excel. Both are critically important to your organization.

Understanding the realities of the individuals on your teams is crucial. Reality-based training, seeing the individual and their specific needs and developing them accordingly, consumes a lot of time and resources. It is critical to assess the individuals' progress in this area; if you don't, the resources applied to reality-based training are wasted.

In the upcoming chapter, Assess, we are going to discuss the Assessment process used to keep our teams aligned by keeping our individual team players aligned and moving forward with their personal training and development. Here, we focus on the importance and relevance of including this type of training and development for individuals in your organization's people strategy. By focusing on each individual's strengths, and helping them develop from those strengths, you will move your teams, and the IOSP as a whole, ahead by leaps and bounds.

People joined our company from all walks of life. We targeted each position to find people who "fit" as well as people who could help us move forward. In all cases, the individuals we hired, who collectively made up our teams, all had individual training requirements. As we explored tools like the Devine Inventory and Strength Finder, we began to understand fully that applying resources dedicated to improving one's weaknesses was not nearly as effective as resources dedicated to building one's strengths.

The better we understood ourselves as individuals, the better we were able to appreciate the diversity of our team and draw on one another's strengths.

One of the best pieces of counsel I received from a mentor was to understand two things:

- You need to know what you know.
- You need to know what you don't know.

If you understand and can answer these two questions, your development path is much clearer and much more meaningful. What is important to note about reality-based training in this chapter is that the need for it is very real and very important to your overall people strategy.

For over 10 years I had the opportunity to work with an extraordinarily skilled guy, and I could not understand why he always deflected opportunities to advance himself. Over time, and after I had been promoted many times, I found out he had a learning issue. He had a very tough time comprehending what he read, which made him feel inadequate, negatively affecting his self-confidence. As the digital age grew and audio books grew, he began to grow. These tools allowed him to compensate for a disability and fulfill his dreams. His reality was that he could not comprehend what he read. Others I met could not write or understand math, or had a variety of other issues that in today's world can be easily offset if we see the strength of the individual and their benefit to the team. The digital age—with online training that allows someone to move at their own pace to overcome some of these issues—has enhanced our ability to deal more easily with individual reality-based training and development.

One of the best things we ever did was to promote a very basic form of individual training—reading. Business and self-help books were an acceptable expense, and fully reimbursed. We celebrated and praised those who would read a book and write a brief book summary for inclusion in our newsletter, or attach it to an email blast. The use of audio books during time on the road was highly encouraged, and we found many of the team began swapping, sharing, and discussing the merits of one book over another.

We also supported members of the team who attended courses put on by a variety of schools, both in class and online, that focused on specific training requirements for the individual. This allowed team members to upgrade their computer skills, reading comprehension skills, foreign language skills, or better manage other issues they faced, such as anger management.

As we move forward into the next chapter, Assess, we will dig into the steps you can take to hold up a mirror to team members so they can see and appreciate themselves for who they are and what they can accomplish.

BEST PRACTICE

Charlie Plumb stood in front of a couple hundred site managers, pacing eight feet to the right and then eight feet to the left. As he paced, he spoke to the group about his experience at the Hanoi Hilton, the name give to the POW camp in Vietnam where he spent many years. During the course of the evening, Charlie drew the crowd into that cell with him, not necessarily to share what life is like as a prisoner of war, but more importantly what it is like to be a prisoner in your own mind. He used the story to plant in the minds of our operational management team the need to lead yourself, create choices for yourself, and not become a victim.

Charlie was just one of dozens of people who were invited over the years to interact with our management teams, providing them insight on how to lead themselves and, in turn, lead others.

Whether it was Charlie Plumb, Dave Ulrich, Ben Shapiro, or countless others, our engagement of these professionals sent a message to our management teams that we recognized them for what they do, what they know, and, most importantly, what they can become. Most of them, upon returning to their site locations, shared and passed that knowledge on to their teams, and their teams passed that knowledge onto their teams.

PROCUREMENT

You can help your IOSP's chances of success if you can help them align their training requirements with those for the employees in your own facilities. Every company who procures inside-outsourcing services uses forms of orientation training for their own internal purposes. Take the time to educate the IOSPs you choose to work in your plants, and educate them as well on how your facilities think and act.

QUICK STORY

Earlier in this chapter, I shared a story with you about Larry and Daniel, the poor victims of misguided pranks. During that same time frame, as part of the improvements in efficiency being implemented at the plant, we began to introduce machines designed to clean factory aisles. The system was cleaner and faster than could be accomplished with a mop and bucket. The units are generally known as ride-on or walk-behind scrubbers. The introduction of these machines allowed us to redistribute up to 80 percent of the existing workforce to new duties. Well, to say that our team members met these new "toys" with any level of enthusiasm would be an exaggeration.

Tony, the site manager, watched an hourly worker walk the machine onto the freight elevator that went to the roof. There were no aisles to clean on the roof. Tony quickly ascended the stairs and arrived on the roof just in time to see the hourly worker walk the machine right off the end of the roof. He walked over as it plummeted to the ground and broke into several dozen pieces. "Why did you do that?" "I guess I just don't want to change?" Yep, those were tough years.

Marcus Buckingham, in his book *First Break All the Rules*, discusses that every high performer wants to be able to state they have the required equipment, materials, and tools to complete their work, and that someone speaks to them regularly about how they can learn and grow. By putting the time into understanding the targeted needs of your team, you can develop targeted training to meet your organization's needs; it is a very simple formula.

Select puts team members into the starting blocks for the race. Train gets them efficiently out of the blocks and into the race.

TAKEAWAYS:

- Training and development is a slow, methodical process that requires stretching each and every day.
- The team needs to be trained to fully understand their new situation, whether it is a new operation, or a new role.
- Training is an investment, often hard to measure. Lack of training has a cost that is easy to measure.
- Don't forget—your team consists of individuals, all of whom have their own unique needs.

PEOPLE

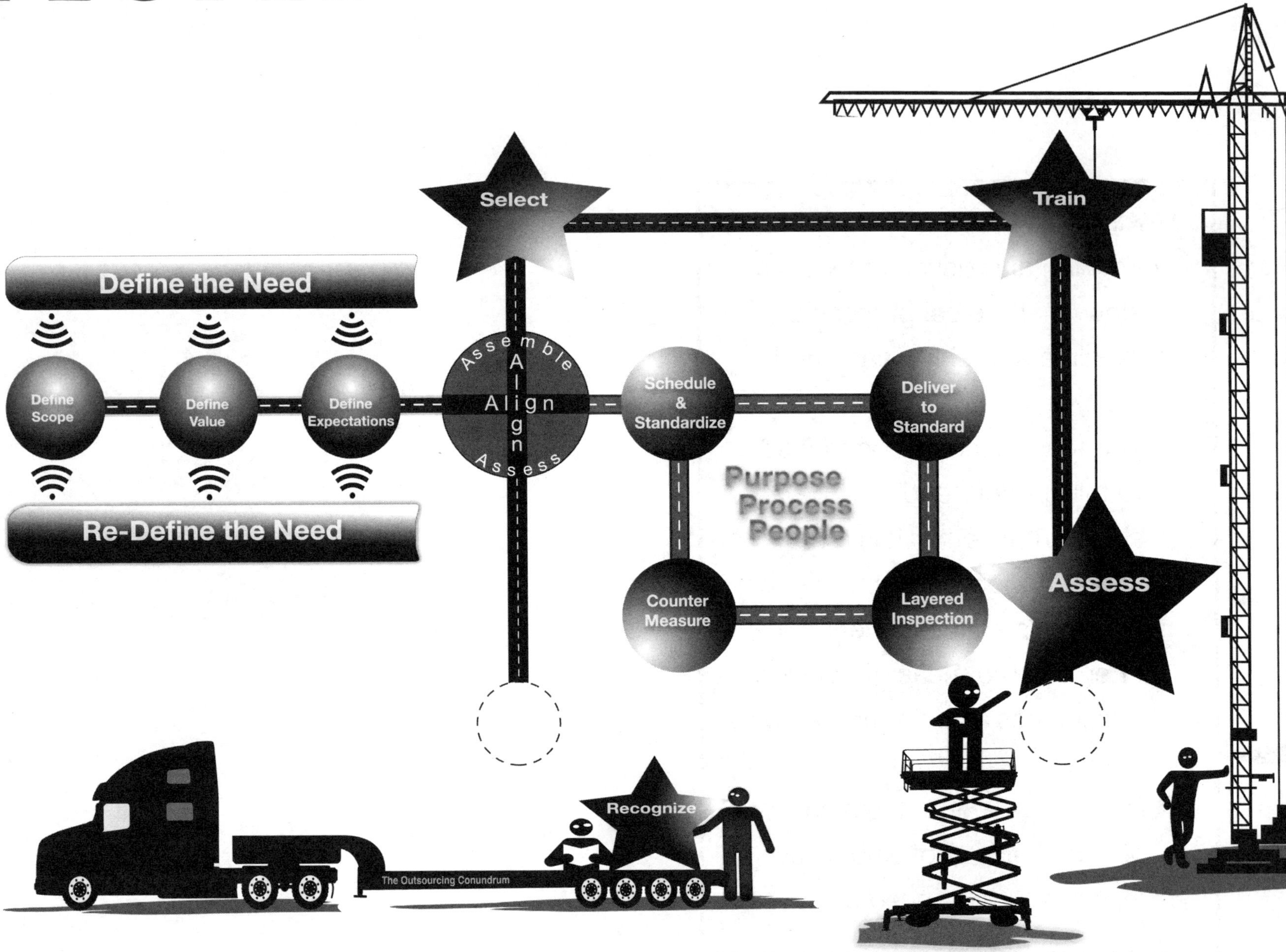

Select
Train
Define the Need
Define Scope
Define Value
Define Expectations
Assemble
Align
Assess
Schedule & Standardize
Deliver to Standard
Purpose
Process
People
Counter Measure
Layered Inspection
Assess
Re-Define the Need
Recognize
The Outsourcing Conundrum

"Everything that irritates us about others can lead us to an understanding of ourselves."

Carl Jung

"Experience is not what happens to you; it's what you do with what happens to you."

Aldous Huxley

"The pessimist complains about the wind; the optimist expects it to change; the realist adjusts the sails."

William Arthur Ward

When I was growing up, the worst days of my life were the days when the school sent me home with my report card. That little piece of paper containing one line for each subject, and a box where the teacher could place a letter followed by a brief notation such as, "Damian needs to listen in class," caused me nothing but heartache. I grew up in the day and age where if you were not doing well in school, it was actually your fault and not the teacher's. Report card day was quickly followed by the dreaded parent-teacher night. As my parents readied themselves to head for my school, I would grab the vacuum and clean my room. I was hoping for the sympathy vote upon their return. The 15-minute parent-teacher meeting, however, always resulted in no TV, street hockey, or any other fun activity for a month. As I refused to learn from this experience, I pretty much went without TV for four months of the year for over 10 years. By the time I was halfway through high school, and after more than 40 parent-teacher meetings, my parents concluded their system was not working. My parents informed me that they were washing their hands of my situation, and my future was now in my own hands. Gee, ya think? My future was always in my own hands, and my successes and failures were mine to bear.

It was around this time that I started my first job as a dishwasher. This was going to be great—my own money, a sense of freedom, my life was now my own, and no more parent-teacher nights. I was ecstatic! After a few months, however, I was called into the head cook's office and given an "appraisal." The cook took out a little piece of paper containing one line for each activity, and a box where she would place a number and a comment. "ARE YOU KIDDING ME?" The only upside was that there was no parent-head cook night. The head cook was actually a great person and she took time to help all the part-time students who were part of her team.

The reality of the situation, which I did not fully appreciate at the time, either in school or in my part-time dishwasher job, is that most people are just as fearful as I was then of the annual assessment, appraisal, and evaluation processes.

In the very early 1990s, my family and I relocated to Cincinnati, Ohio, and I went to work for an IOSP, a company that focused on providing inside-outsourcing manufacturing and support services. Like anyone in a new position in a new company, I was eager and apprehensive to know "how I was doing." By this time, I had been in the workforce for some 20 years and I thought I understood the purpose of the dreaded annual assessment. Not so.

My phone rang and it was my boss, inquiring if I had some free time in the coming month to have a conversation about "how things are going." Was this the code phrase for "the assessment?" Funny thing, though, he went on to ask where I wished to hook up, and if there was any topic in particular I wished to cover while we were together. We set a date, chose an offsite location and, as was typical, my anxiety grew, even though this was not shaping up like any assessment I had experienced before.

After the meeting, I sat back and reflected on what had happened. I felt motivated and energized, with a real sense of belonging and accomplishment. True to my nature, I jotted down the steps to the "assessment meeting."

1. I was invited, instead of being told to be there.
2. I chose the geography, a place I felt safe.
3. I was given the choice of topics to discuss.
4. I was asked if I enjoyed my job, my workmates, and my work situation.
5. I was encouraged to share any new knowledge I had gained.
6. I was asked if there were any areas in which I felt dissatisfied with my results, and if I needed any help to change those outcomes.
7. I was asked about my plans and goals for the future, and if anything could be done to help me with those.
8. Finally, I was asked, if we switched places, what changes would I make to the company?

STAR Overview Table				
	S	T	A	R
Assess	**Situation** Evaluating how the team performed in their situation.	**Training** Evaluating the growth and development of the team.	**Action** Evaluating their attitude by their actions.	**Results** Evaluating the team's ability to meet the measurable targets.

The second thing I did was jot down notes summarizing as much of the conversation as I could recall. What I found was that the discussion fell into four areas:

1. **Situation:** How did I like my situation? My position? My work environment? My colleagues?
2. **Training:** What had I done to improve myself? What did I feel I still needed to do? Did I need any help?
3. **Actions:** By discussing my work situation and rapport with my colleagues, I was actually explaining how I acted and behaved.
4. **Results:** By reporting on my results, I took ownership of my own achievements and was given the chance to request support if required. I was also given the chance to build off of my results and discuss my future ambitions.

The manner in which this assessment was done removed the "fear" from the assessment, allowing me the opportunity to assess myself honestly and not just be assessed by my manager. The purpose of assessment was to encourage and motivate the right behaviors, not dwell on failure.

In the chapter Select, we spoke in great detail about hiring to a set target. In the chapter Train, we discussed training and development of that target. It only makes sense that assessment continually needs to energize the people you have hired and trained, rather than to humiliate and deflate them.

FEAR

In my experience, the biggest hurdle to implementing, sustaining, and mastering an assessment process is overcoming participants' fears. Jay Jackman and Myra Strober, in their *Harvard Business Review* article "Fear of Feedback," discuss the psychological theory that people's recollection of being criticized by their teachers and parents contributes to their fear of assessments and feedback. For most of us, embracing feedback is not natural; it is something that requires training and practice. It is also something that needs to be done in a safe environment, and, like most training, true results cannot be seen immediately. In "Fear of Feedback," Jack and Myra go on to discuss that, without the necessary training to accept feedback, team members can and will resort to some pretty destructive tendencies such as:

- Procrastination – purposely missing deadlines.
- Denial – unwillingness to face reality.
- Pouting – passive paralysis.
- Jealousy – suspicion, rivalry towards others.
- Self-Sabotage – unconsciously undercutting oneself.

For the better part of a decade, I worked alongside a remarkably talented guy, Bill, who could not or would not face his fear and embrace feedback. At one point in his career, he was given the title of Vice President. From all accounts, this decision was a mistake and the title was subsequently taken away. Bill was not what people would call "management material." He was, however, very intelligent, very organized, and very technical, with an aptitude for detail. He just did not "fit" the role of management, and history proved on several occasions that management was not his forte.

Despite several attempts at positive feedback and encouragement, Bill, year after year, chose to move from one destructive tendency to another. He would purposely delay completion of key projects. He slowly lost his colleagues' respect due to his perpetual pouting. Colleagues receiving promotions sent him into complete tailspins. He felt the world was against him, and no one recognized his talents and abilities. His ability to live in denial could put him in the running for an Academy Award.

Shortly after 9/11, Bill entered my office and announced he had reactivated his military status to do a tour in the Middle East. He was drawn back into military life because it offered him rank and title. Bill's tour lasted a year, and, upon his return, he convinced himself he would be offered an upper-management position. When that did not happen, he became even more disgruntled, which eventually led to his dismissal. Bill was strong enough to go overseas and confront an enemy, but he was unable to confront the enemy within. This led him to live his life in a prison of his own making, surrounded by his own fears.

Bill was the epitome of someone who would not accept the reality of his gifts; he had many talents, but executive leadership was not one of them.

Situations like this one with Bill emphasize the need for a much more dynamic tool than the traditional job description to outline the actual expectations of each position and to ensure each position is aligned with our, and our customer's, strategic need.

JOB DESCRIPTION VS. PERFORMANCE MAP

As we have already seen, most things work best when there is a target. This is especially true when you are working with a people process, because people inherently like to see the finish line and know how they stacked up. In the chapter Select, we introduced a tool called the Performance Map, designed to outline clearly the targets for every position in the company. Before implementing Performance Maps, we used traditional job descriptions. A job description does not establish the target behaviors, competencies, or outcomes of the position. It does little more than outline the details and necessary tasks of a job. The Performance Map, on the other hand, provides direction on how to improve one's overall performance, and can also be used to assess overall performance.

The Performance Map allows us to assess how an individual has performed in their situation, any gaps in their training and development, how they acted, and what results they achieved. The Performance Map, unlike a job description, is dynamic and can be changed annually to align with corporate and customer goals, serving as a source of strategic alignment for every member of the team. Chapter 4, Define Expectations, emphasized the need to define the customer's and the IOSP's expectations fully, so those expectations can be communicated to those who actually perform the work. The Performance Map acts as that communication at the individual level, to define the expectation of each individual and to be able assess each person against the current expectation as opposed to an old expectation. As a result, the Performance Map is much more fluid, and much more easily aligned with your organization's, and your customer's, needs.

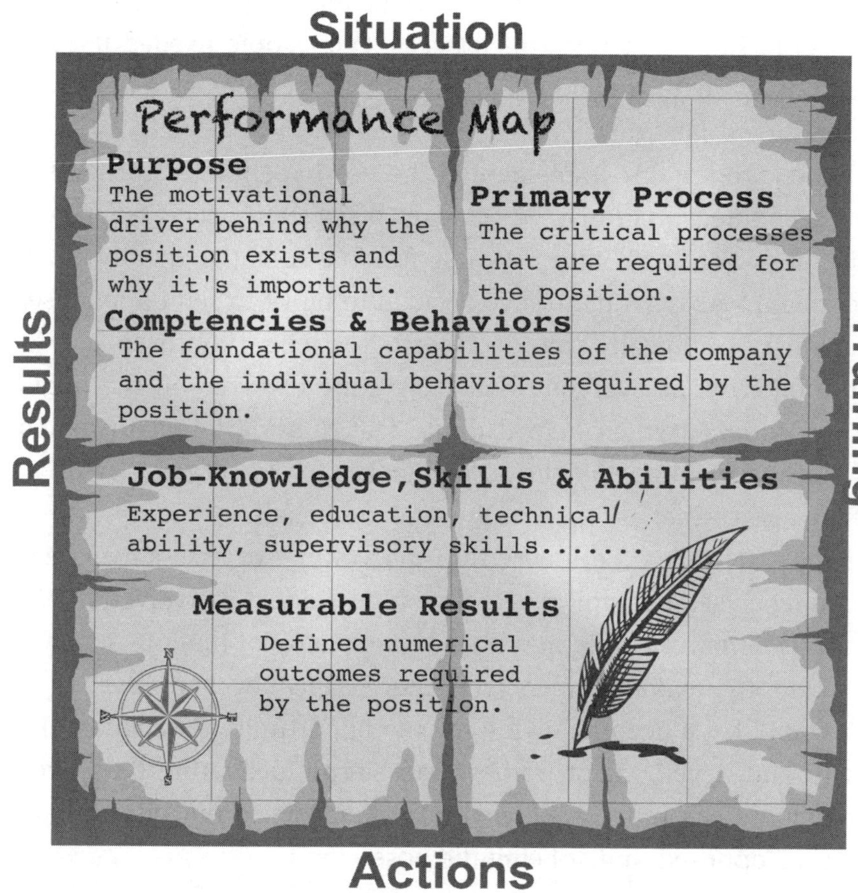

The use of the Performance Map for assessments allows us to answer many key questions that a traditional job description cannot get to the bottom of:

- **Situation:** Does the team member fit? Do they embody our values? Does the position fit them or is a change required?
- **Training and Development**: Does the team member have potential? Has the team member grown? Was there an increase in their job-knowledge, skills, and abilities?
- **Actions:** Did the team member perform? Are their actions consistent with our values and our brand?
- **Results:** Did the team member perform? Did they meet or exceed the metrics outlined for the position?

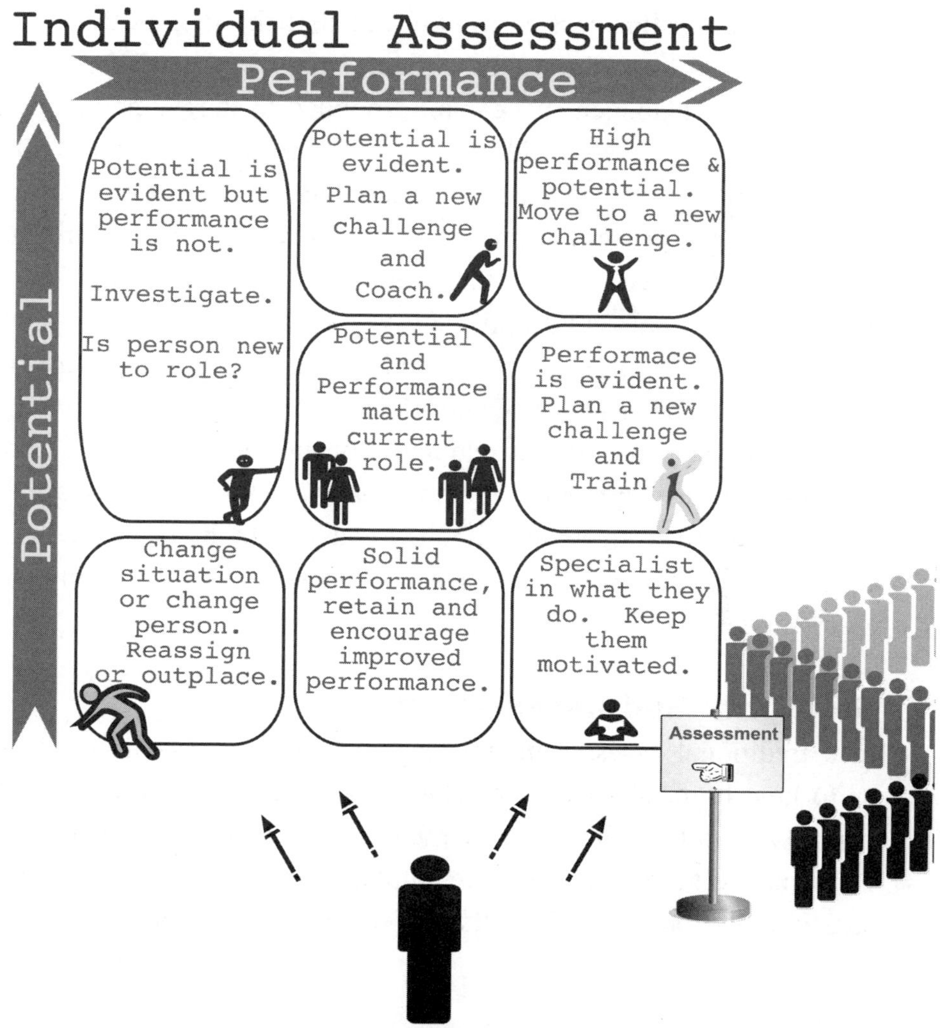

Having the tool to truly answer the questions in each of the four areas provided our company a great advantage as an IOSP. The development of the Performance Map as this tool was a critical step, but how we approached the assessment process with our teams became a more important key to our success.

SELF-AWARENESS

We operated our business at hundreds of sites throughout the world, and it was very important to us as an organization that all our teams, especially our management teams, responded to the changing needs of the customer so we could realign all our people accordingly. Our management teams needed to be adaptable, so it was critical that our assessment process promoted adaptability. We felt that creating a process that developed an individual's self-awareness was key to achieving this goal. Philosophically, we wanted our team members to be able to look into the mirror and assess themselves against the target that had been set for the position.

Our first step was the development of the tools, and our second step was the development of the approach. There were two obstacles that we needed to overcome: abolish fear and embody adaptability. To do this, we adopted the practice of self-assessment and multi-point assessment.

Step One: Self-assessment

In a traditional assessment, the person being assessed is informed as to how he or she is doing. The self-assessment asks team members to assess how they are doing by grading themselves against the Performance Map. It is a simple, subtle change that places supervisors into the position of facilitators of team members' growth and development, rather than being judges of their performance. One of the required training courses for our management teams was crucial conversation. This training and knowledge was a great enabler to becoming more proficient at facilitating meaningful, safe assessments. The word "safe" is key to this process. Our people needed to know that an assessment was not an attack; it was a caring, safe discussion around growth and development.

When we initially implemented the use of self-assessments, they were scheduled quarterly. We quickly discovered, due to our geography and workload, this was not feasible and the quality of the assessment was in jeopardy. We decided to move to semi-annual self-assessments. Ironically this decreased frequency improved comfort and familiarity, as everyone had more time to focus on the quality of the dialogue, which helped dilute fear. It's important to remember that the main goal of the assessment is to encourage growth and development—that is, the quality and outcomes of the assessment process—and not to be focused on the volume of assessments each person receives. In a typical year, I would be directly involved in 25 to 30 assessments, allowing me to view the quality of the interaction. In each case, the team members were more critical of themselves than I ever would have been, allowing me the opportunity to facilitate their growth and development, rather than simply delivering their actual assessment. The process allowed our managers to put on the hat of coach, as opposed to just being the boss.

As the self-assessment process evolved, conversation flowed more easily into discussion of where the team member wished to improve, and that allowed our management teams to facilitate those improvements in alignment with our strategic goals. The self-assessment started the reflective process of self-awareness.

Step Two: Multi-point Assessment

This step was rarely used in the hourly ranks, but became an important tool for assessing members of our management teams. Once a manager had become comfortable with the self-assessment process, the multi-point assessment was introduced. Managers were asked to provide a list of people with whom they had worked, who would be able to provide input on their growth and development. The specific feedback from those participating in the multi-point assessment was anonymous, but the names of the contributors were not, so although they were not able to accurately pinpoint a comment to a person, the managers being assessed knew the group that contributed to their complete multi-point assessment. We found this knowledge to be beneficial overall, as many managers would actually take their feedback and go and sit with those they had asked to participate in order to seek out more clarification on how they could grow and develop. Step Two was a huge step in self-awareness; it was also a big step forward in reducing the fear associated with feedback.

What I found amazing for both myself and for those who reported directly or indirectly to me was that, over the course of a couple of years, the level of openness among the team really grew. The number of people asking to be enrolled in training grew. The number of people reaching out to others to find the best business books to read grew. People were actually writing book summaries and sending them out electronically for others to read. People were openly soliciting help from each other on how to overcome a work or personal issue.

As our comfort level with self-awareness grew, we started to share results from our Devine Inventories. In team meetings, we would chart and present a team's overall behavioral development, quietly allowing individuals to see where they sat relative to the team. It was pretty common during these meetings for members of the team to question the absolute importance of one behavior versus another. This led to great discussion of the need for diversity of opinion and thought, and a continued push to embrace the complementary strengths of a colleague.

A prerequisite for teams attending training at Team Trek was the completion of a personality test. Upon arriving, one of the first things they encountered was sharing the results of the personality tests. With the help and support of our Team Trek partners, we made it possible for people to embrace their personality and the personalities of others, and to understand the need for both. The more our teams were exposed to being aware of who they were, the more their fear of assessment and feedback decreased. Another positive symptom from this focus on self-awareness was how open our management teams had become to seeking out feedback from our customers and passing it on to their teams at the sites.

PLOTTING

We used assessments not only to facilitate an individual's growth and development, but also to do the same for the team as a whole. Taking the idea of assessments one level up the organizational chart, the management group one level above the team being assessed would plot the results of each of the team members' assessments onto the Team

Assessment chart for that group. Plotting on the Team Assessment chart provides a visual talent map outlining who is struggling, who is excelling, and who has met capacity. Thus, individual assessments can be turned into a team development tool, allowing you to identify gaps in the team's performance, as well as opportunities for growth and development.

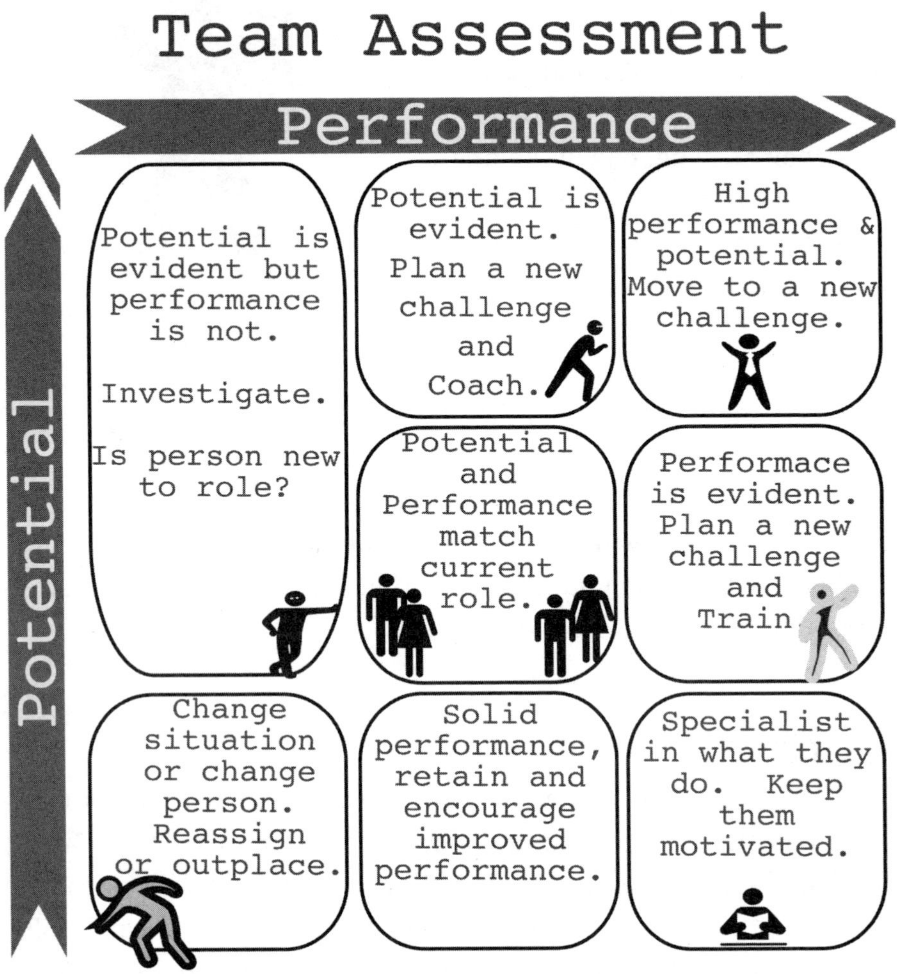

The management team, one level above the team whose assessments are plotted, can review the Team Assessment chart annually. This serves as a "four eyes" approach, providing visibility to everyone in the organization, with a special focus on talent and talent gaps—high-performers with high potential versus low-performers with little potential. One thing we knew about our team was that it was not overly tolerant of low performers. Everyone knew a low performer hurt our brand, so it was critical we knew how to identify them.

To enable us to expedite the overall assessment process, we invested in an online tool called STARway. The tool allowed us to create and store Performance Maps, and to perform assessments online. This provided us phenomenal oversight to monitor and view the assessment process. The database also allowed us to research common themes that could be addressed in our training and development process.

THE BOSS-HOLE

In his book, *The Human Equity Advantage*, Trevor Wilson talks about the "boss-hole." I am sure you are able to relate to this term without the need for too much explanation. Our goal was not to use the assessment process as a means of discipline, nor as a means to identify our "boss-holes." We felt that those who did not perform or did not represent our values or our brand required attention long before we sat down for an assessment. That being said, we are in the service business and, as such, we are in the people business. Often, by their nature, people postpone bad news or move it to another department or group. The use of the Performance Map in conjunction with the individual and team assessment allowed us to face performance issues head on, as well as to flush out the boss-holes who fell through the cracks, and provide them with career opportunities with our competitors.

BEST PRACTICE

Late one afternoon, I got off the bus at Team Trek and was met by Team Trek staff. I introduced myself, and was immediately placed into a group. This was my first visit, and it was our company's first interaction with Team Trek. At the end of the weekend, reflecting on my experience, I was amazed how the staff had sorted the 35 people into such cohesive teams. A year later I was back at Team Trek, this time with our global corporate team. Again we were divided into teams, and again the teams were cohesive.

Several years later, for my own growth and development, I took on the role of facilitator at Team Trek with one of their other customers. While preparing for the incoming group, I learned how Team Trek had mastered the use of the personality test that every participant completed. We spent several hours discussing each participant through his or her personality test, as well as team placement and areas of focus that might need particular attention. I call this a best practice because they had chosen a tool, from many, and had become disciplined in its application and execution. So many times we do not give a process a chance to succeed before condemning it to the failure pile. I find this truer with HR professionals than any other group. The personality test used by Team Trek was a very important detail in placing the right people on the right teams, allowing for a great experience for everyone. Isn't this simply what every IOSP is also trying to do?

PROCUREMENT

At all of the sites where our customer's management group got involved in the routine review of our employees' performance, we performed better. Why? We were able to take the feedback received at such meetings, and align our people to meet goals. In the course of a year, this generally required no more than four hours of plant management's time. Four hours, or 240 minutes, to align the IOSP's team to meet your needs. Huge R.O.I., yes?

QUICK STORY

Probably one of the most effective and efficient assessment processes I ever had the privilege of encountering was the one authored by Mr. Walsh. This guy was a true-blue boss-hole if I ever met one. It was the early 1970s, and my first day with a construction crew in Mississauga, Ontario. As the day began and tasks were handed out, I noticed there seemed to be more people than necessary for the number of assignments. In general conversation with a crew member who appeared to know what was going on, he told me not to worry about it because by the afternoon the herd would be leaned out.

The coffee truck rolled up to the site, and so did Mr. Walsh. He requested that all those who began that morning line up and count off one, two, three. We lined up like you would at a soccer practice, and called out our number. Mr. Walsh requested all the twos to step forward, and then told them they were no longer needed. The termination of the twos was followed by a very motivational speech, informing us all that we would experience the same fate as the twos if we did not perform. As I stood there wondering if I should be grateful for being a three, my informant told me Walsh would do the same thing again at lunchtime. At noon, the coffee truck rolled up again, followed by Mr. Walsh, who asked us to line up and count off one, two. This time he requested all the ones to go home.

Lucky me, I was a two this time, but I really did not see any future in this opportunity, so I informed Mr. Walsh this was my first and last day. This squat, balding, poor excuse for a man walked over, pointed a finger in my chest and called me a quitter. It was then that I programmed the phrase in my head, "Were you born a boss-hole, or do you just work really hard and practice?"

By the time our company crossed into the new millennium, we were operating in 13 countries, at hundreds of customer locations and sites, with hundreds of managers and thousands of hourly team members. It was a daily challenge to keep everyone aligned. The assessment process and tools were a critical piece of that alignment. I would not want to leave you believing that in any way, shape, or form we had everyone rowing in the same direction, but we did do okay, and in general everyone was on the same path. Some walked in the middle, and others chose one side over the other. We embraced our entrepreneurial roots, and as such also bred a certain degree of maverick behavior. The assessment process just helped to keep everything in check.

Select puts team members into the starting blocks for the race, Train gets them efficiently out of the blocks and into the race, and Assess gives them momentum to keep running.

A well-greased and aligned assessment process is one of the greatest gifts you can give to any employee. Everyone wishes to belong to something, to feel valued, and to know his or her contributions count. IOSPs who fail to implement and practice a consistent, disciplined assessment process retard the growth of their people and their organization. As Jim Collins made famous, it is about getting the right people in the right seats on the right bus, and getting the wrong people off the bus, quickly.

TAKEAWAYS:

- The biggest obstacle to an assessment process is fear.
- Fear is something characteristic in human behavior, and arrives as part of the package with every new hire.
- A good assessment process requires the diligent, disciplined use of tools that are easy to use and understand.
- Self-awareness is the antidote to the fear of feedback.
- The primary purpose for an assessment process is to encourage growth and development.

PEOPLE

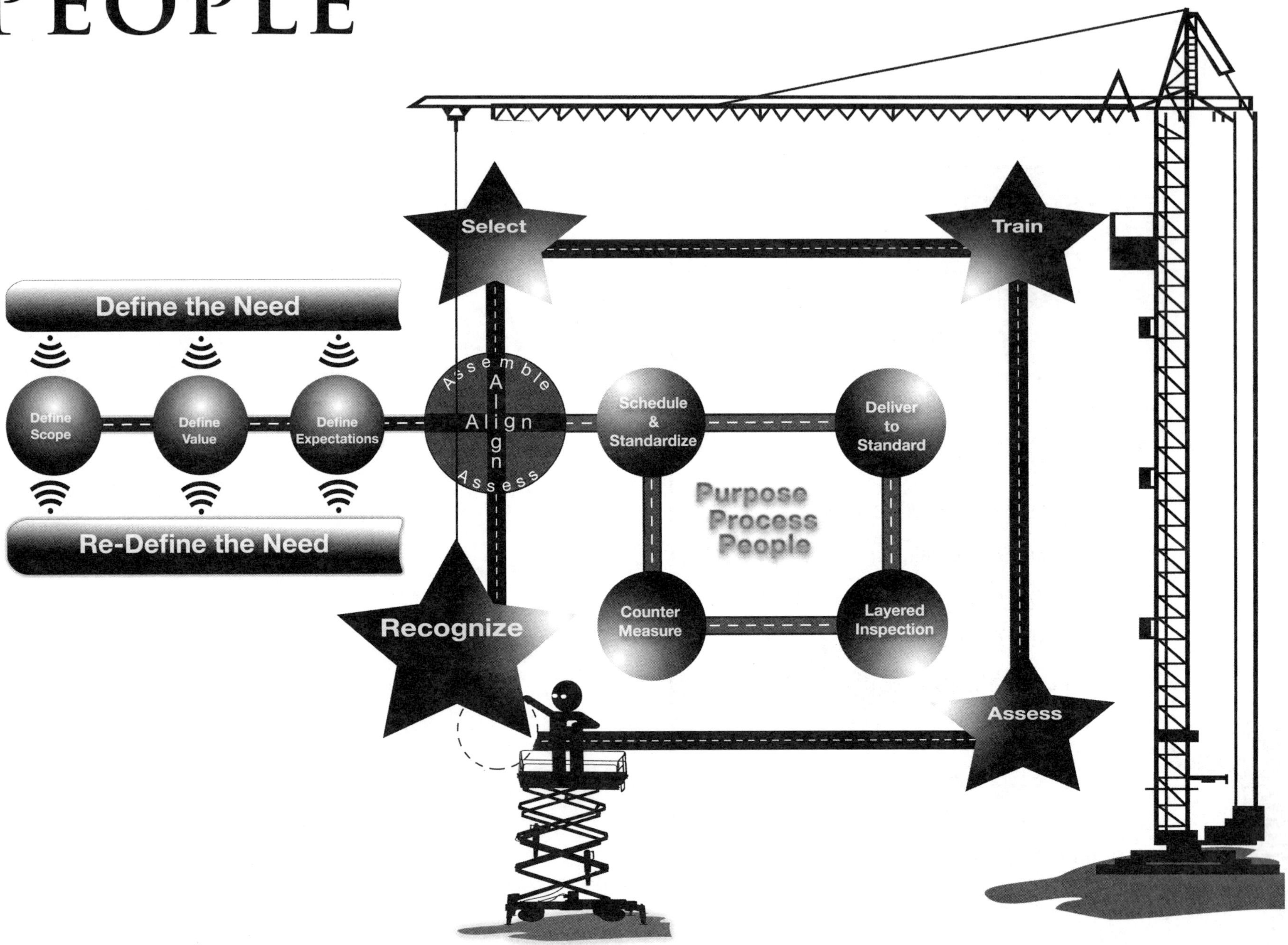

Define the Need
Define Scope
Define Value
Define Expectations
Re-Define the Need
Assemble
Align
Assess
Select
Train
Recognize
Assess
Schedule & Standardize
Deliver to Standard
Counter Measure
Layered Inspection
Purpose
Process
People

> "Employees who report receiving recognition and praise within the last seven days show increased productivity, get higher scores from customers, and have better safety records. They're just more engaged at work."
>
> Tom Rath

> "Research indicates that employees have three prime needs: Interesting work, recognition for doing a good job, and being let in on things that are going on in the company."
>
> Zig Ziglar

Kim Cameron, in his book *Positive Leadership*, discusses the impact of positive versus negative emotions on people. Positive emotions increase a person's ability to cope, to learn, to perform, to make decisions, to be creative, to be social, and to deter negativity.

Over my 40 years in various IOSPs, as I moved through the ranks from an hourly labor position to the "C" suite, I experienced many, many forms of recognition.

- An owner who showed up in the middle of the night to bring a hard-working crew a warm meal.
- An owner who put on overalls and took over the job while the team member was given time to drink a cup of coffee.
- A management team who cooked up extra burgers and hot dogs at a company picnic, and took them back to the plant for those who were scheduled to work.
- A leader who provided lunch, and then spent the entire time walking around, serving his team and picking up dirty plates.
- A leader who sat by the bedside of an employee, and comforted a family, after a mishap at work.
- An owner who took a crew out for a steak dinner after the completion of a critical project.
- A management team who loaded up a U-Haul truck and drove across the country to provide supplies for another team who had lost everything due to a natural disaster.
- A leader who fired an abusive customer.
- Owners who equitably and fairly shared company profitability.
- Leaders who promoted based on performance and potential.
- A management team who worked alongside their hourly teammates to understand clearly and appreciate their working conditions.

In each and every example, the result was the same: a strong, positive feeling of being appreciated, and a strong sense of gratitude that one's efforts were noticed.

STAR Overview Table				
	S	T	A	R
Recognize	**Situation** Recognizing the team for their accomplishments in their situation.	**Team** Recognizing everyone for their ability to work and perform as a team.	**Above** Showing gratitude to the team for going above and beyond what is normally expected.	**Results** Recognizing the team for their measurable performance.

We found that for recognition to be a true source of "real" motivation, it needed to exhibit influence in four critical areas:

- **Situation:** the development of a positive working environment.
- **Team:** the development of a cohesive and caring working team.
- **Above and Beyond:** the identification of individuals who go the extra mile.
- **Results:** the celebration of meeting our annual targets and strategic goals.

The combination of these four areas cemented the foundation of our culture and our brand.

Marcus Buckingham, co-author of *First, Break All the Rules: What the World's Greatest Managers Do Differently*, has spent the last decade helping companies find and motivate their most talented employees. In a 2003 interview with the *Daily Leader*, Buckingham discussed some of the insights behind his book, including the need for leaders to be optimistic concerning their work environment, and also to see those in their work environment as a team of individuals.

Our experience ran parallel to what Buckingham discussed. We were huge advocates of teamwork and what a team could accomplish, but we also recognized the uniqueness of individuals. We realized we would not be successful without embracing and appreciating a strong level of diversity in how people worked and thought. We all shared a vision, and we all shared the belief that people differentiated our company from our competitors, but we also understood and appreciated everyone's individuality. It was important for us not to lose this value by misaligning our recognition process.

In Part 3 we have continually discussed the need for a target.

- We select to a target.
- We train to a target.
- We assess to a target.
- And we also need to recognize to a target.

As we discussed in the previous chapter, Select puts team members into the starting blocks for the race, Train gets them efficiently out of the blocks and into the race, and Assess gives them momentum to keep running. Recognize thanks them and gives them appreciation for running the race, win, lose or tie. If recognition is properly aligned with your other people processes, and if it is truly meaningful, it values the runner and the team and it motivates everyone to run the next race.

Our experience with recognition programs led us to the four focus areas:

- Situation
- Team
- Above and Beyond
- Results

Some IOSPs believe that an annual monetary bonus program will accomplish the goal of recognizing their employees, because they believe it rewards the only reason people work: money. Of course people require money to live, but they often do have options and will gravitate to work where they feel valued. To feel valued, one needs to be recognized. Our customers who understood this basic fact of life also contributed to the recognition process and, as a result, the IOSP were also able to attract higher-performing teams to work at those locations. On many, many occasions, these high-performing teams chose not to take a vacation because they were committed to helping the customer launch a new product and would not let the plant manager down.

SITUATION

We believed that we showed our people the greatest form of respect by providing them with the best place to work. As an IOSP, we provided services in our customers' facilities, so many facets of the work environment were not within our direct control. We could, however, develop the right climate for our employees based on how we interacted with them on a day-to-day basis.

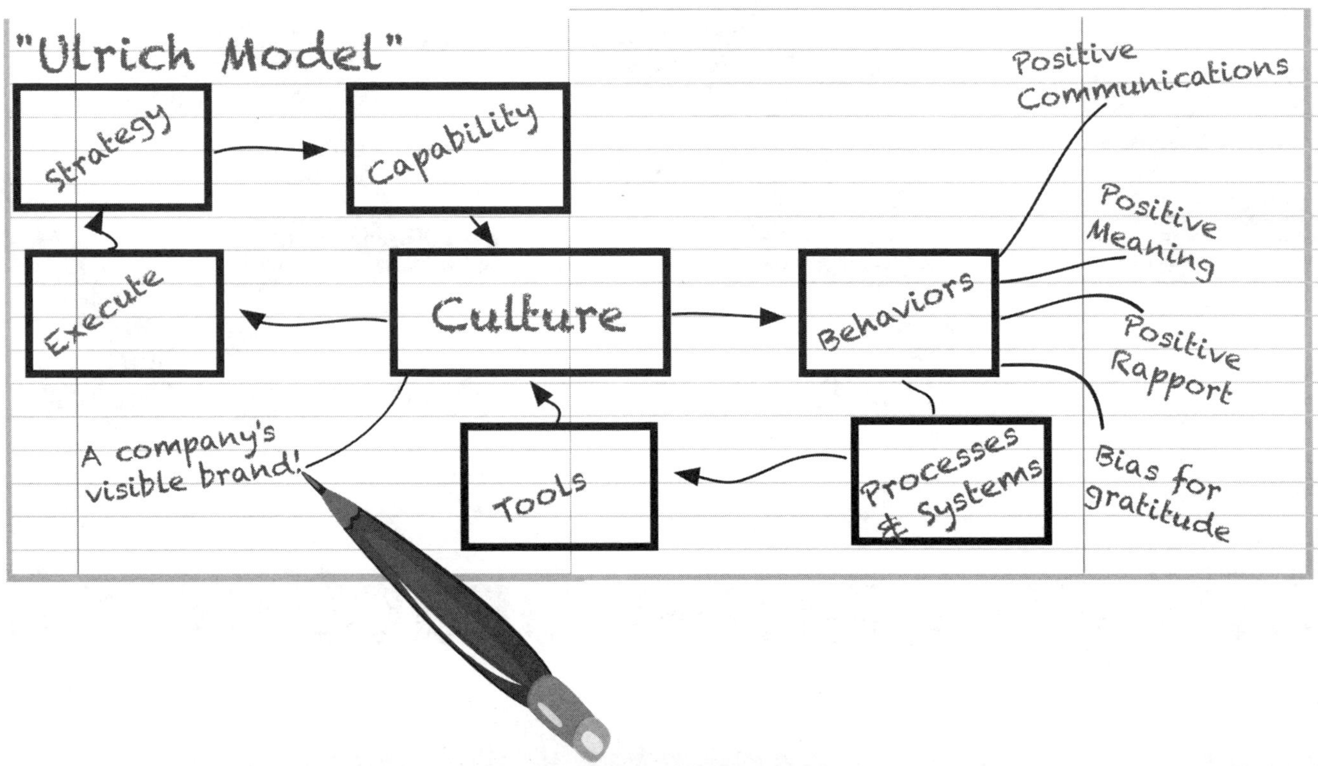

The choice of leader for our sites was critical in developing the right climate. The process we discussed in Select, Train, and Assess helped us to make more "right choices" than "bad choices." In his interview with the *Daily Leader*, Buckingham discussed the irony of managers being put into leadership positions because they are great individual contributors. We have all heard the analogy about the best sales guy being given the sales management position. As we have discussed earlier, we fell into this trap for a period, but with the help of better selection tools we were not only able to select new candidates better, but also to make much better promotion choices.

When I went on plant visits and tours, many team members would make a point of letting me know whether or not the latest supervisor or manager was a good fit and kept the team motivated. Each time a team got a new leader through promotion, that new manager's personality would reset the stage for how that team performed. It was imperative the person promoted was not only technically capable, but also exhibited the required behaviors to improve the team's situation, not worsen it.

If you understand deeply that people are unique and not everything is learnable, then you will be a little more careful about creating a career ladder where individual contributors don't necessarily have to be promoted into a management role to advance their career. The best technicians are not generally the best managers. The best managers create the best situations for their teams; they are sensitive to, and concerned with, the people processes as well as with the actual work at hand.

We performed site surveys periodically (not more than one every two years), to gain an understanding of how team members felt about the situation in which they were working. Buckingham, in his book, *First Break All The Rules*, outlines what is known as the Q12. We performed several different surveys over the years, but, to me, the Q12 worked best for recognizing if the situations at our sites were aligned with our corporate values and strategic goals.

The Q12 survey questions are:

1. Do I know what is expected of me at work?
2. Do I have the equipment and material I need to do my work right?
3. At work, do I have the opportunity to do what I do best every day?
4. In the last seven days, have I received recognition or praise for good work?
5. Does my supervisor or someone at work seem to care about me as a person?
6. Is there someone at work who encourages my development?
7. At work, do my opinions seem to count?
8. Does the mission/purpose of my company make me feel my work is important?
9. Are my co-workers committed to doing quality work?
10. Do I have a best friend at work?
11. In the last six months, have I talked to someone about my progress?
12. This last year, have I had opportunities at work to learn and grow?

I strongly recommend this book to any manager or supervisor whose goal is to encourage and motivate the best from their team. Although we used the Q12 questions in broad site surveys, I also used them very informally during all of my site visits. It was pretty easy during a third-shift team meeting to ask some of the questions and gauge whether or not the team felt they had been praised lately, if they had the proper training and equipment, or if they understood "why we were in business" and "why our customers hired us."

A survey is a great way to recognize a team, by showing that you value their opinions; but if you do not follow up on the surveys, they do a lot more harm than good. We were advocates of town hall meetings two or three times each year, where we brought an entire site team together and outlined for them just how important they were to the success of both our company and our customer. We engaged the customer to speak at town hall meetings to express their gratitude as well, and to outline any new challenges we might need to tackle in the upcoming quarter or year.

Annually we would formally recognize those who, through their actions, demonstrated leadership by creating a positive situation for the teams at work, their families at home, and their communities. Candidates were nominated based on specific criteria, and teammates got together and created presentations in support of candidates. All presentations were given to an executive group, who made the ultimate choice of whom to reward with special recognition. It was a pretty good process, which resulted in the recognition of many very good leaders.

We also recognized those who created positive work situations over the course of their career. A Lifetime Achievement Award was given to seasoned management team members who demonstrated positive leadership over the course of their career, making a significant difference within the industry. Our company president chose candidates. The award was given to the successful candidate at our annual leadership conference, but was given only when there was a recipient worthy of this honor.

Our customer—by including our site management team in their plant or facility meeting, and valuing their contribution—informally recognized our site management team. Including IOSP site management in these meetings also allowed our managers the ability to educate our team further on the impact of our services at that location. Everyone wants to know that what they do each and every day counts for something, and to be recognized for it. You can get a certain amount of satisfaction from performing a task well, but if you can tie your efforts into the production or creation of a great product, it is just that much more meaningful.

In order for a team to achieve success, that team must be put into the right situation. We found that by focusing a certain level of our recognition effort on situation, we continually improved the situation. As we have mentioned, some of the situations we found ourselves in were not conducive to our long-term success, so we decided to recognize that and exit. We also recognized that some members of our management teams did not create a positive situation for our team members, and also asked them to exit—not my favorite form of recognition, but a necessary one.

TEAM

Every Performance Map we created set an expectation for every employee at every level in the organization to be either a great team player, team leader, team supervisor, or team manager. Our success hinged on our people, and our future hinged on our people working together as a team. It only made sense to us always to recognize team performance.

When I visited our sites, I always found it interesting to visit the space where the site teams met. Each year we recognized our sites' performances with what we called a "Premier Performance Award," or PPA. This was an award given to site management teams for meeting their annual targets. The award was proudly displayed on the wall in the meeting room in chronological order. If for some reason a site missed an award, the manager would leave a space on the wall. They would be able to tell you why they missed receiving the recognition that particular year. Some of the teams had awards that spanned over 20 years with one or two years missing, and even the new management team knew the reason why there was a gap on the wall.

After receiving a PPA recognizing the accomplishments of the site team, the management team held a celebration at the site level to ensure the recognition was felt by the team members on the shop floor.

Several of our customers also handed out awards to their suppliers, and, like the PPA, these were also displayed in chronological order on the wall. Again, IOSP management team members could explain why they missed a given year.

Each year we held a leadership conference, during which we informed site management teams of our prior year's results and also the targets for the upcoming year. We diligently set three-year goals for the company, and broke those down into annual targets. Our annual leadership conference was a great two-day celebration recognizing all of those who contributed to our joint success.

On the anniversary years aligned with our three-year goals, we moved the location of the celebration to a resort and extended the conference by a day. This allowed us to celebrate further the achievement of our longer-term strategic goals, and also to communicate the strategic goals for the next three years. Getting hundreds of management personnel from multiple countries all in one place was no easy task, but the effort was always appreciated, and it gave our global teams a chance to reunite and share stories.

It was impossible to bring all of the thousands of hourly team members together for a celebration to recognize their contributions, but site management teams organized breakfasts, lunches, summer picnics, and holiday celebrations to bring teams together just to say, "thanks." To say 100 percent of the people appreciated the effort would be an overstatement, but a lot more did than did not. These types of events also served as subtle reminders to our management teams of who packed their parachutes, and gave them an opportunity to show their gratitude.

Throughout this book, I have mentioned numerous times site visits, "We Serve" days, and third-shift meetings. In each of these cases, the teams were grateful that their management group took the time to come and visit, see what they did, answer their questions, and just let them know they really are important and they matter.

As part of our safety process, we regularly performed safety observations during a scheduled workday. Whether we were doing safety observations, quality observations, or any other management activity associated with the day-to-day operations, we found them great opportunities to recognize the team. Dedicated observation walks served to keep the site safer and working better, but, more importantly, managers being out on the floor told the team their wellbeing and contributions were important to us. Don't forget that these everyday activities that are part of the work to be done can also be extremely valuable opportunities to reinforce good work and good behaviors, to correct how the work is being done if needed, and to appreciate the effort of the employees on the floor. Those small, everyday acts of recognition can often go much further than you could ever imagine.

ABOVE AND BEYOND

If we could build strong, aligned teams at our sites, our chances of long-term, multi-decade success were almost assured. Teams are comprised of dozens of individual-thinking people, with individual desires, ambitions, problems, talents, and obstacles. Our understanding of this individuality and diversity led us to recognize individuals for what we called "above and beyond."

Each and every individual team member contributes to the building of your brand with every activity they complete, and in every interaction with their teammates and with your customer.

At the start of a shift meeting, Doug reviewed changes to the schedule and a few other particulars that affected the night shift team. As he finished up, he called Lindsay to the front of the room and handed her an Achiever Award. Two days before, Lindsay noticed an issue with a welding robot and brought it to the attention of the customer. The customer told Doug that Lindsay's observation saved them ten minutes of potential downtime. Lindsay, by both paying attention and informing the customer, had gone above and beyond, and in turn she was recognized with an "Achiever Award." Lindsay, by her action, improved the value of our IOSP's brand that day.

Thousands of hourly team members in hundreds of sites throughout the world have received an award just like Lindsay. Part of our drive to recognize these unsung heroes was to put their name in our newsletter each month to further the level of recognition. Do not let me confuse you, though. These team members did not go above and beyond in order to get their name in a company newsletter or receive an Achiever Award. They did this because that is what we all did: going above and beyond for the customer was part of our culture and part of our company's brand. The newsletter and the Achiever Award simply told them, and everyone else, that they were appreciated.

Our business relied heavily on receiving suggestions from our team members on how to improve our services. Over the years, we continually adapted and refined our suggestion and innovation programs and processes to keep them fresh and exciting. We had programs that provided a cash reward for implemented ideas and suggestions. We had conferences where the best innovations were shown off, ranked and awarded. We handed out gift cards for suggestions. We continually discussed and debated the best programs and processes, but one thing that was never debated was the absolute need to recognize our employees for their individual contributions. In our company, these small ideas added up to millions of dollars in cost savings each year. Remember the story about Norm in the chapter Layered Inspection, who continually improved his procedure for checking production fluid levels? Our focus on individual recognition motivated many, many Norms to come forward with great ideas.

One thing I did before a site visit was to gather the entire site-related key performance data, a copy of the site organization chart, and also the names of any recent individual Achiever Award recipients or Years of Service Award winners. It was always an enjoyable experience to meet those who packed my parachute. Giving public recognition to people like this is a simple practice that helps build a team by recognizing the individuals on the team.

Programs for recognizing individuals can be time consuming because of sheer volume. HR departments often like to control this process, and make it efficient and effective for them to administer. The results, more often than not, are an efficient and effective, but meaningless, process. The real key to success in this area is to keep the person, the individual, in mind and take the time to say thanks, shake their hand, and personally show your gratitude. Informal acts of gratitude and everyday expressions of appreciation will go further than anything else you could possibly formalize. Think of this in terms of your family: Do you have a formal recognition program, or do you just take the time and appreciate what is done for you on a daily basis? Like so many things, recognizing and appreciating people is pretty simple stuff.

RESULTS

For years and years I have always corrected people who use the word bonus interchangeably with the word incentive. To me they are two absolutely different things:

- Bonus: something welcomed and often unexpected that enhances or accompanies something that is good.

- Incentive: a thing that encourages or motivates someone to do something.

To me, the biggest difference between a bonus and an incentive—and it is a big difference—is that a bonus is a gift given to someone by someone, whereas an incentive is knowingly earned and calculated as the result of meeting set targets. The latter creates a much stronger sense of ownership and control over one's own success. It fosters the understanding that we all win and we all have "skin" in the game.

A well-designed incentive program is self-funding. By meeting set targets, the company increases its bottom line, allowing it the ability to compensate those who contributed to that success. By receiving an incentive, those who contribute see that their efforts have paid off, and they are encouraged to repeat the same behaviors in the following year or quarter.

I'm very opposed to bonus programs, but feel an incentive program is critical to the long-term success of an IOSP.

As an IOSP, we operated hundreds of sites, at hundreds of customer locations, in more than a dozen countries, and to be successful we needed to be decentralized in how we operated. However, we followed a stringent set of guidelines when it came to designing and administering incenctive programs. We expected our on-site teams to be viewed as the local decision makers for the company, and always to act in the best interest of the company. As stated earlier in the book, we wanted our management teams to act like owners. To accomplish this goal, we needed to encourage this behavior and make them stakeholders in the company's success.

In 2010, I met a woman who had been a site manager for about five years. Her compensation plan was based entirely on her base salary, which had not improved much over the years, as growth at the site was stagnant. She was an extraordinarily hard-working person who put in very long weeks, working multiple shifts and weekends. She was getting pretty burned out, and did not see the light at the end of the tunnel. She was accustomed to being given her targets and basically following orders. After a few visits and a lot of dialogue around the principles we have discussed in *The Outsourcing Conundrum*, we created a new mindset. We encouraged her to start thinking and acting like she was a franchise owner.

This simple change altered her entire perspective; she started to think like an owner. We designed an incentive program to enhance this mindset. By 2014, she had tripled the size of her business, top and bottom lines. As a result, her personal compensation and that of her team grew significantly. The compensation growth was 100 percent incentive-based. On my most recent trip to visit with her, she was a totally different person—engaged, on her game, and acting like an owner.

Every site within our portfolio was eligible for an incentive program. It allowed our management teams the ability to compensate themselves further for acting like owners of the business. As a company, it resulted in double-digit growth on the top and bottom lines for two decades. But—and this is an important BUT—it will not work in your favor if you do not have targets set for who you hire, how you train, and how you assess. Setting targets only for results will not lead to sustainable growth and success, but combining targets for results with targets for behaviors, competencies, and fit with your culture is a powerful path to lasting success. Incentive programs are not short cuts, but enhancers that will put your company over the top if you do your homework and practice STAR.

BEST PRACTICE

Bad performance has to be recognized and dealt with just as quickly and efficiently as recognizing good performance. Terminating and firing people is not a fun thing to do, and it is definitely not something you should ever learn to master or enjoy, but it is something you should expedite. If you master what was discussed in the last chapter, Assess, it will minimize the need for you to recognize bad performance here.

In our company, we developed zero tolerance around unethical behavior, and took the time to investigate any and all issues. We erred towards giving people a second chance on a very short leash, but subsequent failure resulted in termination with no regrets. We owed it to our teams to make sure our working situations were very safe and harassment-free. We dealt expeditiously with any conduct visibly contrary to those goals. Moving problem team members from one location to another, or from one department to another, to avoid possible confrontation flies in the face of truly recognizing your team. The practice of moving problem employees rather than dealing with them only compounds the problem and makes the situation worse for everyone. In dealing with problem employees, be very clear about your standards and criteria, and take decisive action if they are not being met.

- Strike One
- Strike Two
- Strike Three

You are out! No one is going to throw you another ball, you do not get to walk to a base, and your game is over.

PROCUREMENT

Recognition is important in any relationship, and all too often the only time many suppliers are recognized by their customer is when things go wrong. The best customers I have ever worked with recognize their suppliers regularly for what they do right. They attend the IOSP's town hall meetings, they take time to tour their facilities and engage with the IOSP's team members, they include the IOSP in production meetings, and, most importantly, and as we have discussed a lot, they set up metrics so everyone is aware of what is expected and everyone can see the finish line.

QUICK STORY

In 1998 I visited one of our sites in Mexico that was celebrating an anniversary. As part of the visit, I was going to hand out Years of Service Awards to several dozen employees who had all been there from the start. We ate lunch at a pretty extravagant restaurant, followed by a small presentation recognizing those eligible for the Years of Service Award. The award was a sterling-silver Cross pen, engraved with each winner's name and our company logo. As each name was called, I shook the person's hand, gave them a certificate, and handed them their pen. I thought this was a pretty exciting day—a chance to meet and mingle with dozens of team members, and show gratitude for all they had done. The funny thing was, I think I was the only one who was excited. Something was very wrong.

The following morning was a Saturday. As we were not due at the plant until late afternoon, I took the time to walk around the small town. In the square downtown was a market where you could buy anything from vegetables, to fresh chicken (really fresh—they were still walking), arts and crafts, and also, if you wanted one, a Cross pen.

You could actually buy a sterling-silver Cross pen for five dollars, or for two dollars if you wanted to haggle a bit. The only downside to the pens was that each one was engraved with the name of one of my team members, and each one bore our company's logo.

After a discussion with the owner of the table of goods, who happened to be one of our second-shift team leaders, I realized what had been bothering me the day before. These guys needed a Cross pen like they needed a hole in the head. We spent more on the pen than they earned in a month. To add insult to injury, the lunch we provided was probably equal to another month's pay.

We had not recognized these employees in a way that was meaningful to them, or in a way that made them feel positive. We had completely insulted them. That afternoon, with the help of my new-found friend, the owner of the table of goods in the market, I came to understand that most of the people who worked for us did not even own a notebook, could not write, and for the most part even had dirt floors in their homes. Why in the name of hell would they need a Cross pen?

Sunday morning, with a ton of help from the local management team who continued my education, we put together a breakfast in the cafeteria. I spent the morning moving from table to table, along with many others from the team, serving breakfast and trying to learn key words in Spanish. The atmosphere was very festive and educational.

In the 40 years I have been in business, I do not ever recall being as embarrassed by my arrogance as I was when we handed out those pens in Mexico. For recognition to be truly meaningful and effective, it should be personal, local, cultural, and sensitive. We changed our policy after this incident, allowing local cultures to do what was best for their local teams.

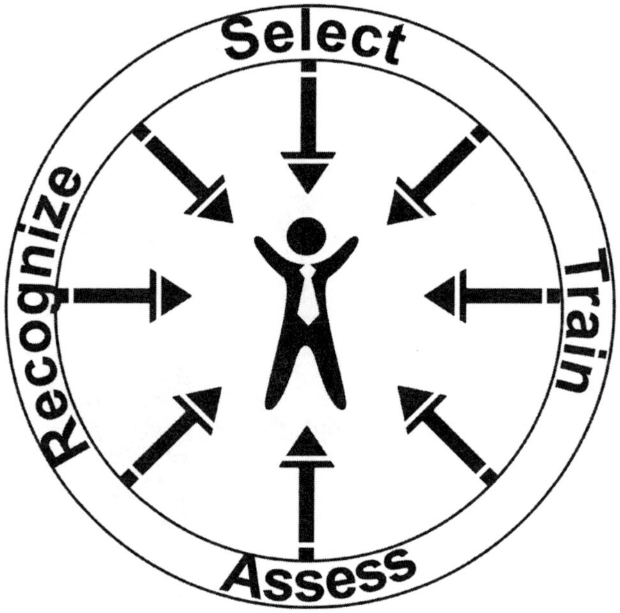

TAKEAWAYS:

- Recognize positive work situations and those responsible for creating them.
- Individual recognition is the keystone to being able to recognize strong teams.
- Individuals build the brand conveyed by the team.
- Incentivize people so they fairly share in the success of the company.
- Those who are recognized should feel like they are being respected and appreciated, not humbled.

EPILOGUE

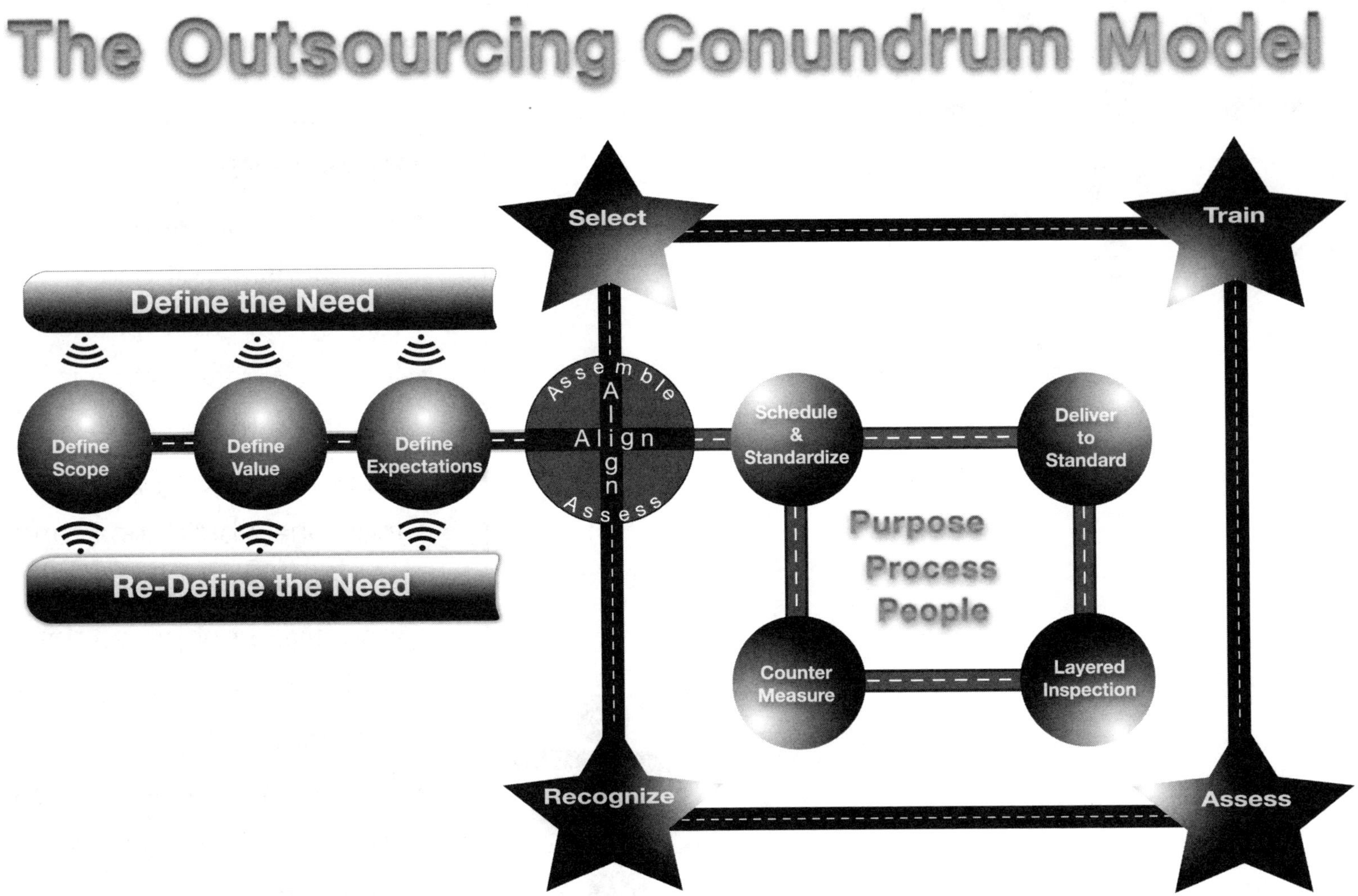

The Outsourcing Conundrum Model
Select
Train
Define the Need
Define Scope
Define Value
Define Expectations
Re-Define the Need
Assemble
Align
Assess
Schedule & Standardize
Deliver to Standard
Purpose
Process
People
Counter Measure
Layered Inspection
Recognize
Assess

DIFFERENT DRUMMERS

If you do not want what I want, please try not to tell me that my want is wrong.

Or if my beliefs are different from yours, at least pause before you set out to correct them.

Or if my emotion seems less or more intense than yours, given the same circumstances, try not to ask me to feel other than I do.

Or if I act, or fail to act, in the manner of your design for action, please let me be.

I do not, for the moment at least, ask you to understand me. That will come only when you are willing to give up trying to change me into a copy of you.

If you will allow me any of my own wants, or emotions, or beliefs, or actions, then you open yourself to the possibility that some day these ways of mine might not seem so wrong, and might finally appear as right—for me. To put up with me is the first step to understanding me.

Not that you embrace my ways as right for you, but that you are no longer irritated or disappointed with me for my seeming waywardness. And one day, perhaps, in trying to understand me, you might come to prize my differences, and, far from seeking to change me, might preserve and even cherish those differences.

I may be your spouse, your parent, your offspring, your friend, your colleague. But whatever our relation, this I know: You and I are fundamentally different and both of us have to march to our own drummer.

David Keirsey (1998), in *Please Understand Me II*

So here we are at the last chapter of *The Outsourcing Conundrum*, the epilogue. I chose to call this last chapter of my business book an epilogue because *The Outsourcing Conundrum* is a factual business story. It is the story of the birth and life of **The Outsourcing Conundrum Model** from 1974 through today.

In an epilogue an author tries to accomplish several things—bring some closure, tie up some loose ends, and discuss the fate of the characters in the story. Some often hint of a sequel to the story.

"Different Drummers," the poem I chose to start this chapter with, has been my companion for more than a decade. The poem reflects how I chose to live both my life and my business life. At my core, I have always been obsessed with the question "why," and I have applied it to many of life's phantom pressures:

- Without a degree you cannot succeed – Why?
- You need to dress the part – Why?
- Get on board with the idea – Why?
- Go along to get along – Why?
- Customers will not pay for value – Why?
- Take the path most trodden – Why?

"Why" drove me to try to find what was unique within myself, and what I have to offer. In my leadership roles, it drove me to set our company apart from the pack, and to strive continually to locate and exploit our uniqueness. If everyone is supposed to march to the same drummer, fall in line, and not challenge the current condition, then what's it all for?

From the moment I walked on the roof in 1974 to high-pressure water-blast the stacks, I was struck by an obvious fact. We can do this better, we can make the work saner, and, most importantly, ***why*** is it in this condition in the first place?

The real main character in this business story, *The Outsourcing Conundrum*, is the model. You have seen the model grow from its birth, part by part and chapter by chapter. The fate of this character, the model, lies in your hands. For over 40 years, I have seen this character evolve through experience and knowledge. In my opinion, there is a sequel out there to be written by another generation of radical drummers.

During dinner one night in the 1990s, my kids were bantering back and forth over the table, and one of them called the other a "poser." The word really caught my attention, and I asked, "What is a poser?"

"You know?" Came the reply

"No, I really don't." They looked at me like I had three heads, or no head at all.

"Dad, poser, a wanna-be, you know faker?"

"Faker, faking what?" I was really into this now.

"Dad, a poser is an imposter, they are not real, and they pretend to be someone else. Get it?"

"I do get it." I felt like I had just passed Nerdy Dad 101.

Over the course of dinner, when I could be heard, I delved into this term "poser." The next day we had a leadership team meeting, and I shared the dialogue from dinner with our team. I asked, "Are we 'posers?'" That is, do we have a unique service offering, or are we following the pack and how do we really know?

The dialogue and discussion that followed over the course of that day and the next few months cemented the three legs, the **3Ps**, of our model:

1. Purpose
2. Process
3. People

We reaffirmed to ourselves that our business was dependent upon understanding our customer needs, our ability to develop and integrate our processes to service those needs, and our ability to attract, motivate, and align our talent to surpass those needs.

I fear that many IOSPs are not taking the time to identify and truly understand where they add value. Instead, they make assumptions as to who is the front-runner, and where they run in the pack. I would like to propose a different path to you. A path riddled with questions to ponder. A path where your company can understand why, where and how it is unique. A path that, if pursued, will allow you to attract the talent with the potential to share in your success. A path to navigate the inside-outsourcing labyrinth, and stay one step ahead of your customer.

I propose that you take whatever time is required to answer the following questions in the first person, where each answer begins with one of the following words:

- Our
- My
- We

PURPOSE

Define the Need:

- Who are our key customers?
- Why do our key customers outsource?
- What do our key customers need?
- Who are our competitors?
- Why are we uniquely positioned to serve our key customers' needs versus our competitors?

Define the Scope:

- What are our key services?
- Are all the components of our key services documented?
- Do our key customers buy our key services?
- What makes us unique in the provision of these key services versus our competitors?

Define the Value:

- Do our key customers agree our key services are unique, and do they buy this uniqueness?
- Do we know the true cost to provide our key services?
- Do we price our services based on our cost or on the value provided to the customer?

Define the Expectations:

- What are the expectations of our key customers from our services?
- How do we measure these expectations?
- How do we rank/trend numerically against these expectations?

Re-Define the Need:

- What is the strategic planning cycle of our key customers?
- How do we re-align to the changes in our key customers' strategies?

PROCESS

Assemble, Align and Assess Processes:

- What are our key, critical processes?
- How do we align them to meet our customers' needs and our own?
- How do we evaluate the condition of our processes?

Schedule and Standardize:

- How do we allocate the right amount of resources to every task or activity we perform?
- How do we gather the knowledge on the best method to perform each task and activity?

Deliver to Standard:

- How do we share the knowledge on the best method to perform each task and activity?
- How do we empower and engage our teams to interact with our customers and evolve the standards?
- What steps are we taking to ensure we do not become complacent?

Layered Inspection:

- How do we inspect the morale and motivation of our team?
- How do we inspect the compliance of our delivery to standard?
- How do we challenge the standard to meet the needs of tomorrow?

Counter Measure:

- How do we build initiative to empower people to act?
- How do we openly share the information so people know how to act?

PEOPLE

Assemble, Align and Assess People:

- How do we label each of the seats in our organization?
- How do we know the number of seats in our organization?
- How do we continually align the seats in our organization with our own needs, and with those of our key customers?

Select:

- How do we develop the right target for each position in the organization?
- How do we hire the right person to sit in that seat and exhibit our brand?

Train:

- How do we train and develop each person to understand the purpose of our organization?
- How do we train each person to understand and perform his or her role?
- How do we train each person to understand the needs of our key customers?
- How do we develop our people as individuals and build resilient teams?

Assess:

- How do we assess each person's contribution to themselves and to the team?
- How do we assess each person's contributions to our customer relationship?

Recognize:

- How do we recognize each person's contribution to the team, and to improving themselves?
- How do we recognize each person's contributions to our customer relationship?

Remember, if it were easy, everyone would be doing it well. It's not easy. Stay the path.

It took 40 years, millions of dollars in mistakes, countless hours by countless people, to get this far. Take this path, move forward, and hopefully write the sequel.

I leave you with my three favorite words, my personal 3Ps:

- **Poser:** Find yourself and your company, and cherish and exploit your uniqueness.
- **Ponder:** Continually question assumptions. If it's too good to be true, it is. If everyone else is doing it, don't.
- **Pursue:** Look through the noise, see the patterns, and seek clarity and direction.

ACKNOWLEDGMENTS

I would not have been able to write this book without the support and insight of family, colleagues, authors, professors, mentors, and seasoned business professionals who have been with me for the past 40 years as sources of knowledge and inspiration.

I hope you enjoyed reading *The Outsourcing Conundrum* as much as I enjoyed its writing.

BIBLIOGRAPHY

American Management Association. *Blueprints for Service Quality*. New York: American Management Association, 1997.

Bossidy, Larry, and Ram Charan. *Execution: The Discipline of Getting Things Done*. New York: Random House, 2002.

Buckingham, Marcus, and Donald O. Clifton. *Now, Discover Your Strengths*. New York: Free Press, 2001.

Byham, William C., Ph.D. *The Selection Solution: Solving the Mystery of Matching People to Jobs*. Pittsburgh: DDI Press, 1996.

Cameron, Kim S. *Positive Leadership: Strategies for Extraordinary Performance*. San Francisco: Berrett-Koehler, 2008.

Cameron, Kim S., and Robert E. Quinn. *Diagnosing and Changing Organizational Culture*. San Francisco: Jossey-Bass, 2006.

Carter, Michael. *The 8-Disciplines: Problem Solving Methodology*. Brea: 6ixsigma, 2012.

Christensen, Clayton M., and Michael E. Raynor. *The Innovator's Solution: Creating and Sustaining Successful Growth*. Boston: Harvard Business School, 2003.

Collins, Jim. *How The Mighty Fall: And Why Some Companies Never Give In*. New York: Harper Collins, 2009.

Collins, James C., and William C. Lazier. *Beyond Entrepreneurship: Turning Your Business into an Enduring Great Company*. Paramus: Prentice Hall, 1992.

Collins, James C., and Jerry I. Porras. *Built To Last: Successful Habits of Visionary Companies*. New York: Harper Business, 1994.

Covey, Stephen R. *The 8th Habit: From Effectiveness to Greatness*. New York: Free Press, 2004.

Covey, Stephen R., A. Roger Merrill, and Rebecca R. Merrill. *First Things First*. New York: Simon & Schuster, 1994.

Fleming, John H., Ph.D., and Jim Asplund. *Human Sigma: Managing the Employee-Customer Encounter*. New York: Gallup Press, 2007.

Gamble, John. *What Your Clients Won't Tell You*. Roswell: Tenacity Press, 2001.

Gamble, John. *Why Good Clients Fire Great Companies*. Roswell: Tenacity Press, 2001.

Gore, W. Gary. *Navigating Change: A Field Guide to Personal Growth*. Memphis: Team Trek, 2002.

Greif, Michel. *The Visual Factory: Building Participation Through Shared Information*. Portland: Productivity Press, 1991.

Hall, Doug. *Jump Start Your Business Brain: Scientific Ideas and Advice That Will Immediately Double Your Business Success*. Cincinnati: Brain Brew Books, 2001.

Heskett, James L. W., Earl Sasser, Jr., and Leonard A. Schlesinger. *The Service Profit Chain: How Leading Companies Link Profit and Growth to Loyalty, Satisfaction and Value*. New York: Free Press, 1997.

Imai, Masaaki. *Kaizen: The Key to Japan's Competitive Success*. New York: McGraw-Hill, 1986.

Kaplan, Robert S., and David P. Norton. *Alignment: Using the Balanced Scorecard to Create Corporate Synergies*. Boston: Harvard Business School, 2006.

Kaplan, Robert S., and David P. Norton. *The Strategy Focused Organization: How Balanced Scorecard Companies Thrive in the New Busienss Environment*. Boston: Harvard Business School, 2001.

Labovitz, George. *The Power of Alignment: How the Right Tools Enhance Organizational Focus*. New York: John Wiley & Sons, 1997.

Liker, Jeffrey K. *The Toyota Way: 14 Management Principles from the World's Greatest Manufacturer*. New York: McGraw-Hill, 2004.

Lowy, Alex. *No Problem*. Bloomington: Author House, 2007.

Lowy, Alex, and Phil Hood. *The Power of the 2x2 Matrix: Using 2x2 Thinking to Solve Business Problems and Make Better Decisions*. San Francisco: Jossey-Bass, 2004.

May, Mathew E. *In Pursuit of Elegance: Why the Best Ideas Have Something Missing*. New York: Broadway Books, 2009.

May, Mathew E. *The Elegant Solution: Toyota's Formula for Mastering Innovation*. New York: Free Press, 2007.

Miller, Robert B., Stephen E. Heiman, and Tad Taleja. *Successful Large Account Management*. New York: Warner Books, 1991.

Osterwalder, Alexander, and Yves Pigneur. *Business Model Generation*. Hoboken: John Wiley & Sons, 2010.

Patterson, Kerry, Joseph Grenny, Ron McMillan, and Al Switzler. *Crucial Conversations: Tools for Talking When Stakes Are High*. New York: McGraw-Hill, 2002.

Porter, Michael. *Competitive Advantage: Creating and Sustaining Superior Performance*. New York: Free Press, 1985.

Shook, John. *Managing to Learn: Using the A3 Management Process*. Cambridge: Lean Institute, 2008.

Slywotzky, Adrian J., and David J. Morrison. *The Profit Zone: How Strategic Design Will Lead You to Tomorrow's Profits*. New York: Times Business, 1997.

Treacy, Michael. *Double Digit Growth: How Great Companies Achieve It—No Matter What*. London: Penguin Group, 2003.

Tufte, Edward R. *Visual Explanations: Images and Quantities, Evidence and Narrative*. Cheshire: Graphics Press, 1997.

Ulrich, Dave. *Human Resource Champions: The Next Agenda for Adding Value and Delivering Results*. Boston: Harvard Business School, 1997.

Ulrich, Dave, Michael R. Losey, and Gerry Lake. *Tomorrow's HR Management: 48 Thought Leaders Call for Change*. New York: John Wiley & Sons, 1997.

Walton, Mary. *The Deming Management Method*. New York: Putnam Group, 1986.

Wiersema, Fred. *The New Market Leaders: Who's Winning and How in the Battle for Customers*. New York: Simon & Schuster, 2001.

Wilson, Brady. *Love at Work: Why Passion Drives Performance in the Feelings Economy*. Toronto: BPS, 2010.

Wilson, Trevor. *The Human Equity Advantage: Beyond Diversity to Talent Optimization*. Mississauga: Jossey-Bass, 2013.

Womack, Jim. *Gemba Walks*. Cambridge: Lean Institute, 2013.

Womack, James P., and Daniel T. Jones. *Lean Thinking: Banish Waste and Create Wealth in Your Corporation*. New York: Simon & Schuster, 2003.

Zook, Chris. *Beyond the Core: Expand Your Market Without Abandoning Your Roots*. Boston: Harvard Business School, 2004.

About the Author

Big Media Group

Damian Scallon is currently a consultant working and living in Cincinnati, Ohio. Prior to becoming a writer and consultant, he was the Vice President of Operations and Vice President of Human Resources at Robinson Solutions and at Voith Industrial Service, with responsibility for several hundred locations throughout Canada, USA, and Mexico. He has spent the last 40 years servicing the automotive industry and has witnessed and participated in the growth of inside-outsourcing.

For more information, please visit:
www.TheOutsourcingConundrum.com